D1602866

Legend into History

and

Did Custer Disobey Orders at the Battle of the Little Big Horn?

Legend into History

and

Did Custer Disobey Orders at the Battle of the Little Big Horn?

Charles Kuhlman

New introduction by Brian C. Pohanka

STACKPOLE
BOOKS

Legend into History original copyright © 1951 and 1952 by The Telegraph Press

Did Custer Disobey Orders at the Battle of the Little Big Horn? original copyright © 1957 by Charles Kuhlman

New material copyright © 1994 by Stackpole Books

Published by
STACKPOLE BOOKS
5067 Ritter Road
Mechanicsburg, PA 17055

All rights reserved, including the right to reproduce this book or portions thereof in any form or by any means, electronic or mechanical, including photocopying, recording, or by any information storage and retrieval system, without permission in writing from the publisher. All inquiries should be addressed to Stackpole Books, 5067 Ritter Road, Mechanicsburg, PA 17055.

Printed in the United States of America

Legend into History first edition, hardcover, in 1951 by The Stackpole Company

Did Custer Disobey Orders at the Battle of the Little Big Horn? first edition, paperback, in 1957 by The Stackpole Company

First combined edition, hardcover, Stackpole Books, 1994

10 9 8 7 6 5 4 3 2 1

Library of Congress Cataloging-in-Publication Data

Kuhlman, Charles, 1872–1959.
    [Legend into history]
    Legend into history ; and, Did Custer disobey orders at the Battle of the Little Big Horn? / Charles Kuhlman ; new introduction by Brian C. Pohanka. — 1st combined ed.
       p.   cm. — (The Custer library)
    First work originally published: 1951. 2nd work originally published: 1957.
    Includes bibliographical references and index.
    ISBN 0-8117-0453-X
    1. Little Bighorn, Battle of the, Mont., 1876. 2. Custer, George Armstrong, 1839–1876. I. Kuhlman, Charles, 1872–1959. Did Custer disobey orders at the Battle of the Little Big Horn? 1994. II. Title. III. Title: Legend into history. IV. Title: Did Custer disobey orders at the Battle of the Little Big Horn? V. Series.
E83.876.K87   1994
973.8'2—dc20   93-34687
                                                    CIP

Introduction

In the vast, rolling prairie of southeastern Montana shortly after sunrise on the 28th of June 1876, a knot of blueclad horsemen reined up on a ridge overlooking the valley of the Little Big Horn River. The sunburnt, bearded faces of those in the vanguard reflected all too clearly the exhaustion and strain of the past three days. Seven companies of their regiment had battled a cleverly concealed and numerically superior foe, sustaining a loss of more than one hundred killed and wounded. Only the timely approach of reinforcements had spared them possible annihilation at the hands of their Sioux and Cheyenne antagonists.

The minds of these officers and troopers of the Seventh U.S. Cavalry were clouded with ominous speculation. What had happened to Lieutenant Colonel George A. Custer and the five companies under his immediate command? The battered battalions of Major Marcus Reno and Captain Frederick Benteen had heard nothing from their regimental commander since the dispatch of a courier on the afternoon of June 25. As the harsh, impartial light illuminated the rugged terrain east of the river, the soldiers' worst fears were realized. The hillocks and coulees were dotted with the bodies of more than two hundred men and some seventy slain cavalry horses.

As the troopers rode onto the fatal battlefield, they confronted what Lieutenant Edward Godfrey called "a scene of sickening, ghastly horror!" The flyblown bodies blackening in the hot western sun were stripped naked, scalped, mutilated, and bristling with arrows. The skulls of most of the dead had been crushed with Indian warclubs; some bodies were decapitated, others quite literally dismembered. "It would be impossible to put in print the sight that met our eyes at that place," Sergeant Charles Windolph recalled; "it was impossible to recognize any of even one's closest friends."

The fact that Reno's and Benteen's wounded had to be evacuated and the necessity of General Alfred Terry's relief column continuing the campaign against the Sioux and Cheyennes required that Custer's dead be buried quickly. Their senses overwhelmed by the awful task, few of the burial party displayed much inclination to explore the battlefield. No organized effort was made to plot the locations of the slain or the ejected shell casings that would have denoted the firing positions of soldiers and Indians.

Little Big Horn's gruesome aftermath haunted every survivor and provided a nightmarish undercurrent to the second-guessing, dissentious wrangling, and bitter recriminations that followed the Indian-fighting army's greatest disaster. Much of this debate, including the army's 1879 court of inquiry, centered on the actions of Major Reno, Captain Benteen, and their subordinates. The details of Custer's maneuvers, like his strategic motivation, remained controversial and obscure.

Latter-day students and historians of Little Big Horn similarly found themselves stymied by a lack of concrete evidence regarding Custer's fate. There were, of course, numerous Indian accounts of their great victory over the soldiers; but many white researchers dismissed these stories as self-serving and hopelessly contradictory. Most authors were content to focus on Reno's and Benteen's engagement, which was controversial enough in its own right. For these writers the movement and deployments of the Custer battalion must perforce remain an unsolvable mystery; the "Last Stand" was the stuff of legend, not history.

In the mid-1930s a newcomer to the field of Custeriana named Charles Kuhlman decided to tackle the "Custer Mystery" head on — to transform the legend into history.

Charles Kuhlman was born in Davenport, Iowa, on January 15, 1872. Both of his parents were German immigrants, his father Wilhelm Kuhlman a veteran of the Prussian Army, and Charles and his six siblings were reared in a bilingual household where English was the second language.

When Charles was a child, his family moved to Nebraska, where his father operated a farm near Grand Island. Tall, powerfully built but shy and retiring, young Kuhlman displayed marked scholastic ability, and after graduating from a Grand Island high school entered the University of Nebraska. He received his B.A. from that institution in 1897, and in 1900 an M.A. in European history. Pursuing his academic career in Europe, Kuhlman studied in Leipzig and Paris, and obtained a Ph.D. from the University of Zurich, Switzerland. Much of his postgraduate study centered on the French Revolution, specifically the role of the Jacobin Society, on which subject he ultimately hoped to publish a definitive history.

Returning to Nebraska, Kuhlman married his college sweetheart, Minnie Wilkinson, and assumed the post of Professor of European History at his alma mater. He seemed well on his way to a promising academic career when tragedy struck. Always somewhat hard of hearing, an illness rendered Kuhlman almost completely deaf. He gave up his position on the university faculty, moved to Loveland, Colorado, and became a farmer.

Kuhlman's agricultural background, coupled with a life-long interest in botany, enabled him to pioneer a number of horticultural innovations including a strain of hull-less corn and an improved variety of cabbage. By 1916, when Kuhlman and his wife and four children settled on a farm near Billings, Montana, his creative agronomy had made him a profitable agricultural wholesaler. The former professor never completely abandoned his academic pursuits; in 1920 he published a monograph titled "Pacifism, Unifying Thesis of Social Reform," and he continued to pursue his research on the Jacobins.

Misfortune again struck Charles Kuhlman in his late fifties. The Depression severely undermined the family's economic resources, and in 1929 his beloved wife, Minnie, died. The loss compounded the introversion resulting from his deafness, and Kuhlman lapsed into a melancholy so profound that his daughter-in-law Fay (Mrs. Fred Kuhlman) recalled that the "despondency threatened to destroy him." She and her husband "prepared his food and took care of him" on their farm near Billings.[1]

Fred and Fay were in the habit of taking Dr. Kuhlman on Sunday drives. One such excursion, in the early 1930s, brought them to the Custer Battlefield, which along with its adjacent national cemetery was then under the administration of the War Department. As the elder Kuhlman walked about the grass and sagebrush, dotted with the marble markers where Custer's soldiers had fallen more than fifty years earlier, and climbed Last Stand Hill to the monument atop their mass grave, he seemed to undergo an almost miraculous emergence from his crippling depression. The enigmatic fate of the doomed battalion, the disputed orders that had led 210 troopers to disaster, and the tactical evolution of their final battle presented Charles Kuhlman a daunting intellectual challenge. His seemingly hopeless lassitude gave way to scholarly fervor—a determination to unravel and solve "the Custer Mystery."

By the end of the 1930s Charles Kuhlman had become an energetic and outspoken member of a small and dedicated fraternity devoted to the field of Custeriana. Working in the little cabin or "gardener's shack" (as some visitors recalled it) in which he lived on the grounds of his son's farm, Dr. Kuhlman maintained a voluminous correspondence with Fred Dustin, Colonel William A. Graham, E. A. Brininstool, and dozens of other Little Big Horn buffs. He maintained a long-standing if occasionally cranky friendship with these fellow enthusiasts, with whom he chose to disagree on a number of important issues.

Unlike many students of the battle—amateur historians, journalists, or retired army officers—Kuhlman's research was grounded in the academic disciplines of his early career. His conviction that history was a "science" formed the foundation of his approach to Little Big Horn. He strove to be open-minded rather than permit bias to color his interpretation. In this he differed markedly from the fervently anti-Custer (and thus pro-Reno) leanings of Dustin and Brininstool. Most significantly, Kuhlman stood in contrast to Graham and other battle historians in his refusal to dismiss the movements and deployments of Custer's ill-fated battalion as forever "unknowable."

Kuhlman's theoretical approach was twofold. First, a "synchronization [of] time and space" juxtaposing Reno's and Benteen's *known* movements with Custer's *possible* movements would markedly narrow the range of possibility to a *probable* course of events. Second, and most importantly, Kuhlman believed the marble markers on Custer's field—denoting the positions of the dead troopers—provided the key to an accurate "visualization" of tactical deployments, and the sequential evolution of the Last Stand.

Since the marker locations became the cornerstone of Kuhlman's theory of the Custer battle, and because they are an intrinsic element of his 1951 opus *Legend into History — The Custer Mystery,* it would be well to review their somewhat controversial history.

We now know with reasonable certainty that at the time of

the fatal battle the Custer Battalion numbered 210 men, though it had initially been larger. Two couriers (Sergeant Daniel Kanipe and trumpeter Giovanni Martini, or John Martin) had been dispatched to hasten Captain Benteen's companies and the mule-borne pack train. Additionally, at least four and possibly as many as seven troopers had straggled behind the column, ultimately linking up with the Reno and Benteen battalions.

Burial parties reported interring between 202 and 206 men on Custer's field—virtually all of the doomed battalion. There were few shovels on hand, and these initial "burials" were hasty and inadequate, more often than not a scant covering of earth and sagebrush thrown atop the mutilated bodies where they lay. In the case of twenty-eight dead who had perished in the eroded cul-de-sac known as Deep Ravine, soil from the steep embankments was simply broken off and rolled down on top of them. Wooden stakes cut from abandoned Indian lodge poles were pounded into the ground at most of the individual gravesites.

In the summer of 1877 an army contingent led by Captain Michael Sheridan (General Philip Sheridan's brother and aide) returned to Little Big Horn to exhume the bodies of Custer and most of the other slain officers. At that time, and again in 1879, military personnel policed the bone-strewn battlefield and reinterred the scattered remains. In 1881 yet another detail gathered all the bones that could be located and placed them in a mass grave atop Custer Hill—within several feet of the spot where Custer had fallen. Their resting place was marked with an imposing granite memorial inscribed with the names of the slain.

In the late spring of 1890 Captain Owen Sweet was dispatched to Little Big Horn with his company of the 25th U.S. Infantry. He had been given the unprecedented and daunting assignment of erecting headstone-like markers at the places where Custer's men had fallen fourteen years earlier, and from whence they had been exhumed in 1881. Sweet did the best he could under the circumstances, placing the markers wherever he found depressions in the ground, vestiges of the original wooden stakes, or where "rank vegetation" indicated the soil had once held human remains. There was clearly more than a little guesswork involved.

Captain Sweet's detail irrevocably complicated the task of future battle historians by erecting 246 stones where no more than 210 men had died — apparently placing those intended for Reno's and Benteen's dead on the Custer portion of the field. Moreover, it seems that rather than set twenty-eight markers for the men killed in the eroded washout known as Deep Ravine, Sweet chose to erect these stones at more geographically stable portions of the field.

Charles Kuhlman apparently never saw Captain Sweet's May 15, 1890, report of the marker detail, and mistakenly blamed an early battlefield superintendent for erecting the extra stones. Over the years six more markers were added, bringing the present number on Custer's battlefield to 252.

"Some of the markers are out of place," Kuhlman admitted, "though it is improbable that many of them are very far out of place." In the 1980s archaeological surveys confirmed Kuhlman's assessment. The partial remains of thirty-four troopers, overlooked by the reburial detail, were found in context with the markers. The forty-two spurious headstones, plus the twenty-eight that should have been placed in Deep Ravine, seem to have been set immediately adjacent to accurately placed ones, since at most "paired" markers the fragmentary remains of only one individual were found.

In 1940 Kuhlman printed 250 copies of a forty-six-page monograph titled *Custer and the Gall Saga,* which for eleven years remained his principle contribution to the literature of Little Big Horn. He was determined not to publish a detailed reconstruction of the battle until he was thoroughly familiar with military sources, the marker locations, and the lay of the land. Whereas author Fred Dustin made only one visit to Custer Battlefield, and Colonel Graham passed up his only opportunity to do so, Dr. Kuhlman's proximity to the battlefield enabled him to make numerous — possibly hundreds — of visits to the site, and he would often camp at a nearby location with his family and friends.

Noted Western historian Robert M. Utley, who worked as a Park Service seasonal ranger at Custer Battlefield in the 1940s following its establishment as a national monument, provides a vivid recollection of Dr. Kuhlman:

> He was a very tall, very gangly figure with leathery face and hands and horn-rimmed glasses. . . . From my post at the monument, I often saw him moving slowly along the edge of Deep Ravine pondering his conception of what happened there. He had been completely deaf much of his life and thus led a highly inner-directed existence . . . he was one of the

most cerebral beings I ever knew—a distinction probably heightened by his inability to communicate with the world outside his mind. Despite his deafness, he was not reticent in sharing his theories. He spoke volubly, even discursively, in a high-pitched monotone, and one communicated with him only by writing on a pad of paper he always carried with him. He was alike a pathetic person but also an admirable one for the adjustment he had made to his infirmity. Whatever one thinks of his theories, his intense field work gave him the most intimate knowledge of every fold and crevice in that battlefield. . . ."[2]

Addison Bragg, former reporter and columnist for the *Billings Gazette,* remembers Dr. Kuhlman as a pleasant conversationalist with a ready smile. His humble one-room residence was lined with bookshelves and files. Well into his eighties, Kuhlman could often be found working away in his vegetable garden, or taking long walks ("mooning," he called it) along the rimrocks above Billings. During these excursions Kuhlman would ponder his theories of the Last Stand, occasionally pausing to jot down ideas. Bragg recalls that it was Kuhlman's habit to purchase spiral notebooks, which he would laboriously unwind; then he would type his manuscripts and carefully rewind the wire spirals into the paper.

Charles Kuhlman was a year shy of his eightieth birthday when the publication of *Legend into History* brought the eccentric intellectual to the forefront of Little Big Horn historians. Six years later the Stackpole Company published the monograph *Did Custer Disobey Orders at the Battle of the Little Big Horn?,* in which Kuhlman convincingly refuted criticism of Custer's actions and provided a well-crafted defense of the flamboyant commander's strategic motivations. But it is undoubtedly *Legend into History* for which Charles Kuhlman will chiefly be remembered. It was, as he admitted, a book for "specialists," and the study quite quickly assumed almost cult status among students of Custeriana—a reputation that it maintains to this day.

Because of Kuhlman's reasoned, tightly constructed and clearly presented account of Custer's last battle, his theories were most persuasive and hence widely accepted. His influence extended beyond Little Big Horn enthusiasts to the National Park Service. Two years after the publication of *Legend into History* nine interpretive markers were emplaced on Custer Battlefield bearing inscriptions that closely followed Dr. Kuhlman's reconstruction of the engagement.

It is thus important to note several areas in which Kuhlman may have overlooked or misinterpreted the historical record.

Rational and objective as Kuhlman professed to be, like many of his peers he remained deeply skeptical of Indian accounts. He doubted the integrity of the interpreters and journalists who had chronicled the warriors' tales, and was stymied by seeming contradictions. To Kuhlman's scientific mind, not only were the stories told by Sioux and Cheyenne veterans of Little Big Horn "unverifiable," he concluded that "no consistent account has ever been given by them." Had Kuhlman chosen to pursue and examine the scores of Indian recollections compiled by his historical precursors, he would have found that the same "synchronization of time and spacial relationships" he applied to the military's maneuvers provides for an equally valid synthesis of Indian movements. In fact most seeming "contradictions" in Indian accounts are explained by the specific time and place that a given warrior entered the fray.

Central to the thesis expounded in *Legend into History* is Kuhlman's belief that Custer massed his five companies on the hill where he would later make his last stand, then deployed them in a holding action intended to cover the anticipated arrival of Reno and Benteen. When those battalions failed to make their appearance, Indian assaults prompted Custer to initiate a coordinated effort to fight his way southward to the other elements of his scattered regiment. Kuhlman's theory of a north-south flow of battle is strongly refuted by Indian accounts, as well as by archaeologists whose microscopic examination of ejected shells enabled them to identify and track the movements of individual weapons across the battlefield. Moreover, numerous excavated shell casings from Henry and Winchester rifles (as opposed to the Springfield Carbines carried by the troopers) refute Kuhlman's assertion that "very few [Indians] had magazine firearms." Indeed, the most important revelation emerging from the recent archaeological surveys was that Custer's men were not only outnumbered, they were outgunned as well.

It is to Kuhlman's credit that he refused to fall prey to the common impression that Custer's fight was from the very outset a beleaguered, desperate struggle against thundering Indian hordes. Kuhlman correctly assumed that the Sioux and Cheyennes had no cohesive strategy other than to cross the river and engage the soldiers who threatened their village. He also realized that by and large the warriors fought dismounted—tying their ponies to sagebrush, warily creeping up coulees and ravines and sniping at the troopers from increasingly shorter range. Thus, while Kuhlman's reconstruction of Little Big Horn can be challenged in many of its specific details, the overall sense of gradually escalating combat ultimately leading to military collapse and annihilation is essentially valid.

Until cancer began to take its inevitable toll on the once strapping octogenarian, Charles Kuhlman continued his agrarian pursuits (for a time he served as head gardener at Rocky Mountain College), and began assembling his long-anticipated history of the Jacobin Society in the French Revolution. Kuhlman succumbed to his illness September 18, 1959, leaving that work unfinished. But *Legend into History* will remain a lasting monument to Charles Kuhlman's intellectual tenacity, a model for all who seek to know the truth of "The Custer Mystery."

Brian C. Pohanka
Alexandria, Virginia

---

1. Fay Kuhlman, introduction to 1977 reprint of *Legend into History*, The Old Army Press, Ft. Collins, Colorado.
2. Letter, Robert M. Utley to Brian C. Pohanka, August 4, 1993.

LEGEND
into
HISTORY

The Custer Mystery

✰

**An Analytical Study
of the
Battle of the Little Big Horn**

✰

BY CHARLES KUHLMAN, PH.D.

THE STACKPOLE COMPANY
HARRISBURG, PENNSYLVANIA

THE CLIMAX

© Brown & Bigelow, St. Paul, Minn., U. S. A.

Contents

Maps and Illustrations

Foreword

THERE is little need for another study of *what* happened at the Battle of the Little Big Horn, considered from the standpoint of objective results, for they have already been repeatedly cataloged. And, except for the action on Custer Field, the *how* of the event has been largely cleared up. What remains in violent controversy is the *why* of the results. This leads us directly to the mental reactions of the participants in the face of what they encountered from the time they left the Yellowstone until the battle was over.

If we wish to understand why Custer, Reno, Benteen, or any of the troop commanders did what they did, we must, in imagination, ride at their elbows and try to see what they saw at any given time and place, the nature of the terrain, what they knew or believed, about the position and numbers of the enemy, the whereabouts of the different detachments of the regiment, and try to understand their doubts and perplexities resulting from insufficient information. In addition to this we must constantly have in our own minds a panoramic view of the whole area involved, as well as a fairly accurate idea of the minor details of the topography that are of military significance, and remember that the responsible officers learned of these details, for the most part, only as they came to them.

The present study is, therefore, concerned chiefly with this *why*. It represents an effort to do what, as far as we are aware, has never been attempted before except for certain limited phases of our subject. That is to say, I have sought to explain in a systematic way the *why* of the battle not so much by dint of quotation from the sources as by subjecting these sources to a rigid analysis in order to discover what they seem to spell after all definite inconsistencies have been canceled out. It is a large order that leaves ample room for self-deception and other types of error.

Sustained analysis calls for close attention and the habit of logical thinking as well as an open mind, a mind as far as humanly possible unencumbered with irrevocable convictions. This applies to the writer and the reader alike.

The confirmed partisan will be interested in this book, I hope; but he will not like it. The desultory reader in search of new stories interesting as collector items may find it somewhat dry, although I should be sorry if this were the case. But the nature of the task assumed left me no choice if I wished to be intelligible; for the analytical type of narrative does not lend itself effectively to the scientific technique of copious quotations and the punctilio of citation to the authority for every statement made. This book is, therefore, addressed primarily to the readers who are already familiar with the chief sources and the more important narratives already available. Needless to say, the two types are not wholly incommensurable. They overlap in many places in such a way that the story can be told by direct quotations that are self-explanatory, and thus in themselves form the necessary links in the chain of cause and effects. Wherever this was possible I have used the quotation method.

Objective events cannot be fully understood until we have localized them in both time and space. In other words, time and space are our indispensable orientation points. When, therefore, we read an account in which one or both of these points are missing, we are not much enlightened. We encounter this difficulty even in describing the Reno fight in the valley, although in this case we have a cloud of witnesses far above the average in both intelligence and a sense of personal integrity. The Maguire map, made a few days after the battle, does not contain the necessary data to locate the battlefield. We are forced to resort to constructive reasoning based on topography and the testimony of the officers and enlisted men participating in the fighting here, to identify the field. Our first orientation point here is a certain ravine that can be definitely located with reference to the troops. Another fairly well established orientation point is the location of the Uncpapa Indian camp, also with reference to the troops. The description of the field itself by the participants can be applied in several points to two different localities; but only one of them can be reconciled to the *two fixed points*—the ravine and the Indian camp.

It seems rather absurd to pontificate on the necessity of keeping order in both time and space. This is axiomatic, and everyone knows it; but the fact is that it has been too frequently neglected in practice, as has also the fact that in this subject we are concerned with three-dimensional space; for the topography was a decisive factor in bringing about the events as they actually occurred rather than in some other way and with a different result. I found it impossible to really get anywhere before I had brought a reasonable degree of order into these three factors, time, space, and topography; or, to put it more concretely, had constructed a synchronization showing where, at any given moment, the several detachments of the regiment were with reference to each other and the Indians, the whole limned against the topography as a background. It is by the use of these factors that the wheat is largely screened from the chaff in the oral accounts we have. The difficulty is not in any lack of evidential material. There is a great mass of it. The trouble arises from its contradictory character. But that part of it that is clearly irreconcilable with the three fixed orientation points is obviously untrue and to be rejected no matter what the source. Science has no respect for authority, though scientists may respect persons who have by their accomplishments become "authorities."

There is nothing exceptional in this inconsistency of the sources. It is more nearly the rule than the exception in any historical subject for which a considerable amount of source material exists. It is, therefore, obvious that no coherent narrative can be produced unless there is selection and elimination. In 1940 I published a booklet; *General George A. Custer and the Gall Saga.* It was favorably received by the U. S. Cavalry Journal and a friendly reviewer for the *Chicago Daily News* who, however, felt some qualms when he noted that I had obtained my results largely by using only those Indian accounts that tended to prove my conclusions. Well, my dear reader, would you expect me to establish my conclusions by using only those accounts that are irreconcilable with them?

But a "wisecrack" is a shabby answer to an honest doubt resulting from a misconception. The answer is that no historian worth his salt chooses his sources to suit his thesis. He uses some in preference to others because he thinks they are nearer the truth. He studies all the sources he has but does not accept all of them any more than a man sorting apples accepts all of them if he finds that some of them are bad. He refers them all to certain points of control, if such there are that are known to him, which eliminates those that are not consistent with this control, wholly without reference to any thesis he may have. In a systematic work on historical method this subject is treated under a section called "Control of the sources," in which the technique of control is explained. But, as in all pretentious constructions, it all boils down to systematized common sense. The only reason for formulating it is the fact that, as someone has said; "The trouble with common sense is that it is so uncommon."

If the reader will turn to chapter 6 of the present narrative he will find a type of control in which one witness, or source, is played against another in such a way that certain facts emerge in which there was no conscious choice on my part. He will find another type of control in that part of chapter 9 dealing with Custer's passage from Medicine Tail Coulee to the battlefield. In chapter 5 the same kind of control is used for the testimony of Captain Benteen and his officers concerning the distance they had covered in their scout to the left. They thought it was about 14 to 15 miles. Actually it was less than half that distance, but there is no way of proving this from oral evidence alone. But they all said that they watered their horses at a certain morass after they came back to the trail about a half mile above the morass. We have Benteen's word for it that this morass was four miles from the point where they had left the trail to go on this scout, and this has been confirmed by speedometer readings of several different makes of cars. When the reader comes to this chapter he will see how this works out to a conclusive demonstra-tion.

The judge on the bench faces this problem of control in every case based on oral evidence, or testimony. To reach a decision he must pick his way through a mass of conflicting statements by the witnesses, and I believe the legal profession will support me in saying that the judge's decision, if he is worthy of his office, usually represents as near an approach to the truth as is humanly attainable.

Selection and rejection are, therefore, inseparable from the writing of history. No selection, no history. But the selection is not made to support a thesis already formed. The thesis grows out of the selection, not the other way about. What is selected is the product of the analysis without reference to pre-conceived ideas. The word "selection", therefore, points to a misconception; for there is no selection in the sense implied by my critic. There is a presentation of the evidence that has withstood the analysis with reference to the known facts. When the test-facts are not conclusively established we attain only probability or plausibility.

Another friendly critic expressed a natural doubt that the head-stones, or markers, on Custer field can be safely used to reconstruct the action here. He admits they can be so used if they actually stand on the spots where the bodies of the troopers were found; but it is urged that in view of the many conflicting accounts of the original burials and re-burials, we cannot be certain that the markers now stand where the men fell.

To a certain extent this criticism is valid, I think; for there seems to be little room for doubt that some of the markers are out of place, though it is improbable that many of them are very far out of place. There are, however, something like 40 markers that are wholly spurious, set up at random many years after the battle, where no bodies were found. But, as stated in the narrative, these, while not in most cases individually identifiable, were placed in the south skirmish line and inside the fence around the Custer group at the Hill, where they do not affect the reconstruction of the action materially.

What, for the want of a better term, we may call the legitimate markers were set up by Captain Owen J. Sweet of the 25th U. S. Infantry, in 1890, fourteen years after the original burial of the bodies. Fourteen years is a long time, and since the burials of 1876 are known to have been skimpy, what reason have we to believe that Captain Sweet was able to identify the gravesites when he came to set up the markers?

Let us for the moment ignore the history of these graves and their bodies, or skeletons, and ask: "How does the number of markers set up compare with the tallies reported at the time the burials were made? Major Reno, in his report to General Terry dated July 5, 1876, said they buried 204. Captain Benteen, writing to his wife a week after the battle, said 203, as also did Sergeant John Ryan many years later. Lieutenant Bradley, in a letter to the *Helena Herald* of July 5, gave the number as 206. Godfrey's tally was 212. Up to 1896 there were only 202 markers on the field, the number still carried on the Geological Survey special sheet attached to the contour map of the Custer Battlefield area. The same number was reported by Superintendent Grover Wessinger in a letter to headquarters in 1896, in which he asked for 41 headstones, saying that there were 263 names on the burial register but only 202 stones on the field.

There is here a minor difficulty because of the headstones for Lieutenant Crittenden and Mark Kellogg. Mr. Dustin informs me that the former was set up by Crittenden's father and the latter by the *New York Herald*. Were they included in the 202 reported by Wessinger though they were not official? My own guess is that Captain Sweet set up 202 marble headstones and two wooden headboards for Boston Custer and Armstrong Reed, a discrimination which aroused the ire of a local citizen at the time who insisted in a letter to the *Miles City Journal* that they should have the same markers as the troops because they had died fighting. This makes 204, the exact number of burials reported by Major Reno, or 206 if we include the markers for Crittenden and Kellogg, under the assumption that Wessinger did not count them. In 1935 and 1936 I counted and re-counted the markers four or five times. At the last two counts the tally stood at 246 and I let it go at that. If we now add to the 204 officially set the 41 asked for by Wessinger, we have 245.

Turning now to the history of Custer's dead, we find that there is substantial agreement as to the general nature of the first burial, though there is noticeable here the usual tendency to exaggerate. To emphasize the skimpiness of these burials—or to excuse it, such as it was—we are left with the impression that only a half dozen or so of spades and shovels were at hand. It is, therefore, worthwhile to quote what the careful and unexcitable Colonel Gibbon said on this subject. "The Seventh Cavalry remained on the bluffs during the night," (27th to 28th) he said, "and early the next morning moved down to the scene of Custer's conflict, to perform the mournful duty of burying the remains of their slaughtered comrades. This would have been an impracticable task but for the discovery, in the deserted Indian camps, of a large number of shovels and spades."

There is also a general impression that wolves tore the bodies to pieces and scattered the bones all over the field, but just how extensive these depredations were is a matter of doubt. The Cheyenne warrior, Wooden Leg, who with a party of his tribesmen visited the field around the middle of December—six months after the battle—told Dr. Marquis that he could not recall seeing any graves that had been disturbed by wolves, though he had noticed that they had been feeding on the dead horses. In any case—and this is the important point for our purpose—there cannot be the slightest doubt that the graves were easily found by the burial party in 1877. In fact a correspondent of the *Chicago Times* who was present at the re-burials, wrote that "All the graves of both officers and men were discovered without difficulty."

But concerning the re-burials of 1877 and everything thereafter, there is still the widest difference of opinion. The late Dr. Marquis, for instance said in his pamphlet, "Custer's Soldiers not buried," published in 1933, that no re-burials whatever were made at any time except in the trenches around the base of the Monument set up in 1885, according to him. We shall see presently that the monument was erected in 1881, but whether at that time only the bones on the surface or all still underground were also buried in these trenches, seems still open to debate.

In spite of all this Dr. Marquis was of the opinion that the present markers "serve as important helpers in a study of that tempestuous and panicky scramble in 1876."

Mr. Fred Dustin, author of a truly monumental work on our subject, thinks the re-burials of 1877 were just a repetition of the original burials—a mere gesture as described by General Scott who, as a young lieutenant, was present as the work was nearing completion and himself covered a few skeletons with earth.

All this is entirely out of line with the strictly contemporary accounts both as they appear in official documents and in a letter by a correspondent of the *Chicago Times* mentioned above. This correspondent said that a troop of cavalry, whose members had been supplied with willow cuttings, was deployed in skirmish line and marched back and forth over the field so as to cover the ground for miles around. "In a few hours," he said "the thin layer of dirt had been removed from the bones of over two hundred soldiers, and the remains re-interred in the same trenches, but rather more decently than before. Three feet of earth tastefully heaped and packed with spades and mallets was put upon each set of remains, and the head marked by a cedar stake."

This account, so far as it concerns the nature of the re-burials, is fully confirmed by the findings of Captain Luce while going through the records in the archives of the Seventh Cavalry at Fort Bliss. The work was done by Troop "I", wiped out in the fight except for the men in the packtrain and those on detached service elsewhere, but recruited during the intervening period. According to these records there was a real burial, something more than mere re-piling of earth on skeletons lying on the surface.

Within a few weeks after this work had been done Generals Sherman and Sheridan visited the field. Sherman was on his way to Fort Ellis and merely inspected the field enroute. But Sheridan, at Sherman's suggestion, had both the Custer and Reno fields re-combed for any remains Troop "I" might have missed. He ordered his aide, Major General George A. Forsyth, to organize a working party for this purpose. About 70 men who had come with Sheridan were divided into three detachments, each under command of a commissioned officer. They spent four hours in their search and reported finding 17 skeletons, or parts of skeletons, which they buried, where, Forsyth's report, dated April 8, 1878, does not say. "We found" says the report, "that as a general rule, the graves were in as good condition, as under the circumstances and considering the extreme lightness of the soil and the entire absence from it of clay, gravel or stones, could have been expected . . . The soldiers' graves were generally grouped together in four distinct places, and with two exceptions where wolves had dug for prey, were well covered. On the side of a ravine where a number of bodies had been buried, we found several skeletons that had been exposed by rains, as the soil is as easily washed as so much ashes."

The last statement in all probability refers to the bodies of the "E" Troop men in the deep ravine south of Custer Hill. The men who buried the members of this troop the year before found the bodies in such condition that they could not go on with the work in the usual way because they were overcome by nausea. They therefore shoveled earth on them from the top of the banks of the ravine, leaving a condition under which Troop "I" might easily have overlooked several bodies. As I have tried to show in the body of the narrative, these skeletons must have been taken up in 1877 and buried on the line the troops held just before the Indians struck. The subsoil in this ravine is, indeed, as light as ashes and easily washed away. I have been over practically every foot of the field many times and feel certain there is no other ravine where men were buried in loose soil. The only other place where men were buried on the side of the ravine is where the second platoon of "L" Troop fought, and here the soil is not as loose as ashes, and the drainage area of the ravine is so small that the washing even in a heavy shower cannot be very great. In fact the bottom of this ravine is now grass-grown, and must have been even more so in 1877, before over-grazing by sheep had killed the taller grasses here as elsewhere over the West. This work was done on July 21, 1877. In submiting Forsyth's report to General Sherman, Sheridan said, among other things, "I then visited the main portion of the battlefield myself, and found all the graves neatly raised as in cemeteries inside civilization, and most, if not all, marked with headboards or stakes." And in a final paragraph: "I am half inclined to think, strange as it may appear, that nearly all the desecration of the graves at the Custer battlefield has been done by curiosity hunters in the shape of human coyotes. I have myself known one or two cases where bones were exhibited as relics from the Custer battlefield."

And the present writer can testify from personal knowledge that the "coyotes" are still busy on the Custer field where their presence and identity is established by the many chipped headstones.

From a report of Captain G. K. Sanderson, 11th U. S. Infantry, dated Fort Custer, Montana Territory, April 7, 1879, and addressed to the Post Adjutant, we learn that the field was again searched for remains of the dead. "I found it impossible to obtain rock within a distance of five miles," runs the report. "I accordingly built a mound as illustrated below, out of cordwood, filled in the center, with all the horse bones I could find on the field, in the center of the mound. I dug a grave, and interred all the human bones that could be found, in all, parts of four or five officers bodies. This grave was built up with wood for four feet above ground, well covered, and the mound built over and around it. The mound is ten feet square, and about eleven feet high, is built on the highest point, immediately in rear of where General Custer's body was found."

"Instead of disenterring remains," the report continues, "I removed (renewed?) all the graves that could be found. At each grave a stake was driven, where those previously placed, had fallen."

"Newspaper reports to the effect that bodies still lay exposed are sensational, from a careful searching of the ground. A few remains now buried beneath the mound, was all that could be found."

Captain Anderson believed that the large number of horse bones had given rise to the sensational stories, which was his reason for gathering them up.

"The whole field presents a perfectly clean appearance, each grave being re-mounded," says the report.

The report itself does not indicate when this work was done: but I am under the impression that the commander of such a working party usually makes his report immediately after completing his task. A single platoon could have done this work in about three days if it was well planned and the necessary materials were at hand. If the report was dated immediately after the work was finished we are safe in saying that from July 21, 1877 to the close of March, 1879, very little washing out or other disturbances of the remains had taken place, but that sensational stories were afloat about unburied bodies lying exposed on the field.

The next reference I have to work done in connection with the remains of the dead on all three battlefields, takes us to the spring and summer of 1881, when, under the direction of Lieutenant Charles Francis Roe stationed at Fort Custer, the granite monument was erected on Custer Hill. Mr. Dustin, searching for the report of Lieutenant Roe in the printed reports of the War Department, failed to find it, but did find General Terry's report from which he quotes the following in a letter to me: "July 6, 1881, Lieutenant Roe, Adjutant, Second Cavalry, placed in charge of the Custer battlefield, left Fort Custer with Troop "C," Second Cavalry, Lieutenant Fuller commanding, to establish a camp near the Little Big Horn battlefield, between the first and second crossings of that river, to erect the monument and collect and inter the remains from the battlefield around the site of the monument."

I do not know if the report of Roe still exists: but shortly before his death Mr. W. A. Falconer of Bismarck, North Dakota, sent me what seems to be a summary of it. In his covering letter he said that very few people knew of this, but did not say where he obtained it, and before I got around to ask him for this information, he passed on. There is, however, no doubt whatever in my mind that it is authentic.

This summary is as follows: "Lieutenant Charles Francis Roe, while stationed at Fort Custer, Montana Territory, in the spring and summer of 1881, February to August, 1881, hauled the three large pieces of granite weighing 14,000, 12,000 and 10,000, from the bank of the Big Horn River to the Custer battlefield, and erected the Custer Monument where it stands. He also dug a trench ten feet from the base of the monument on four sides for the remains. He gathered all the remains he could find from the Custer battlefield-Reno Hill and the Valley—and they were buried around the monument, making three burials of the remains. Roe says that wherever he found the remains of a man, he planted a stake well into the ground. Work completed July 29, 1881."

This brings us to within nine years of the time the headstones were set up. It will be seen that up to this time there had been small chance of the gravesites being lost. If during the succeeding years rains and the trampling of stock tended to obliterate them there were still the stumps of the stakes driven in 1877 and 1881, for these were well driven down and could not be pushed over. They might rot or be broken, but the parts that were left in the ground could have been easily found and serve as a guide in 1890 in those cases where the vegetation and the evidence of disturbed soil was not conclusive. The fact that the number of headstones set up corresponds so closely to the number of burials reported in 1876 is good evidence that Captain Sweet did his work carefully and placed stones only where there was clear evidence of a grave. This construction is supported by the fact, reported in the *Billings Gazette* for May, 1890, that he was expected to place 228 stones. We know, however, that he placed only 202.

All this leaves out the probability that Lieutenant Roe, or someone else, made a map or diagram showing exactly the location of each gravesite, if the skeletons were really taken up in 1881. The idea of ultimately removing all the remains to Custer Hill and erecting headstones on the gravesites, had been under discussion as far back as 1879, for it is mentioned by Captain Sanderson in his report discussed above. It would therefore have been an inexcusable piece of negligence to fail to make such a diagram. Captain Sweet's report, in which there may have been a reference to such a diagram, could not be found by Captain Luce when he searched for it in the records of the War Department.

But—putting the cart before the horse—the most convincing evidence that the present markers, with few exceptions, stand where the men were killed, is the almost automatic manner in which the action unrolls before our mental vision once we have established a few key-facts concerning the relative positions of the troops and the Indians when the fighting began. If the markers did not stand approximately where the men fell we should sooner or later come to a major impasse. But nothing of the kind happened. There are alternative explanations for a few of the isolated markers, but none I have been able to imagine for the groups, which all drop closely into the dynamic pattern of the overall action, cause and effect immediately obvious and in many cases confirmed by Indian accounts, sometimes long after the chain had been constructed.

Orientation Summary

A preview of the tactical movements of the several elements of Custer's command on June 25, 1876, as reconstructed by the author. The reader is invited to refer to the map facing page 1 and the maps on pages 247 to 251 for orientation purposes.

THE strategic movements outlined in General Terry's orders to Custer and Gibbon were based on the general impression that the Indians were located at the headwaters of the Rosebud and the Little Big Horn. Custer was to go up the Rosebud to block their way past the head of the Wolf Mountains, while Gibbon was to intercept them if they fled downstream.

But late in the afternoon of the 24th of June Custer discovered, as he neared the site of the present town of Busby, that the Indians were in much greater force than had been believed and were only about 30 miles ahead, as indicated by the freshness of the trail, and were, therefore, 50 miles or so farther downstream than had been supposed, if, indeed, they had as yet reached the river.

This enormous discrepancy between the facts and the general impression upon which the orders were based, led Custer (for reasons detailed in the narrative) to stick to the trail instead of continuing up the Rosebud as his orders advised him to do. He decided to cross the Divide between the Rosebud and the Little Big Horn that night (24th to 25th), conceal his command during the day (25th), locate the Indians during the day (25th), and during the night move into position to strike at dawn on the 26th, the day Gibbon was expected to enter the valley of the Little Big Horn from the north.

This plan was abandoned when, a little before Noon, he received information which convinced him that his command had been discovered by the Indians.

Good tactics now demanded an immediate advance. So the command was halted as it reached the Divide and organized for a reconnaissance in force in order to pick up as much information as possible as they went along. Benteen was assigned 3 troops for a scout to the left; Reno received 3 troops, and Custer retained 5 under his immediate command. The remaining troop under McDougall was left to serve as guard for the packtrain. A few minutes after Noon the advance began, Benteen moving off at a left oblique, Reno along the south bank of Sundance (now Reno) Creek, Custer over the Indian trail along the north bank.

Benteen, having gone as far as he thought advisable, returned to the trail a little before 2 o'clock, about 4 miles behind Custer and Reno who were then nearing a single tepee four and a half miles from the Little Big Horn. Here they flushed a small band of warriors who fled down the trail. At the same time a heavy dust was seen in the valley, which was taken to mean that the Indians were in wild flight. Custer at once ordered Reno to go in pursuit.

Reno went down the trail at a fast gait, crossed the river and galloped down the valley about two and a half miles, then halted to fight on foot. After about 15 to 20 minutes he moved into the edge of some timber along the sides of a basin some fifteen feet below the plain; fought here for another 15 to 20 minutes, while the Indians converged on his command from every direction. Not having men enough to cover his defensive position, he remounted his command and retreated to the bluffs east of the river where, in about 10 to 15 minutes, he was joined by Benteen, and by the packtrain about an hour later.

Meanwhile Custer, after Reno had left, proceeded slowly down the trail for some distance, turned to the right diagonally toward the river, and then rushed up the slope northwestward at a furious gallop; halted his command near Reno Hill, and with his staff rode forward to the edge of the bluffs, arriving there a few minutes before Reno went into dismounted action in the valley about a mile and a half to the west. He remained there for perhaps 5 minutes and then resumed his march downstream. As the column neared the high ridges now officially designated as Weir Point, he sent Sergeant Kanipe with an order to the packtrain to hurry forward.

At Weir Point Custer once more halted the command and from the top of one of the ridges surveyed the Indian camps and the terrain downstream. Then on again northeastward down a deep ravine leading to the head of South Medicine Tail about two miles straight east of the Middle Ford. After going about 300 yards he sent Trumpeter Martin with the now famous order to Benteen to come on, be quick and bring the packs.

Coming to the head of South Medicine Tail he followed it down for about a mile, then halted for 15 to 20 minutes. At the end of this period he sent the Gray Horse Troop down the coulee and with the remaining 4 troops turned northeastward toward the head of a high ridge about a mile east of the battlefield, and followed its curving crest past the head of North Medicine Tail.

While Custer was making this detour, the Gray Horse Troop moved down South Medicine Tail to within about a half mile of the Ford, and then left it to go to a fairly high ridge about a half mile to the north, engaging in a light skirmish with a few warriors who had come up from the Ford. At the ridge they dismounted, deployed as skirmishers, and slowly moved toward North Medicine Tail down which Custer was now coming to pick them up. As the two detachments neared the point where they were about to meet Custer fired several volleys down the coulee scattering and driving back the warriors who had come up from the Ford. Then the Gray Horse Troop rejoined Custer and the whole command rode northwestward to Custer Hill and halted. Here they stood for an hour or more strictly on the defensive with only two troops engaged in a light and almost harmless skirmish.

Meanwhile on Reno Hill there was divided command, doubt, indecision, hesitation, delay. But most disastrous of all, a premature move by Captain Weir and his troop, that deceived Custer and led him to a responsive action which, unsupported, sealed his **doom**.

Acknowledgments

IN my study of the Battle of the Little Big Horn, begun in 1935, I have been extraordinarily fortunate in the extent and character of the assistance received from voluntary co-operators whose names are listed below. Much of this came unsolicited and without price, though it sometimes involved both expense and considerable labor. While it is true that some who are specialists in the subject contributed more than did others, I wish to assure all alike of my sincere appreciation of their kind and unselfish service. Without their extensive co-operation it would have been quite impossible for me to assemble the data necessary for a narrative worthwhile from the historical point of view. My repeated thanks therefore, to

CAPTAIN E. S. LUCE, U. S. Army, retired, quondam member of the Seventh U. S. Cavalry and veteran of the First World War, from whom I received a typed copy of the *Chicago Times* record of the Reno Court of Inquiry, together with numerous official documents, a number of little-known manuscripts, valuable data from the records in the office of the Superintendent of the Custer Battlefield Cemetery, now the Custer Battlefield Monument, and finally a map showing the distribution of cartridge cases and other remains east and southeast of the Battlefield, including the discovery of the iron stake marking the spot where the body of Sergeant Butler was found.

E. A. BRININSTOOL, who needs no introduction to the students of the battle and of Western history in general, to whom I am indebted for the loan of a typed copy of the Official Record of the Reno Court of Inquiry, supplemented by the loan of letters by other students some of whom were participants in the battle or connected with the campaign, not to mention his own letters full of details as well as background. Also his own narratives on Benteen, Reno, and more recently his fully documented account of the betrayal and killing of Crazy Horse.

FRED DUSTIN, Author of "The Custer Tragedy," last, but by no means least of the trio who have from the beginning responded unfailingly to my numerous requests for the raw, primitive, objective facts upon which any narrative whatsoever must ultimately rest. Although we disagree radically on almost all major points in controversy, he has nevertheless frequently searched through his vast accumulation of material for a specific datum required for the correct interpretation of groups of facts already in my possession. For this extensive and time-consuming service I am sorry to say I have been able to make only a slight return. Our correspondence, if printed, would fill several large volumes.

The late R. S. ELLISON, formerly president of the Stanolind Oil Company, for extensive excerpts from the field notes of W. M. Camp.

The late W. A. FALCONER of Bismarck, North Dakota, for some little-known newspaper articles and books "out-of-print."

COLONEL W. H. OURY, D. S. M., veteran of the Spanish-American and First World War, U. S. A., retired, for answering a long list of hypothetical questions. Or, to put it concretely: Confronted with a given situation, what would an experienced soldier do about it?

JUDGE FRIERSON H. RICE, for the loan of books and many letters.

The late BRIGADIER GENERAL HAMILTON S. HAWKINS, U. S. A., to whom I am indebted for extremely valuable details involved in Cavalry action, and encouragement to proceed with my studies after the publication of my pamphlet, *General Geo. A. Custer and the Gall Saga*, in 1940, which certainly did not come amiss to a civilian working on a purely military problem. He also made a prediction as to what, in a general way, I would almost certainly find if I continued on through to the end in the spirit of the pamphlet. As it turned out he proved to be an excellent prophet!

COLONEL W. A. GRAHAM, U. S. Army, retired, author of "The Story of the Little Big Horn," (Military Service Publishing Co.) for some material that led to the solution of some vexing problems in connection with the location of Reno's skirmish lines in the Valley and the burial of the bodies of the Gray Horse Troop found in the deep ravine south of Custer Hill. Also for other material, and a critical reading of my manuscript.

COLONEL ELWOOD L. NYE, U. S. Army, retired, for minute details on cavalry marches, and critical reading of parts of my manuscript. Also for a considered statement for publication, regarding the risks habitually taken by the Cavalry in our Indian wars after the close of the Civil War.

LIEUTENANT COLONEL BRICE C. W. CUSTER, for a critical reading of the completed manuscript, and comments.

R. G. CARTWRIGHT, for many Indian accounts, discussions, and a map locating remains found over the whole battlefield area. Also for interviewing Charles Windolph to secure answers to questions submitted by me.

GEORGE G. OSTEN, for loan of books and other material, and trips to the battlefields and over the trail to Busby.

H. G. YOUNG, surveyor of Rosebud County, for checking up on the terrain of the Indian campsites between Tongue River and Rosebud Creek, and other details about the ground in this area.

DR. RAYMOND A. BURNSIDE, Lt. Colonel, Army Medical Corps, for material, discussions and trips to the field.

GRACE STONE COATES (Mrs. Henderson Coates) for loan of material.

Glendolin Damon Wagner (Mrs. Michael Wagner), for loan of material.

My daughter Edith, now Mrs. Robert R. Rachmanow.

Robert R. Rachmanow, formerly of the Coast Artillery and instructor at Camp Callan, California, with the rank of Major.

My son Robert and his wife Hazel.

My son Fred and his wife Fay.

My daughter Evelyn and her husband James R. Lanier; who have taken turns driving me to the battlefields and environs, and made innumerable photographs covering the battlefields and more or less the whole battlefield area.

And finally, my grandson, Fred Arthur Kuhlman, for repeatedly driving me to the battlefield in his car, chiefly for recording distances and for experimentations to determine at what points Custer's command could have been seen by anyone stationed on the Benteen position on Reno Hill.

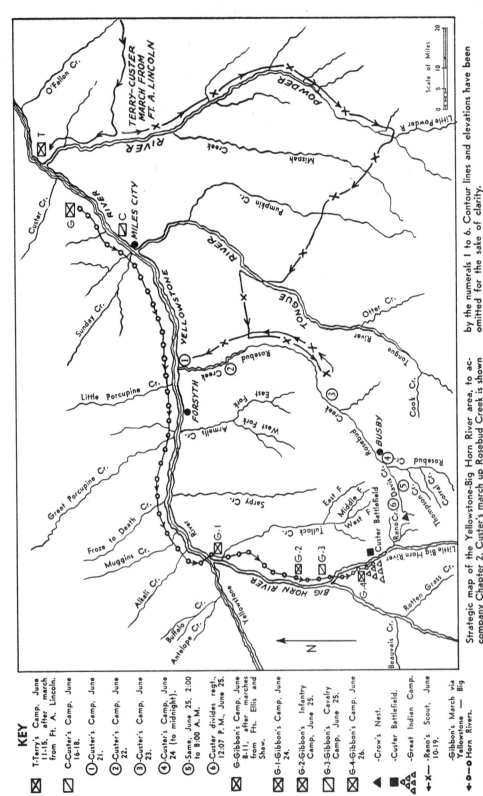

KEY

⊠ T−Terry's Camp, June 11-15, after march from Ft. A. Lincoln.

◻ C−Custer's Camp, June 16-18.

① −Custer's Camp, June 21.

② −Custer's Camp, June 22.

③ −Custer's Camp, June 23.

④ −Custer's Camp, June 24 (to midnight).

⑤ −Same, June 25, 2:00 to 8:00 A. M.

⑥ −Custer divides regt., 12:07 P.M., June 25.

⊠ G−Gibbon's Camp, June 8-11, after marches from Fts. Ellis and Shaw.

⊠ G-1−Gibbon's Camp, June 24.

⊠ G-2−Gibbon's Infantry Camp, June 25.

◻ G-3−Gibbon's Cavalry Camp, June 25.

⊠ G-4−Gibbon's Camp, June 26.

◀ −Crow's Nest.

■ −Custer Battlefield.

△△△ −Great Indian Camp.

−×−×− −Reno's Scout, June 10-19.

−○−○− −Gibbon's March via Yellowstone — Big Horn Rivers.

⬩○○○ −Horn Rivers.

Strategic map of the Yellowstone-Big Horn River area, to accompany Chapter 2. Custer's march up Rosebud Creek is shown by the numerals 1 to 6. Contour lines and elevations have been omitted for the sake of clarity.

CHAPTER 1

General Introduction

W E ARE TODAY in the clear concerning the essential facts about the Battle of the Little Big Horn except the action on Custer field. That is still regarded by many students as a mystery beyond the stark fact that every man in the battalion was killed. But how? Only the Indians knew the answer to that question, and they have told a thousand tales, many of them lurid, some of them fantastic, and all of them disjoined and "spotty."

The field itself, as it was found immediately after the battle and as it was until a few years ago, is almost unbelievably provocative to the imagination. It is a place where the ghosts walk in broad daylight; a place of ravines, gulches and ridges, in part still as desolate and lonely as it was on the day of the battle. Over a space roughly rectangular and about a third by a half mile in extent are marble slabs set, apparently, in the primitive sod, each supposed to mark the spot where a member of the Seventh U. S. Cavalry fell late on a sultry Sunday afternoon in 1876. They are scattered by twos and threes or in larger groups. Some of them stand alone a hundred yards or more from their nearest neighbors, suggesting a despairing moment for some unknown soldier before he crumpled under the blow of a warclub, bullet, or the shaft of an Indian bow.

Except for the markers south of Custer Hill, the first impression is that the battalion of five troops had in some way been shattered into a number of formless masses in which no trace of military order remained, and were then destroyed like a band of frightened sheep. Some writers seem to have had something of this sort in mind. Captain Benteen, going over the field two days after the battle, virtually so represented it. It was a panic rout, he said. No lines were formed except in one place. Nor was there any evidence that a stand had been made except by

1

General Custer and a group of men at the foot of the hill. "You can take a handful of corn and scatter it over the floor and make just such lines," he said. "There were none. The only approach to a line was where five or six horses were found dead at equal distances like skirmishers. At the head of them were five or six men at about the same distance, showing they had jumped off and were trying to get where Custer was. It was the only approach to a line on the field." Again: "Lines could have been formed, but lines were not formed; they probably had no time to form lines * * * The position of the bodies on the Custer battlefield indicated that the officers did not die with their men, for only three officers were found with their companies. All the officers except Keogh, Calhoun and Crittenden were on the line with Custer. That would not be the fact if the command was over-whelmed making a stand. If there had been a charge the officers would have led it * * * The officers' bodies, including Custer's, were in a position indicating that they had not died in a charge; there was an arc of a circle of dead horses around them."

Captain Benteen gives two other significant facts. He said he counted 70 dead cavalry horses and two Indian ponies on the field. Lieutenant Godfrey counted the dead horses around the Custer group and reported that there were 39. We have it, then, that over half of the horses killed on the field were shot for breast-works in one place.

This was about all the senior captain of the Seventh Cavalry could make of it two days after the battle-a panic rout. The objective facts, except for the dead horses and Indian ponies, can still be verified. They are exact with one exception. The five or six men he mentions in the Custer line were not of Calhoun's Troop "L," but in all probability of Tom Custer's Troop "C." Lieutenant McClernand saw these bodies before they were buried, and his account leaves little doubt that they belonged to the latter troop. The bodies of Calhoun's men were found on the northeast corner of the field. In the absence of other evidence the deductions of Benteen were natural, except that men in a panic are not likely to abandon their horses.

We have heard a man who believed himself a thorough stu-dent of the battle make the cynical remark: "Custer and his whole outfit were drunk." Another with the magic letters "Ph.D." after his name, who had visited the field only once, said he had seen enough to convince him that Custer was "crazy." Many of the thousands of visitors who annually drive up and down the miscalled battleridge no doubt come away with similar impressions.

Writers like Hunt, Byrne, McLaughlin and others, basing their narratives on stories by the Sioux, concluded that Custer's men were overwhelmed by Indians charging on their ponies and knocking the troopers off their horses in hand-to-hand combat.

This is wholly at variance with everything the Cheyennes have had to say; and the confused, fragmentary accounts of innumerable others indicate that nothing of the kind occurred. It is in itself extremely improbable as being out of accord with the Indians' usual method of fighting; and 210 men, more or less, armed with breech-loading carbines and Colt revolvers are not as easily bowled over as nine-pins.

If Custer's men had been attacked pell-mell by mounted warriors, they would have rallied for a countercharge, presenting a narrow front in close formation, giving them the full advantage of heavier horses and superior organization and thus minimizing the disadvantage of inferior numbers. But nothing of the kind happened. In any case, had the Indians charged *en masse* and mounted, it is a certainty that they would have left more nearly a hundred dead ponies on the field than the two found by Benteen.

All the Cheyennes—and this was *their* fight in particular—stress the point that the Indians did not fight mounted, but left their ponies concealed in ravines and gulches out of range of the troops. Only those who were demonstrating on the slope toward the river and engaged in long-distant sniping during the first phase of the battle, remained mounted. Later a few warriors on the outskirts of the position fired from their ponies. Those toward the river southwestward merely provided a cardboard front designed to impress Custer with their prowess and force to prevent his making a move toward the village. They had no intention of attacking mounted from this direction, and the evidence is that they did not at any time do so. They served, however, to distract attention from those warriors who were crawling up the ravines all around the defensive position the troops had taken.

Byrne and Van deWater believe that the Indians foresaw exactly where Custer would go, and surrounded the place now known as Custer Field long before he arrived, leaving a narrow opening through which he obligingly entered the trap. Then they greeted him with "a thousand rifle shots," "advanced in wave upon wave" and in a few minutes wiped him off the map.

The late Dr. Thomas B. Marquis, conforming in this instance to a literal reading of what his Cheyennes friends had told him, represents the whole command as having been lined up on the crest of the so-called battleridge, with the warriors crawling up from both sides, firing their rifles and loosing a constant stream of arrows as they advanced. Soon the horses were stampeded carrying with them the reserve ammunition in the saddlebags. This caused instant, universal panic and wholesale suicide among the troops. The Cheyenne warrior, Wooden Leg, said the Indians did not kill over 25 to 30 soldiers. The rest killed themselves or each other. There seems to have been a fixd tradition in the tribe that either whiskey or the Everywhere Spirit had made the troops insane. They could not understand suicide to escape death in fighting, since, as a rule, the Indians do not make captives of warriors, and they, therefore, fight until they are killed, if they cannot escape. Since in such cases death is inevitable, it seems to them an evidence of an unbalanced mind to kill themselves rather than to continue fighting and killing enemies until they are themselves killed.

Wooden Leg thought that if the troops had not committed suicide the Indians would have abandoned the fight and moved out of reach of the troops. This is in all probability true; for, if Custer had remained in the defensive position originally assumed, the Indians would have broken camp at dusk. They had expended much ammunition in their fight with Crook and were fast using up what they had left without doing much damage. They could not come closer and into the open without incurring the heavy losses certain to result from a mounted charge by the troops, a short, hard hit-and-run blow, heavy execution with revolvers at short range before a counter-blow could be struck in the Indian fashion. The warriors were far too smart to risk such losses voluntarily. Neither their weapons nor their organization enabled them to cope with the troops in this kind of fighting. Instead of coming into the open where mounted action by the troops was possible, they confined themselves to crawling up the ravines both north and south of the ridge and up the deep, steep-sided depression northwest of the hill.

The Cheyennes admit that they had not been able to do serious harm to the troops as long as they remained in their defensive position. But when Custer sent the Gray Horse Troop into the broken ground south of the hill they struck hard and destroyed the troop in a few minutes. But even so their losses were heavy, for they say that more Indians were killed here in the few minutes of close-quarter fighting than anywhere else on the field.

And there was something else that made the warriors reluctant to engage in an all-out fight against Custer. Reno still held the bluffs nearly opposite the south end of their village. They did not know how many other troops might be coming against them. Some of them knew that Reno had been reinforced. Had Custer held back and the nearly harmless sniping continued, they would soon have learned that another force of about 130 troopers had joined Reno. With over 200 menacing them at the lower end of the camps and over 300 on the other end, with the possibility that many more were close at hand, prudence suggested that they remove their families and property to a safe distance before committing themselves to a decisive action. In fact there is every reason for thinking that they wished to avoid fighting altogether, and that they fought Custer only because he had surprised them and compelled them to fight to keep him out of their camps.

This view may appear as inadmissable to those who, like Benteen, ascribe supreme confidence and aggressiveness to the Indians, citing the fact that the warriors had gone twenty miles out of their way to fight General Crook. It would be more reasonable to suppose that they attacked Crook because of nervousness over his nearness to their camps. But even this attack was made against the advice of the older chiefs who could see that if Crook went down the Rosebud they could avoid him by going up the Little Big Horn, and that there was as yet no need of fighting. If, on the other hand, he continued on westward and came down the Little Big Horn, they could backtrail to the Rosebud and on to the Bad Lands, if necessary.

The chiefs constituted what we today would call "The Policy-Making Council," and their advice was ordinarily accepted and obeyed, though it could not be enforced if it was disregarded. At the head of this council now stood the Uncpapa medicine man, Sitting Bull. Their policy was to avoid fighting if that was found to be possible. They had already twice restrained the warriors from going on the warpath against Crook. About a month before the battle a small band of Sioux near the mouth of the Rosebud had an oral and sign talk across the Yellowstone with LeForge and Mitch Bouyer of Gibbon's scouts. They said that they did not want to fight the whites; explained that they had left the agencies because they were starving and merely wanted to be let alone to hunt and live south of the river, promising to stay on

their side and asked the troops to stay on the other. "Tell that
to your chiefs," they ended. The Cheyenne warrior, Wooden
Leg, told Dr. Marquis: "Many young men were anxious to go
for fighting the soldiers. But the chiefs and old men all urged
us to keep away from the whites. They said that fighting wasted
energy that ought to be applied to feed and make comfortable
ourselves and our families. Our combination of camps was simply
for defense. We were within our treaty rights as hunters. We
must keep ourselves so."

It is undoubtedly true that the Indians expected trouble during the summer; but they were not seeking it. In any case, if
they were compelled to fight they would certainly do it as nearly
as possible on their own terms. This meant keeping their non-
combatants out of reach of the troops at all times, while the
warriors maneuvered and fought the enemy when fighting was
unavoidable. They were experts in these tactics, in which their
casualties were usually very light. On the other hand, they knew
from bitter experience that cavalry in an Indian village made a
frightful mess of things, destroying tepees and other property,
killing ponies, women, children, and old men. It is well to remember these things while studying the Battle of the Little Big Horn.

The picture of the Custer battle most widely held has been
gained chiefly from melodramatic paintings after the fashion of
a Verboekhoven. We have all seen something of the kind, either
on canvas or the screen. We see General Custer in heroic posture,
a hefty revolver in each hand, sending death and destruction into
a horde of Indians charging mounted from all sides, the few
surviving troopers scattered about in disorder, standing or kneel-
ing, a surprisingly large percentage of them in the act of firing,
as if neither their pistols or their carbines required re-loading
except semi-occasionally. We do not know definitely how this conception originated. It did not spring into existence full-fledged
like Athene from the head of Zeus. There was little on the field
as found by Reno's men when they came to bury the dead that
could have given rise to it, though some of the officers said a
desperate struggle had taken place at the Hill where Custer had
entrenched himself. There was no indication of a general rally,
as we hope will become apparent later in our study.[1]

There must have been less than 30 unwounded enlisted men
in "Custer's Last Stand," besides 6 to 7 officers. Godfrey said
42 bodies were found behind the semi-circle of dead horses.
Wallace said 20 to 30. But during the fighting there were also

7 men behind dead horses on top of the knoll in the rear of the main group, but they were not killed until after they had run away toward the river. Moreover, when the group was formed Troops "F", "I" and "L" were still virtually intact. It has already been noted that Benteen found only 2 dead Indian ponies on the entire battlefield.[2] It would indeed have been something of a miracle if some 35 men behind breastworks had killed only 2 ponies before they were ridden down and killed. We do not believe such a miracle occurred, and therefore do not believe either that there is any truth in the lurid canvasses to which we have referred.

Needless to say, the military students are not guilty of such atrocities in the guise of history. The first of such students to attempt a systematic description of the action was Captain E. S. Godfrey who commanded Troop "K" in Benteen's battalion. This was published in the *Century* magazine for January, 1892; and while we cannot at all subscribe to his findings, it must be admitted that the article presents a number of very useful facts and is wholly free of verbal extravaganza.

Godfrey represents Custer as coming to the field from the east. When he came to a point in the deep ravine about a third of a mile from the Calhoun position he halted, dismounted Troops "I" and "L" under Keogh and Calhoun respectively, and sent them at "double time" to the east end of the ridge, Calhoun deploying with his left presumably at the point where the ridge makes a right angle by turning southwest. Keogh took position on Calhoun's right, both troops facing southwest toward the river. Then Custer passed along the rear of this line, posted "E" under Lieutenant Smith on the right of Keogh, and with the remaining two troops, "C" under Captain Tom Custer, and "F" under Captain Yates, went on to the knoll now known as Custer Hill. The horses of Keogh and Calhoun were left in charge of holders in the usual way but without a guard, where the troops dismounted.

Up to this point the picture is clear, but from here on the action is lost in an impenetrable fog. We are told that the men of "E" in some way and at an unspecified time left their position and drifted to the line south of the hill, so that now there are two separate battles going on, one by Keogh and Calhoun and the other by Custer. No explanation is made of this seemingly needless dispersal of the troops in the presence of the great force of warriors, or why the horses of Keogh and Calhoun were

left a third of a mile from their troops. Both skirmish lines were
now "up in the air" to be flanked at will by the enemy and no
reserves to take care of such a move; no obvious position to be
held or defended, or that could be defended with the troops
available. The Hill could have been defended only if all five
troops were used for that purpose. As a rear guard Keogh and
Calhoun, a half mile away, could not be of the slightest service in
defending the Hill. The south skirmish line, as shown by the
markers, was not posted for defense. It was on the most exposed
ground to be found there. The ravines and ridges on the west
in front of the line, and the ravine in the rear, sheltered the
warriors while the troops were in the open, dismounted and holding their horses by the reins; or at least those of "E" were
standing in this way.

And what became of the horses and their holders of Keogh
and Calhoun left back in the ravine a third of a mile from where
the troops were deployed! Godfrey says they were destroyed by
Gall who stampeded the horses and killed the holders in a surprise attack by coming up the ravine from the ford. But no dead
men or horses were found here. We shall see in a later chapter
that the bodies of the holders and some of the horses were found
on the east wing of the battleridge, where they would have been
in front of Calhoun's skirmish line, according to the Godfrey
conception.

And there are other facts irreconcilable with Godfrey's conception. It has been noted that the troops north of the ridge were
in column of platoons, the marching formation, when attacked.
Keogh's troop was destroyed while in this formation. How are
we to reconcile this with a standing fight on the ridge? Had Keogh
withdrawn from the ridge and prepared to flee before losing a
man? According to the markers not a dead man was found on
the ridge where his men are supposed to have stood. Did Keogh
try to run away while Troop "F" to the west of him stood to
fight it out, leaving its dead scattered up and down the slope
between his own men and those with Custer?

We are absolutely forced to the conclusion that the three
troops north of the ridge and on the east wing of it, were never
lined up on the ridge at all and were marching off the field when
attacked. Were they running away deliberately leaving Custer in
the lurch? Or have we here the evidence of the "panic rout"
Benteen thought he found?

Unless we answer these questions correctly we cannot understand how the battle was actually fought. In the present chapter we are merely establishing certain crucial facts and pointing out the problems to be solved. On the face of it Custer alone burned his bridges and prepared to fight it out at all costs.

We turn now to look at our subject from the Indians' point of view, and here again we find the evidence endlessly conflicting. Some Indians say that they knew of the coming of the Seventh Cavalry long before they reached their village. The bulk of the evidence, however, is that the actual attack was a complete surprise. That does not rule out the possibility that it was known the cavalry were in this part of the Indian Country. The fact, however, that Reno was almost upon them before they saw him seems conclusive proof that no attack was expected at the time. As explained in Chapter 4, the first evidence they had of approaching troops was the smoke from the Lone Tepee set afire by the Arikara scouts in advance of Custer. The action of the herd boys in rushing in the ponies and the presence of a few warriors up the valley who signalled to the camps, caused the news to spread through the village. We have no definite evidence that warriors were up the valley, but there are statements in the testimony of some of the officers which suggest that such was the case. By the time Reno was within about a mile of the upper end of the village, warriors appeared in numbers sufficient to cause him to dismount his command as he neared the timber instead of charging as he had been ordered to do. But there was no confidence on the part of the Indians that the troops could be kept out of the village. There was panic among the non-combatants. Women ran about screaming frantically for their children, gathering them together and fleeing to the benchlands to the west or northward down the valley. Others took down tepees and carried away such of their possessions as were readily portable.

And the panic among the leading chiefs, other than the war leaders, was hardly less for a time than that of the women. Sitting Bull is said to have fled in such haste that he left one of his children behind. Many Indians have denied this story, some saying that he did his full share of the actual fighting But if he was at the council of chiefs he seems to have been unable to check the panic of its members; for Red Horse, a member of the council says that when Reno charged down the valley he and four women were digging wild turnips. He ran to the council lodge where the chiefs were assembling to decide on a course of action.

But they did not deliberate. Instead they all ran out again and "talked in every direction," a phrase accidentally eloquent.

Since these chiefs were respected for the wisdom they were supposed to possess it may be assumed, we believe, that any information concerning the vital interests of the tribes would be conveyed to them promptly. It follows, then, that since these chiefs clearly did not know of the approach of the Seventh Cavalry, no one else then in the camps knew it. This would seem to dispose definitely of the theory that the wily Sitting Bull had for weeks or months maneuvered to lead the troops into a trap which was finally sprung successfully on the Little Big Horn. All the apparently trustworthy evidence we have shows that, on the contrary, he had done his best to persuade the tribes to keep out of the way of the troops.

The Indians in the camps were not aware of the approach of the Custer battalion until after it had crossed Medicine Tail Coulee. A number of Indians have said that they saw it long before it had gotten that far; and this is probably true. For there were undoubtedly a few Indians east of the river at different points opposite the village. Sergeant Kanipe speaks of a small body of warriors ahead of Custer as he approached the bluffs near Reno Hill, and we know that Martin's horse was wounded while he was returning with Custer's message to Benteen. But it does not seem that any of these Indians reported what they had seen before Custer came into view as he left Medicine Tail.

Much has been written about the strategy of the Indians in this battle, Colonel Graham asserting that it was superior to that of the White man. We have to confess that we have found no evidence which to our civilian mind indicates that they used any strategy whatever other than to rush forward pell mell to place themselves in the path of the advancing troops and then after the troops had halted, filtered into the depressions near them, without any order or plan at all.

The truth seems to be that the Indians could not execute an elaborate plan even had they been able to conceive one; for the war chief could not move the warriors about as a military commander maneuvers his troops. He led an unorganized band whose movements were largely unpredictable and out of his control. There were no fixed units for evolutions on the field. He could not by a brief order direct a given number of warriors to attack a certain point in the enemy position and secure the prompt action so often decisive in battle. Indeed, he could not command at all in the sense we attach to the word. He led, advised or suggested what should be done, but no one was under obligation to obey. His only authority was that of personal prestige. The number of warriors who followed him varied with circumstances. If he wished to make a raid against an enemy he might announce it publicly and those who thought they might in some way profit from it might go with him. There were no muster rolls or formal enlistments and, therefore, no chief knew in advance what he would have to work with. If he had a definite objective that required a certain number of warriors he would have to change or abandon it if the requisite number failed to report. This was true even when the fate of the whole tribe was at stake.

During the Custer action many warriors loitered in camp, or moved about aimlessly, undecided as to whether to go out and fight or wait until the troops actually rode into camp. There was a custom among the Cheyennes and Sioux that at least one man in each family must participate in a battle which concerned the tribe as a whole, but he was not compelled to follow any chief. He could, without subjecting himself to criticism on any legal ground, fight entirely on his own initiative. This is what hundreds of them did throughout the series of actions known as the Battle of the Little Big Horn. Nor did the tribal warriors remain together on any part of the field. The members of the different tribes were everywhere intermingled. Not even the members of the relatively coherent warrior societies fought as a unit. The Cheyenne chief, Two Moon, was with Crazy Horse of the Ogalala Sioux, together with members of other tribes, north of the ridge, while the leading Cheyenne war chief, Lame White Man with other Cheyennes was on the south part of the field among Ogalalas and others.

Nor does it seem that there was any conscious co-operation among the chiefs in a large way. There had been neither time nor opportunity to prepare a plan of any kind, however embryonic. Warriors entered the fight as they got ready. The ponies of many of them were in the herds on the benchlands when the alarm came, and we can imagine that it was not, in many cases, an easy task for a warrior to secure a mount. There were no ponies in the camps except the few regularly kept there by the camp police. Many stopped to put on their special war dress, paint and secure their "medicine." Some of them did not get into the fight at all because when they arrived there was no longer room for

them near the troops. They remained outside the ring of warriors who were doing the fighting, and "swirled all round him,"
on their ponies, firing over the heads of the warriors between
them and the troops. Back of them, toward the close of the fighting, was a dense crowd of old men and boys the troops on Weir
Point mistook for warriors.

If we wish to understand the Custer action we must know
when the warriors arrived and at what points they entered the
area where fighting occurred. In general it may be said that they
crossed the river at three points. One of these was the Middle
Ford near the Cheyenne camp. This ford is at the base of the
fan-shaped drainage area known as Medicine Tail Coulee, with
its two large ravines, or dry runs, one of which extends straight
eastward for about two miles, the other slightly east of north
and passing about a third of a mile east of the Calhoun position.
It was the latter ravine, called North Medicine Tail on some
maps, that was first used by the warriors in going against Custer
as he was approaching from the east. Few, if any of the warriors
used this route after Custer had reached the Hill. Those who
crossed at the Middle Ford turned to the left and went parallel
with the river until they came to the deep ravine leading to the
southwest corner of the field. The second ford used is the one
opposite the mouth of this ravine straight south of the Hill. The
warriors using these routes spread partly over the river slope
southwest of the Hill, and filled the ravines south of the ridge.
Crazy Horse crossed the river farther down and passed to the
rear of Custer's position by way of the ravine running up to the
battleridge from the northwest.

Further details of these movements will be given later; but
it should be stated here that in none of this is there any discern-
able plan or concerted action. Custer had surprised them. They
believed he intended to attack their camps, and they did the immediately obvious thing to place themselves in such a way as to block
his advance. After Custer had halted on coming to the Hill, and
more and more warriors arrived, they began to crawl further up
the ravines on both sides of the ridge, until the troops were almost
encircled. This was later distorted into a "trap" set in advance
by the sagacious Sitting Bull and his war-chiefs among whom Gall
towered above all the rest.

Gall's pre-eminence as the chief who, through extraordinary
shrewdness and general ability, outmaneuvered and destroyed
Custer was a thing of gradual growth. This is not to say that he

was not a prominent chief at the time of the battle. We are merely pointing out an exaggeration which leads to a distorted view of the battle. The fact is—and it can be clearly proved—that Gall and his immediate following did little real fighting against Custer's battalion. The troops they destroyed were already defeated and were virtually driven into the arms of Gall's concealed warriors. It required little skill or courage to kill them. On the other hand, Gall probably did play a leading part, if not *the* leading part, in the fight in the valley. Because he was the only really prominent chief who lived for many years after the battle, his followers had the opportunity to proclaim his prowess to the white man who was only too glad to find a superman to save his face. His only real competitor for fame was Crazy Horse who was killed during the summer of 1877, the victim of a lying interpreter who mistranslated his acceptance of General Crook's request that he and his warriors should take part in the campaign against Chief Joseph's Nez Perces.³ The result of this treachery was his arrest and death at the hands of his guards; which left the field to Gall only a year after the battle.

It was not until after the fiftieth anniversary of the battle that we obtained a number of key-facts by the use of which the mystery of Custer field can be cleared up. Through the cordial intermingling of Red and White during the ceremonies on the field on this occasion the fear of reprisals still in the minds of many Indians was largely dispelled. They now felt that the heart of the white man was good toward them and that it was safe for them to tell him what they remembered of the fight. Of this increased confidence the late Dr. Thomas B. Marquis (deceased 1935) of Hardin, Montana, took full advantage. He had been at one time physician for the Cheyennes at the Lame Deer agency and had come to understand and like these people. He invited them to his table and to help themselves to his tobacco. This was something any unspoiled Indian would understand and respond to with a glad heart, and particularly was this true of the Cheyennes who, though not mawkishly sentimental, possessed a wealth of true sentiment for which few have given them credit, since all Indians were supposed to be "dirty," "lousy," and good only when dead. When, therefore, Dr. Marquis asked them to tell him the truth about the Battle of the Little Big Horn—and a good many other things—they responded with an almost pathetic eagerness, going to no end of trouble to get him what he wanted. He seems to have been careful not to ask "leading questions." If he entertained theories of his own the fact is not evident in the material he published.

One of the products of his years of research is the book *A Warrior Who Fought Custer,* a book reminding us of the Greek Classics. The warrior in question was a Cheyenne named Wooden Leg who was about 18 years of age at the time of the battle and had participated in both the Reno and Custer fights. When, in telling his story, he was in doubt he said so. In such cases, if the point was important, others were called in to clear it up if possible. A good example of how carefully the work was done, is the fixing of the locations of the various camps during the battle. This seems to have occupied them several years, a number of Cheyennes at different times going over the ground with Dr. Marquis; and there is little doubt that on the resulting map these camps are correctly located. To a large extent these findings can be verified from other accounts, but only in a very general way. Dr. Marquis corrected a mistaken idea seemingly held by all writers concerning the extent of the village usually represented as stretching from the site of Garryowen to opposite the battlefield. Everyone in Reno's command knew the southern limit but no one seems to have seen lower. Benteen had been farthest down stream when the troops were at Weir Point, and he gave the length of the village as 4 to 5 miles. After the battle they found campsites opposite the battlefield and naturally concluded that the village had extended over this ground on the 25th. The Cheyennes corrected this misconception by explaining that all the camps were moved downstream after the close of the Custer fight because it was the custom to abandon a camp as soon as possible after a death had occurred in it. All the tribes had lost some men whose bodies had been brought from the field by relatives, or through wounded who had come in and died. Their own camp was farthest downstream a trifle below the mouth of Medicine Tail Coulee before the removal. This is a very important fact. No end of mistakes have been made in an attempt to reconstruct the Custer action because of this misconception.

In general it may be said of these Cheyennes that they have "debunked" the Little Big Horn event. All the heroic posturings and melodrama vanish. The brush of the Verboekhovens and Davids is replaced by that of Verestchagin depicting the sordid and ghastly realities. The Indians, so far from having known everything in advance, confidently planning and setting a "trap," were themselves surprised, unprepared and badly frightened. The

Cheyennes scoffed at the reported exploits of this or that chief, the legends about the killing of Custer and the treatment of his body, pointing out that no one knew he was there, or that it would have meant anything in particular to them if they had known. And again, had they known him and had known that he was in command of the troops no one could have recognized him in the dust and smoke after they had come close enough to identify anyone whomsoever, that the day was hot, the whites and Indians both sweating profusely and soon so covered with grime that even friends hardly recognized each other; that they supposed at the time that they were fighting the same troops they had fought on the upper Rosebud eight days before, and did not suspect until the 26th that it was not Crook they were fighting. Their suspicion was aroused by their discovery of several bodies of Arikara killed in the valley fight, and they remembered that they had seen only Crows and Shoshoni with Crook. Not until months later did they learn that it was Custer they had fought, and then it was not the fact itself but the importance the whites ascribed to the event that impressed them most. The white man's talk and behavior seemed to indicate that the leader of the troops on the Little Big Horn must have been the great chief of all the soldiers in the country, and they took their cue from that and began to respond as they were expected to do, so that by and by what had been up to then merely an extraordinarily big day's work now began to take on truly epic proportions that called for heroes among themselves worthy of the event. Their ideas of military rank and organization are known to have been rather nebulous. In all probability they did not know on the day of the battle that the "chief" who led the men on Custer field was also the commander of the rest of the troops they were fighting.

But there is small occasion for us to make sport of this, for we were not much better informed about the Indian chiefs, their rank and authority, than the Indians were about our own military set-up. Thus it was the habit at the time to refer to all the Indians absent from their agencies as "Sitting Bull and his hostiles," as if he had been the commander in chief of the whole warrior force of the Sioux and Cheyennes, instead of being merely an Uncpapa medicine man in whose "medicine" these Indians had great confidence. The truth is that Sitting Bull was to the Sioux and Cheyennes, in essentials, what most of the Hebrew prophets were to the Israelites under similar circumstances, a great moral and political leader of his people menaced by the greed and

debaucheries of a more numerous race farther advanced in the
field of organization and material utilities.

Sitting Bull has been called a coward because he did not fight
at the Battle of the Little Big Horn. The truth is that no Indian
expected him to fight. There were many other able-bodied Indians
who did not fight. Fighting was the prerogative of all able-bodied
males between the ages of about 17 and 38 years. Men over 38
fought only under exceptional circumstances. They might fight if
they did not have at least one son in the battle. Under ordinary
circumstances the young warriors took it as a reflection on their
own courage and ability if men over 38 joined in the fighting.

These facts must be taken into consideration in estimating the
warrior strength of the village. Such estimates were usually based
on the number of tepees in a camp or village, a method sometimes
complicated by the presence of wickiups, counterpart of the army
"pup-tent." It was assumed that the latter were occupied ex-
clusively by warriors who were either unmarried or in the field
without their families. As a matter of fact many warriors still
attached to the parental tepee slept in these wickiups during the
summer, as did very old people for whom there was scant room
in the tepees of their sons or other relatives. It will be seen from
this that guessing the number of warriors from the number of
family tepees and wickiups was a hazardous business. No
wonder, then, that estimates of the warrior force on the
Little Big Horn ranged from less than 1500 to 4500 or
more. No complete count of tepees and wickiups seems to
have been made, though the figure of 1800 tepees was mentioned at the Reno Court of Inquiry in 1879. Whether or not this
covers both campsites we do not know, but the natural assumption is that it does. However, as only a few family tepees were
set up on the second campsite it is not possible to even venture
a rational guess as to how much this double count affected the
estimate. Some wickiups also were constructed here, but probably not many, since the weather was hot and fair. The Indians
had been up until near dawn the night before, feasting and danc-
ing, and the events of the day had kept them busy, and since
they could sleep comfortably in the open wrapped in their buffalo
robes, it is improbable that any great number took the trouble
to construct shelters.

Taking the estimate of 1800 tepees to illustrate what his
method of computation involves, and counting 7 people to the
tepee (in the well-known letter of Major Brisbin to Captain

Godfrey, the number said to have been used in estimating the population in the village on the Rosebud reported by Major Reno, was given as 6 to 7), we have a total population of 12600. This is not far from some estimates made later. Dr. Marquis reached the conclusion that the village Custer attacked contained about 12000 souls. The Indian agent, James McLaughlin, put the number at 10000.

Assuming a population of 12600, about half of which would be males of all ages, we have 6300 as a basis for further analysis. The warrior force was composed of all able-bodied males between the ages of about 17 and 38, the Cheyennes told Dr. Marquis. Some allowance must be made for the physically weak, the permanently disabled and chronic invalids. It would seem a fairly safe assumption that at least half the males were either above or below the military age, leaving at the most about 3000 warriors. This would be nearly—1 warrior out of every 2 males in the population, an astoundingly high ratio—too high without much doubt.

Captain Benteen, who was a careful observer, wrote his wife a week after the battle that "three thousand warriors were there." This was undoubtedly his real opinion, for he had at this time no reason to indulge in such wild exaggerations as characterized his testimony on the subject at the Court of Inquiry nearly three years later. But the most careful and experienced observer might easily be off several hundred in either direction where such a large number is involved. Nevertheless we believe that Benteen came as near the truth as we shall ever come. This is because his figure is about the same as is obtained in estimating from the number of tepees, which we have said is almost certainly too large. The explanation of this seeming inconsistency is found in the wickiups mentioned by several of the officers. We pointed out a moment ago that not all of these wickiups were occupied by young warriors present without their families. But it is fairly safe to assume that *some* of them were so occupied by young bucks resentful of the restraints and semi-starvation at the agencies, eager for fame and the excitement of the chase and its accompanying feasting. Their numbers would reduce the abnormally high ratio of one warrior to every two males in the total population produced by the formula usually employed in these estimates. But when all has been said that can be said with any degree of plausibility, we have only a very shaky approximation because our primary data are too indefinite for anything better. Perhaps it would be best to say that the warrior force numbered between 2500 and 3000.

As is the case with nearly everything else concerning the Battle of the Little Big Horn the extent and character of the Indian armament is also in dispute. Some writers, among them Colonel W. A. Graham, would have it that all, or nearly all the warriors were armed with magazine rifles, chiefly Winchesters and plentifully supplied with ammunition. The Indians have denied this, and it is in itself improbable because of the high price of both the guns and the ammunition. The arms found in possession of the Indians when they surrendered do not bear out this contention. The Cheyenne, Wooden Leg, told Dr. Marquis that among the more than 500 Cheyenne warriors he knew of only two who possessed magazine rifles, that only about half of them had fire arms of any kind, and that he believed that the proportion among the Sioux was about the same. Also that the muzzle-loader was preferred by many because the charge for it could be measured as the circumstances demanded; and that, further, they had very little ammunition for their better guns and not much for the rest. Also they explained that on Custer field the bow was used more effectively than fire-arms because the bowman could remain concealed throughout. There was no telltale puff of smoke to reveal his position. He could shoot his arrows in a long, high curve to drop on men and horses, inflicting wounds and causing confusion if they did not actually kill. The flat trajectory of the rifle made it necessary to raise the body high enough to see the target. The arrows were shot in the general direction of the troops and horses. The vast majority of them undoubtedly missed, but as the Indians had plenty of arrows, this was not very important, since only a small percentage of the thousands they shot needed to strike trooper or horse to cripple and demoralize and finally bring disaster. This method could have been used with deadly effect against the Custer group crowded together on the exposed slope with the knoll behind them, betraying their position to warriors who could find shelter by the hundreds behind the ridge only a little over 60 yards to the west and southwest. The Indian warrior seldom overlooked such an opportunity, and we believe that he did not do so in this instance.

CHAPTER 2

Setting the Stage

General Terry Moves to Trap Sitting Bull.
His Much-Debated Order to General Custer

WHEN the column of Brigadier General Alfred H. Terry, coming from Fort Abraham Lincoln, and that of Colonel John Gibbon composed of troops from Forts Ellis and Shaw, Montana, made contact during the second week in June the latter had been playing "hide and seek" and exchanging shots for a month with raiding parties of Indians who were undoubtedly members of a village discovered May 16 by Gibbon's scout leader, Lieutenant James H. Bradley. This village was then located on the Tongue River about 35 miles from its mouth. An attempt made to attack it the next morning failed to get started because the cavalry horses could not be induced to swim the raging torrent of the Yellowstone then in flood. On the 27th of May Bradley learned that this village had crossed over to the Rosebud and was then located about 18 to 20 miles from the Yellowstone.

All quiet now on the Yellowstone! This second scout south of the river had been undertaken because the Indians had ceased to annoy the camp of the troops at night and nothing had been seen of them elsewhere for some days. And when Gibbon met Terry on the *Far West* (steamer) he learned that the Dakota column had found no signs of Indians anywhere along the line of their march. The impression, and to some extent the belief, began to spread that the Indians had left this part of the country and that there would be no fighting at all on the expedition.

In the Gibbon column there were, according to Bradley, six companies of infantry numbering about 220 enlisted men; four troops of cavalry, 186 enlisted men, under Major James S. Brisbin; about 20 non-combatants; 23 Crow scouts, two interpreters, and the guide, Mitch Bouyer. A grand total of about 450.

The Dakota column was composed of the whole of the Seventh Cavalry under Lieutenant Colonel (Brevet Major General) George

19

Armstrong Custer; three companies of infantry, a battery of Gatling guns, and some 40 Indian scouts, mostly Arikara. The column left Fort Lincoln on May 17 and reached the Powder River at a point about 25 miles from its mouth, the second week in June. Here it halted while Terry went downstream to board the *Far West* and meet Gibbon, known to be coming down on the north side of the Yellowstone.

As already intimated, no one knew at this time what had become of the Indians Bradley had seen on the Rosebud on the 27th of May, though Gibbon's Crows undoubtedly told him that it was a near certainty they were on the way to the hunter's paradise at the headwaters of the Rosebud, the Little Big Horn and the western tributaries of the Tongue. Terry's order to Custer later was clearly based on this assumption. These Crows knew that at this very time a village of over 200 lodges of their own tribesmen was engaged in hunting in this region, their scouting parties sharply on the alert against the Sioux and Cheyennes, roving eastward as far as Crook's camp on Goose Creek, and possibly even farther, though their tepees had been set up west of the Big Horn in the vicinity of the ruins of Fort C. F. Smith. This, not the lower part of the Little Big Horn valley, was a "favorite haunt" where the Crows had frequently clashed with the Sioux and Cheyennes because of the abundance of game to be found there. This fact was, after the disaster, deliberately obscured by the partisans of General Terry to prove that he knew when he made out the order to Custer, that the hostile village then was where it was later found, having guessed it would be there because it was known to be a "favorite haunt" of the Indians. We shall see in a later chapter that it was an unexpected circumstance that caused the Indians to turn downstream instead of upstream as they had intended to do when they first entered the valley of the Little Big Horn.

There was, however, the possibility that the Indians on the Rosebud had turned back eastward into the Bad Lands in the Powder River area where also there might be others, and that the whole Indian population might be escaping from the jaws of the trap composed of Crook's command on the south and Terry's two columns on the north. Terry, therefore, decided to send Major Reno with six troops of the Seventh Cavalry to scout this region before committing himself definitely to a campaign southwestward. Reno was to go up the Powder to the mouth of the Little Powder, cross to the headwaters of Mizpah Creek and follow it down back to the Powder, then cross to Pumpkin Creek and on to the Tongue which he was to follow to the Yellowstone where he would find the rest of the regiment.

After Reno had left on his scout Custer moved with the rest of the Dakota column to near the mouth of the Powder where the base camp was now being established by bringing up supplies from Fort Buford and Stanley Stockade with the assistance of the *Far West* and three companies of infantry under Major Orlando Moore. The three companies of infantry in the Dakota column were assigned to Moore to complete the garrison of the post.

This done the Seventh Cavalry stripped to light marching order. The wagon train, band, tents were left behind. The officers, or some of them carried "pup-tents," and Custer retained his headquarters tent. The mules from the wagon train were made to serve as pack-animals, a clumsy makeshift enforced by necessity. Then, taking along Lowe's Gatling guns, Custer moved on to the Tongue where, according to his orders, Reno was to have joined him by marching down the stream from the south. But Reno, disobeying his orders, has passed from the Powder across the headwaters of both Mizpah and Pumpkin creeks directly to the Tongue, which he followed down about 8 miles and then crossed over to the Rosebud to a point a little below the site of the Indian village discovered by Bradley on the 27th of May. Turning upstream, he marched for about 12 miles and then turned back, reaching the Yellowstone on the evening of the 18th. The next day Reno marched downstream to near the mouth of the Tongue, sending one of his Indian scouts to notify Terry of his arrival. Terry received this message late in the evening, and to spare both men and animals a useless march and countermarch, at once sent his personal aide, Captain Robert P. Hughes, to order Reno to remain where he was and wait for Custer to join him.[4]

The command was re-united during the morning of the 20th, and Terry, after obtaining the full report of Reno, outlined his plan of attack, explained it to Custer, then returned to the *Far West* which, about mid-morning of the 21st reached the rendezvous at the mouth of the Rosebud. Within an hour of his arrival he ordered Gibbon to march back to Fort Pease with his whole command.

As Gibbon's men were passing the mouth of the Rosebud they saw the long line of the Seventh Cavalry against the background of the Little Wolf mountains, coming over the high bench or tableland. About 2 o'clock Custer arrived and went into camp on a flat between the tableland and the river. Soon after this a conference was held by Terry on the *Far West*. Present at this conference were Custer, Gibbon, Brisbin and perhaps several others. Terry now went into the details of his plan, and there can be no doubt that all concerned understood it perfectly. A fairly accurate map covering the area of the proposed operations was laid on the table and an attempt made to synchronize the movements of the two columns. It was a very simple plan which left no room for obscurities *as to intent,* and there is no more doubt that it was approved by both Custer and Gibbon than there is about its being understood. But while the intent was clear it took account of many contingencies which are reflected in the order to Custer reproduced below. In a military textbook or Field Regulations, such an order would be called a "Letter of Instructions" or, perhaps, a "Letter of Advice," as a later commander of the Seventh Cavalry, General Forsyth, called it in a letter to Mrs. Custer. The nature of the task imposed ruled out any other type of order. This does not imply that Custer was free to do as he pleased. It does mean that he was given discretion concerning the measures employed in attaining the objectives sought should the circumstances prove to be substantially different from what they were assumed to be.

Camp at the mouth of the Rosebud River,
Montana Territory,
June 22, 1876.

Lieutenant-Colonel Custer, 7th Cavalry.
Colonel:

> The Brigadier General Commanding directs that, as soon as your regiment can be made ready for the march, you will proceed up the Rosebud in pursuit of the Indians whose trail was discovered by Major Reno a few days since. It is, of course, impossible to give you precise instructions in regard to this movement, and were it not impossible to do so the Department Commander places too much confidence in your zeal, energy and ability to wish to impose on you precise orders which might hamper your action when nearly in contact with the enemy. He will, however, indicate to you his own views of what your action should be, and he desires that you should conform to them unless you shall see sufficient reason for departing from them. He thinks that you should proceed up the Rosebud until you ascertain definitely the direction the trail spoken of leads. Should it be found (as it appears almost certain it will be found) to turn to the Little Big Horn, he thinks

that you should still proceed southward, perhaps as far as the headwaters of the Tongue, and then turn toward the Little Big Horn, feeling constantly, however, to your left, so as to preclude the possibility of the escape of the Indians to the south or southeast by passing around your left flank. The column of Colonel Gibbon is now in motion for the mouth of the Big Horn. As soon as it reaches that point it will cross the Yellowstone and move up at least as far as the forks of the Big and Little Horns. Of course its future movements must be controlled by circumstances as they arise, but it is hoped that the Indians, if upon the Little Horn, will be so nearly inclosed by the two columns that their escape will be impossible. The Department Commander desires that on your way up the Rosebud you should thoroughly examine the upper part of Tullock's Creek, and that you should endeavor to send a scout through to Colonel Gibbon's column with information of the result of your examination. The lower part of the creek will be examined by a detachment of Colonel Gibbon's command. The supply steamer will be pushed up the Big Horn as far as the fork of the river if the river is found to be navigable for that distance, and the Department Commander, who will accompany the column of Colonel Gibbon, desires you to report to him there not later than the expiration of the time for which your troops are rationed, unless in the meantime you receive further orders.

Very respectfully your obedient servant,

E. W. SMITH
Captain 18th Infantry
Acting Assistant Adjutant General

There has been a great deal of criticism of General Terry over the supposed obscurities and loose-jointedness of this order. But the trouble is not in the order. It is perfectly clear to anyone not blinded by his own prepossessions derived from "hindsight." Conceiving the order *as a whole and returning it to its proper setting as understood at the time it was written,* it becomes completely evident that Terry foresaw the possibility that, before the columns made contact again, *both* might be operating quite outside the "views" expressed in the order. This is clearly shown in what is reserved for Gibbon in such phrases as "Of course, its (Gibbon's command) future movements must be controlled by circumstances as they arise," and "move up *at least as far as the forks* of the Big and Little Horns." Why these reservations, if not to make it plain to Custer, and of record, that each column as it advanced must be guided by circumstances as it found them, not by the long-distance guesses upon which the order was predicated. As Custer said in his letter to the *New York Herald,* dated June 22, they were acting on the "general impression" that the Indians would be found at the headwaters of the Little Big Horn and Rosebud.

Terry's uncertainty of the whereabouts of the Indians is betrayed also in a dispatch to Sheridan dated June 21 in which he says "I only hope that one of the columns finds the Indians." The same uncertainty is found in his Report to Sheridan in which he says "This plan was founded on the belief that at *some point* (italics our own) on the Little Big Horn a body of hostile Sioux would be found; and although it was impossible to make movements in perfect concert, as might have been done had there been a known fixed objective to be reached, yet, by the judicious use of excellent guides and scouts which we possessed, the two columns might be brought within co-operating distance of each other, so that either of them which should be first engaged might be a waiting fight-give time for the other to come up."

The best guess the three commanders, Terry, Custer, Gibbon, could make was that the "fixed point" was near the headwaters of the Rosebud and Little Big Horn. Actually that "point" turned out to be about two days' march farther downstream, as Custer guessed late on the evening of the 24th. What he did about it will be discussed in the next chapter.

"In all the welter of lies and distortions that cover the facts of the subsequent week, none charge disagreement or even demurral in the cabin of the *Far West.* Yet, something strange happened there. Some spiritual blow was dealt Custer, who entered expectant and emerged profoundly depressed." (F. F. Van DeWater in *Glory Hunter*). There is little doubt that Custer emerged from the conference in an abnormal state of mind, but we know neither its exact nature nor the cause of it. Was it due to a vague intimation or premonition stemming from the subconscious psyche, as has been hinted? It may have been; or it may be that he sensed the hostility of Major Brisbin which flared up violently soon after Custer had left the boat. The conference had lasted from about 3 o'clock to near sundown, as nearly as can be determined, a long time for the "truculent" (we are borrowing Mr. Van DeWater's adjective) Major to keep his attitude effectually concealed. Perhaps Custer felt that his man would prejudice his standing with General Terry while he, Custer, was away on a difficult assignment which, because of its many doubtful factors, might easily lead to failure for which he was certain to be blamed by the envious or the sycophantic in the entourage of the commander. Of the latter there were several on Terry's staff of whom both Lieutenant Bradley and Lieutenant McClernand spoke with something resembling a mild but thinly veiled contempt—"flippant," Bradley called them. They admired Custer as a great soldier-until he met with disaster. Then they accused him of disobedience while his body still lay unburied where it had fallen, long before they could possibly have possessed the necessary data on which to base so grave a charge. Had Custer possessed the power to read the future he might have foreseen that someone then near the person of General Terry would change the words "sufficient reason" in his orders, to "absolute necessity" in the copy made of them in Terry's copybook!

CHAPTER 3

Custer Goes in ''Pursuit of the Indians''

THE conference on the *Far West* seems to have broken up around sundown, and in the early dusk Custer left the steamer, accompanied by Terry and Gibbon. When they arrived at Custer's tent they stood for a few minutes talking together, then shook hands and Terry and Gibbon left. It would seem that out of this simple act of courtesy on the part of Terry and Gibbon there later grew up the story culminating in the affidavit published by General Miles in his *Memoires*. This is to the effect that in a conversation after the conference Terry gave Custer *carte blanche* for the strategic movements outlined in his orders. The affidavit, as Colonel Graham has shown, is a bare-faced fraud. It is on a par with the forgery committed in Terry's copybook in which the words "absolute necessity" are substituted for "sufficient reason" in the original. In both cases the forger betrays his own doubt in the soundness of his position.

After Terry and Gibbon had left, Custer had officers' call sounded and gave his instructions for the march to begin at noon the next day. In his *Century* article of January 1892, Godfrey said that each troop commander was ordered to carry on his packmules fifteen days' rations of hardbread, coffee, and sugar, and twelve days' rations of bacon. Each trooper was to carry on his person or in his saddlebags 100 rounds of carbine ammunition and 24 rounds for his revolver, while 24,000 rounds for the carbines were to be carried on the packmules. Each man was also to carry 12 pounds of oats on his horse. When Custer suggested that they should take an extra supply of forage, and several officers protested, saying the packmules were in poor condition and would certainly break down under the load, he replied impatiently that they could do as they pleased; that it was only a suggestion, but that they would be held responsible for their commands; that they would

27

follow the trail for fifteen days unless they caught the Indians
sooner; that they might not see the supply steamer again, and that
they had better take an extra supply of salt, since they might have
to eat horsemeat before they got through.

Some time after dismissing his officers Custer went back to the
Far West, for what purpose is not clear from any evidence in our
possession. In the meantime the steamer had carried Low's battery
of Gatlings to the north side of the Yellowstone in order that it
might overtake Gibbon's command, and brought to the south
side six Crow scouts, Mitch Bouyer and probably George Herendeen, who were to go with Custer because his Ree scouts were unfamiliar with the ground over which they were to march. Herendeen had been engaged to carry Custer's report of what he might
find on the upper Tullocks, as required in his orders.[5]

A number of other officers also went to the *Far West,* some of
them to make a night of it, it is said, at cards and drinking. Among
them were Major Reno, Tom Custer, Calhoun, and Captain
Keogh. At one time Reno and Lieutenant Carland of Baker's
company on board as guard for the boat, stood up together, arms
over each other's shoulders, and sang "Larboard Watch."[6] At a
late hour Keogh came to Carland and asked him to draw up his
will for him.[7]

But there was one man aboard who was not in a mood for any
of these things. This was Major James S. Brisbin, the "old blather-
skite"[8] who commanded Gibbon's four troops of cavalry. Sourly
he had come to General Terry earlier in the evening and upset
his peace of mind concerning the "wild man" he had "turned
loose" to go up the Rosebud in pursuit of the Indians. After
listening to his diatribe for some time Terry said rather sharply;
"You do not seem to have confidence in Custer." "None in the
world. I have no use for him," replied Brisbin.[9]

The upshot of Brisbin's interference, if we may trust his word
in this, was that Custer was offered Gibbon's cavalry to strengthen
his command. This offer Custer declined, saying he had all the
force he needed, that the Seventh Cavalry, as a homogeneous body,
could accomplish as much as the two combined.[10]

Brisbin says also that it was he who offered Custer Low's
battery, Low having requested him to make the offer. After obtaining Terry's permission, Brisbin went again to Custer and explained
Low's desire to go with him. Custer said "yes," but returned an
hour later and said "I don't want Low. I am afraid he will impede
my march with his guns." He made no reply to Brisbin's urging to

reconsider, but went into the boat and repeated to Terry that he did not want Low.

The gatling guns were drawn by four condemned cavalry horses.

There is a strong suggestion in the evidence that, if "there was sound of revelry by night" on the *Far West*, it was otherwise in the camp of the Seventh Cavalry. The campsite, if we have identified it correctly, could not have been a cheerful place at night. It is a low, level flat, irregular in shape and only a few feet above the water of the Yellowstone. Along the east and south sides are steep banks 25 to 50 feet high, ending on the east end in a forbidding headland along the base of which washes the river which here heads into the bank, or cliff. On the upstream end the flat narrows to perhaps 30 to 40 yards. Here the bench is lower and can be negotiated by horses, and it may be that at the point where it turns sharply toward the river, the Seventh climbed out after passing in review, as a sentence in Gibbon's description suggests.

It was a gloomy place in a wilderness, and it would not have been an unnatural thing for those who are sensitive to their environment to have had forebodings or premonitions, as is said to have been the case. Custer's personal orderly, John Burkman, recalled his impressions some fifty years afterward in talks with the late I. D. O'Donnell from whose notes Glendolin Damon Wagner has constructed an eerie picture of that night. Something of this also clung to the old soldier, Colonel Gibbon, and runs as an undertone through his language, as will be seen in a moment. According to Godfrey both Custer and Wallace betrayed evidence of unusual psychic experience for several days as they marched up the Rosebud, the latter seeing an evil omen in the event when Custer's headquarters flag blew down twice and twice fell backward, as the command was halted near the remains of a Sundance Lodge on the 24th.

The supplies for the march had been unloaded from the *Far West* before reveille on the 22nd, and by noon the regiment was ready to move. General Terry, accompanied by Colonel Gibbon and Major Brisbin, rode to a knoll or low ridge near the upper end of the camp toward the Rosebud (the camp was about two miles below the mouth of the creek) and waited there for the regiment to pass in review.

To the imaginative there is always a vague suggestion of the *morituri te salutamus* in the formal military Review or Dress Parade. In retrospect this became pre-eminently so of the last

Review of the Seventh Cavalry under Custer. Its setting in the primitive wilderness, the character of the day, and the tragic fate that was soon to overtake so many of the participants, made this inevitable. Frederick F. Van deWater has succeeded admirably in presenting the picture as seen through this romantic and emotional lens. Drawing together all the dramatic elements in the event he has, with his usual literary skill, given it an epic sweep and the panoramic glamour of a dream.

Here is Colonel Gibbon's factual account of what appeared to the physical eye. We learn from him that "a very heavy, cold wind was blowing from the north," which kept the *Far West* moored to the bank of the Yellowstone until 4 o'clock. It was not a beautiful day, as Mr. Hanson and General Edgerly want us to believe. It was, on the contrary, one of those blustery, depressive throw-backs from late March or early April which those who have lived long in the foothills region know and would gladly do without.

Of the review Gibbon wrote: "At noon next day (22nd) General Terry, myself and Major Brisbin, rode to the upper end of the camp to witness the departure of Custer and his fine regiment. The bugles sounded the "boots and saddles" and Custer, after starting the advance, rode up and joined us. Together we sat on our horses and witnessed the approach of the command as it threaded its way through the rank sage brush which covered the valley. First came a band of buglers sounding the march, and as they came opposite to General Terry wheeled out of the column as at review, continuing to play as the command passed along. The regiment presented a fine appearance, and as the various companies passed us we had a good opportunity to note the number of fine horses in the ranks, many of them being part blooded horses from Kentucky, and I was told there was not a single sore-backed horse amongst them. General Custer appeared to be in good spirits, chatted freely with us, and was evidently proud of the fine appearance of his command. The pack mules, in a compact body, followed the regiment, and as that approached Custer shook hands with us and bade us goodby. As he turned to leave us I made some pleasant remark, warning him against being greedy, and with a gay wave of his hand he called back: "No, I will not," and rode off after his command. Little did we think we had seen him for the last time, or under what circumstances we should next see that command, now mounting the bluffs in the distance with its little guidons gaily fluttering in the breeze."

And so, as in a vision, we see them as they ride away through a desolation of sage brush, a land of stunted growths harsh and sterile to the minds of those who had come from the lush prairies of the central plains, on in pursuit of the Indians,

> With tattered guidons spectral thin
> Above their swaying ranks
> With carbines swung and sabers slung,
> And the gray dust on their flanks,[11]

the chilling blasts on their backs seeming to hurry them on to their bloody sweat on the Little Big Horn.

Ten miles up the Rosebud they made camp for the night at the base of a cliff on the west bank of the creek, a thin trickle of a stream three to four feet wide and a few inches deep. Today the Rosebud, except in times of flood, is little more thas a succession of pools, and hardly comes up to what our fancy pictures it because of its name. The official report of Lieutenant Wallace, who kept the record of the march, shows it was about the same in 1876.

That evening, according to Godfrey, Custer's mind was again under a cloud. As he talked to his assembled officers "there was something undefinable about him that was not Custer," he says. His usual self-sufficiency and assurance were absent, and in their place was a dependence on and an appeal to the loyalty of his officers. After the assembly had been dismissed, Godfrey, Wallace, and McIntosh walked together toward their bivouacs for some time in silence. Finally Wallace said: "Godfrey, I believe Custer is going to be killed." "Why, Wallace, what makes you think so?" "Because I have never heard Custer talk that way before."

But this was not the impression the assembly made on Benteen. In an unfinished paper supposed to have been written in 1891 or 1892, he said:

"In the evening (of the 22nd) the orderly trumpeter was sent to notify the officers that General Custer wanted to see them at his headquarters and after the arrival of the last officer General Custer commenced his talk; which was to the effect that it had come to his knowledge that his official actions had been criticized by some of the officers of the regiment at headquarters of the Department, and that while he was willing to accept recommendations from the junior second Lieutenant of the regiment, he wished the same to come in proper manner; calling our attention to the paragraph of Army Regulations referring to criticism of action of commanding officers, and said he would take the necessary steps

to punish, should there be recurrence of the offense. I said to
General Custer, "It seems to me you are lashing the shoulders of
all of us to get at some; now, as we are all present, would it not
do to specify the officers whom you accuse?" He said, 'Colonel Benteen, I am not here to be catechised by you, but for your own
information will state that none of my remarks have been directed
toward you.' Then, after giving some excellent orders as to what
should be done in case of attack on our bivouac, the meeting of
the officers was over, and each adjourned to his palatial "puptent."

This sounds very much like the real Custer, who had been quite
himself a few hours before as he waved his farewell at the conclusion of the review. Nor is there any trace of anxiety in the long
letter he had written to the *New York Herald* that morning, other
than the fear that the Indians might have seen Reno on his scout
and fled. So far was he from having any misgivings of the outcome if an encounter did occur, that he ridiculed Reno, who had
had only half the regiment, for not pursuing the Indians and
bringing them to bay after discovering that he could have over-
taken them in a day and a half. On this evening Custer was still 8
miles or more from the point where the Indian trail struck the
Rosebud from the east. He had, therefore, no information he
did not possess before leaving the Yellowstone. In his letter to
the *Herald* he said that the camp Reno had discovered had contained 380 lodges. Godfrey says that on this evening Custer had
remarked that the Reno report indicated a warrior force of 1000,
but that from his own study of the report of the Commissioner
of Indian Affairs in regard to the number of hostiles usually absent
from the agencies, they might find as many as 1500 but not more
than that; a statement Colonel Hughes, for his own *ex parte*
objectives, distorts into "According to Godfrey, Custer himself
stated in terms that they would have to face three times that
number," thus turning an *improbable maximum into an absolute
minimum.* Hughes was using the estimate of 500 to 800 given
in General Fry's *Comments* published with Godfrey's article in
the Century. This makes Custer say that they would *have* to meet
1500 to 2400 warriors. The object of this distortion is, of course,
to point up Custer's supposed rashness as contrasted with Terry's
caution, an intellectual dishonesty with which the literature on
the Battle of the Little Big Horn is, unfortunately, replete.

Under date of June 23 we find in the official report of Lieutenant
Wallace that "Orders were issued last night that trumpet signals
would be discontinued, that the stable guards would wake their

respective companies at 3 A. M., and that the command would march at 5. General Custer stated that short marches would be made for the first few days, after that they would be increased."

It is worth while to note the implications in the last sentence. A "few days" would have brought them into the valley of the Little Big Horn if they followed the trail across the Divide, as everyone well knew. Then what were the final long marches to accomplish if, as his critics say, he had from the beginning intended to disobey the conditional injunction *not* to follow the trail? Custer was here repeating what he had already told General Terry, that his marches would, at first, be about 30 miles a day; which shows that in his mind was the picture of long distances not to be covered in a few days. In his mind the Indians were either at the headwaters of the Rosebud or Little Big Horn, or on both, as he had said in his letter to the *New York Herald*. The emphasis in his orders to guard against the escape of the Indians past the headwaters of the Rosebud shows that Terry was of the same opinion. In another place we shall show how desperately Colonel Hughes labored to obscure this fact.

All the campsites passed on the 23rd were old, Wallace reported, but everything indicated a large body of Indians. Every bend of the stream bore traces of some old camp, and their ponies had nipped almost every spear of grass. The ground was strewn with broken bones and cuttings from buffalo hides. The total distance marched for the day was "over 30 miles." Camp was made at 4:30. The last of the packtrain did not come into camp until near sundown; which means about four hours after camp was made. On this day the packtrain was escorted by Captain Benteen with three companies. Incidentally Benteen informs us that they came very near losing Dr. Lord who was so seriously ill that he fell far behind the packs and just managed to drag himself into camp long after dark. "He declined tea and wanted nothing to eat or drink," wrote Benteen.

Under date of June 24 Wallace reported; "The command marched at 5 A. M........After we had been on the march about an hour, the Crow scouts came in and reported fresh signs of Indians, but in no great numbers. After a short consultation, General Custer, with an escort of two companies, moved out in advance, the remainder of the command following at a distance of about half a mile........ At 1 P. M. the command halted, scouts were sent ahead, and the men made coffee. The scouts got back about 4, and reported a fresh camp at the forks of the Rosebud. *Everything indicated that the Indians were not more than thirty miles away.* (Italics our own). At 5 P. M. the command moved out, crossed at the left bank of the Rosebud; passed through several camps. *The trail was now fresh, and the whole valley scratched up by the trailing lodgepoles.* (Italics own own). At 7:45 we camped on the right bank of the Rosebud. Scouts were sent ahead to see which branch of the stream the Indians had followed. Distance marched today about 28 miles."

We leave the rest of Wallace's report here, to discuss what the march up to this time had disclosed, and to introduce some evidence never before, as far as we are aware, used in this connection.

The halt at 1:00 P. M. was near the frame of a large lodge which had been used by the Uncpapa in connection with a medicine, or sundance, here a purely tribal affair attended by many members of other tribes but in which they took no active part. Godfrey says that at this halt officers' call was sounded, and that at the assembly they were informed that the Crow scouts had discovered fresh signs, the tracks of three or four ponies and of one Indian afoot. It would seem that Godfrey here confuses the two halts made this day, the first around 6 A. M., the second from 1:00 to 5 P. M.; for what he says of the discovery by the Crows corresponds to what Wallace reports for the first halt. The tracks of the ponies and that of the lone Indian constituted the first evidence of the recent presence of Indians on the trail. It did not signify much, but it was enough to put Custer on the alert, hold a short conference with his officers and personally lead an advance guard of two companies. But what the Crows reported during the second halt brought him up sharply; for here was something wholly unexpected, something that might call for action radically different from what was contemplated in his orders. The Crows had been over the trail made, evidently, only a day or two before by the large body of Indians coming from the agencies to join the camps on the Little Big Horn. They had not followed the Indian trail down the Tongue, i.e., the course taken by the rest during their spring wanderings, but had crossed over to the Rosebud a little above the site of the Sundance lodge, where, as related in the report of Wallace, the troops struck it soon after resuming the march at 5 o'clock. The trail was now so fresh that it indicated the Indians were not over 30 miles away. The Sundance could not have been held much later than June 10, or about two weeks before Custer passed the spot, as will become evident from the Cheyenne account given below. There is no reason for thinking that there had been a sudden large increase in the number of Indians in the camps at this place. What gave Godfrey this impression was undoubtedly the trampled condition of the ground near the Sundance lodge, caused by the large number of spectators at the ceremonies.

Following is a greatly condensed account of the gathering of the tribes and their movements down to the Battle of the Little Big Horn, as found in the excellent work of the late Thomas B. Marquis, under the title: *A Warrior Who Fought Custer.*

The first impetus to this concentration was given by the attack of General Reynolds in command of a detachment of General Crook's force, on a Cheyenne camp of about 40 lodges on the upper Powder River, March 17. These Cheyennes fled eastward to Crazy Horse and his Ogalalas camped on another branch of the Powder, and the two together then joined Sitting Bull with the Uncpapas on still another tributary of the Powder 15 to 20 miles downstream. As they moved about in the Powder River country, gradually working toward the Yellowstone, contingents from the Minniconjous, Sans Arcs, and Blackfeet joined them and formed their separate camp circles. These six camp circles formed the nucleus around which was built the great village as, during the spring small bands from time to time joined their tribesmen under the general lead of Sitting Bull, Uncpapa medicine man. By the middle of May they had arrived on the lower Tongue River 15 to 20 miles from the Yellowstone. From here they crossed over to the Rosebud as related in Chapter 2.

They made their first camp on the Rosebud about May 23 or 24 and[12] remained there for five or six days. It was this camp, 18 to 20 miles from the Yellowstone, Bradley saw on May 27 on his second scout to the Little Wolf Mountains.

About the 29th of May they moved about 12 miles upstream, camped for one day, and then moved 12 to 15 miles to their third camp. The next day they went on to their fourth camp opposite the site of the present Lame Deer where they remained for five or six days.

While in this fourth camp a band of Cheyennes arrived from the agencies and reported that "lots of soldiers" were coming to fight the Indians. This created considerable stir, and a scouting party of 11 Cheyennes, including the narrator, Wooden Leg, went out to look for soldiers, going to the Tongue over the divide by the low pass over which the Lame-Deer-Ashland road now runs. From the Tongue they passed on to the Powder, which they followed upstream to near the mouth of Lodge Pole Creek (Clear Creek on some maps), just across the Montana-Wyoming line. Here they discovered a camp of soldiers. They waited until dark to make closer observations; but when they approached the camp near midnight they found it empty. The next morning they followed the trail of the soldiers in a northwest direction and found them camped on Crow Creek near its mouth at the Tongue. They circled around to the left and at dusk crossed the Tongue and concealed themselves on the west side of the valley. From the top of the bluffs the next morning they saw some Indians riding away from the camp, and soon after noted preparations for departure among the soldiers. Six members of their party then started for the upper Rosebud, and at dusk the remaining five followed and reported that the soldiers also were coming toward the Rosebud. They slept there that night, and early the next morning hurried downstream to report to the camps. They found that the Indians, after remaining for five or six days in their fourth camp, had moved to the fifth camp where the Unc-papas had held their Sundance, and then moved to the sixth camp within about 10 miles of the mouth of Davis Creek, where they still were when the scouting party returned.

This brings a number of things into focus, lifting the mystery from the trail which had so intrigued the members of the Seventh Cavalry as they passed over it.

The scouting party had left the fourth camp on the fourth day after its establishment. Going back over what has just been said, we see that this must have been around June 5 or 6. A day or two later they moved to their fifth camp where the Sundance was held. The account does not tell us how long they remained at this camp, but because we can fix the dates of several later camps we know that the Sundance camp must have stood from about the 7th to the 10th of June. The move to the sixth camp could not have been made later than the 12th or 13th, for the scouts returned not later than the 13th.

The news brought by the scouts created great excitement. Many of the young warriors wanted to go out and fight the troops, but the older chiefs dissuaded them. Instead five or six Cheyenne scouts were sent to observe the further movements of the troops, while the village moved to its seventh and last camp on the Rose-bud, the Cheyennes, as always, in the lead. They halted on the east bank of the creek, the Cheyenne camp being directly opposite the mouth of Davis Creek.

Wooden Leg could not recall how long they remained here, but thought it was more than one day. We know, however, that they left here on the 15th and went up Davis Creek to near the Divide and made camp in a wide ravine entering Davis Creek from the north. The next day, June 16, they crossed the Divide and camped at the forks of Reno Creek, four and a half miles from the Little Big Horn.

Soon after arriving at this campsite, the Cheyenne scouts sent out shortly after the return of the first scouting party, came in and reported that the troops were now on the upper branches of the Rosebud. This news created genuine alarm among the women, who at once packed up all articles not needed for immediate use, some of them even taking down their tepees and getting them ready for transportation. The young warriors again wanted to go out and fight. But again the principal chiefs, after holding council, advised against fighting, and sent out heralds announcing their decision.

But this time the warriors refused to accept the advice of the chiefs. As dusk came on they got together and went up the south branch of Reno Creek and the next morning attacked General Crook's command as it was marching down the Rosebud. As is well known, the battle resulted in Crook's retreat to his base camp on Goose Creek, after the warriors had withdrawn from the fight.

The day after the battle, that is, June 18th, the Indians moved down Reno Creek for a short distance, then turned south across the bench and camped in the valley, east of the river and just south of the old Busby road. They left one tepee standing at the forks of the Creek. It contained the body of a warrior killed in the fight with Crook. This was the "Lone Tepee" which figures so prominently in all accounts of the march of the Seventh Cavalry.

The Cheyennes say that when they came to this camp their intention was to go upstream. Although we have no direct evidence on the point, it is altogether probable that it was the great abundance of game usually to be found on the well-watered table-land and slopes on the upper reaches of the Tongue and Little Big Horn, that led to the decision. It was this region that was the "favorite haunt" of the Indians, not the lower part of the Little Big Horn valley. This is undoubtedly the reason for the "general impression" that the Indians were near the headwaters of these streams. The "general impression" was the guess of the Crows serving with Gibbon, it is fairly safe to assume. Early in June a Crow hunting party of over 200 lodges was camped near the ruins

of Fort C. F. Smith, where Frank Grouard, Louis Michaud, and
"Big Bat," scouts from Crook's command, found them during the
second week in June. These Crows were evidently in communication with the Crows in Gibbon's command, and had received
news concerning not only Gibbon but of the hostile Indians as
well. They knew that Gibbon had attempted to attack these
Indians, then on the lower Tongue, but had desisted when the
horses of "one company" were drowned in the Yellowstone.[1a]

It was a purely fortuitous circumstance that caused the Indians
to change their plan and go downstream instead of upstream.
Except for this the "general impression" would almost certainly
have been correct, and the Battle of the Little Big Horn would
have been an entirely different story. The Indian hunters had
discovered vast herds of antelope on the benchlands west of the
Big Horn in the neighborhood of the mouth of the Little Big
Horn. So, on the 24th of June they turned about, crossed the
Little Big Horn and moved to the place where Custer found them
the next day. When Reno attacked them some of the women had
already begun to take down their tepees preparatory to the move
that day to the mouth of the Little Big Horn.

It is an interesting speculation as to what would have happened
if Custer, instead of attacking on the 25th, had continued up the
Rosebud, and the Indians had gone into camp at the mouth of
the Little Big Horn where General Terry and Major Brisbin
with only four troops of cavalry—about 160 men—arrived before
daylight of the 26th dog-tired after a weird night-march through
rain and stygian darkness, over a terrain of successive ridges,
ravines and gulches, and the infantry still 12 miles downstream on
the Big Horn!

We find, then, from the clear and circumstantial accounts of
the Cheyennes that the Indians were on the Rosebud from May
23 or 24 to June 15; that when Reno found their first campsite
it was a full three weeks old. Dr. DeWolf, who accompanied
Reno on his scout, says in his diary that they followed the trail
for only 12 miles; from which it follows that they saw only the
first and second campsites, possibly only the first. When Custer
came to them they were nearly a month old; but since he passed
over in two days the same ground the Indians had taken approximately three weeks to traverse, the trail and campsites must
have appeared ever fresher as he proceeded until, on the 24th,
they came to the last campsite which had been abandoned only
nine days before, but was overlaid by a trail made much later.

We left the command halted at the remains of the Sundance lodge. The officers' call mentioned by Godfrey was undoubtedly sounded soon after Custer had received the report of the Crow scouts who had returned about four o'clock. It was probably at the conclusion of this assembly that Custer went to the Arikara to have a talk with them. This incident is related by Red Star as follows:

The whole army stopped here and ate dinner on a hill. Custer came to their camp with his orderly, the one who carried his flag for him. The Arikara were sitting in a half-circle.— Custer sat down with one knee on the ground and said: 'What do you think of the report of the Crow scouts? They say there are large camps of the Sioux. What do you suppose will be the outcome of it all?'

In reply to Custer's question, Stabbed jumped up and hopped around to show how the Arikara acted in a fight to minimize the chances of being hit, and suggested that the troops should adopt the same tactics, instead of standing still to be shot down "like buffalo calves."

"I don't doubt you, Stabbed," Custer replied. "What you say seems reasonable. I know you people. You are tricky like the coyote. You know how to hide, to creep up and take by surprise."

Other officers now came up and stood around the fire, while Custer told the Arikara that all he expected them to do in the battle was to capture many Sioux horses. He ended by promising to befriend them in Washington if they were successful in the campaign.

Custer was now thoroughly disillusioned about the "general impression." Certainly the Indians who had made the fresh camps and trails had not yet reached the headwaters of either the Tongue or the Little Big Horn. They were only a day's march ahead. Moreover, they were far more numerous than anyone had believed them to be. "The whole valley was scratched up by their trailing lodgepoles," said Wallace. "We knew that 8,000 to 10,000 Indians had passed over that trail" said Benteen less than three years later.

But as yet they did not know "which branch of the stream the Indians had followed." Although it was thought altogether probable that they had crossed to the Little Big Horn, there was nothing certain about it. We can see today that they might have gone up the Rosebud if the Cheyenne scouts had not brought word that the troops were coming to the upper branches of that stream. They were safe in going to the Little Big Horn if Crook came down the Rosebud, for he would have left the way open for them to go up the Little Big Horn and pass eastward back to the Tongue and the Bad Lands, as Terry had feared they would do if they discovered the approach of his command. This point was emphasized in his orders and orally by both Terry and Gibbon. When, therefore, camp was made at 7:45 the Crows were once more sent ahead to clear up this point. They returned in about an hour and reported that the trail led across the Divide to the Little Big Horn.

We have found no direct evidence that anyone in the command knew that the fresh trail and campsites were made by a second body of Indians after those whose trail they had been following had left the Rosebud. It would seem that had such an important fact been known, Wallace would have mentioned it in his report. This, however, is not conclusive. Unless other evidence points in the same direction, it is usually unsafe to assume the non-existence of a fact because a witness who, presumably in position to know of it had it existed, fails to mention it. The fact may have been known to the Indian scouts, and they may have discussed it with Custer. It is, of course, possible that they may have noticed that the fresh trail was super-imposed on an older one, but that they were in doubt as to whether or not this necessarily meant that the fresher trail had been made by a second band of Indians. The more recent trail could have been made by the original band whose traces of an earlier occupation had been partly obliterated by a heavy rain the Arikara noted as having fallen while the Indians camped here, as shown by the trenches around the tepee-sites.

If Custer knew that to the original band which, according to his own estimate, might possibly contain 1500 warriors, there had later been added a body of Indians whose trailing lodgepoles had scratched up the whole valley of the Rosebud, there was, indeed, something to worry about. Since the general impression was that the Indians he was sent in pursuit of, had gone to the upper Little Big Horn region, those who had made the fresh trail could not yet have joined them. But if the first band had not gone either far up or far downstream, had remained together or within supporting distance, the addition of the second band would complete the assembly of the most formidable Indian force ever gathered to face the White enemy. Only direct observation could supply satisfactory answers to these questions. The

Crows did not pretend that, from the Crow's Nest, they could do more than determine whether or not there were Indians on the Little Big Horn. The trail itself had already told them that much, though it indicated nothing regarding their exact location on the stream. It may as well be said here that next to nothing of the valley can be seen from the Crow's Nest. The benchlands beyond can be seen in places.

After receiving the report of the Crow Scouts around 9 o'clock, Custer sent a sergeant to notify the officers that he wished to see them at his headquarters. According to Benteen it was then pitch dark, which means that it must have been about 10 o'clock, official time. The only order given was that the command would march again at 11 o'clock, at which time, Benteen says, it did march. But because of difficulties Captain Keogh experienced in getting the packtrain across Mud Creek, they were delayed for an hour and a half.

This business out of the way, Custer went to the camp of the scouts located across the Rosebud from the rest of the command. While he was talking with the Crows Lieutenant Varnum came in from the trail "pretty well tired out." Custer then came to Varnum and said the Crows had informed him that on the Divide there was a high hill they called the Crow's Nest from which, at daylight, they "could tell by the rising of the smoke whether there were Indians on the Little Big Horn or not. He wanted some intelligent white man to go with these Crows and get from them what they saw and send back word to him. I told him I supposed that meant me, and it ended in my going. I took with me Charles Reynolds, five Crows and eight or ten Rees."

One of these Rees, Red Star, says that only six of his tribe and four Crows went with Varnum, and names all of them. When these Arikara reported at headquarters, Custer, through Gerard, gave them their instructions, and the party started on its mission. Varnum says that he reached the Crow's Nest about 2:30 and lay down to sleep, but was called to the top of the hill in an hour or less. They tried to show him an immense pony herd, but he could not see anything. Nevertheless he wrote a note to Custer saying the village had been located, and sent it about 4:45. Custer received it about 8 o'clock, he says.

In the meantime the command had marched up Davis Creek for about 6 miles and halted at dawn to await news from the scouting party on the Crow's Nest. Coffee was made by some of the men, but the water was so alkaline that it was almost impossible to drink it. Some of the men did not make breakfast, but at once lay down to sleep. The unfortunate horses would not touch the water and in addition were left standing saddled for a good five hours.

Red Star did not take Varnum's message directly to Custer, if the Arikara Narrative is to be believed. Instead he went to the camp of the scouts where he was greeted by Stabbed and Bloody Knife, proud of the distinction that had come to one of their young men. Custer, perhaps because he sensed that it might be some time before these primitive children finished what they deemed the appropriate ceremonies, came to the scout camp accompanied by Gerard, and asked Red Star in the sign language if he had seen the Dakota. Red Star replied in signs that he had, and handed him Varnum's note.

The Arikara Narrative goes on to say: "By Red Star's side were Bloody Knife and Tom Custer. Custer said to Bloody Knife by signs, referring to Tom: 'Your brother there is frightened; his heart flutters with fear; his eyes are rolling from fright at this news of the Sioux. When we have beaten the Sioux, he will then be a man.' "

We have quoted this passage largely because Godfrey all through his *Century* article, represents Custer as having been constantly in a state of semi-trance, lost in reverie. He represents him thus in this instance. "The General wore a serious expression," he says, "and was abstracted. The scouts were doing the talking, and seemed nervous and disturbed. Finally Bloody Knife made a remark that recalled the General from his reverie, and he asked in his usual quick, brusque manner: 'What's that he says?' The interpreter replied: 'He says we'll find enough Sioux to keep us fighting for two or three days.' The General smiled and remarked: 'I guess we'll get through with them in one day.' "

Actually it took them a little longer than one day to "get through with them."

In the Arikara Narrative, where, if anywhere, we might expect to find it, we look in vain for the repeated heroics Bloody Knife is credited with in the stories told by the half-breed, William Jackson, to whom we are indebted for the conception of Mitch Bouyer as a male Cassandra.

We suggest that the historical truth is something like this: When Custer came to the camp of the scouts after the arrival of Red Star, he found the Arikara somewhat excited. To reassure them he made the facetious remarks about his brother Tom.

Bloody Knife, sensing the mild reproof in the pleasantry, replied, in effect; "Granted, but it will take us two or three days to finish the job and make a man of brother Tom." There can be little doubt that Custer, as well as the Indian scouts, was uneasy about what might await them on the Little Big Horn, but that getting "jittery" about it, and showing it, would certainly not help matters. The Indian scouts knew that as far as they themselves were concerned they could safely run away almost any time even after the fighting had begun, but we shall see in a moment that they probably understood that the troops could not do so; that they would have to fight regardless of the odds.

Nowhere in the narrative of the Arikara is there as much as a hint that they felt Custer had treated them arrogantly or their services with contempt. If, in the interview described above, he had given Bloody Knife the impression that he took the coming encounter too lightly, he corrected that impression on his return from the Crow's Nest. According to both Red Star and Young Hawk he told the Arikara that there was serious work ahead that would try their courage. He is reported to have said, among other things: "Boys, you are going to have a hard day. You must keep up your courage. You will get experience today." Their mentor, Stabbed, immediately took up where Custer had left off, exhorting them to be brave and obey Custer's orders. His morale talk was followed by the ceremonial rubbing of a certain kind of clay on their chests to serve as a protective "medicine" in battle. This did not signify that they all expected to be killed, as is sometimes suggested. It was a rite any normal Indian would have undergone before undertaking a dangerous mission of any kind, and had no great tragedy occurred in this instance, it is unlikely that any mention whatever of this ceremony would have been made. We have to do here with the distorting shadows the event cast backward.

Before going to the Crow's Nest Custer had ordered the command to resume the march at 8 o'clock. It started a little after 8 and continued until about 10:00 when, within a mile or so of the Divide, it halted once more until 11:45. It was here that Custer rejoined it on his return from the Crow's Nest.

Before Red Star had finished his breakfast he was called to lead Custer and his party to the Crow's Nest. His story here is interesting chiefly for what he says of a colloquy between Custer and Half-Yellow-Face. While at the Crow's Nest the scouts had discovered six Indians they took to be Sioux scouts from the

camps leaving the vicinity of the Hill. Half-Yellow-Face insisted
that these scouts would report the presence of the troops to the
camps and that the Indians would then attack if Custer did
not attack them. Custer replied angrily: "I say again we have
not been seen. That camp has not seen us. I want to wait until
dark and then we will march. We will place our army around
the Sioux camp."

"That plan is bad. It should not be carried out," retorted
Half-Yellow-Face. He insisted that Custer must attack at once.

It would seem, then, that not all the Indian scouts were of
Bouyer's opinion—or the opinion ascribed to him—that the only
thing left for Custer to do was to run away as fast as his horses
could carry the command.

This incident would also seem to show that Custer was
chagrinned at the thought that his approach had been discovered,
else why the angry reply sounding like that of a man half-con-
vinced, exasperated, but as yet clinging to his plan to postpone
his further advance until the next day. The delay would have
given him time to send a messenger to Terry with the information that the Indians were present in much larger numbers and
much farther downstream than anyone had supposed, and what
he proposed to do. He was now opposite the headwaters of the
Tullochs, and a man like Herendeen who knew the country
could, if mounted on a good horse, have reached Gibbon's advanced units in, perhaps five or six hours. It was Godfrey's
opinion that Custer had intended to send such a messenger. But
the discovery of his command by the Indians, as he believed,
forced his hand and the pace of events to such an extent that the
sending of a messenger had become pointless at least as far as
any assistance from Gibbon was concerned. Things would come
to a head within the next few hours, whatever might be found
on the Little Big Horn when he got there.[14] It may be admitted
that he should have sent a messenger nevertheless; but it is il-
logical to say that he purposely refrained from doing so because
he wanted all the glory for himself, for, as just stated, the fight
would begin long before a messenger could have reached Terry;
so that any glory there might be in the fight would have been
reaped in any case. He knew also that Gibbon could not possibly
reach the field until some time on the 26th. It is possible that
in the rush of events the subject slipped his mind. Something of
this nature happened to Benteen who failed to send a messenger
when he knew, had he happened to think about it, that he

should have done so, though there may not have been in this case a specific order enjoining him to do so. There were a number of more or less costly "slips" in connection with this battle, as we suspect there have been in the vast majority of others. These will be pointed out as we come to them.

When Custer left the Crow's Nest his temper was on edge because of two exasperating uncertainties. Doubtless he had hoped to obtain more exact information about the enemy than the view from the Hill had supplied. There might be a camp or village at the place indicated by the scouts. Assuming that there was, how many Indians were there in it? He evidently did not believe this could be determined from the Crow's Nest. The Indians, experienced as they were in such matters, were not infallible in their observations and deductions. We have only to read the narratives of Colonel Gibbon and Lieutenant Bradley to learn how often these same Crow scouts had been at fault earlier in the campaign. He had looked carefully through field glasses and had not seen anything at all that suggested the presence of Indians at this point. Varnum had not been able to see anything either, though he had looked at daylight when the signs would be plainer than later in the day. Mitch Bouyer and Reynolds had certainly done likewise. They had all drawn a complete blank in the up-stream region, for no mention of it is made. But the freshness of the trail and its size proved that a large body of Indians were not far away. The necessary information could have been obtained during the afternoon and night. But now came Half-Yellow-Face and insisted that the command had been discovered, and that it was necessary to attack at once, which was perfectly true, granted the fact of discovery. This meant striking blindly, taking, among other things, the chance that the bulk of the Indians were up-stream with the way of escape open to the south. On returning to the command he learned that Sergeant Curtis of Yates' troop had found several Indians at a box of hardbread lost on the trail during the night march. These Indians, when approached, had fled toward the river, and it was, therefore, assumed that they were scouts from the hostile camps. They were, in fact, scouts from a small band of Cheyennes on their way to their tribesmen on the Little Big Horn. Several others had been noted spying on the camp.

Custer, now convinced that he had been discovered, assembled his officers, told them of the results of his observations from the Crow's Nest, what his scouts had said about a great village downstream on the river, the doubts he held concerning their findings; that he had intended to conceal the command for the rest of the day, send scouts to learn definitely where the Indians really were located, and attack the next morning. Since, however, the command had been discovered, it was necessary to atack at once to prevent escape of the Indians. He ordered the troop commanders to send a detail of one non-commissioned officer and six enlisted men to take charge of the packs of their respective companies, adding that the first company commander reporting to him that this had been done, should have the lead. Benteen was the first to report and was told to move to the head of the column. Captain McDougall, the last to report, was assigned to guard the packtrain.

The command now moved to the Divide where it was again halted and organized for a reconnaissance in force on a wide front. Captain Benteen was given troops "D", "H", and "K"; Major Reno "A", "G", and "M", and McDougall with "B" left to guard the packtrain. The five remaining companies "C", "E", "F", "I", and "L", Custer retained under his personal command. These assignments made, they crossed the Divide a little after Noon, and a few minutes later Benteen received an order to scout to the left, which later caused so much controversy.

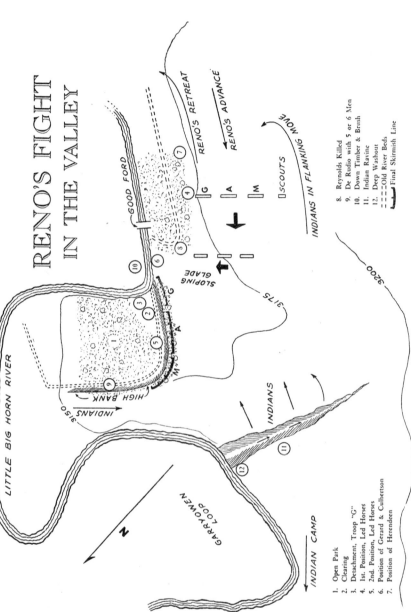

RENO'S FIGHT
IN THE VALLEY

LITTLE BIG HORN RIVER

GOOD FORD

RENO'S RETREAT

RENO'S ADVANCE

SCOUTS

INDIANS IN FLANKING MOVE

3175

3200

SLOPING GLADE

HIGH BANK

INDIANS

INDIANS

INDIAN CAMP

GARRYOWEN LOOP

3150

N

G

A

M

1. Open Park
2. Clearing
3. Detachment, Troop "G"
4. 1st. Position, Led Horses
5. 2nd. Position, Led Horses
6. Position of Gerard & Culbertson
7. Position of Herendeen

8. Reynolds Killed
9. De Rudio with 5 or 6 Men
10. Down Timber & Brush
11. Indian Ravine
12. Deep Washout
---- Old River Beds
└┘ Final Skirmish Line

The above illustration includes the principal terrain features and movements of the opposing forces pertinent to Reno's fight in the valley, following his approach march down the valley after crossing the Little Big Horn at Ford A. The author believes that Custer, from the fight on foot, and that he moved at once to attack the Indians from the opposite flank, simultaneously drawing the main body of the hostiles away from Reno preparatory to reassembling the entire regiment for concerted action on a more favorable part of the field.

CHAPTER 4

Reconnaissance in Force

Major Reno's Fight in the Valley

THE division of the command at the Divide and the order to Benteen to scout to the left show that Custer was not convinced that what the scouts had told him, even if substantially correct, was all of the story. There might be a village, and possibly a large one, at the place they had pointed out, though he had not been able to see any evidence of it. But even if this were true it did not necessarily follow that no other camps existed elsewhere along the stream; and if such camps did exist it was important to know about them before he became seriously involved in fighting anywhere. Since no time remained to clear up these uncertainties, he adopted the only remaining alternative by advancing with his whole force on as wide a front as was practicable and compatible with safety.

Our oral evidence here is too vague, too susceptible of variant readings for us to be positive on the minor details of what was in Custer's mind. His actions are a better guide than his words as reported years later. None of the dispositions made at this time had any reference to a plan of battle. No data for the formulation of battle tactics were as yet at hand. What was being done now was for the purpose of securing such data and at the same time move as rapidly as possible to deprive the enemy, as far as might be, of the initiative. For, whether the Indians were in one village or in several, it was important to move against them. If they fled, the sooner the troops moved to pursue or intercept them the greater the chances of success. If the warrior force was dangerously large, as there was considerable reason for thinking it might be, Custer risked destruction if he waited to be attacked, as Half-Yellow-Face had more than hinted. Colonel Hughes was aware that this danger had existed. He understood the military problem confronting Custer after he had been discovered; but

49

he evaded the issue in two *ex parte* statements, neither of which is true. In one of them he says that Custer was still 40 miles from the village when he went into camp on the evening of the 24th and was, therefore, nothing like "nearly in contact with the enemy," leaving the reader to infer that if he had remained there or continued up the Rosebud he would not have been discovered[15] and all would have turned out as Terry had planned. We have shown elsewhere that the distance was only a little more than half that—23 miles on the map used by General Terry and 22 on the modern survey. In the other statement he says that Custer need not have feared being attacked, because the warriors could not have left their village unprotected while they were away fighting.[16] But they had done just that eight days before when they attacked Crook only a few miles up the Rosebud from the spot where Custer camped on the evening of the 24th.

The principle in military science Custer foresaw might be used against him had been understood for ages, and had often been used with crushing effect. The warriors he was about to attack had demonstrated it perfectly in the battle just alluded to. Poorly armed as compared with Crook's troops, inferior in numbers, probably, they "all but whipped him," writes Colonel W. A. Graham in "The Story of the Little Big Horn." Stated abstractly, this principle is that a numerically superior (and under certain circumstances a numerically inferior) light armed force using missile weapons and possessing superior mobility, can destroy a more heavily armed but less mobile force with greater striking power, as long as it has ample room to maneuver. This is especially true when the terrain is exactly suited to the training and tactics of the light armed and correspondingly unfavorable to the heavy armed, which was exactly the situation in the case in hand.

Custer, with a force less than half that of Crook, and with no infantry, was doomed if the full force of the warriors attacked him while he was in the rough ground east of the Little Big Horn, provided the warriors were willing to pay the price.

There is one important exception to this principle. On open ground the advantage of the light armed and mobile force is largely nullified if the weapons of the more heavily armed enemy materially outrange their own. This applies only to the actual stand-up-and-knock-down business of fighting. On such ground as that over which Custer was marching the range of the weapons was of little importance. On Custer field the bow was used as effectively as firearms.[17] As long as the Indians were free to hang on the rear and flanks of the troops, dodging from cover to cover, the superior organization and weapons of the cavalry availed them nothing. The only way to deprive the warriors of this advantage was to move against their camps, compelling them to concentrate in defense of their non-combatants and property, leaving the initiative, the freedom to maneuver, to the troops.

To the military folks things of this kind are a matter of routine. They read the facts almost automatically in the light of the military maxims they have at their fingertips. Aside from the fact that it was impossible to fight Indians effectively in the Bad Lands, or semi-Bad Lands, there was the question of supplies and the safety of the wounded. General Crook, though only a day's march or so from his base, refused to pursue the Indians when they withdrew from the action, not because he could not have continued to drive them for a day or two. He returned to his base because he knew that driving the Indians from one position to the next would get him nothing except a constantly increasing number of dead and wounded, dead and crippled horses, ending in so restricting his movements as to put him on the defensive, followed by ultimate destruction before he could get back to his base of supplies where, in a good defensive position and with plenty of ammunition he could defend himself indefinitely.

Colonel Gibbon, after enumerating the many difficulties encountered in campaigning against Indians, wrote: "One other element enters into this system of warfare, for which, as yet, no adequate provision has been made. This is the care of the wounded, who cannot, as in civilized warfare, be left in hospitals on the field of battle. An Indian is rarely defeated until he is dead, and he not only kills every one of his enemies he can find, but wreaks his vengeance on his dead body. Hence a very small number of wounded men is sufficient to temporarily paralyze the offensive operations of a large body of troops.[18]

After Benteen had left the head of the column at the Divide, or soon after crossing it, Reno turned slightly to the left and marched down along the left or south bank of Sundance (Now Reno) Creek. Custer followed the Indian trail along the north bank. They moved along about parallel with each other for nearly 8 miles when, at 2 o'clock, Custer waved to Reno to cross over. About a mile from here they came to the forks of the creek where they found a single tepee with a dead warrior in it.

Although this tepee and the campsite on which it stood had
been abandoned exactly a week before, we must remember that
the trail the troops were following was believed to have been
made only a day or two before. This, taken in connection with
two or three other things now observed, led Custer to believe
that the Indians who had camped here had only just pulled out
and were now in wild flight. Gerard, who had ridden to a nearby
knoll, saw a small band of warriors fleeing down the trail. He
shouted to Custer: "Here are your Indians running like devils."
About the same time a dust cloud was seen in the valley of the
Little Big Horn four and a half miles in their front. It was assumed that this dust was stirred up by the Indians who had
camped here until frightened away by the approaching troops.[19]

This deduction, natural under the circumstances, was very wide
of the mark. What undoubtedly happened was something like
this: The Arikara, riding some distance in advance of the column,
on coming to the tepee, first slashed open one side of it and then
set it afire. The thick smoke from the buffalo hide attracted the
attention of the herdboys attending the ponies belonging to the
upper camps of the Indians, the nearest of which were about two
and a half miles from the ford where Reno crossed the river.
There can be little doubt that this was the first intimation the Indians had that the troops were almost upon them. The herdboys rounded up the ponies in haste, and rushed them toward
the camps, those in the valley raising a great dust cloud because
the grass here had been closely cropped and the ground trampled
into the consistency of an "ashbed," as Lieutenant Wallace put it.
Warriors in or near the upper camps, seeing the commotion, rode
up to investigate, and were still there when Reno arrived at the
ford about a half hour later.[20]

There can be little doubt that Custer had hoped to postpone
actual fighting until he had received word from Benteen. That
is really implied in a reconnaissance of this kind. It is, moreover,
suggested in his order to Benteen to "ride rapidly," and by his
own dawdling on the trail. The distance from the Divide to the
Lone Tepee was eight and a half miles, and he had taken over
two hours to cover this distance. The regulation cavalry walk
is 4 miles an hour. His average gait had, therefore, been only
a trifle faster than a walk. And after sending Reno to attack
he still moved slowly for some distance, as if hoping Benteen's
column would come into view. There was nothing unreasonable

in such an expectation; for, on Benteen's own word, the belief was that he would not have to go far to find what he had been sent for. And in actual fact, at 2:15, when Reno received the order to attack, Benteen was watering his horses at a morass only four and a half miles back on the trail; which is to say, only a little over a half hour's trot behind Custer. But with the Indians apparently in panic flight instant pursuit with the troops at hand seemed preferable to action later on with a larger force. So Custer seems to have reasoned; for when Gerard reported the flight of the small band of warriors in their immediate front he ordered the Indian scouts in pursuit, and when they refused to go, sent Adjutant Cooke with the order to Reno to take as fast a gait as he thought prudent and charge the Indians when he came up with them, and that he would be fully supported. The exact word-ing of the order is not known, but this was the sense of it. It was given about 2:15, according to Lieutenant Wallace's estimate of the time. Wallace was the official record-keeper of the march, and his statements as to time are to be accepted in preference to those of others unless there are convincing reasons for questioning them; and the hour given here is an extremely important orienta-tion point for the construction of the whole temporal series from the Divide on to the time the fighting began on Reno Hill about an hour before sundown.[21]

Reno went down to the river at a fast clip, probably at 8 to 9 miles an hour, an alternate trot and gallop, according to one or two officers. With him went Reynolds, Herendeen, Gerard and Lieutenant Hare with most of the Indian scouts. Mitch Bouyer and four Crows, Goes-Ahead, Hairy Moccasins, White-Man-Runs-Him, and Curley, remained with Custer. For some reason not fully ap-parent, Adjutant Cooke and Captain Keogh also went as far as the ford. Just as Reno was starting out Lieutenant Varnum, who seems to have passed along over the bench to the left of the column, rode up to Custer and reported that from a high point he had seen a large body of Indians in the valley, then hurried on after Reno. At ford the column mushroomed more or less so that it was necessary to re-form it after crossing. The horses were thirsty, and some of them were permitted to drink, while others were forced across and merely got their noses into the water as they moved through it. The river here makes a long loop northeastward, and along the upstream side of it is a very high bank, the end of the tableland sloping up to the south bench. While the troops were crossing the scouts, or some of them, rode to the top of this and looked over the treetops down the valley. They called to Gerard, who was just east of the ford, that the Indians were coming up the valley in great numbers. Gerard shouted this information to Major Reno, who made no reply, but continued forming the troops in three parallel columns as the men straggled out of the river to the open ground in the loop. Being aware that Custer believed the Indians were fleeing, and that it was important for him to know that they were not, Gerard looked for Cooke, met, or overtook him 75 to 80 yards from the river and told him what the scouts had said. Cooke promised to report it to Custer, and left. When Gerard got back to the river the command was about 500 yards down the valley. He hastened after it with several of the scouts who had waited for him at the ford.[22]

At the Court of Inquiry Major Reno said: "I crossed the creek and formed my battalion with two companies in line and one in reserve. I had been a good deal in Indian country and was convinced they were there in overwhelming numbers. I sent word back twice, first by a man named McIllargy, my striker, to say that the Indians were in front of me in strong force. Receiving no instructions, I sent a man, Mitchell, a cook—that was some minutes after I was convinced that my opinion was correct. I still heard nothing and so proceeded down the valley to carry out my orders. My first thought was to make my charge with two companies and hold the third in reserve as a rallying point, but when I saw the number of Indians I sent my adjutant to bring the third company into line." Describing the progress down the valley a little more in detail, when they started out from the ford, Company "A" was on the right, "M" on the left, and "G" in the rear, the latter being brought on the line while they were on the gallop. After going about two thirds of a mile they came to a rise in the ground, and here the individual companies were brought "On the left into line," according to Captain Moylan commanding Company "A." This was probably done because, at the moment, the Indians were rushing up as if to attack. Lieutenant Varnum, riding with the scouts to the left and a little in advance of the command, said: "There was a large body of Indians some distance off running toward us and back and across the prairie in every direction, kicking up all the dust they could, and it was impossible to tell their number. At this time they were running away, then circling back and making a heavy dust. All of a sudden they stopped and turned back, and as they did so I glanced back and saw the column deploying into line. It moved forward and we rode on, working to the left of the line."

From here on the command seems to have moved at the gallop to where the skirmish line was formed. Lieutenant Hare gives us the clearest account we have of the location and movements of the warriors at the beginning of the action. He said: "Up to the time the command was dismounted and a skirmish line formed, there were probably 40 or 50 Indians riding around and firing. As soon as the command dismounted, 400 to 500 came out of a coulee about 400 yards in front of us, and moved to our left and rear. I could see the upper part of the village, probably 400 to 500 tepees. I was a little in front of the line about 200 yards to the left near the foothills. When the command halted, the Indians who had been riding back and forth were about 200 to 300 yards away. As fast as they came out of the coulee they would fire from their horses. They were riding to the left, going into the foothills and coming down again. During the time we were in the bottom there were always Indians in our front, 200 constantly, maybe more."

The location of[23] the coulee mentioned by Hare should be carefully noted, for it is a very important orientation point in identifying the position of the troops. Just above the point where it enters the river it is a wide and deep washout large enough to have concealed several hundred warriors. Immediately above this it is now for some distance merely a flat, shallow slough, having been filled in with soil washed down by irrigation of the land on both sides. Still farther up it is mostly a steep-sided trench five to six feet wide and about four feet deep. It is easily identified on the map of the U. S. Geological Survey of the Custer Battlefield Area where it is indicated by a green, dotted line. There is no support in the evidence for the contention of some writers that the coulee out of which the Indians came ran down from the benchlands directly opposite the Indian camps. Others besides Hare said it was a few hundred yards directly in front of the troops as they rode up. In cross examination Reno said: "I then knew nothing of the topography, but it afterwards developed that had I gone 300 yards further the command would have been thrown into a ditch 10 yards wide and three or four feet deep. The Indians were in it, and the command would never have gotten that far; by the time they had got within a few yards most of the saddles would have been empty and the horses killed." It is useless to attempt to describe the battle before we have discovered the battlefield and noted its features that were of military significance. The accounts of participants are, for the most part, incomprehensible before this has been done.

We have today two views concerning the location of the skirmish line. The first, in time, is that of General Godfrey as shown on the map accompanying his article in the *Century Magazine* and reproduced on the Geological Survey. For this no support whatever can be found in the testimony of participants given at the Court of Inquiry.

The other is that of Fred Dustin, the result of a long and careful study which at one time came very near the solution of the vexing problem. Unfortunately, in our opinion, Mr. Dustin abandoned his original conception after making a visit to the field in 1938. He learned from a local resident that the loop in the river opposite Garryowen Station had not always extended as far southwestward as it does today. Until 1923 the river was still flowing through this loop, and because it threatened the right of way of the Burlington and Quincy railroad a channel was dug through the narrow neck of land at the upper end, thus turning the water out of the whole loop. Mr. Dustin, building on the fact that the river, until cut off, was constantly working southwestward, and having in mind the position of the skirmish line as shown on the Maguire map, assumed that at the time of the battle the current at the point where it turns northwestward continued in that direction instead of turning southwestward as it is now shown on the map; and then assumes further that at an earlier date the river *did* flow southwestward. In this way he obtains the old riverbed which appears vaguely in the accounts of some of the participants.

But up to the present time we have been unable to find any evidence that the loop was ever dry before the cut was made in 1923. However, granting Mr. Dustin's assumptions, certain passages in the testimony of the officers can be fitted into this construction. On the other hand the great bulk of the testimony is absolutely irreconcilable with this conception.

Our own conclusions regarding the battlefield are illustrated in the accompanying sketch. By referring to this the reader can check on our narrative, including the quotations from the sources we have used. We have seen from the testimony of Major Reno that the skirmish line was formed about 300 yards from the coulee out of which the Indians were coming to go to the rear of the troops around their left flank. This would mean that the line at first stood about where the headstone for Lieutenant McIntosh now stands. Lieutenant Wallace said: "When we first engaged there was a loop of the Little Big Horn in front of our right wing; to the left was open prairie, and in front of that we could see a ravine out of which many Indians were coming."

Several witnesses testified that the line advanced a hundred to a hundred and fifty yards and was finally brought into the edge of the timber "By the right flank." The line, therefore, never crossed this ravine and consequently could not have stood on the Garryowen loop.

The old river channel mentioned by the officers was not at the Garryowen loop, but along the three sides of the first bench lying along the left bank of the river in its northeastward course east of the Garryowen loop. The Maguire map shows this clearly, marking in both the old river course and the high bank above it. The complaints of the officers at the Court of Inquiry that the map did not represent the ground correctly, did not refer to this part of it. They described the basin or first bench as it is represented on the map. What seems to have confused them was the fact that the basin and the skirmish line were not in the right place with reference to the course of the river as they remembered it. Actually the river in its westward course here heads straight for the old channel along the south side of the basin instead of running nearly parallel with it, as shown on the map. The line of timber to the right of the line was not opposite the open loop of the river as it appears on the map. It ran nearly parallel with the flat, closed end of a loop. The strip of timber was a good 210 yards long and comparatively narrow, and was probably not an integral part of the narrow fringe along the two sides of the basin. The timber, as represented on the map is both too wide and too short. The length of the strip of timber can be roughly determined from the testimony. Herendeen's account shows that the line must have deployed at least 50 to 75 yards below the point. The line advanced 100 to 150 yards to near the timber fringing the basin, giving us a minimum of 200 and a probable 225 yards.

All this is so far out of line with the map that the officers could not, off-hand, make a clear explanation of just what was wrong with it.

We have already explained that the basin along the edge of which the skirmish line was finally posted was carefully drawn and in considerable detail. The only criticism of it was that there

was not as much large timber in it as is represented. There were
a few large trees and heavy brush.

As an explanation of the whole confusion we suggest that the
sketch of the basin was originally drawn on a detached sheet and
was intended as an "inset," but was misplaced when it was transferred to the general map. Take it bodily from where it stands
and place it as we have it on our sketch, readjust the direction of
the skirmish line, mark in the line of timber on which the line
deployed, and we have a map that corresponds closely to the
testimony.

Captain Moylan said the basin was 200 yards wide at its upper
end, 150 to 200 at its downstream end, and that it was 30
feet below the second bench on which the troops stood. Lieutenant
DeRudio said the bank was 10 to 12 feet high—"maybe more"—
and so steep that it was impossible to get down except over the
pony trails found there. Lieutenant Hare said the basin was
200 yards wide at its lower end and that the bench bordering
it ran into the river. The bench he refers to here is obviously
the narrow strip running down between the first bench and the
Garryowen loop which the river struck at the lower end in its return course westward. He thought the basin contained about ten
acres.

Many years after the battle Thomas O'Neil of "G" Troop,
who had been a member of a detachment of 20 men on a scout
to the lower end of the bench while the fighting was in progress,
said: "It was discovered that at some previous time the stream
had run close to our bank position, but had changed its course
farther away about three hundred yards, which left a ditch in our
rear. We were ordered to lie down on the edge of this bank—our
horses being held behind us."

As already stated, this bench, or basin, contained a scattering
of trees with heavy underbrush between them. At the upper end
next to the river, there was a clearing the exact extent of which
we do not know. Above this on the second bench, in a southeast
direction, there seems to have been a patch of ground bare of
timber and brush, or nearly bare, as we infer from the Gibbon
account which here seems to be confirmed by Lieutenant Wallace
who was here with part of "G" Troop on the extreme left of the
line after it faced about. He said there was no protection for them
here against the fire of Indians across the river some fifty yards
away. The final position of the horses was in the brush at the
western side of this clearing on the first bench. About the middle

of the bench there was another open space, some officers called the "park," in which some tepee poles had been left standing on which some meat had been left to dry. This is represented on the Maguire map much larger than it actually was, if our impression from what DeRudio, who crossed it, said is right.

The clearest description we have of the ground to the right of the line where it stood before entering the edge of the timber, is found in the testimony of Captain Moylan who said: "The right of the line was 200 yards from the river; perhaps not over 150; the first 30 yards being timber, the rest only a tree here and there and scattering underbrush. In the timber was heavy undergrowth."

This, except for the distance to the river, is constructively supported by the testimony of Gerard and Herendeen who were in this strip of timber from almost the beginning to the end of the action. The timber in question stood on the second bench and seems to have run about parallel with an old riverbed which Gerard called a "little creek" below a cutback 6 to 8 feet high, between the first and second benches. It seems clear that Moylan believed the river, which was several hundred yards beyond to the northeast, ran along this cutbank. In using the Geological Survey map we made the same mistake, and consequently at first located the skirmish line 150 to 200 yards too far to the east. The "little creek" begins at the point where the downstream course of the river loop in which Gibbon pitched his camp turns to the right back toward the bluffs east of the valley, the little creek continuing on diagonally to the second bench, which it follows past the point where the right of the line stood, and finally turns northeast, leaving a tongue of land of the second bench between itself and the actual river just above the turn it makes to form the loop in which lies the basin we have described.

The right of the line did not come near the river until it moved to the edge of the timber fringing the basin. It went there on the command "by the right flank," a march in single file east, or northeastward. This must have been followed by a "left oblique," or "By the left flank" to reach the timber in the original front, though neither of these commands are mentioned. Nor is there anything to show whether or not the head of the file actually forced its way through the thick underbrush on the original right, or whether or not there was a clear spot here between the strip of timber and that on the bank above the basin, as we have inferred from the testimony of Gibbon and Wallace.

In this maneuver the command as a whole may have moved eastward 150 to 200 yards to come near the river, which at this point has cut a considerable distance into the basin since 1876, as we have indicated on our sketch.

The Geological Survey does not show the "little creek" to the right of the line, because it is absorbed, as it were, in the 25 feet interval on which the survey was made, a fact which has caused us a good deal of confusion through the unconscious assumption that at the time of the battle the river ran along the border of the second bench. It has already been pointed out that Captain Moylan seems to have had the same misconception. After this mistake was discovered the remaining obscurities of consequence were cleared up, though not without a searching re-study of the evidence involving several trips to the ground.

In connection with this re-study we wish to make special acknowledgment to Colonel W. A. Graham, who was responsible for it and whose assistance, given from his own extensive knowledge of the sources, we have had throughout the re-study, ending in a personal meeting at the home of Mr. E. A. Brininstool in Hollywood, California, in March, 1950. Here, with the necessary maps supplied by our obliging host, the remaining obscurities were cleared up subject to checking on the ground. This check was made in the summer of 1950 and it confirmed the conclusions reached at the conference.

Some of the new information gained from the re-study have been incorporated in the preceding pages. The rest follow, it being understood that Colonel Graham can not be held responsible for all details and minor constructions.

The re-study began in the fall of 1949 when Colonel Graham sent us a sketch of the Custer battlefield area he had found in the *New York Graphic* for August 13, 1877, the year after the battle. This sketch had been used at the Reno Court of Inquiry, and Captain Benteen had marked in the position of Reno's skirmish line where it was first deployed and also its farthest advance. This definitely confirmed our own conclusion as to the loop on which the final stand was made.

With the line correctly placed and with a truer conception of the nature of the topography, much of the testimony, and in particular that of Sergeant Culbertson and Fred Gerard, that had been incomprehensible before, now became clear and significant. Incidentally the picture of the ground as drawn by Colonel Gibbon at the Court of Inquiry, of which no one had been able to make sense, suddenly flashed out clear and absolutely confirmed Benteen's identification of Reno's final position. Colonel Graham, with the assistance of General Godfrey, had tried to read this riddle, and both had drawn a complete blank. We had tried it at intervals for about fifteen years with precisely the same result. But discussions, comparisons, suggestions, breed ideas underground that sometimes come into focus in the conscious work a-day mind, according to Freud and a host of others who have delved into the subconscious.

Gibbon said that the river loop on which Reno made his stand was the third or fourth from the one in which he, Gibbon, had camped, and identified it unmistakably by the fact that here the river cuts sharply into the second bench. This is the fourth loop and the *only* one of the four that comes anywhere near the second bench. And, as if this were not sufficient, he remarked that he had seen several of Reno's dead horses in the brush opposite the turn of the river a little downstream from the point where it cuts into the second bench.

This cutbank is in a tongue of land from the second bench and runs upstream along the left, or south bank where it is shown on the Maguire map much larger than it really was. At the time of the battle there seems to have been a knoll or narrow ridge here right over the cutbank, making a considerable slope southward that was probably bare of timber and brush. Both Gerard and Culbertson speak of being here on "the brow of the hill." If there actually was such a knoll or ridge it has either been levelled down for the farmstead now located there, or the river has washed it away. Looking at it from the south the slope is evident enough today, though the tongue of land is little, if any higher than the second bench. Looking at it from the other side, that is, from the first bench we unconsciously gain the impression that the place is higher than the second bench to our right where there is a bank of 12 to 15 feet while the sheer cliff of the tongue of land to the left is 25 feet or more because the river here is about 15 feet below the level of the first bench. But be that as it may, there is no doubt that Gerard and Culbertson referred to this tongue of land and thus located themselves on the map and in consequence made their testimony intelligible.

We are now prepared to narrate what happened on the battlefield as located and described.

As already explained, the skirmish line was formed near the site of the present headstone for Lieutenant McIntosh. Its right rested on a narrow strip of timber running parallel, or nearly so, to an old riverbed 150 to 200 yards from the line. Troop "G" under McIntosh held the right, "A" under Moylan, the center, and "M" under French, the left. For a few minutes a mixed group of scouts and civilians, under Varnum and Hare, stood about 200 yards to the left of French. Among them were, besides the Arikara and several Crows, the two Jackson brothers, half-breed Blackfeet, Reynolds, Gerard, Reno's orderly, Davern, Herendeen, and probably the Negro Dorman. Still farther toward the foothills was the Arikara, Bobtailed Bull, if his fellow tribesmen are to be believed.

The Indian scouts left the line almost as soon as they halted, if, indeed they formed a line at all, and thereafter conducted themselves as Indian always did in a fight, each a law unto himself and seeking his own objectives in his own way, if he did not wish to fight as a member of a closely co-operating group formed to meet a specific and immediate threat, or some other strictly limited action. Even so each fought in his own individualistic manner. The officers who later accused them of having fled in wild panic simply did not understand this. The evidence indicates that all except four Arikara who crossed the river to run off some Sioux ponies, as they claimed Custer had instructed them to do, stayed in the fight.[24]

The rest of the group here remained for a few minutes to fire some shots at the Indians coming out of the ravine, but finding their bullets dropping short, they went to the timber where the led-horses had been taken, where we shall meet some of them again later.

The line remained in the open for perhaps 10 to 15 minutes, some of the men firing wildly into the air, according to Varnum. There was, as far as we can determine from the evidence, very little to shoot at for the men on the right at this time. Most of the Indians in sight were off to the left and out of range for even the small group there, as noted above. There probably were some Indians along the Garryowen loop where they could easily drop down into the washout at the mouth of the ravine used by the Indians to turn the left of the line—perhaps some of those who had retreated before the troops as they came down. The bullets that wounded several men in the line, must have come from this direction or from the timber on the bank of the basin. The fact remains, however, that we have no definite or clear picture of what the troops were firing at before they entered the timber. The impression left is that this firing was, for the most part, a reckless waste of ammunition. Some of these wildly-fired bullets undoubtedly landed in the Uncpapa camp 800 to 1000 yards away beyond the river loop where they may have caused some damage and added to the general panic among the non-combatants. Gall is reported as saying in 1886 that his two wives were killed during the fighting in the valley, and that this made his "heart bad."

At this point Reno's summary is helpful, though it needs correction. "We were on the skirmish line under hot fire for 15 to 20 minutes," he said. I was on the line near Captain Moylan when word came to me that the Indians were turning our right. I left Lieutenant Hodgson to bring me word of what went on there and went with Company "G" to the bank of the river. I suppose there were 40 men in the Company. When I got there I had a good view of the tepees and could see many scattering ones. It was plain to me that the Indians were using the woods as much as I was, and scattering. Lieutenant Hodgson came to me and told me they were passing our left, and I told him to bring the line in, round the horses."[25]

After the line had been brought into the edge of the timber and faced about, it formed a curve with the rounded angle of the high bank bordering the basin in its rear about opposite the center of "M" Troop half of which then faced the foothills across the valley. Back of the new left of the line was the clearing down in the basin and a thin belt of timber on the bank except, perhaps, for a short distance next to the river. It was to the downstream side of this clearing Reno went with a *part*, not the *whole* of Troop "G." Reno's testimony throughout is full of loose, inaccurate statements. Moylan, who was as careful as Reno was careless, testified that the "greatest part" of the troop was taken down on the bench, as did Varnum and Wallace. It is very important to remember this if we wish to understand how and why this troop came to grief through no fault of its enlisted men.

What this detachment of "G" Troop was to accomplish is not made entirely clear in the testimony. To say that it was to prevent the Indians turning the right of the line does not, at first, seem to make sense. As a partial explanation we quote the following from Thomas O'Neill. "Twenty men under Lieutenant McIntosh (of whom I was one) were ordered to deploy in skirmish line and scout the brush, in order to ascertain if the Indians could attack us from the rear. We found thick underbrush and vines and some cottonwood trees growing on this place and at the head of it, a very deep cut and washout. As we discovered no Indians between us and the river, the Lieutenant came back and reported........ But we observed that they were forming in great numbers on our left, where they could deliver a flank fire. It was thought by the officers that they were forming for a charge on that end. A brisk consultation was held by the officers, who shouted back and forth from their positions on the line."[26]

To understand this we must assume that by the time this scouting party got back the troops had moved into the edge of the timber and faced about, making the former "right" of the line now the "left."

After this detachment returned from the scout it was deployed along the river on the farther side of the clearing, presumably in order to fire on Indians across the river who were, no doubt, heading for an easy ford some distance above the point where the river cuts into the second bench. Colonel Gibbon mentioned this ford in his testimony. Once across the river these Indians could approach the line through the brush on the first bench south of the tongue of land described some pages back. In the meantime the Indians who had turned the original left of the line were now approaching, or entering, the strip of timber on the upper end, so that in a comparatively short time the two converging columns would have taken possession of the whole strip and be in position to pour a heavy, slanting cross-fire into the line, forcing the men to take refuge behind the high bank, where in all probability they would soon have been exposed to the same kind of cross-fire from across the river. It should be explained here that in the loop of the river there was a good deal of dead and down-timber as well as tangled underbrush; and, as Gibbon said, it was agreed that had the Indians gained possession of this, as they could easily have done, it would have been necessary to dislodge them. But there were no reserves for such a purpose, and it would certainly have been suicidal to rob the line under the existing circumstances.

Both of these movements threatened the led-horses, and Varnum, when Moylan called his attention to this, rode back onto the bench, passed through the clearing and on to the left of the line and on to the horses. He called for "A" Company to follow him with the horses and led them to the rear of their company position. "And then, I guess, the whole of the other companies followed me," he said.

This made the horses relatively safe for the moment but did not remedy the weakness in the position of the command; for this was not the only movement by the Indians threatening immediate disaster. Although McIntosh had found no Indians in the brush on the bench itself, they were moving upstream against the exposed right of French over the high tongue of land bordering the bench on the northwest. Even before McIntosh could have returned Wallace called DeRudio's attention to Indians approaching from this direction. DeRudio went with 5 or 6 men of Company "A" to investigate, going down on the bench by way of one of the pony or buffalo trails. He crossed the clearing, and as he approached the "park," saw the Indians on the high ground to his front and left. Taking his men in this direction he posted them on the high bank at the base of which ran the old riverbed, or "creek," as he called it, explaining that he believed it was a "dry creek." He and his men remained in this position for about 10 minutes, he said, firing at Indians coming upstream. Then the trumpeter of his company ("A" Company; DeRudio having taken the place of Varnum when the latter was put in command of the scouts) came with his horse and said: "Lieutenant, here is your horse." I said, "I don't want my horse." The man said: 'They are going out', and the men I had with me immediately mounted their horses. I tried to check them, but they would not listen to me. I stopped at the creek trying to keep the men steady as the last man passed me. I noticed the guidon of the company on the bank of the creek, and I told him to go and get it before he went out. The man said it was too hot there for him, and he continued on his way. I thought it was not very hot, and went and got the guidon myself. It was not more than 40 feet which I had to go back. I crawled up to the top of the bank and grabbed the guidon, and there were 20 to 30 Indians coming, not more than 40 or 50 yards from me, scattering as they saw the head of my horse over the bank. They fired a volley at me and I dropped down."

This incident is timed by the following questions and answers.

Question. By that time (the time DeRudio secured the guidon) had the command all gone out?

Answer. Yes sir, those that were with me.

Q. Had the *command* gone out at that time?

A. The left was going out.

What became of these panicky "A" Company men? Did they reach their company in time to go out with it? We shall have more to say about them presently, in connection with a mysterious order by an officer who has never been identified.

About the time DeRudio and his men were on the high bank some hundreds of yards in rear of the line Herendeen had an encounter with Indians in the timber a little upstream from the place where the led-horses had been taken at the beginning of the action. He, with Reynolds and Gerard, had come here from the extreme left of the line soon after its development and tied their horses near those being held there. On leaving the place he had become separated from Reynolds and Gerard and had then gone upstream in the timber, where he remained until the line ceased firing on being ordered to mount, then started downstream to get his horse. Before he reached it 20 to 25 Indians came to within 40 to 50 yards of him, and he stopped to fire 7 to 8 shots at them. When he got to his horse he found all the rest gone. Mounting, he rode downstream into the clearing, where he found Major Reno and the men of companies "A" and "M" mounting for the retreat to the bluffs. He saw one company in line near the river. This was, of course, the platoon of Company "G" which had scouted downstream through the brush, and had taken position here on its return. No officer was with them. Like Casabianca, they remained at their post because no order had come for them to leave it. Their commander, Lieutenant McIntosh, had gone in search of Reno to report the result of his scout and had not yet returned. Wallace was with the other platoon in the line at the left of "A" Company. More about them later.

A crisis in the battle had now arrived and an instant decision must be made. Irremediable disaster threatened if the line remained much longer where it now stood. This had become apparent to others besides Reno.

While DeRudio was on the high bank to the north he had noted that farther down across the river a very large body of Indians was coming through the sparse timber there. Sergeant Culbertson had also seen them, and so had Reno who instantly understood that they menaced the whole rear of his position. He had nothing with which to meet this Indian force estimated at 700 to 800, except the 20 men detached from "G" Troop. At the same time, as already noted, another body of Indians was moving downstream to pass to the left of the line. Others were coming over the high ground bordering the bench on the northwest, as we have seen from DeRudio's account. The underbrush on the bench in rear of the line offered covered approach to hundreds of Indians. The plain in front of the line was covered with hundreds of warriors from the Garryowen loop clear across the valley. Bullets were already falling among the horses in the brush at the west end of the clearing where a number of them were killed.

In the face of this situation Major Reno acted promptly, though it is fairly certain that he asked the opinion of his troop commanders before he gave the order to mount. We have already quoted O'Neill to that effect; and Private W. C. Slaper of "M" Troop, wrote years later: "It was said before Reno gave the order to mount and retreat, he rode up to Captain French and shouted: 'Well, Tom, what do you think of this!' Captain French replied 'I think we had better get out of here!' Reno thereupon gave the order though I did not hear it."[27]

The manner in which this order was conveyed to the men on the line led to a great deal of criticism, the charge being made that many did not receive it, and that, in consequence, unnecessary losses were incurred. To this Reno replied that he sent his Adjutant, Lieutenant Hodgson, to give the order to French and himself gave it to Moylan and McIntosh, and that it was the duty of the troops commanders to see to it that their men received it.

Technically this justification may seem watertight; for, if it be argued that the men should have been summoned to their horses by trumpet, the troop commanders, who had their own trumpeteers, could have done so, and the fact that they did not do so shows that they did not think it necessary. Under ordinary circumstances communication of orders by voice may serve reasonably with cavalry, though DeRudio said that the trumpet was ordinarily used even on the drill-ground. But here the circumstances were quite exceptional because of the timber and the wide dispersal of the men. It is clear enough from his questions that Recorder Lee believed the order should have been given by trumpet and that losses were incurred because it was not so given. DeRudio, who was particularly pressed on the point, and who was evidently of the same opinion though he did not want to say so, was finally driven to say that Major Reno was a good "drill-master" whose voice carried far enough for all the men to have heard it. The absurdity of this becomes apparent when we remember that wherever Reno might have been when he gave the order, some of the men would have been 200 yards away, while 70 grains of black powder were exploding at the rate of about two per second, on the average, to say nothing of the firing by the Indians. In any case we know on Reno's own word, that he did not shout the order to the whole command, but passed it to the troop commanders who do not seem to have possessed stentorian voices.

W. C. Slaper wrote: "I could hear nothing but the continual roar of the Indian rifles and the resonant bang-bang of cavalry carbines, mingled with the warhoops of the savages and the shouts of my comrades." DeRudio and his men several hundred yards away to the north did not hear the order, nor did Davern who was on the extreme left of the line. He went to his horse when he saw the "G" Company men run for theirs. The command was well on its way when he cleared the timber. He was slightly delayed because he found a "G" Company horse tied to the bridle of his own, and he stopped to turn it over to a sergeant of that company he met in the timber as he was going out. Varnum and Hare, foot-loose after the Indian scouts had left the line, likewise failed to hear the order. Gerard[28] and the half-breed, William Jackson, were late in getting out because, like Varnum, they did not understand the meaning of the shout they heard, "Charge, charge, we are going to charge!" raised by the horseholders. When they saw the troops tearing across the plain they waited, expecting them to return after making the charge. When they did not do so, they started after them. But before going very far they saw that many Indians were between them and the troops. Believing they could not get through, they returned to the timber.

When Varnum came out of the timber only a short distance behind "A" and "M" he was still under the impression that the "charge" was not a retreat to the bluffs but an attack in the ordinary sense of the term "charge."

We have found no absolutely conclusive evidence that any men of "A" and "M" *who were on the line* when the order was given, were left behind, except Sergeants Culbertson and McDermott of "A" who did not hear the order. Like many others they heard the shout "We are going to charge." They went out with Wallace, presumably because they were too late to go out with their company. The men of these companies, or most of them, mounted in the clearing in an orderly way, then individually scrambled up the bank by way of the pony or buffalo trails, passed through the narrow belt of timber on the second bench on which the line had stood, and formed in column of fours in the open. Though Moylan stated definitely that all but one of his men were in place when they started out, there is reason for thinking that the 5 or 6 men who had been with DeRudio got back too late to go out with their company and came through with Wallace instead. For Herendeen, who had left close on the heels of "A" and "M," but returned when his horse stumbled and ran away, said that as he neared the timber on his way back he heard an officer on the other side of it call out; "Company "A" men, halt. Let us fight them. For God's sake, don't run."

After pin-pointing on the map and the face of the clock all those who testified, we find that this officer must have been Lieutenant Wallace who was at that moment trying frantically to mount the panicky "G" Company men of his neglected platoon which had stood at the left of "A," after searching vainly for his company commander, McIntosh. It should be explained here that Wallace was not, technically, on duty with his company. He had been detached to keep the itinerary of the march and was at liberty to go where he pleased in the performance of his duty. This fact may have caused him to hesitate taking command of the company longer than he would have done had he been on duty as second in command. The circumstances certainly called for all possible haste in getting the men to their horses, especially those in the platoon that stood near the river on the farther side of the clearing.

The accounts of Varnum and Herendeen show that they must have passed each other not far from the timber. It could, therefore, not have been Varnum's voice Herendeen heard down on the bench. DeRudio, we know, did not again make contact with any group of men other than Gerard, O'Neill, and William Jackson, after those who were with him off to the north had left him. Hare's own account excludes him from consideration here. McIntosh was lost from sight until some time after Herendeen had regained the timber. But the accounts of Varnum, Culbertson and Wallace show that he, Wallace, left the timber only a minute or two behind Varnum. This points directly to Wallace as the officer who called on the "A" Company men to halt. There is other evidence pointing to the same conclusion.

Herendeen said that among the 12 men who remained in the timber with him were one or two wearing caps with the letter A, but added that headgear among the troopers was frequently exchanged as fancy or caprice dictated, and that therefore these men were not necessarily from "A" Company.

If the failure to use the trumpet caused any losses, it was mostly in "G" Company, which was so completely shattered that it ceased to count as a fighting unit for the rest of the day and was, in all probability, not good for much on the 26th. As we shall see in Chapter 6, when the combined commands of Reno and Benteen moved out late in the afternoon to join Custer, Wallace had only 7 men. After they returned to Reno Hill he could find only 3 men for the skirmish line. Where were the rest of the 40 the company is said to have contained? The official casualty list shows 14 killed, including McIntosh, and 2 wounded. The killed were not reported separately for the two days, but it is extremely improbable that any "G" men were killed on the Hill either on the 25th or the 26th. That leaves 22 men unaccounted for when Wallace posted the company on their return from Weir Point.

The explanation for this extraordinary fact is not far to seek. One man, Thomas O'Neill, we know, bolted from the "Casabiancas" and returned to the timber after his horse was killed. The 12 men who came out with Herendeen were, with the possible exception of two, almost certainly "G" Company men, two of them wounded. All of these were without much doubt among the numerous skulkers with the packs of whom both Reno and Benteen complained.

Assuming the company contained 40 men, and that all the men with Herendeen were "G" men, it will be seen that after Wallace arrived on the Hill he should have had 14 men instead of 7. This is only approximate, for no roll calls, if any were made after the dispositions at the Divide, have come down to us, and we know that some men were not serving with their companies. For instance, McIllargy and Mitchell belonged to Company "I," but were with Reno on the 25th and carried the two messages for Custer Reno sent soon after starting down the valley. Davern, one of Reno's orderlies for the 25th, was a member of "F" Company. Reno said he supposed that "G" Company contained 40 men. There may have been a few more or a few less. We have no record of any "G" men killed before the retreat began.

Assuming that our narrative up to this point is approximately correct, we have the following picture: "8 men of "G" Company went out with Wallace or bolted from the line while he was searching for McIntosh, or after he had gone out. Since, according to O'Neill, the platoon on the farther side of the clearing contained 20 men, and only 12 came out with Herendeen, 8 of them must have made a break to go out with Wallace, or "on their own," though we cannot be certain of their number, for some of the men of the platoon on the line next to Moylan may have found their horses killed or missing when they came to mount them, and chose to remain in the woods rather than risk a flight in the wake of the column. But the general situation suggests that most of the men with Herendeen belonged to the platoon at the river. How many of the 28 were mounted when they started out there is no way of determining. 14 of the 28 were killed on the retreat, leaving 14 who should have been with Wallace when they started to go to Custer. After returning to Reno Hill Wallace should have had, in addition to the 14, the 10 unwounded men who had arrived with Herendeen a few minutes after he started to go to Weir Point, a total of 24 instead of the 3 he was able to place on the line. The other 21 were skulking among the packs!

Here is the list of casualties for the three companies in Reno's battalion, compiled from Appendix D in Captain E. S. Luce's *Keogh, Comanche, and Custer.* Captain Luce's compilations were made from the official record in the archives of the War Department.

	Killed, 25th and 26	Wounded, 25th	Wounded, 26th
A	8	4	3
G	14	2	0
M	12	5	5
	34	11	8

Since the "G" men wounded on the 25th were almost certainly hit in the valley fight, "G" Company incurred no wounded on the Hill, a strong suggestion that few of its members were on the line on the 26th, and hence little likelihood that any of them were killed. The 14 dead were left along the line of retreat. This is the probability, not a proved fact—an approximation.

We have tried to show what happened to Company "G." It remains to show why it happened.

Part of the explanation is to be found in the separation of the company into two platoons operating several hundred yards apart. A more important cause was the absence of McIntosh at the critical moment when the command was in the act of disengaging. He had left his post to report the results of his scout to Reno, and, as far as our evidence goes, was not seen again until after Wallace had gone out, when he came to what was left of his company on the bench. This was, evidently, before Herendeen had made his way back to them. According to Dustin, a trooper named McCormick offered him his horse, with the remark that they were all as good as dead anyway, an offer McIntosh finally accepted and hurried after the command the head of which must by this time have been across the river. He was killed before he got to the river, but there is no general agreement as to the spot where his body was found. It is extremely doubtful that he was killed where his present headstone stands. Mr. Dustin writes us that he is in possession of much evidence going to show that the headstone has been moved a number of times to suit the convenience of the farmers here. Our own guess is that he was killed a hundred yards, more or less, from the river.

We can only speculate as to what detained McIntosh. Reno testified that he had given him the order in person. Assuming this to be true, why did not McIntosh go at once to his men and order them to mount? A plausible answer is that he went in search of his horse. Why his orderly did not bring it to him is another subject for long-distance speculation. Had the orderly, like Wallace, searched for him and failed to find him? Was the "G" Company horse Davern found tied to the bridle of his own, McIntosh's mount? Had the orderly tied it to Davern's horse, which was close to the horses of "G" Company, to make certain that someone would find it—McIntosh himself, perhaps, when he came to mount his men, and then gone out with Wallace or the stragglers? All horses not in charge of orderlies or belonging to footloose members of the command, were supposed to be in charge of horse-holders so that in case of need they could be rushed quickly to their dismounted holders, or be together where they could be secured without loss of time if the men were ordered to their horses.

Coming back to Companies "A" and "M," we recall that they formed in column of fours outside the timber. It is impossible to determine definitely whether or not they stood here an appreciable time waiting for "G" Company to come up. The indications, however, are that they did not wait at all, but went out even before all of their own men were in place. This much we can say in spite of Moylan's statement that all but one of his men were with him when he went out. Aside from this Moylan's testimony contains nothing direct on the point in question. Nor does that of Dr. Porter. This leaves us only Major Reno and Herendeen. Herendeen's account leaves the impression that no halt of consequence was made here. Reno said he stood for ten minutes at the place where Bloody Knife was killed. The careful historian will attach little weight to this. Except for a few details that may or may not throw light on the subject, we shall have to be content with

Looking west from Greasy Grass Ridge. Across the river is the site of the 3-mile long Indian Camp. At the extreme upper left dimly appear the key bluffs which highlight the "Weir Point" and "Reno fight on the hill" episodes. (Photo by Edith Kuhlman 1936).

The Ravine up which Reno's troops retreated after the fight in the Valley. The Little Big Horn can be seen at the foot of the bluffs. (Photo by Edith Kuhlman 1937).

Varnum's summary that "the retreat from the woods was hasty and the rear of the column disorganized." Although Varnum did not see the formation he was in position to know that they did not wait long for him after he heard the shout of the nearby horse-holders; "We are going to charge." He was at the extreme right of the line and instantly rushed to his horse tied or in charge of his orderly near the other horses. He found a number of men already mounted in the clearing, while other still blocked the passages through the brush into the open. This caused him some delay. The men went up the bank as soon as they were ready and Varnum followed them. When he got out of the timber "A" and "M" were some rods out on the plain.

This cry, "Charge! Charge! We are going to charge," coming from the horseholders, is in itself significant; for the men who made it were in charge of horses whose riders had not shown up to claim their mounts. They were the most experienced troopers of their units, anxious about the less experienced, knowing that something was amiss, or the men would all have come in together, or nearly so. It was not their business to call the absent ones, but since those whose duty it was to see to it that they got to their horses seemed to be off the job, they did what they could to let everyone know that the command was re-forming for some kind of move. There can be little doubt that their shouts saved lives.

If, as Moylan claimed, all his men were in their places when "A" and "M" left, we wonder at the crowd Varnum found when he came to get his horse. They were not the "G" Company men who came out with Wallace, for they left with Varnum who was a few minutes ahead of Wallace. The most plausible inference is that they were mostly "A" and "M" Company men who caught up during the bolt to the river, as did a number of others, among them Hare and his orderly. And we think it a near certainty that the five or six men who had been with DeRudio, as related some pages back, did not get back to go out with their company. DeRudio said that the right of the line had gone out by the time his men left him. The "right" in this case, meant French and possibly Moylan. In any case we know that the two companies left together. DeRudio's 5 to 6 "A" Company men could therefore, not have gone out with them, if DeRudio is to be believed; and he seems to be supported by Herendeen's statement that, as he was returning to the timber after his horse had thrown him, he heard an officer calling on some "A" Company men to halt. "A" Company must have been at this time at least half-way to the river.

The Indians on the plain upstream do not seem to have made any move to attack the troops as they came into the open ground. But an undetermined number had, as we have seen, moved downstream behind, or through the narrow strip of timber near which "A" and "M" now stood in column of fours. They were, Herendeen thought, the same he had exchanged shots with a few minutes before. While the troops were mounting and forming in column they worked their way through the thick underbrush to within a few yards of the two companies standing in parallel columns about 15 yards apart, Reno at their head, mounted, and near him Bloody Knife, also mounted. Concealed in the edge of the underbrush they fired into the troops at the murderously close range of about ten yards. A bullet crashed through the head of Bloody Knife, spattering blood and brains into the face of Reno. Another struck French's striker, Henry Klotzbucher, who toppled from his horse screaming horribly "O my God, I've got it!"

The full details of what happened immediately after this will probably never be known with absolute certainty. But we have the essentials. Herendeen believed that Reno became badly flustered when Bloody Knife was killed and Klotzbucher screamed, ordered "Dismount," promptly changed his mind and ordered "Mount," then dashed away followed by the troops. This, like one or two other accounts, while substantially true as to objective fact, is misleading; for it leaves the impression that the troops were *stampeded* by Reno putting spurs to his horse and fleeing.

While it is probably true that the men in the two companies were at this time at near-panic level, they went out in column formation and under orders adapted to the circumstances; "Forward," "Trot," and "Gallop." This we have from Captain Moylan, perhaps the coolest-headed officer present and in position to hear.

What has been generally overlooked in discussing this incident is the controlling fact that neither Reno nor anyone else knew how many Indians were in the brush here. Herendeen had seen only 20 or 25, but said that more were coming when he saw them. Moylan had seen just twice that number, and believed that there may have been several hundred. It is easily seen that 200 Indians, or even half that number, could in a few minutes have completely wrecked the two small companies while they stood in column of fours. Such a heavy fire as they could have delivered, especially if directed against the horses, would have killed or wounded a great many of them, and turned the rest into a frantic, plunging mass out of control of their riders or holders long enough for the Indians to rush in from the plain and the brush and destroy the two companies bag and baggage. When the volley was delivered from the brush Reno must have instantly perceived this possibility, and his first instinctive, or semi-automatic reaction could well have been to dismount his men to place them more nearly on a par with the Indians. But as a cavalry commander of long experience his first conscious rationalization would have told him that, while this might meet the immediate threat, it could not save him from ultimate destruction; for the hundreds of Indians on the plain, whose attention was now closely focused on the troops, would have rushed on the horse-holders the moment the dismounted men entered the brush to fight. In short, he seemed to be, and quite possibly was, in a serious ambush, and the only thing to do was to get out of it before the trap was fully sprung, Hence the quick countermand and what, from the point of view of the battalion as a whole, was a virtual *sauve qui peut*[29] scramble to get away.

We have stated the objective facts as they appear to us in the testimony of the witnesses. We leave it to the reader to decide for himself whether or not Major Reno's reaction to them indicates that he was so badly frightened that he fled in the manner he did without justification on military grounds.

From the skirmish line in the edge of the timber to the point where the command crossed the river, is about a mile and a quarter over the curved route followed. The troops, 'A" on the right, "M" on the left, and Wallace with men from all of the three companies, far in the rear, tore over the ground at a fast gallop, and reached the river probably in 5 to 6 minutes. Behind them, like the tail of a comet, came the forlorn hopes, mostly "G" men, a-horse and a-foot. Some of the former, among them Varnum and Hare with their orderlies, got through though Hare's orderly was killed at the river and Varnum's wounded. It does not seem possible that any of the latter could have succeeded in doing so. Benteen, looking down on the scene from the bluffs near the upper ford, thought he saw 12 or 13 men in skirmish line being killed by Indians riding through the line back and forth. It must have been among these stragglers that the bulk of the casualties occurred, or at least the greater number of those who were killed.

Most of the Indians attacking the troops on their way to the river were on the right flank just beyond effective pistol range, firing as they galloped parallel with the column. This position gave them a great advantage in that they could use their rifles.

The troops could use only their revolvers, since it is next to impossible to fire a carbine to the right from the back of a horse at the gallop, and hit the target. Varnum and several others were under the impression that all the Indians were armed with Winchesters which they "pumped" into the column from across their pommels. This is more than doubtful, for we have today nearly conclusive evidence that only about half the Indians possessed firearms of any kind, and that very few of them had magazine rifles. It would, however, have been natural for those with the best weapons to lead in the attack. Some of them rushed up close when they saw a man who had emptied his revolver, Wallace said, and some close encounters occurred in this way. But that could hardly have happened except among the disorganized troops at the rear. There were a few Indians on the left on the same side of the river as the troops. There were hundreds of them on the other side of the river, or more properly, on the first bench between the river and the troops, who had crossed at the ford indicated in our sketch; but there is little evidence that many of these left the first bench to fire on the troops. We have no positive direct evidence that any of them did. It is, however, difficult to account for the presence of the Indians on the bluffs ahead of and to the left of the troops unless we assume that they came up the right bank. There is, in fact, an account by a member of a group of Indians east of the river near the bluffs, that must have come up the right bank, but hurried downstream again when they learned that troops were approaching the lower end of the camps. We know, of course, that some of the Indians who rode at the right of the troops and those following them, crossed the river to the right and no doubt also where the troops had crossed, or, in fact, anywhere here where it was possible.

When the troops got to the river they found the left bank to be 4 to 5 feet high. They went over it pell-mell into water about belly deep to the horses. On the other side the bank was cut by a buffalo trail too narrow to permit more than one horse to pass at a time. Many troopers headed for this outlet, resulting in some crowding and confusion. But it was not impossible to get out in other places. We know that Varnum and Davern crossed below the trail, and Hare and Culbertson above it, and there must have been many others who did likewise, or the crossing could not have been made in 3 to 5 minutes, as reported by Wallace, which seems in any case, an underestimate.

Most of the Indians turned back before reaching the river. The few who went beyond it inflicted some casualties, but did nothing to justify the lurid accounts of fighting hand-to-hand in the water and a hail of bullets from the right. Only one or two men were killed in the crossing, Wallace said. Several others were wounded or killed near the river on either side. Hodgson's horse was shot in the river and himself wounded in the leg. One or two troopers helped him to the east bank. Whether or not he received further assistance or stumbled on alone to the spot where his body was found, is not known. Wallace said he was killed 50 yards from the river by Indians on the bluffs. Sergeant Culbertson, who led Reno's searching party soon after Benteen arrived, said they found his body "a little up the hill," which would be considerably farther than 50 yards from the river.

No attempt was made to cover the crossing. When Sergeant Lloyd, at the suggestion of Culbertson, asked Captain French to do something to protect the wounded, he replied: "I'll try, I'll try," but we have found no evidence that either he or anyone else made any attempt to cover the crossing. On the contrary several of the witnesses said flatly no such attempt was made.

Nor, in going from the river to the top of the bluffs, was anything done to restore the formations disrupted in crossing. Indeed, it was impossible to climb the steep, irregular slope in any way except "at will." Dr. DeWolf and his orderly started up a ridge at the left and were killed when about half-way up to the 8-10 feet ledge against which the ridge ended. The rest went up the large ravine to the right, which divides a little above the mouth at the plain. The left, or north branch, offers by far the easiest way to the top, but whether or not this, or both were used we have not been able to determine. The south branch divides again as it nears the top. Up to the point of division its banks are so high and steep today that it is doubtful if any but a specially trained horse could climb them, to say nothing of the dense tangle of shrubs and trees now choking it at places. It is easy to get out at the point where it branches. In one of these clumps of bushes and trees Sergeant Culbertson's party, returning from the river found a "G" Company trooper who had lost his horse and, evidently, also his nerve. This man represented one extreme. On the other extreme was the hard-boiled specimen mentioned by Godfrey, who somewhere in the nerve-shattering retreat had taken time out to lift a Sioux scalp which he waved nonchalantly at the troops on the hill as he came up.

It seems that it was Captain Moylan who halted the retreat and begun reforming the scattered troops in line on the slope of the bluff. Later Reno appeared and said this was not a good place to make a stand. The men were then mounted, and after counting fours, moved to the crest of the bluff a little to the north of where the monument now stands. We have been unable to learn how they were posted. When Benteen was questioned on this point at the Court of Inquiry, he replied: "They were not in line of battle but scattered around, I suppose, to the best advantage. They all thought there was a happier place than that, I guess."

The last part of this reply, which caused a ripple of laughter in the court room, may have been suggested by an exchange of compliments between Recorder Lee and Captain Moylan when the latter was on the stand. Nettled, it would seem, by the skillful manner in which Mr. Gilbert had led Moylan to give answers that appeared to minimize greatly the degree of demoralization of the command when it arrived on the hill, he came back with questions that verged on taunts of cowardice. "Leading" questions were not barred at the Inquiry, and Mr. Gilbert was a past-master in the art of leading witnesses. Was it not better, he had asked Moylan, to be dejected on the hill than dead in the timber, and Moylan had replied: "Well, I would rather be dejected on the Hill than dead anywhere." (Laughter). Very politely, and repudiating any thoughts of criticism or scorn, the Recorder asked: "Would it not have been better to be dead in the timber than dishonored on the Hill?" Replied Moylan: "I do not know that that is a proper question to put to me. Very few men but would prefer to die in the timber than be on the Hill degraded."

This was during Moylan's re-direct examination. When this had been concluded, Major Reno asked Moylan: "Did you feel degraded when you reached the top of the Hill?" "Not particularly so," replied Moylan.

Moylan had not lost his nerve nor forgotten his training during the run to the bluffs. When about half-way to the river he had dropped back to about the center of his company to be in better position to see what was needed, if anything, to bring his men through with the minimum of loss. He was clearly of the opinion that Major Reno should have done likewise for the battalion, but evaded direct statements to this effect. But he was under no illusion as to the extent of the danger the command had passed through and in which it still stood on arriving on the Hill; for, when he met Sergeant Culbertson soon after reaching the crest of the bluffs he named some fabulous price for which he would not sell his horse!

When Varnum was asked how the command felt when it reached the Hill, he replied: "I don't know how the command felt, but I felt personally that we had been badly licked." Lieutenant Hare, on meeting his troop commander, Lieutenant Godfrey soon after the arrival of Benteen, shook his hand enthusiastically and said: "We've had a big fight in the bottom, got licked, and I am damned glad to see you."

There was no dissent from Reno's contention that it had been necessary to leave the timber position, if we disregard the testimony of the two civilian witnesses, Gerard and Herendeen. General McClernand, a lieutenant at the time of the battle and serving as engineer officer in Gibbon's command, wrote many years later in the U. S. Cavalry Journal, that when Terry arrived "many of the criticisms were severe." His own opinion was that "The timber area was too large for a force as small as a squadron of three small troops to hold indefinitely, but it was a strong position and one in which Reno might have maintained himself for a considerable period, possibly several hours."

If a check-up had been made immediately after all the stragglers had arrived, it would have shown 49 to 50 dead or missing, not counting the Indian scouts, and 7 or 8 wounded. Among the casualties were 4 commissioned officers, namely Lieutenants McIntosh, Hodgson, DeRudio, and Dr. DeWolf. Herendeen with 12 to 13 enlisted men rejoined the command as it was moving out toward Weir Point late in the afternoon. Gerard and William Jackson came in soon after midnight on the morning of the 27th, followed a little later by DeRudio and O'Neill.

It was finally determined that the loss in the valley fight and during the retreat to the bluffs, was three officers, McIntosh, Hodgson and DeWolf, and 29 enlisted men. Of the Arikara, Bobtailed Bull, Bloody Knife and Little Brave were killed. Of the Crows, Half-yellow-face and White Swan, the latter was severely wounded.

As nearly as we have been able to determine, the command went into action about 3:05-10 and arrived on the hill about 4:15. About 10 minutes later, 4:25, Benteen came up.

CHAPTER 5

Captain Benteen's Scout to the Left

With Companies D, H, and K.
12:10 to about 1:50 to 2 O'clock

THERE is almost as great a difference of opinion concerning Benteen's scout south of the trail as there is about anything else connected with the Battle of the Little Big Horn. Both its object and extent are in dispute. It is contended on the one hand that Custer ordered it in deference to Terry's suggestion that he should feel constantly to his left to prevent the escape of the Indians around his left flank. On the other hand it is asserted that the scout was pointless, the orders given in connection with it vague and in part senseless. Another view is that Custer wanted Benteen to go into the valley of the Little Big Horn and attack the Indian village from upstream, or to head them off if they fled on being attacked from the north. Lieutenant Edgerly expressed such an opinion at the Reno Court of Inquiry. Lieutenant Godfrey seems to have believed that the scout was simply a part of a reconnaissance in force—which was, essentially, the nature of the advance from the Divide to the River—the exact location, strength and distribution of the Indian force not being known as yet.

What the Indian scouts had told Custer on the Crow's Nest did not settle these points. There might be a village where they said they could see the evidence of one. But this did not prove, or even imply, that no other camps existed elsewhere along the stream. No intelligent, or at least no adequate, plan of attack could be formulated until these points had been determined. Recorder Lee's questioning of Benteen shows clearly that he held the same view. The whole striking force of the regiment was advancing on a wide front to make contact with the enemy for the purpose of attack or maneuvering for position as soon as the necessary information was at hand. It is nonsense to talk of a plan of battle existing while the regiment was still at the Divide.

In any case, an encounter with a body of Plains Indians at mid-
day called for extremely fluid battle tactics. If the Indians were
separated into several bodies considerable distances apart, the detachments making the attack would have to be left almost wholly
to their own resources, probably, because of the extremely mobile
tactics of the warriors, if we may speak of tactics on the part of
a body of warriors each of whom was a law unto himself, seeking
his own objectives in his own way.

Godfrey's conception of Custer's plan is, we believe, substantially correct. Did Captain Benteen understand it? If so, did he
co-operate loyally to carry out Custer's intentions?

At the Reno Court of Inquiry Benteen testified, in substance,
as follows:

I left the trail near the Divide at 10 minutes after 12 by the
watch of Lieutenant Wallace, with an order to proceed to a line
of bluffs 4 or 5 miles away.[30] I was to send an officer with six men,
in advance, ride rapidly, pitch into anything I might find and
send back word at once.

I chose my First Lieutenant, Gibson, and six men of my own
troop to ride in advance, but was myself with my orderly in advance of Gibson most of the time.

I had gone perhaps a mile when the Chief Trumpeter brought
me an order from Custer saying that if I found nothing at the first
line of bluffs I was to go to the second line of bluffs.

I had gone about another mile when the Sergeant Major
came with an order directing me to go into the valley if I found
nothing at the second line of bluffs. I thought it was rather a
senseless order. It meant, literally that I was to go valley-hunting
ad infinitum. I did not know what I was expected to find. I supposed I was to hunt up some Indians. I might have gone 20 miles
without finding a valley. At my farthest point I must have been
about 15 miles from Major Reno. I knew the Indians had too
much sense to go into such rough ground unless they had no
alternative. Finally I concluded I had gone far enough, and seeing no reasonable prospect of finding a valley, I ordered the return to the trail where I thought I might be needed.

The questioning now turned to the trail with the object of
locating Benteen at different times with reference to the other
detachments. In replying to these questions Benteen said that he
came back to the trail some distance above a morass where he
halted to water his horses; that the packtrain was then about a

mile back on the trail, its leading mules rushing into the morass just as he was leaving it. The Lone Tepee, he said, was about 11 miles (actually 8¼) from the point where he had left the trail on a "left oblique" as he started out on his scout. It was 7 miles (actually 4½) from the morass to the tepee, and 4½ miles to the river from the tepee.

It is worthwhile to note here that Benteen struck the trail about a mile ahead of the packtrain. Since the packtrain advanced at an average rate of about 3 miles an hour and arrived at the morass just as Benteen was leaving it he must have been at the morass at least 20 minutes; for he came to the trail about a half mile above the morass[81] and gained upon the packtrain in traversing this distance, since he was going considerably faster than the latter. Our best guess is that he was at the morass 25 minutes.

It will be noted here also that we have, in a general way, a check on the time Benteen spent on his scout. The packtrain had started about 20 minutes later than the rest of the command,[82] or about 12:30. If it was still a half mile from the morass when Benteen struck the trail it had made only three miles while the latter was on his scout.[83]

We now return to the testimony of Benteen. About a mile beyond the tepee, he said, he met a sergeant (Kanipe of Company C) who brought an order for the commander of the packtrain. He told the sergeant that he, Benteen, had nothing to do with that, that the packtrain was in charge of Captain McDougall, and that it was about 7 miles back on the trail.

About a mile farther on he met Trumpeter Martin (of his own company H) with a written order reading: "Benteen—come on—big village—be quick—bring packs. W. W. Cooke. P. S. Bring packs."

He asked Martin about Custer and received the reply that th Indians were "skedaddling." Since the Indians were running away he thought there was less need for him to go back for the packs, and that, in any case, he could not have expedited them, since a sergeant had already gone to do that; that it would have taken him an hour and a quarter to go back for them and bring them to the point where he then was.

At this time he was riding with his orderly 400 to 500 yards in advance of his command. Captain Weir was about 200 yards behind him. He waited until Weir came up and then handed him the order he had just received. He asked him no questions and Weir returned the order without comment.

When the column came within hearing distance he ordered
a trot, but did not think this increased the pace, because they had
been on the trot all the time since leaving the Divide. As he neared
the river he saw down in the valley 12 to 13 men in skirmish line
parallel to the river. They appeared to have been beaten back
and the Indians were riding back and forth through the line
demolishing it.

Four or five hundred yards to the right and east of the river, he
saw 3 or 4 Indians he took to be hostiles, but on riding up to
them he saw they were Crows. (Really Arikara). They told him
there was "pooh-poohing" going on. Then, off to the north, he
saw some troops on a hill. He did not know that Custer and Reno
had separated, and thought this was the whole command, and
that it was whipped. He rode on to the hill and came upon
Major Reno who had ridden forward several hundred yards to
meet him.

He showed Reno the order and asked him if he knew where
Custer was. Reno replied that he did not; that he had been sent
to charge those Indians on the plain; that Custer through
Cooke had promised to support him with the whole outfit, and
that that was the last he had seen or heard of him. "Reno's men
appeared to be pretty well blown, and so were the horses."[34]

When Benteen was asked what time it was when he arrived at
the morass he replied that, considering the distance traversed in
his scout, it must have been about 3 o'clock. What time was it
when he met Martin? About 3 o'clock, answered Benteen. What
time was it when he met Reno. About 3 o'clock!

In a fragment supposed to have been written in 1891 or 1892,
Benteen said it was about 1 o'clock when he came to the morass.
Godfrey thought it was about 2 o'clock when they struck the trail
again about a half a mile above the morass, which is somewhere
near the truth, as far as we can determine today.

How far was it before Custer's column passed from view,
asked the Recorder?

The last he had seen of Custer's command, replied Benteen,
was the Gray Horse Troop going at a dead gallop. This was about
three-quarters of an hour after he started on his scout.

How far away was the Gray Horse Troop when he saw it?

"It might have been 5 or 6 miles, and it might not have been
one."

The commissioned officers on this scout, besides Benteen and
Gibson of Company H, were Captain Weir and Lieutenant Edgerly

of D Company, and Lieutenant Godfrey commanding Company K. Benteen and Gibson led the column with Company H followed by D, the actual command of which Weir usually left to Edgerly. Godfrey brought up the rear. His lieutenant, Hare, was with Varnum in command of the scouts, as will be remembered from the preceding chapter. From the Divide on Varnum with some of the scouts moved along on the left, while Hare with the rest seems to have ridden on the trail just ahead of Custer, for they were at the lone tepee when they arrived there. Varnum came up with the rest a few minutes later. These details are recalled here for the convenient orientation of the reader.

Concerning the extent of the scout Godfrey said that the first line of bluffs was about 3 to 4 miles distant, that at the time they turned back they were about 5 miles from the trail, and that the total distance traversed in the scout was 13 to 15 miles.

Edgerly thought that the line of bluffs was about 2½ miles distant, and that they covered about 14 miles before they struck the trail again.

The questions of military importance here are:

1. Were Custer's orders given in connection with the scout as indefinite as Benteen said they were?

2. Did Benteen understand what he was expected to find and do?

3. Did he do what Custer wanted him to do?

4. What were the distances traversed from the Divide to Reno Hill?

The testimony of the officers does not contain direct answers to any of these questions. It leads us instead into a maze of contradictions and impossibilities. Some of the distances mentioned would have brought them into the valley of the Little Big Horn before they could have gotten back to the trail. Their march, practically parallel with the trail after they reached the first line of bluffs, as the Court stated in its report, and never much more than a mile from it, could at no time have taken them 15 miles from Major Reno who was never more than that from the point where the trail crossed the Divide from which all had started out after battalion assignments had been made. Nevertheless we can today answer satisfactorily, or nearly so, all except the first of these questions. It is impossible to check on the two oral orders brought respectively by Chief Trumpeter Henry Voss and Sergeant Major William H. Sharrow. Both were killed with Custer, and when the orders were delivered no one except his orderly was near enough to Benteen to hear them repeated, unless it was Captain Weir who may at times have been riding with Benteen. But Weir had died before the Court was convened, and, as far as we know never expressed himself on the subject, though it is reported that he did refuse the importunities of Whittaker for a statement derogatory to Reno and Benteen. Godfrey was at the rear of the column and could not possibly have had firsthand knowledge of these orders. Edgerly expressly stated that he had heard only the first of the three orders which was given by Custer in person directly to Benteen.

The answers to the second and third questions depend on the conclusion we reach in connection with question 4, so we take up the latter first.

The seemingly hopeless muddle over the distances involved in the scout and over the trail can be cleared up by making use of the known constants we have. One such constant is the modern survey. Another is the landmarks mentioned by participants and still identifiable. A less reliable but still useful check are certain points in time which can be fixed in the objective events with a reasonable degree of accuracy and to which other events can be correlated.

Turning back to what Benteen said in reply to questions concerned chiefly with his progress along the trail, we note that the distance from the point where he left the trail to the Lone Tepee was 11 miles, and that from the morass where he watered his horses to the tepee was 7 miles. Actually these distances were 8½ and 4½ respectively. This leaves 4 miles as the distance from the morass to the point where he left the trail. He said he came back to the trail some distance above the morass—half a mile, according to Edgerly. In any case he was off the trail for less than 4 miles. But to keep an even figure and to give Benteen the benefit of any doubt there may be, let us say 4 miles. Since he left the trail at a "left oblique" and returned to it at a "right oblique," we have a triangle with a base of less than 4 miles measured on the trail, angles of 45 degrees at the base and 90 degrees at the apex, if we ignore the fact that after going only about a mile they turned to the right and rode parallel with the trail, thus cutting off the apex. Had they gone the full distance at the left oblique and then turned back at the right oblique, the sides of the triangle would have been about 2.8 miles each, or 5.6 miles, the total distance traversed in the scout. Subtracting the base of 4 miles we have 1.6 miles. That is to say that, theoretically, and other things being

equal, Benteen was under a handicap as compared with the rest
of the command, of 1.6 miles in going from the Divide to the
river. Some allowance, however, must be made for detours, the
roughness of the ground, and possibly also halts to enable Gibson
to make observations and keep ahead of the column, though no
mention is made of halts in the accounts we have. Edgerly said
that Gibson made four to six trips to the higher points for observation. Stated in time, it is not unreasonable to say that this handicap was an hour's march, more or less. Custer and Reno were a
little over two hours in going from the Divide to the Lone Tepee,
a distance of 8½ miles. Their rate of march was, therefore, 4 miles
an hour, the regulation cavalry walk.

If we could not identify the sites of the morass and the tepee
this would not be conclusive. But we know definitely that the tepee
stood at the forks of the creek, and there is only one place between
the tepee and the Divide where such a morass could have been.
It is a small flat near the mouth of a ravine running up from the
creek in a northeasterly direction, and is exactly 4 miles from the
Camp marker, as measured by the speedometer of a Dodge sedan.
The Camp marker stands on the Divide where the trail crossed it.

In August, 1939, Captain E. S. Luce and Mrs. Luce, I. D.
O'Donnell, and the writer, were guests of Mr. George G. Osten
of Billings, Montana, on a trip to Busby. On the return the speedometer of Mr. Osten's car was read from the Camp marker to a
point opposite Reno's crossing of the Little Big Horn. As already
stated the distance from the marker to the morass was shown to
be 4 miles. From the morass to the site of the tepee the speedometer
registered 4½ miles. From the tepee to opposite Reno's crossing,
4 miles instead of 4½ as given by Benteen. The difference is
accounted for by the fact that the present road runs over the
bench about a half mile south of the trail to the ford.[35]

Benteen's estimates, therefore, are seen to be exact except for
the distance between the morass and the tepee, which he gave as
7 miles instead of 4½. The present road may be somewhat off
the trail at several points and this may in a small degree account
for the difference.

We have, then, the following distances: Benteen 15½ miles;
speedometer 13 miles, after making the allowance as indicated
above. These are the total distances from the Divide to the river.
The straight-line measure on a map of the Department of the
Interior, Indian Bureau, is exactly 12 miles.

This brings us near enough to the truth to dispose definitely of the fantastic 15 miles scout and the statement that at one time Benteen was 15 miles from Reno. Except for about a half hour he was never more than 7 from either Reno or Custer, and for most of the time less than that. This becomes apparent when we locate him at different times with reference to Custer and Reno.

According to Godfrey, Benteen struck the trail on his return at 2 o'clock, a half mile above the morass, Edgerly said. This would be five miles from the tepee. At 2 o'clock Wallace, riding with Reno, looked at his watch and later estimated that they were then fifteen minutes' ride from the tepee—a mile at the rate they were going. It follows, then, that Benteen was at this time only 4 miles behind Custer and Reno.

But for the next half to three-quarters of an hour Benteen fell farther behind, both because he remained at the morass 20 minutes to half an hour, according to Godfrey, and because both Custer and Reno increased their pace to almost a gallop at 2:15. Custer, it is true, moved slowly for a mile or two from this point but soon made up for it after turning off the trail, as will be more fully discussed in Chapter 9. After this Benteen began to make up the lost ground, so that when he arrived on Reno Hill about 4:25 Custer was again only 4 miles or slightly less than that away and still a mile from the hill on which he died. (Detailed evidence in Chapter 9)

Nevertheless it is not true that Benteen loitered on the scout or along the trail. The 20 to 30 minutes he spent at the morass cannot be called loitering, in view of the fact that he had just returned from a hard ride over rough ground and in intense heat. His horses were tired and needed a rest if they were not to become unfit before the day was over. That he had not dallied on the scout is sufficiently evident from the fact that he struck the trail again ahead of the packtrain which had started only 20 minutes later than he had himself.

This makes it clear also that the countercharge to the effect that Custer had sent Benteen out of supporting distance, on a "wild goose chase," "valley-hunting *ad infinitum*," is likewise untrue; and Benteen might have saved himself trouble and embarrassment in trying to prove that he had. An unembellished recital of the facts would have cleared him of the charge of loitering and left a much better impression of his own reliability as a witness, to say nothing of suspicions aroused by transparent evasions. These evasions, plus the grossest kind of exaggerations, both painfully evident today, did not serve his cause at the time or with the historians later; for, what he tried to conceal from the Court and his contemporaries generally, he had already revealed in letters to his wife, to be confirmed after his death by Lieutenant Gibson who admired and defended him to the end, showing a sentiment which was, regrettably, not mutual, as appears in the correspondence between Benteen and Theodore Goldin and elsewhere in Benteen's writings.

We are now ready to take up questions 2 and 3; Did Benteen understand what he was expected to discover and do, and, Did he do what Custer wanted him to do?

With one important qualification, the answer to both questions is "Yes."

On July 2, 1876, Benteen, on board the *Far West*, wrote his wife "I was ordered with Companies D, H, and K, to go to the left for the purpose of hunting for the valley of the river—Indian camp, or anything I could find."

Two days later he wrote his wife another letter in which he returned to the subject of his scout in the following words: "I was ordered . . . to go over the immense hill to the left, in search of the valley, *which was supposed to be very near by.*" (Italics own own).[86]

There was probably not an officer in the regiment who did not know that there was only one river Benteen could be expected to find in this direction, namely, the Little Big Horn. It was not just *a* valley or *a* river, but *the* valley and *the* river. The use of the definite article in both cases leaves no doubt whatever that he knew what river and what valley Custer had in mind. At the Court of Inquiry Recorder Lee sought in vain to elicit from Benteen the admission that he understood Custer had referred to the valley of the Little Big Horn, not to some hypothetical valley that had been overlooked years before by the officers and troops at Fort C. F. Smith, situated within a day's march or so of the terrain in question, and by Captain Ball of Gibbon's command two months before. The upper Little Big Horn country became known during the years when the Bozeman trail was in use, as had the upper part of the Rosebud whose middle course was traced in dots on the map used by General Terry, while the upper part was represented as definitely known.

Godfrey, who seems always to have suspected the truth, wrote Gibson in 1898 to confirm his belief. Gibson, in replying to his question, said that from his last observation point he had with the aid of Benteen's field glass looked far up the valley of the Little Big Horn without seeing any signs of Indians, and had so reported to Benteen who had then given the order to return to the trail.

This should leave no doubt in any unbiased mind that Benteen knew the object of his scout and understood Custer's "plan" as far as any plan could as yet have been formulated. He understood that his column was acting as the left flank of the full striking force of the regiment in a reconnaissance in force, and that he was to make certain that no Indians escaped up the valley or remained there as a menace to the flank or rear of the command if the whole body of hostiles elected to fight.

The die-hard partisan may still insist that we are reading implications into the return to the trail that are not there in fact; that the assumption that Beneen did so because he knew he had found what he had been sent to find, is mere speculation; that if Gibson had meant this he would have said so in so many words.

The answer to this is that he later did say so in so many words. Under date of April 28, 1915, he wrote George D. Yates, son of Captain G. W. Yates, killed with Custer: "Colonel Benteen was not guilty of either treachery or disobedience of orders. His orders were . . . to take his battalion to the left . . . and if he found any Indians trying to escape up the valley of the Little Big Horn, to intercept them and drive them back in the direction the village was supposed to be. After going some distance and to facilitate the movement as much as possible Benteen ordered me to pick six men on the strongest horses, and to hurry over the hills as quickly as possible to see if there were any Indians trying to get away . . . and to send back a man or signal, and said he would get all there was left out of the horses, which were jaded. Should he find nothing he was to pick up the trail again and follow it on."

In his official report, dated July 4, 1876, Benteen said that Custer's instructions were that, as soon as he became convinced that "there was nothing to be seen of Indians, valleys, etc., in the direction I was going, to return with the battalion to the trail the command was following."

At the Court of Inquiry Benteen said, in reply to a direct question, that he disobeyed his orders in returning to the trail; that the Court might consider his action as "Providential" or whatever it chose to call it.

We have it, then, from both Benteen and Gibson, that if no

Indians were found the battalion was to return to the trail and rejoin the command. The evidence proves that Benteen carried out his orders faithfully and expeditiously. What he actually did does not seem to be open to any criticism whatsoever. But there was one serious omission, it seems to us, which was certainly not intentional. It was undoubtedly an oversight. For, was it not very important that Custer should know as soon as possible that there were no Indians upstream, and if so, should not a messenger have been sent at once bringing this information? The object of the reconnaissance was to obtain as much information as possible to enable Custer to formulate his tactics and give orders to carry them into effect. The sooner he had this information the better would be his chances to bring all his available troops into position. Had Custer overlooked this detail in the orders he gave Benteen, or taken it for granted that Benteen would send a messenger because it was so obviously the thing to do under the circumstances?

Let us, as nearly as possible, place ourselves in Custer's position at this time. The Indian scouts had told him there was an immense village in the valley which, from the nature of the terrain he could see was probably some distance downstream from the point where the trail crossed the river. He had said that he thought the scouts were mistaken; but of course he knew that the Indians were *somewhere* in the valley "not over 30 miles away." (On the evening before). No one had seen signs of a village elsewhere. He might, therefore, as well follow the trail. If they should be upstream Benteen would soon discover the fact, since the valley was supposed to "be very near by." He had told Benteen to ride rapidly, evidently so he would soon know definitely whether or not there were Indians upstream, and also that he, Benteen, would not fall too far behind, or Custer be too far away if he did find Indians and needed assistance. It was hardly reasonable to expect Benteen to overtake him after returning from his scout, but a messenger on a good horse could have done so; for until Custer came to the Lone Tepee, he moved at a walk, as if expecting a messenger with the information he so evidently needed before attacking any considerable force of Indians. Had such a messenger been sent the moment Gibson reported the valley upstream clear of Indians he might have reached Custer before he gave his ill-advised order to Reno. He would have needed a tough horse, for Benteen was then five miles or more from Custer. But since Custer was expecting a messenger, or at least on the lookout for one, he might have seen him some distance back on the trail and waited for him before taking any decisive action. This is merely stating the logic of known facts. The messenger might have come too late; but there is no doubt one should have been sent, and little doubt in our mind that Benteen later regretted that it had not occurred to him to send one.

In the face of the facts definitely established, it does not matter that Benteen said that the last he saw of Custer's column was the Gray Horse Troop going at a "dead gallop." And he is equally unconvincing when, in reply to a question as to how far away the Gray Horse Troop was when he saw it, he said: "It might have been five or six miles and it might have been one," a typical Benteenism frequently resorted to when he wished to conceal a fact he thought might be used against himself or someone else he wished to shield. The absurdity of such a statement coming from an experienced soldier necessarily trained in the kind of observation involved here, is at once apparent, and the motive of the evasion is equally apparent.

We have seen in a previous chapter that Custer learned on the evening of the 24th that he had to deal with a much larger force than had been anticipated. Benteen testified that they knew there were 8000-10,000 at the end of the trail they were following. That might mean 2000 to 2500 warriors. Whether or not Custer also estimated the strength of the enemy at this figure we do not know; but had Benteen reported that the valley upstream was clear of them, he would have had reason to think that the scouts might, after all, be right in their interpretation of the signs they said they could see. And it must not be forgotten that until Benteen reported that he was returning to the trail Custer could not know where he was unless he saw him, and would therefore not know where to find him without loss of time. He might, indeed, conclude from the fact that he received no message, that Benteen had found no Indians. But this was not certain, for a messenger might be waylaid by skulking Indians, or fail to arrive for some other reason such, for instance, as an injury to his horse in going fast over rough ground. Needless to say, there is here no question of wilful negligence or deliberate treachery. Those who make such charges cannot have taken the least trouble to understand the character of Benteen.

His orders showed Benteen that Custer was not convinced the Indians were all gathered in one village. Benteen was so convinced, if he expressed his true belief on this point at the Court of Inquiry. He expressly said that he returned to the trail because he thought he would be needed there. He also knew that if he informed Custer that he was mistaken in thinking the Indian force might be scattered up and down the valley in the usual fashion—that there were no camps upstream—Custer would be warned of the danger of attacking with only two thirds of the regiment—8 companies. Had a messenger with this information reached Custer at the Lone Tepee, it is conceivable that Reno would not have been sent to attack. The messenger would also have told him that Benteen was only a few miles behind. Knowing then that he had the whole Indian force before him and between himself and Gibbon, he could afford to wait until Benteen came up, or send him instructions at once, which would have reached him in less than half an hour; for Benteen was then at the morass only 4½ miles away and about ready to leave it. A messenger would, therefore, have met him after going only about 3 miles, probably less than that.

We are here merely reconstructing the picture, not charging Benteen with responsibility for what happened to either Reno or Custer. Custer might or might not have halted where he was until Benteen came up, and if he had the losses might have been greater than they actually were. For the full warrior force would then have swarmed up against him while his command was strung out for four or five miles in the narrow valley of Reno Creek, in places a veritable death trap. Not threatened front, flank and rear, they would have known exactly what to do, and would have had 6 or 7 miles in which to harass and maneuver while the village moved away. It would have been the Crook fight all over again with the odds in their favor at least four times greater; for Crook had over 1400 men, among them 250 good Indian warriors and enemies of the Sioux, and also a considerable body of infantry. On the other hand, the Indians had been re-inforced by hundreds of warriors since the fight with Crook.

It can be reasonably urged that had Custer known the whole truth about the force of the Indians he would not have sent Reno with the kind of order he gave him, and probably not into the valley at all, but posted him somewhere on the bluffs in the neighborhood of where he later took his stand to serve as part of a multiple threat, bluff and mystification, as well as a support to what remained back on the trail in case the warriors should attack here in great force while Custer was making his way down to the lower end of the village. It is because Custer was only by degrees disillusioned as to the meaning of what he saw while at the Lone Tepee that we find so much difficulty in understanding what he did from this point on. This is discussed in detail in chapter 9.

This brings us finally to the question that has been and still is hotly debated between the partisans of Custer and those of Benteen. It is maintained by the latter that Custer had no reason to expect assistance from Benteen, because he had sent him out of supporting distance. They have the word of Benteen and of the officers who were with him on the scout, to support their contention. It was only because Benteen disobeyed his orders by returning to the trail, that Custer's messengers were able to find him, they assert. The partisans of Custer deny this, but make no attempt to refute directly the statement about distances made under oath. They merely point out that Custer evidently did know that Benteen was not far behind him, for otherwise Adjutant Cooke would have given Trumpeter Martin specific instructions to enable him to find him in the jumble of ravines and ridges south of the trail. Instead of this Cooke merely told Martin to ride back on the trail, return after delivering the message, if he thought it was safe, otherwise remain with his company. To this might well be added the further observation that, had it not been known that Benteen was back on the trail Martin would not have been sent at all, for he was little more than a boy, spoke and understood English with difficulty, was relatively inexperienced, and not too intelligent.[37] If Benteen was thought to be still on his scout far away in the rough ground an experienced sergeant with a good horse would have been sent.

But how could Custer have known that Benteen was back on the trail? It is possible that he saw him; but that is doubtful, for in that case he probably would not have waited as long as he did before sending him some kind of instructions. It would seem more probable that he deduced it from data he possessed before giving the order for the scout, confirmed later by what he certainly discovered the moment he came to the high bluffs east of the river opposite the Indian village. From here he could see far up the valley of the Little Big Horn and note that there were no Indians in that direction. Therefore Benteen had not seen any there either; and since the valley was "supposed to be very near by" (The Divide) he had not gone very far before securing the desired information and returning to the trail. Because Custer had not received this much-desired information from Benteen he was certain to look for it himself at the very first opportunity.

Had Benteen guessed that Custer had reasoned in this way? When Recorder Lee asked him: "Could either yourself or General Custer have known what was behind that second line of bluffs without sending someone to ascertain?, he replied: "He could have found out by following the trail he was on," which was not an answer to the question asked though a fairly good indication of what was on Benteen's mind. He might have enlightened the Court by telling it what he had told his wife more than two and a half years before, a week after returning from the scout. But that would have dynamited his whole case as he had presented it in his direct examination. The Recorder slept on this and came back with a handful of prying questions that stabbed straight at the truth which had been so laboriously camouflaged.[88]

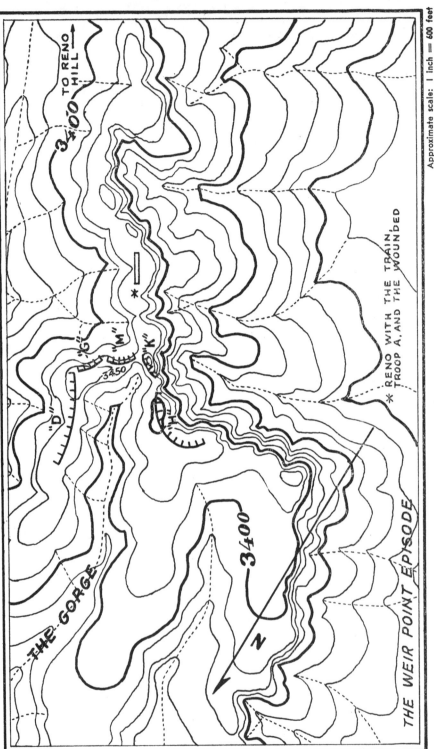

THE WEIR POINT EPISODE

Approximate scale: 1 inch = 600 feet

3400 TO RENO HILL →

* RENO WITH THE TRAIN, TROOP A. AND THE WOUNDED

THE GORGE

3400

N

Moving out from Reno Hill in an abortive, uncoordinated and virtually undirected attempt to form a junction with Custer three miles to the north-west, the six troops of the Reno and Benteen battalions took temporary

The author maintains that (a) from Custer Field the General saw the troops on these ridges and at once modified his own troop dispositions to facilitate the expected junction; (b) the Indians, aware of the movement

[CHAPTER 6]

The Weir Point Episode

5:00-7:45, June 25th, or later

THE attempt of Major Reno to join General Custer late in the afternoon of June 25th was, of all subjects before the Court of Inquiry, the most delicate for the officers who testified concerning it, and especially so for Reno and Benteen. Although only Reno's conduct was under investigation, the rest would have been less than human had they not felt themselves more or less under attack, or at least under suspicion. This natural feeling caused them to assume an attitude of extreme caution which was reflected in their testimony, to the complete mystification of the unwary students who accepted their stories at face value. Their self-protective reaction took the form of evasion, misplaced emphasis, and statements so general or indefinite that they blurred or concealed certain details which, had they been revealed at this time, might have served hostile critics as a basis for charges of both incompetence and cowardice. This did not mislead the court in any matter pertinent to the inquiry, and was not intended to do so. It was intended for the general public against whose criticisms Reno was seeking protection. Indeed the failure of Recorder Lee to press his questions at the right junctures leads to the inference that a tacit understanding existed that an opportunity should be given for this kind of back-firing, provided that the necessary facts for a just decision should be furnished at the same time. This was a natural and human thing to do, since a soldier has practically no defense against civilian criticism no matter how unjust it may be. I am not finding fault with it. I find it necessary, however, to "edit" the testimony rather drastically in order to uncover the objective facts concealed behind the camouflage.[39]

The earliest reference we have, in an official document, to the Weir Point Episode, is found in Major Reno's report dated July 5, 1876.

97

"I moved to the summit of the highest bluff," says the report, "but seeing and hearing nothing of Custer, sent Captain Weir with his company to open communication with the other command. He soon sent back word by Lieutenant Hare that he could go no further, and the Indians were getting around him; at this time he was keeping up a heavy fire from his skirmish line. I at once turned everything back to the first position, and which seemed to me the best."

Nothing could be more misleading than this. In the first place, Weir was not "keeping up a heavy fire from his skirmish line" at "this time." It will become apparent later that it is very doubtful that Weir's troop fired a single shot or was even deployed at this time. It was not on the high ridge over ten or fifteen minutes (Hare later said ten minutes) before it turned back, not on Reno's order, but on the suggestion of Hare or Weir's own motion. The troop suffered not a single casualty either at this time or later, while on the ridge. At this time nothing was "turned back" except this troop, because nothing else had as yet gone out. We have here the beginning of the myth it was thought necessary to build up, that the troops at Weir Point were, from the beginning, heavily engaged. The myth was completely exploded by Lieutenant Godfrey.

Instead of ordering Weir out in advance to open communication with Custer, Reno refused him permission to go when he asked for it, and a violent altercation ensued, overheard by several persons near them. Having been refused permission to go with his troop, Weir called his orderly and rode in the direction of the firing downstream beyond the hills; whereupon Edgerly, thinking permission had been granted, mounted the troop and followed. Within about fifteen minutes Reno sent Hare after him to tell him to open communication with Custer, and that he, Reno, would follow with the rest as soon as the packtrain came up.

Whether Reno changed his mind because of the report brought from the packtrain by Hare, or was only avoiding an issue he might have lost had he permitted it to appear openly, no one can say. Although Weir had asked permission of Reno, it was an open question whether the latter possessed authority either to give or refuse it. Weir belonged to Benteen's battalion, and Benteen had a written order from Custer to "come on—be quick—bring packs," which he had not yet executed in full, and until he had done so he could logically refuse to obey the orders of any other subordinate regardless of rank. In fact Weir himself was in doubt on this point, for he told Edgerly he would ask Reno *or* Benteen for permission to go. Not until Benteen ceased in his efforts to carry out Custer's order in full would the general rule apply making him subject to the orders of Major Reno. When, later, on Weir Point, he admitted in effect that he could not go on, his mandate from Custer logically expired.

For reasons not apparent to me the Court of Inquiry ignored this point, though some of the questions by the Recorder suggest that he may have had it in mind. There is no doubt whatever that Benteen acted on the assumption that he held an independent command until they turned back from Weir Point. In the pamphlet by E. A. Brininstool, second edition; *The Custer Fight. Captain F. W. Benteen's Story of the Battle of the Little Big Horn*, he is quoted as follows:

"About this time I saw one of the troops of my battalion proceeding to the front, mounted. It was Captain Weir, who sallied out in that direction in a fit of bravado, I think without orders. That was about a half hour after we arrived. It was before the packs came up. Upon this I followed with the other troops, Major Reno having his trumpeter sound the halt continuously and assiduously; but I had to get in sight of what I had left my valley-hunting for."

There is no doubt of the fact that Benteen with his remaining two troops followed Weir before Reno was ready with the rest, but it was considerably later than a half hour after his arrival, and it is certain that Captain French with Troop M went out about the same time, probably with Benteen, for they arrived at Weir Point together. Hare testified that soon after Benteen arrived Reno sent him, Hare, to the packtrain with orders for it to hurry up as fast as possible, and to send forward the ammunition; that he met the train after going about a mile and a half; had two mules with ammunition cut out and hurried in advance of the train; that he got back and reported to Reno in about twenty minutes and was then sent to Weir.

In 1910 Hare told Mr. Camp that he left to go to the packtrain ten minutes after Benteen arrived, which is to say, at 4:35 according to the time series we are following. He was, then, back to Reno at 4:55. We shall probably be nearer the truth if we say 5:00, for 20 minutes is a short allowance for the three-mile round trip and the time to attend to the order. He told Camp also that, as he reported to Reno, he saw Weir's troop some distance on the way to Weir Point, which means that it was not over 700

yards away, for Edgerly led it down the ravine running to the
left of and parallel with the long, high ridge beginning about 700
yards down stream from Reno Hill, and as soon as the troop
passed the head of this ridge it would be out of sight. The two
ammunition mules were, of course, some distance behind Hare,
and we learn from the testimony of Godfrey that Benteen waited
until the ammunition arrived, before starting out. Since he did not
want ammunition for his own men and did not take any, we assume that he waited for French's men to replenish their supply,
and that French, therefore, went out with Benteen.

Benteen could, therefore, not have left as early as he says he
did, about 4:55. It must have been all of 5:25 instead, and about
5:45 when he reached Weir Point.

In the meantime Hare had returned from Weir Point and
reported to Reno that he had used his, Reno's name to order Weir
to return. This is what Reno said in his testimony, but Hare
told Camp in 1910 that he had not ordered any company to turn
back from Weir Point. In coming back Hare must have met
Benteen within a few hundred yards of Reno Hill, for he says
that while he was making his report he looked up and saw
Weir's troop joining "the command." The command was, of
course, Benteen's, but he fails to warn us against our natural
assumption that the term covers all the troops except Weir's,
and that Reno was leading it. In another connection he seems
actually to go out of his way to confirm us in this wrong assumption, for he says that he did not think Reno could have been
dilatory in starting to go to Custer, judging from where he met
him on his, Hare's return from Weir. The truth is that he did
not "meet" him at all. He found him still on the Hill. But at a
pinch he could justify his statement by saying he used the word
"command" in a technical sense, as a single unit, no matter how
disposed, and that the part of the command to which he referred
happened to be under the immediate command of Benteen. Hare
was not the only one who spoke in this ambiguous way.

Reno did not leave his position on the Hill until after Benteen
had reached Weir Point and posted the troops there, including
Weir's company which had turned back with him.

How do we know this? We know it from the testimony of
Varnum and Herendeen. Varnum tells us that Reno ordered
him to bury the body of Hodgson still lying where they had
found it near the river. He waited until the packtrain came up
so he could secure some spades. He then took six men and started

out, but when about two-thirds the way down he saw a civilian
(Herendeen) and 12 enlisted men approaching from the river.
He waited for a few minutes and then turned back, Wallace
having called to him that the command was moving out. He
thought it took him 20 to 25 minutes, coming and going. When
he got back he found that all except Moylan and a few others
had gone. Had Reno gone with them?

The answer to that question is furnished by Herendeen. He
said that when he got to the Hill Reno called him to interpret
for him and Half-Yellow-Face, the Crow scout. Reno asked the
scout to explain why the Indians were taking down their tepees,
and was told they were doing so because they were going away.
A few minutes later Reno asked why the Indians were putting
their tepees up again, and Half-Yellow-Face said he did not know.

This would seem to show pretty conclusively that Reno waited
for Moylan to get ready to carry the wounded before he left to
head his column composed of McDougall, Moylan, and Wallace
with 7 men of Troop G disrupted during the flight from the
timber. The 12 enlisted men who accompanied Herendeen must
have, for the most part, belonged to this troop, but, as we see,
did not arrive in time to go out with Wallace.

When did Reno leave the Hill to follow Benteen? We cannot
fix the hour except within very wide limits, because the data are
too indefinite for anything better than that. It is, however, fairly
safe to say that it was 6 o'clock or later. We assume from here on
that it was 6 o'clock.

Reno headed his column for only a few minutes before he left
it to confer with Benteen on the western spur of the Weir ridges.
The column halted when the head of it arrived to within about
200 yards of Weir Point and remained there until Reno returned.

We lost track of Hare for a while after he reported to Reno
on his return from Weir. He was not at the Hill when Reno set
out and did not hear the order to go downstream or know who
gave it, he tells us. We find him again at the conference between
Reno and Benteen just mentioned and then lose him again until
he turns up at his own company, K, posted on the south end
of the western spur, and commanded by Godfrey. More about
this in a moment. It is necessary at this stage of the discussion
to show how things stood at Weir Point when the movement
downstream had been completed.

Five troops, counting the remnant of G under Wallace,
reached Weir Point and mounted the ridges as shown on the map

illustrating this chapter. Four of them arrived there with Benteen
before Reno left the Hill position with the rest, namely H led
by Benteen in person, K, Godfrey, D, Weir, M, French. Wallace
started out with Reno's column, but found its pace too slow, it
seems, for he left it to join those already on the point.

These five companies, the whole maneuverable battle-force,
were posted as follows: Weir took position on the east ridge, deploying probably with his right at the point where the ridge
drops away 25 to 30 feet in a steep decline. French followed
but did not close up with Weir, so that when Wallace arrived
he found room between the two for his 7 men. Benteen mounted
the west spur and took his company down about a half mile,
he said, and planted a guidon to show Custer his position, "if
he was down there." Godfrey halted his company on the hillside
just below the south end of the west spur. He brought it up later,
after Benteen had withdrawn with his company and passed him
on his way back to Reno Hill.

Since the testimony is confusing and in part conflicting, there
is still a difference of opinion concerning the disposition of the
troops here. This makes it necessary to go into some detail to
show the basis for my constructions.

The following is taken from the official record of the Court
of Inquiry. Lieutenant Hare testifying. Questions by Recorder
Lee.

Q. State, if you can, where Major Reno went at the time that
movement (from Reno Hill to Weir Point) was made. Did he go
to the position Captain Weir occupied?

A. He was going to that high point when I went away. No,
he went to the right (he meant to say left as is clear from what
immediately follows) of it. There were two divides. Captain Weir
went to the one on the right, and Major Reno to the one on the
left a little farther downstream. (Since Reno was here to confer
with Benteen, it follows that Benteen was on the west ridge, or
spur.)

In reply to another question, Hare pointed out on a map
the positions occupied respectively by Weir and Reno. Questioned
still further, he said "Captain Weir had to go to the rear by a
ravine below, before he could come to the position occupied by
Major Reno."

Q. How did he join Major Reno's column?

Hare, ignoring the misconception evidenced by the reference
to Reno's column which was not there, replied: "He came back

and headed off a little coulee." This "little coulee" is the narrow, shallow end of the deep ravine between the two ridges. It is where the two ridges joined before the road was put through a few years ago. Edgerly, in referring to the same incident, said Weir rode back along the east ridge to get to Reno. Anyone who has been here will easily see that Weir did this to avoid the steep sides of the two ridges he would have had to negotiate had he ridden straight across from his company to where Reno was in conference with Benteen.

Q. Did the rest of the command reach the Indians there?

A. (The question was partly evaded.) "Captain Weir and Captain French were the only ones who engaged the Indians till within about three or four hundred yards of the final stand. Then Captain Godfrey engaged them."

We shall come back to this later, when it will appear that this answer conveyed more misinformation than fact.

Wallace had already said that the head of Reno's column had come to within about 200 yards of Weir's position when it was met by Reno and turned back. What Hare said concerning the position of the various units on Weir Point is fully confirmed by Edgerly, except that the latter said distinctly that Benteen's company instead of Weir's was farthest downstream. Edgerly said that when D Company joined Benteen, French and Godfrey, it moved on with them; that Benteen took the most advanced position; that D went to a spur at right angle to his position; that French formed in the rear of D and Godfrey in the rear of French.

We need to form a clear mind-picture of the troop dispositions at Weir Point, for without it important parts of the testimony remain incomprehensible.

First, it must be pointed out once more that Reno's column was never on either of the two ridges at Weir Point; that it was ordered back by Reno on his return from his conference with Benteen, when the head of it had come to within about 200 yards of Weir's position.

When and where was this conference, who were present, and what decisions were made?

It has already been shown that Reno could not have started downstream until 6 o'clock or later. It must, therefore, have been ten to fifteen minutes after 6 when he reached Benteen for the conference; for the distance from Reno Hill to Weir Point is a mile and a third.

As to the place on the ridges where the conference was held,

Hare, replying to a direct question, said "He was standing on the top of that highest point when he made that remark." The remark in question was Reno's saying that he did not think that a good place to make a stand.

This highest point is the south end of the west ridge.

Present at the conference were Benteen, Reno, Hare, Weir, and Davern, Reno's orderly. There is nothing in the record to indicate the presence of anyone else. Godfrey, whose troop was right below the hill, seems to have remained with his command, for nothing in his testimony suggests his presence at the conference.

Asked who selected the position for the final stand, Hare replied: "I heard Captain Benteen say to Major Reno that he thought that was the best position (Reno Hill) and Major Reno answered that he thought so too."

This does not necessarily conflict with Benteen's statement that he was for halting where they were so as not to be rushed over before they could form for defense. There is, however, good reason for thinking that he never made any such suggestion at the time, because there was not then anything to indicate that an attempt would be made to rush them before they could form their lines in the chosen position. Neither in his testimony at the Court of Inquiry nor in his interview with Mr. Camp in 1910 does Hare mention this suggestion by Benteen, though in both cases he touches upon the Reno-Benteen conference. This suggestion of Benteen, if accepted, would relieve him of responsibility for an oversight which came near causing a disaster.

Having decided to return to Reno Hill, Benteen started back with his company, either leading it himself or having Gibson do so, while Reno turned back to his own column. As he came down from the high ridge he passed Godfrey and his company standing on the southern slope. Godfrey testified that he had not taken his company to the crest of the ridge until some time after arriving but had gone personally to the top to look around. In answering a question concerning the troop farthest down, he said he could not see where they were because of intervening hills, which tells us that he could not have mounted the ridge until after Benteen had withdrawn his company from its advanced position. If it had still been there he could not have failed to see it, for the head of the west ridge is the highest point there and from its crest both ridges are in full view. I have been on this point many times and know positively.

The conjecture lies close at hand, therefore, that as Benteen passed his troop commander, he ordered him to take position on this highest point, since this ridge was left bare of troops after Benteen had withdrawn his own company, leaving those on the east ridge exposed to a sudden flank attack by Indians coming up under cover of the west ridge. What further orders he may have given him, and what orders were given and by whom to Edgerly, French and Wallace, is likewise a matter of conjecture, for the statement of Hare that Reno had ordered Weir and French to cover the retreat, is open to serious question quite aside from his own statement to Mr. Camp in 1910 that he did not remember who gave the order to fall back. It would, however, have been somewhat extraordinary, if when he passed Godfrey, he had not explained briefly that they had decided to return to their original position, prepare for defense and make the long overdue camp to restore men and animals to fit them for the fight which was certain to come sooner or later. Any good soldier would have attended to this at the first opportunity.

But for the moment it had become clear that the Indians were still interested elsewhere. Benteen's company had not fired a shot while in its advanced position, according to Charles Windolph, one of his troopers still living, who declares also that not a shot was fired by any of the other companies at this time, and that there was not an Indian in sight except those miles away around Custer.

Most of the witnesses contrived to leave the impression that Weir's company was under heavy attack from the time it arrived on the ridge, Reno saying that he, Weir, kept up a heavy fire even during his first brief venture in advance of the rest. Benteen said that they had been there only a few minutes before the gorge filled with warriors rushing up to attack. In some instances similar statements can be explained as possibly due to the late arrival of the witness. This is true, for instance, of Varnum who, moreover, qualified his statement by saying that the warriors were scattered and 700 to 800 yards away. Varnum had come late because Reno had sent him to bury the body of Hodgson, and when he returned he helped Moylan with the wounded before going to Weir Point.

It was left to Godfrey to brush aside all this talk about a heavy engagement at Weir Point. Because there is more than just the severity of the fighting involved, I give his testimony in some detail.

Q. Describe the movement (to Weir Point and back) fully, from the time it began till it returned.

A. After the packtrain came up (He means the two ammunition mules, no doubt) the command mounted and moved down the river, till the advance came to that high point indicated by the figure "9." Three companies, I think, were up to that point. I know my company was about the third, and it was a little below on the hillside, and I went to the top to take a view of the country. While I was there, the Indians started from some position they had ahead, apparently about three or four miles. (This was, of course, after Reno and Benteen had left). They started toward us and the companies were ordered to dismount. My company was placed in skirmish line, I think, with M, which was at the high point. Soon after getting into position, I saw the packtrain and part of the command moving to the rear. I remained in position, however. The general understanding is that when part of a command moves, the rest follow, if they don't have orders to the contrary. I waited there some time. The companies on the ridge, on the high point and below, were firing. Lieutenant Hare came to me and told me the command was ordered back, and that I should mount my company and follow the command . . . I then drew in my skirmish line, mounted my company and started back. I had gone but a short distance when Captain French's company came down the hill, passing to the rear very rapidly, and soon after Lieutenant Edgerly, with D Company, came down the hill quite rapidly. The Indians followed them to the crest of the hill, and began a very heavy fire on them. As soon as I saw the Indians I dismounted my company, and as soon as Lieutenant Edgerly and his company had passed, I commenced firing on the Indians and drove them back behind the hill. Soon after that I received an order from Captain Benteen, through Lieutenant Varnum, to send in my led-horses and fall back. I was executing that movement, and when coming near a high ridge, I directed Lieutenant Hare to take ten men and occupy a high point to the right, facing down river, when Trumpeter Pennell (Pennwell?) came to me with Major Reno's compliments, saying I was to fall back as quickly as possible. I recalled Lieutenant Hare and fell back to the line where the command was.

Q. How far down was the general movement by the command?

A. Some went beyond where Captain Weir went. I could not see how far they went because hills would intervene. They went below toward the ford "B."

That is to say they went down the west ridge, not the other, not the one from which Edgerly and French fled, which runs for some distance at nearly a right angle to the one on which Godfrey was stationed. The "they" refers to Captain Benteen and his company H. But how careful Godfrey was in not naming Benteen, and in not betraying the fact that he was the first to withdraw from the Point! This could not have been for the benefit of the Court, since the fact implied nothing derogatory to the mind of a soldier. To a civilian critic this withdrawal might serve as proof that "this treacherous cur" had deliberately stampeded the whole command when it was a question of saving Custer!

Q. When you got down to that advanced position, were there Indians confronting the command, or engaging it at the time?

A. No sir.

Q. Who halted the command, or why was it halted?

A. I don't know.

Strange lapse of intelligence in so fine a soldier! The command had gone to the Point under Benteen. No other officer with authority to halt it was present. Nevertheless, the command was halted when no enemies confronted it. Again, "this treacherous cur." Not if faithful "Goddy" could help it!

Q. What could be seen down river?

A. Lots of Indians.

Q. What did they appear to be doing?

A. I formed the impression at the time that their attention was directed down the river. I supposed, hearing but little firing from them—only an occasional shot—that General Custer's troops had been repulsed, and they were watching his retreat.

Godfrey had, indeed, observed carefully. The great crowd of Indians were nearly three miles away, and yet he had detected the fact that they were not then interested in the troops on Weir Point, but in something in the other direction. What he did not know is that nearly all those he could see were not warriors but non-combatant old men and boys. The Indian accounts, especially those of the Cheyennes, make this quite clear.

Q. How near was the command to the Indians when it went downstream?

A. I think about three or four miles.

Q. They remained there till the Indians came up?

A. Yes sir, those companies did.

Q. Was the engagement severe in and around there, or was there any engagement at all resulting in casualties?

A. No sir; no severe engagement at all.

Q. What were the casualties during the advance?

A. I don't think there were any casualties before the troops started back.

Q. I believe you have stated that you do not know by whose order the backward movement was made.

A. I do not know.

Q. Was there much firing on the part of the Indians down at the Point up to the time the command started to go back?

A. No sir.

Q. Describe it.

A. They were firing occasional shots.

Thirteen years later, in his article in the *Century*, Godfrey gives us the missing link, as it were, between Custer firing his last shots and the puzzled troops on Weir Point. He said that toward the last he heard some shots that seemed to be a great distance off. Immediately after these shots a great dust cloud arose on Custer field out of which finally rode the crush of warriors from which the troops fled back to Reno Hill.[40]

Into this, like a hand in a glove, fit the stories of the Cheyennes about the non-combatants, old men and boys, dashing onto the field on their ponies when the shout went up that all the soldiers had been killed, raising a dust that "nearly choked me," as Kate Bighead put it.

For the most part the cloud of Indians the troops on Weir Point had seen were these old men and boys who surrounded the field like expectant vultures after it was seen that the Indians were winning. They were especially numerous to the left, near the river, Godfrey said, and were moving about slowly as if watching something, as, in fact, they were. They were, however, too far away for the troops to see that they were not warriors. Taking them to be warriors, it was natural for them to conclude that the fight was about over, or they would have been busier than they seemed to be.

Custer's troops were not on the high ridges, as will appear later in Chapter 10 and as can still be determined by the visitor to the field from the distribution of the markers. There was no real fighting on the east wing of the battleridge, the part of the field in the foreground for the troops on Weir Point. Troops F, I, and L fought on the north slope of the ridge and in the upper ravine, while Custer was on a lower ridge south of the Hill. Those in the south skirmish line were completely hidden from anyone on Weir Point. On a clear day the markers for the Custer group can be seen from the Weir ridges, but toward the end of the fighting the Indians stirred up a good deal of dust with their ponies, and the smoke of their more or less random firing added to the murk, which must have almost completely blotted out the lower or northwestern part of the field for anyone looking on from the southeast. This was true especially for Custer Hill where the fighting continued for some time after it had ceased elsewhere. The last shots mentioned by Godfrey may have been a spurt of firing when the last survivors on the top of Custer Hill ran away toward the river, the warriors they had been fighting running to the top of the hill and sending a volley after them. Fired from the top of the hill, and toward the south, these shots would have been heard more clearly than others fired from the ravines and in the opposite direction as most of them were. This is merely a plausible conjecture based on known circumstances.

This gives us the best check we have for fixing the time the Custer battle ended. It will be seen from the detailed account of the troop movements that the last shots heard were fired at least as late as 6:30, and probably somewhat later than that. For Reno did not reach Weir Point before 6:10 to 6:15, and his orderly, Davern, who went with him said they remained about 15 minutes; which brings us to about 6:30; and Godfrey did not hear these last shots until Reno was well on his way back to Reno Hill or already there.

It must have been well after 7 o'clock by the time the last of the command got back to Reno Hill. Davern looked at the sun about the time the fight began and estimated that it was less than an hour high, which would have been about 8:00 in the time carried by the regiment.

From this it will be seen that the Custer fight lasted until 6:30 or later. This is entirely out of line with the impression the testimony made on the members of the Court of Inquiry which, in its decision, accurately reflected the surface indications of the testimony, saying that when the troops arrived on Weir Point they saw no evidence that Custer was still fighting. Both Reno and Benteen were especially emphatic in their opinion that Custer and his command had been wiped out long before they started downstream to join him."

But this was not the impression they had left on the mind of Lieutenant Maguire right after the battle. Maguire, reporting to the Chief of Engineers for the fiscal year ending June 30, 1876, said of the action on Custer field: "This part of the fight did not, from all reports, last over two or three hours."

Two or three hours!

What a difference time and circumstances had made! In the testimony the estimates ranged from fifteen minutes to an hour and a half.

Since Maguire could not have had any reports except those of the very same officers (with the exception of Weir, French, and Gibson) with whose testimony we are dealing, we are given an opportunity to see to what extent their statements were influenced by the fact that they were under attack. Speaking to Maguire at a time when events were fresh in their minds, and when they had no reason for thinking that their part in the battle merited the public reprobation it later received, they spoke openly and, without doubt, honestly. They were not then conscious that their failure to go on from Weir Point could be, with some plausibility, represented as a damning fact. This discrepancy, if anything, washes them of the charges of cowardice and deliberate betrayal; for had they felt guilty they would have been as cautious in speaking to Maguire as they later were at the Court of Inquiry.

Nor would it be fair to lay the whole discrepancy to a conscious effort to put the best face on the event. As soon as they learned what had happened to Custer they knew they had looked on his field of battle for a good hour or more while he and his men were fighting for their lives and wondering why the troops they could see through the dust and smoke did not rush to their assistance. That was too painful a thought to carry through life and it is one of the few kindly dispensations of Mother Nature that She had so constituted us that we, without being aware of it, so gloss over the reality as to alleviate the emotional distress as far as possible. So far do many of us carry this process that, after we have suffered an irremediable disaster, we at once set about persuading ourselves that it really does not matter greatly, that it is, perhaps, a blessing in disguise, or even a part of God's design for our salvation. This is the inner or psychic side of the ceaselessly active process of adjustment, and the historian who ignores it will be constantly lost in blind alleys, or led to conclusions that fall short of both the inner human and the external objective truth. If, on the other hand, he will practice an honest introspection he will be less inclined to adopt the role of an Olympian sitting in judgment on the quick and the dead alike, and restrict his labors to the modest task of understanding and explaining, leaving the stones to be cast by those who are without

sin. Far too often have the prosecutor and the judge spoiled the
historian.

It still remains to analyze the testimony of the two officers
technically responsible for what was done or left undone—Major
Reno and Captain Benteen.

From what has gone before it is easily seen that the movement
to and from Weir Point was without order or unified direction.
The Court was to determine whether or not Reno had performed
his duty in a soldierly manner, and here was a fact which seemed
to imply that his conduct had been considerably short of perfec-
tion; and it was this fact which caused both Reno and Benteen
to make the reckless statements characterizing their testimony.

Although Benteen's conduct was not under investigation he
actually out-did even Major Reno in distorting facts. The following from his testimony contains a few germs of facts, but they
are so misplaced as to produce a wholly false impression. "I left
one company on the ridge," he said, "with instructions to send
back their led horses dismounted and to hold that ridge at all
hazards; mind you, I was looking after things probably more
than it was my business or duty to do; this company when we
got back to the place where we were corraled had left that point
and were coming back as rapidly as any of the others. I then
sent Captain Godfrey's company to another hill to check the
Indians until we formed and told him he was alright and that
he would be looked out for and they got in alright."

Captain E. S. Luce, in comparing the *Chicago Time's* account
with that in the official record, comments: "In an account written
apparently some years after the battle Benteen narrates the episode
as follow: 'Reno came to the same point (Weir's Point) after I
had thrown Captain French's company in line at right angles
to the river, to hold that point dismounted, till Weir's troop got
through, and then to retreat slowly, and I would have that part of
the command looked after; this did not finish as well as I had
hoped and expected however, from the facts of the Indians not
making the most of the opportunity, and Lieutenant Godfrey
carrying out his instructions more faithfully and in a more soldierly manner, we had time to get some kind of line formed.'
Captain Luce continues: "Hare, who was with Godfrey in the
retreat, asserts, in a statement of June 11, 1929, that this movement saved Reno's command from annihilation; that it was taken
wholly on Godfrey's initiative, and that the remainder of the
command was then out of sight; while Godfrey in his several

references to the episode, says, in effect, that he acted without orders."

But Hare told the Court of Inquiry quite a different story. "When we got to the high hill, the highest point there," he said, "the Indians returned and attacked them. Major Reno said the position would not do to make his fight on, and he selected a point farther up on the bluff, and ordered Captain Weir's and Captain French's companies to cover the retreat back to the point. They covered the retreat to within a few hundred yards of the line, when Captain Godfrey's company was dismounted."

There is not a single grain of truth in the last sentence.

At this point things are so involved, there are so many statements that must be corrected because they convey either more or less than the truth, camouflage that must be removed to reveal the facts behind it, that it is almost impossible to decide where to begin.

Who, if anyone, ordered the troops on Weir Point to do this or that? Reno said that the whole movement to Weir Point and back was made under his orders. We have already shown that both Weir and Benteen moved downstream in the face of his opposition if not his positive orders, and that he himself followed with what was actually little more than the impedimenta. In spite of this he said that he led the command downstream, with three companies on the left, two on the right, the packtrain in the middle, and scouts out on the flanks. We can almost hear the band!

It is perfectly clear that Edgerly, commanding in place of Weir who had not returned to his command after attending the conference, knew nothing of an order to cover the retreat. He failed to say that he had received such an order, or an order to retreat without reference to covering the retreat of others. He acted like a troop commander who had no orders of any kind, which is, I believe, the fact. He could not make up his mind to face the Indians resolutely where he was or to retreat while he could still do so in a safe and orderly manner. This is equally true of Captain French whose company was next to Edgerly's after Wallace had withdrawn. He told Edgerly the order to retreat had been given. This Edgerly doubted and told French so; which proves that French was merely guessing that such an order had been given, or Edgerly would not have disputed his word. French betrayed his own doubt by hesitating for five minutes, and then, because the warriors were almost upon them, and because he saw Godfrey retreating, he repeated that the order had been given, mounted his troop and went out at the gallop. If he had really received the order, why did he hesitate? Such an order is simple and definite, leaving no room for doubt and hesitation. If anyone had brought it to him he could have named the messenger to Edgerly whose indecision nearly resulted in his falling into the clutches of the warriors before he could mount his frightened horse.

By turning back to what has been quoted from Godfrey's testimony on the question of this order, it will be seen that there is here the same mystery. He had not received the order, he said, and did not know who gave it. But while he was still in position on the ridge, Hare came to him and told him the command was ordered back. The same indefiniteness as in the case of Edgerly and French—"the order has been given." Who had given Hare the order? A troop commander wants to know whose order he is executing, both to protect himself against possible censure and to know to whom to report. Therefore the rule is for the messenger to name the officer whose order he carries, and that rule is usually observed even if the messenger happens to be the adjutant of the commanding officer, as Hare was in this case.

As stated, Hare came to Godfrey with the "order" while the latter's company, Hare's own, was in skirmish line on the high south end of the west ridge. From this point he could have tossed a pebble into French's line and without raising his voice much above that of ordinary out-door conversation, given the order to Edgerly. If he had been sent by either Reno or Benteen with an order to retreat why did he not deliver it to French and Edgerly? Each company commander here was "on his own." Both Reno and Benteen knew this and so did Hare, because no one had been assigned to command this "rear guard," as Reno called it. It was, therefore, necessary to deliver the order to all three separately.

In my opinion all this mystification and misrepresentation had just one main object, namely, to conceal the fact that no orders whatever had been given to the troops left on Weir Point after Reno and Benteen left to prepare for camp and later eventualities. The troops were left there merely to observe and keep back the few scattered warriors firing an occasional shot from a distance of 700 to 800 yards. The Indians from whom trouble might later come were several miles away and seemed then not to be interested in the troops on Weir Point. Moreover, it was getting late in the day for a serious attack by Indians who were known to be averse to fighting at night. Both Reno and Benteen were, therefore, "caught napping" by their sudden swift approach, which made it necessary for the company commanders to decide what to do before orders could be asked for or sent. Had this been admitted it would have furnished material for endless criticism and defeated the object sought by Reno in calling for the Court of Inquiry. Also, it would have been conclusive evidence that their talk about a heavy engagement, already foreshadowed in Reno's report of July 5, 1876, was merely a build-up to justify a retreat before a public unable or unwilling to see that the real justification for retreat lay not in any actual attack, but in the vast aggregation of Indians several miles away in their front, as was, in fact, admitted by several witnesses when pressed, among them Benteen, Hare, and Varnum. The unglossed truth would, in the eyes of the Court, have washed them clean of all charges of cowardice or deliberate betrayal, but would not have protected them from the harpies of the press, their real accusers, since the army had never preferred charges against anyone on the score of his conduct during the battle.

Was there, then, nothing at all behind the talk about this mysterious order which everyone pretended had been given, but of whose source all, except Hare, professed complete ignorance? I think we are fairly safe in assuming that Hare invented the order because he saw that it was urgently needed at a time when he, who alone possessed authority to give it, was not in position to give it. He was Reno's adjutant; but Reno was a mile or more away and knew nothing of the sudden rush of warriors and the resulting emergency. There was no time to send for instructions. When, therefore, Hare returned (we do not know where he went immediately after the conference; but presumably he accompanied Reno or Benteen for some distance on their way back) and saw how things stood at Weir Point—grasped the fact that if the troops did not withdraw promptly they would become so heavily involved that it would be impossible to escape without considerable loss and at the same time make it difficult to form properly at the Hill—he, as Reno's adjutant, advised Godfrey to retreat, hoping that French and Edgerly would follow. Godfrey was his troop commander, and the two were on excellent terms. Benteen had assigned Godfrey to the position where Hare found him, and his instructions had evidently been such that he did not feel justified in leaving it unless something wholly unexpected happened that called imperatively for the exercise of discretion on his part. Shall we say that Hare, who had been present at the conference, knew more definitely what was in the minds of Reno and Benteen than did Godfrey, convinced him that a retreat under the existing circumstances would be fully approved regardless of any instructions he might have received at the time he assigned him to his present position, instructions which had made him hold his ground when he really knew he should withdraw? I think it nearly certain that this is all there avere was to this "order."

If we time the movements of Godfrey, French and Edgerly, this conjecture is strongly reinforced. French certainly saw Hare come up and talk to Godfrey, for, from his position on the ridge he could see him approach for the better part of a mile; and as he was certainly waiting for orders it would have been strange had he not looked in the direction from which orders would come if any were given. When he saw Godfrey mount his troop after talking with Hare, he knew that he was going back and guessed that Hare had brought an order to retreat; so he turned to Edgerly and said that such an order had been given. But French did not go at once. He waited until Godfrey actually started, then repeated to Edgerly that the order had been given, mounted his troop and started after Godfrey, followed by Edgerly. The sequences here are suggestive.

Only about an hour and a quarter before this Hare had taken the same kind of responsibility in advising Weir to turn back from his first venture to this point. There had been no urgency in this case. But there was great urgency now, and Hare went as far as was necessary to get the troops back without actually ordering them back. In his interview with Mr. Camp on February 7, 1910, he said he could not remember who had given the order. Neither could he remember correctly the logical action that should have followed such an order, had it been given, but did not, namely an orderly retreat by French and Edgerly covering the withdrawal of the rest, actually only Godfrey, for Wallace had left some time before and got back at a walk.

Recorder Lee had all along probed diligently to discover what orders Reno had given or failed to give, to determine whether or not he had exercised command in a reasonably efficient manner. The order in question here was needed for Reno's vindication, and Hare obligingly supplied it. The little invention was in the interest of justice, not against it. Moreover, it probably saved the command from serious loss if not from something worse. Hare was an excellent soldier and proved it here.

But this invention made necessary another. Reno, said Hare, had ordered Weir and French to cover the retreat, so "cover" it they did—according to Hare—up to within a few hundred yards of the line. Since Hare was with Godfrey all the way back he must have known that this is not true, for French and Edgerly made no attempt to cover the retreat. On the contrary, they fled in such haste as to threaten disaster to the whole command, as Hare himself told Mr. Camp. Godfrey intervened not "within a few hundred yards of the line," but within about 60 yards of Weir Point, according to Edgerly. That this is substantially true is shown by the fact that Godfrey's fire halted the warriors at the ridge and drove them back behind it. That Godfrey did not exaggerate the effect of his fire is indicated by Edgerly's statement that he promised to go back for one of his troopers dropped from the saddle by the fire of the Indians as they topped the ridge.[a] There could have been no question of that had the Indians not received a decided check at this point.

The testimony of Benteen did not help Reno's case as it was intended to do, as Benteen himself seemed to realize before he was through with it when he interjected the remark: "Mind you, I was probably looking after things more than it was my business or duty to do." Toward the end Reno saw that the testimony as a whole showed that the Weir Point episode had been a complete mess; that from the beginning to end there had been a lack of unified action; that at no time was the whole command organized for the kind of work ahead, the short, hard push to break through to Custer and at the same time protect its impedimenta. It would seem that it was his realization of this fact that caused him at the last moment to ask for permission to testify in his own behalf. He tried to conceal his motive by having his counsel make the request on his own motion rather than at his, Reno's desire, persisting even after the Recorder had pointed out that such a request must be made by himself in written form. With this requirement he finally complied after the Court had proved adamant and had assured him, in response to the inquiry of his counsel, that no lack of a sense of delicacy would be imputed to him if he did make the request. When on the stand he stated without qualifications that everything had been done by his own orders, and that he had personally led the movement downstream!

The Court was not called on to pronounce on the character of this movement unless it found Major Reno responsible for what was done or left undone. If our analysis is anywhere near correct it is evident that no fair-minded person could hold him responsible. Before he could have formulated a consistent plan, before the whole of the packtrain had arrived, the power of direction was taken out of his hands, first by the independent action of Weir and then by Benteen in moving out in defiance of Reno, with virtually all the troops available for the firing line. Even if we assume that, under the regulations, he could command Benteen—which seems to me very doubtful—it still remains true that he possessed no means to enforce his orders if they were disregarded. And Benteen proves by his own words and actions that, both before and after his mandate from Custer had, presumably, expired, he followed his own sweet will in giving orders, not only to the troops of his own battalion but to those of Reno as well.

The impatience (not to give it a harsher name) on the part of Weir, laudable as it was in intent, led Custer to make a premature move that turned a safe holding action into a series of ambuscades for his troops which resulted in destruction.

But there is no reason for thinking that this general mismanagement of the attempt to go to Custer changed the outcome in any material way as far as the fight on Reno Hill is concerned, because, fortunately, the disaster which threatened for a moment was averted by Godfrey in throwing his company across the Indian front and checking the rush of the triumphant enemy with a volley at fairly close range, showing them that there was at least one "chief" among the white people who was not in a panic, whose medicine was still working. A few hours before these soldiers had fled from the valley, leaving their trail littered with dead men and horses. No one had then turned about to fight. They had shot them down from the flank, stabbed them with lances, and beaten them with clubs and pony whips. And now, when French and Edgerly fled, seemingly in terror, they crowded after them, expecting another orgy of safe and easy killing. The action of Godfrey, therefore, came as a dash of ice-water on their heated anticipations, which undoubtedly made them more cautious as they approached the lines on Reno Hill.

And so, finally, we come to the ever mournful "might-have-been"which has hovered over the tragedy from the day of its occurrence. Was it possible for Reno and Benteen to have saved Custer and his men? Knowing, as we do today, (what was not known at the time) the extreme nervousness of the Indians, the fact that at first they were merely fighting a delaying action to permit them to escape at night, it would appear as not only possible but probable that the tragedy could have been prevented by Reno's command had it advanced resolutely in compact formation, and without such a false and deceptive start as that of Captain Weir. It was Custer's response to Weir's appearance on the high ridge that led to the disaster, as explained in chapter 10. Custer was perfectly safe as long as he remained in his position on the Hill. He did not require any assistance there. and hence there was no need for Reno to make haste. But it *was* necessary that after he, or any of his troops, *did* start they should come through promptly in order to support any commitments of Custer to facilitate their passage. Captain Benteen was quite right in saying that he thought that Custer could take care of himself; for, had the latter confined himself to the sole task of looking after his own immediate command, nothing would have happened to him beyond the few casualties resulting from the mostly long-distance sniping to which the Indians confined themselves until he made his seemingly aggressive move south of the Hill. Had that move been supported by the rapid advance of Reno's whole command, it is very doubtful that the Indians would have committed themselves to the all-out attack on the south line. They would have incurred too great a risk of being caught between the two commands and roughly handled before they could have avoided the close-quarter fighting that would have resulted from the converging movement of the troops. The Indians never did this kind of fighting if they could avoid it. unless they could spring a surprise or the enemy was extremely weak.

On the other hand, had Reno made no move at all nothing serious would have happened to either command; for it cannot be too often repeated that the Indians did not want a fight here —or anywhere else. We have their word for that; and we would know it just as well without their word. We need only to place ourselves in their position to be convinced of it. They were fighting merely for a chance to move their village out of the immediate reach of the troops. After that had been done they might have become very dangerous enemies to Terry's whole force, as they had been to Crook whom the warriors, against the advice of the Council, attacked because he was coming too close to their camps.

The difficulty in the view I am presenting is not in the facts. It is in ourselves; in the picture built up in our minds from the kind of stories spread for years after the tragedy, a blurred picture of a wild, panicky scramble, of horror, torture, death and obscenity from the first shot to the last. In this there is no room for Custer with only part of his command engaged in a light and all but harmless skirmish, the rest standing in reserve nearby, while with his field glass he scans the troops on Weir Point two to three miles away. The very idea of such a thing is at first startling, incongruous, to our phantom-ridden minds. When I made my first tentative suggestion that Custer had seen Weir on the high ridges and had responded by deploying the two companies south of the Hill, a friend of mine and a life-long student of the subject, was amazed that I could for a moment entertain an idea so utterly wild and contrary to what he accepted as definitely established facts. He said, in effect, that he had been inclined to look with tolerance upon the speculations of a novice, but that if I now intended to urge this seriously—Well! Just a case of another good man gone wrong; and all that could be done about it was to draw the cloth over my dead sanity, breathe a regretful *requiescat in pace,* and sadly turn away.

And yet, does not the idea suggested become completely obvious the moment we stop to consider the facts upon which it is based? The Weir Ridges can be seen plainly with the unaided eyes from Custer Hill when general visibility is not abnormally low. Through field glasses troops on them, especially mounted troops, would stand out like a forest against the skyline. Custer was expecting these troops to be on his trail. He had sent two very urgent messages ordering them to follow him with all possible speed. Would it not, then, have been most extraordinary if he had not been watching constantly for their appearance? And if he had watched, could he possibly have failed to see them? Can anyone who has been on Custer Hill and noted how clearly Weir Point stands out, doubt that Custer saw the troops there? Nor would General Custer have been the only one who was watching the trail. Cooke, Tom Custer, and many others would have been certain to do so.

Nor did the officers on Weir Point have much doubt of this; for Benteen, though he insisted that Custer field is not visible from Weir Point, nevertheless planted a guidon to attract Custer's attention, Reno explaining that it was thought that its fluttering would be noticed more readily than the horses.

There can be little doubt that every officer on Weir Point knew where Custer was fighting, though they could not see the troops. They, or most of them, knew also that he had been fighting for at least an hour. What they did not know was his desperate need of reinforcements, or that he was being completely wiped out. But the Court of Inquiry did not possess the independent means of checking on the testimony such as we have today. It gave Reno the benefit of the doubt to which he was entitled under Anglo-Saxon conception of justice, and in my opinion its decision on his conduct was fair and just, whatever it may have thought of the manner in which the attempt to go to Custer's assistance was managed.

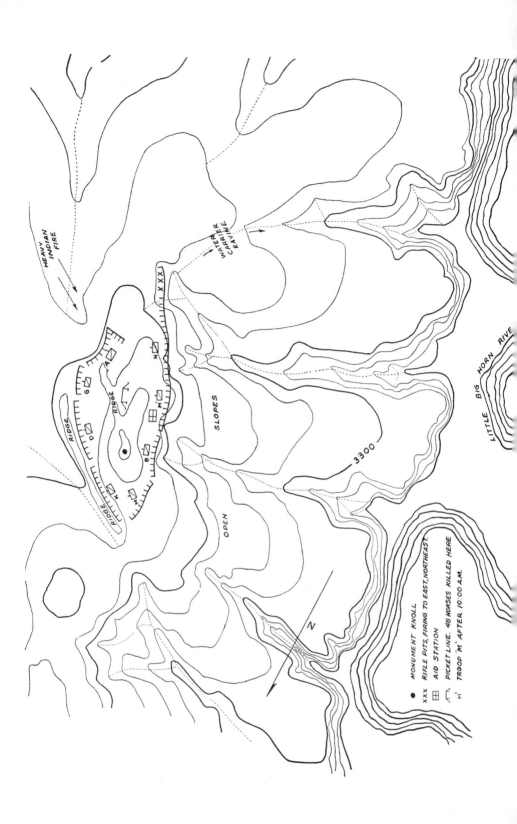

HEAVY INDIAN FIRE

WATER CARRIER RAVINE

LITTLE BIG HORN RIVER

MONUMENT KNOLL

RIDGE

RIDGE

RIDGE

SLOPES

OPEN

3300

N

● MONUMENT KNOLL

xxx RIFLE PITS, FIRING TO EAST, NORTHEAST.

⊞ AID STATION

⌒ PICKET LINE. 48 HORSES KILLED HERE

m¹ TROOP 'm¹ AFTER 10:00 A.M.

[CHAPTER 7]

Major Reno's Fight on the Hill

June 25th and 26th

WEIR POINT, from which the troops fled at the approach of the Indians, was by far the best defensive position in the whole battlefield area. Had it been nearer water there can be small doubt that it would have been selected instead of Reno Hill. In the preceding chapter it was pointed out that when the decision was made to withdraw from this position there were no indications that the Indians contemplated making an attack in force; that, in fact the day was so far spent as to make such an attack improbable during the short time remaining before darkness set in; and that the idea of camping to recuperate men and animals while the opportunity existed, seems to have been foremost in the minds of Reno and Benteen when they withdrew with part of the command. We must remember that no one at this time believed that Custer and his command were being completely wiped out. It was therefore necessarily in everyone's mind that the Indians would still have to reckon with him for the rest of the day and on the morrow. So, while it was desirable to occupy the strongest position available, it had also become urgent to see to the care of the men and horses to keep them fit. In fact the impossibility of securing water at Weir Point was given by Reno as a reason for not making his stand there. In our opinion it was the decisive factor, though Lieutenant Wallace gave a different reason. He explained at the Court of Inquiry that the troops occupied two nearly parallel ridges and that they had no means to defend the ravine or gorge between them on the downstream end. This becomes quite unconvincing when we examine the ground, for no Indian force however strong would have subjected itself to such a heavy, short-range crossfire as they would have received here. It would have been impossible for them to keep under cover while crawling up between two skirmish lines

---

Surrounded on all sides by the Indians who were flushed with victory after wiping out Custer's five troops 4 miles to the northwest, the combined battalions of Reno and Benteen, deployed in a tight ellipse on the military crest of Reno Hill, fought a bitter defensive battle on the evening of June 25 and all day June 26, when the Indians withdrew on the approach of General Terry's column.

◄━━━━━━

fifty feet or more above them. Two strong Cossack posts within easy supporting distance from the main body could have held them far enough back to make the packtrain and horses in the *cul de sac* on the upper end where the ridges joined, absolutely safe. The skirmish lines on the ridges would have had the crests for protection here as much as such crests would have served them anywhere in this area, more so, in any case, than on Reno Hill. There were no other elevations of approximately equal altitude except across the immense depression to the east, and the crest of the ridge there is more than 800 yards from the nearest point on the Weir ridges; which is to say, out of effective range.

In short, the Weir Ridges formed an almost perfect defensive position considered solely from the standpoint of actual fighting.

The Reno Hill position was vulnerable in several particulars. It was, however, by far the best available after abandoning Weir Point. Colonel Gibbon thought it was "extremely weak" because of the near-by broken ground in which the warriors could find perfect cover, and higher points from which they could fire on the troops. To this may be added the fact that it was impossible to cover the whole position without exposing large sections of the line to long-distance cross-fire. The greater portion of Benteen's line was thus exposed from both the northeast and the northwest, resulting in heavy casualties on the 26th. Godfrey, Weir, and Wallace were similarly exposed to fire from the southwest, but from a much smaller number of Indians.

Several officers described the position as being in the form of a saucer with one side broken out. This is true of that portion lying between the Monument knoll and Benteen's position. It was through this break in the rim of the saucer that the Indians fired upon the animals ranged around the improvised hospital, killing and wounding many of them. Commenting on this Gibbon said: "Then the manner in which the animals were exposed was very bad for the command. I think I counted some 48 dead animals in one small valley just to the west of the main position." This small valley was the saucer-shaped depression in which the animals were coraled, for there is no other such valley immediately west of the position. The ground to the west is a rather wide and fairly open slope, so much so that the Indians did not attempt to make much use of it.

As soon as Reno and Benteen became aware that the warriors were rushing up to attack the troops still on Weir Point, they began preparations for defense. Benteen, leaving his own troop to be posted later, turned to Wallace, who for some reason not explained in the record had abandoned his position between Weir and French and returned, and said: "Wallace, put the right of your troop here; his answer was 'I have no troop, only three men.' Well, I said, stay here with your *three* men and don't let *them* get away. I will see you are looked out for'—Colonel Reno was on the left—forming the same line—which was not a line, but an arc of a circle, rather irregularly described, too, and when we met about center, my own troop remained to be disposed of; so I put it over almost as much ground as the other six companies occupied protecting left flank and well to the rear, just on the edge of the line of bluffs, near river."[43]

Wallace did not let his three men "get away." They remained and served as "guide" or point of reference for posting the rest. When Edgerly arrived with "D" Troop he formed on the left of Wallace, that is, downstream from him but not quite closing up with him, it would seem. We do not know definitely where French was stationed. He came in ahead of Edgerly and probably deployed his troop behind the little ridge at the point where he struck it, while Edgerly passed behind his line as it was forming, his men taking interval from French's right, which may account for the gap between "D" and "G", which was closed after the firing ceased, by "D" extending its line to close with Wallace. After McDougall had returned the packtrain and retrieved the platoon he had loaned Moylan to assist in carrying the wounded, Benteen directed him to take position to the left of French, and facing in the direction of the Indian village. Moylan with "A" was stationed in the depression, or shallow ravine at the right of Wallace, with his right wing turned rearward at a right angle. Benteen's line was formed along the high south and southwestern rim of the saucer, its left extending toward Moylan's right, but a little farther south to be up far enough to be able to fire on the Indians facing them on the ridge here. Godfrey,[44] last to come in, distributed his men among those of "B", "D", "M", and "G", which would seem to show that these troops had been posted in a closed line or nearly so, leaving no room for Godfrey's men to form *as a troop*. We learn from the testimony of the officers that there was a gap between "M" and "B", and by deduction, also between "D" and "G", for after the firing ceased "D" was extended, or moved somewhat to the right, and the gap between "B" and "M" closed in some way not explained. But it seems rather obvious that "M" was moved to the left to close up with

"B", and that this movement of "M" and "D" in opposite directions opened a place between them for Godfrey's Troop "K".
Edgerly said definitely that on the 26th "K" stood next to "D"
on the left. It is altogether probable that in this re-arrangement
"B", as a whole, was moved farther to the left, so that at least a
part of it faced west instead of northwest; for that must have
been its position when it charged the Indians on the afternoon of
the 26th, because the Indians he was asked to drive out were
close enough to Benteen's line to shoot arrows into it.[45]

As Mathey was preparing to corral the packmules Benteen
ordered him to send the men in charge of the company packs to
the line. Mathey gave the order and turned loose the packmules,
one of which Benteen later caught as it was running away toward
the river with 4,000 rounds of ammunition. About dark, at
Reno's order, he took the 6 or 7 civilian packers and started to
build breastworks, chiefly for Moylan's line which had no protection whatever, using breadboxes and whatever else that was at
hand that would serve.

Within a few minutes after the line had been formed the
Indians swarmed up and soon had the position surrounded, or
nearly so. It does not seem, however, that any serious attack was
made up the long slope from the river on Benteen's right either
on the 25th or the 26th. Charles Windolph, who was stationed
here, says that the line was very thin here. He is not certain that
even so there was not a gap between Benteen's right and Mc-
Dougall's left. But everywhere else the fire was very heavy, and
before it ceased at dusk 18 men had been killed and 46 wounded,
according to Reno's Report to Terry of July 5th. This, however,
must be a mistake. The figures correspond to the total losses for
the two days fighting on the hill. Since the action did not begin
much before 8 o'clock it could not have lasted over about an
hour and a half, though to the tired, hungry and frightened men,
it seemed to stretch on into the ages. Edgerly said it lasted about
an hour and a half, which gives us a clue to the time it began,
supporting the evidence given in the preceding chapter.

Nor was there any rest after the Indians had withdrawn. No
rations were distributed, and it is probable that most of the men
went without supper because they were, in effect, ordered to remain on the line to throw up breastworks. Some of them, however, left their posts and went to the packs to help themselves.
But the packs had been removed hurriedly and dumped at random, resulting in a thorough scrambling of the saddlebags of

the individual troopers and the impedimenta of the twelve companies.⁴⁶ Further confusion was necessarily created by the civilian packers when they rummaged through this tangled mass to obtain material for breastworks. When the hungry troopers came to search for something to eat many of the breadboxes had undoubtedly already been carried off to the line, and those that remained were mixed up with other gear. This resulted in a good deal of pulling and hauling on the part of the men to get what they wanted and in some actual stealing of personal belongings, which was later greatly exaggerated in order to excuse Reno's unprovoked attack on the civilian packer, Frett. We can deduce the approximate truth from the testimony of Reno and Lieutenant Mathey. Questioned about rations, Reno said; "The men were ordered to carry their own rations for three or four days, I think. I am not positive about that, because, as I say, I was not consulted. It was in order that the packtrain, which was limited in its capacity of transportation, should be relieved as much as possible. For that reason the rations were taken and were in the hands of the men and on the horses. The rations in the packtrain were under the charge of the company commanders.

When Mathey was on the stand he was asked: "Were rations distributed to the command that night?"

Answer. "I do not know. I do not think the men had much that night."

Question. "Were rations distributed the next morning, or did the men help themselves?"

Answer. "I believe they did. I heard something about it. Anybody could have taken rations."

Question. "Did you hear any special complaint about the packers?"

Answer. "I heard some rations were taken, but I do not know whether it was done by soldiers or packers. There was nothing to prevent anyone helping himself. I don't suppose anyone would have interfered if he had seen the men taking rations."

The innuendo of Major Reno that because the men were supposed to carry their own rations, they had no excuse to go to the packs for them, is rendered questionable by the statement of Captain McDougall: "Then I went at nightfall to get some hardtack for my men and a box of ammunition." Evidently, then, the men of Troop "B" carried no rations, or at least no hardtack; and one can imagine what freshly cut bacon would have done to saddlebags during the intense heat unless it was wrapped in grease-proof paper, a luxury it is not likely the cavalry carried.

There was little sleep for the command that night. Most of the men remained on the line to dig rifle-pits, or throw up heaps of earth to conceal their heads from the Indians, and to serve at least to some extent as protection against bullets.⁷ But there were few tools to work with. Wallace, Moylan and Edgerly reported that there was only three spades, the latter saying also that there were only two axes at hand. For the most part the men used tincups and knives. Benteen, after sending for spades and not receiving any, made no attempt to fortify, not thinking it necessary, as he explained to the Court.

During the night there was naturally a great deal of speculation concerning Custer. What had become of him? Where was he? Why did he not rejoin them. What was his actual situation?

All the witnesses who testified at the Court of Inquiry—Wallace, Varnum, Moylan, Mathey, Edgerly, Godfrey, McDougall, Benteen, and Sergeant Culbertson—agreed in saying that they had no suspicion that Custer and his command had been destroyed. Opinions as to his whereabouts and actual situation differed, though Benteen said "It was the belief of the officers on the Hill during the night of the 25th that General Custer had gone to General Terry and that we were abandoned to our fate."

This idea may have been the ruling one among the enlisted men, at least for a time, for there is a hint to that effect in the testimony of Godfrey and Wallace, the latter saying "There was a great deal of swearing about Custer running off and leaving us." According to Godfrey "There was an impression among the men that Custer had been repulsed and had abandoned them. I had no such impression, however." Godfrey said further "Captain Weir and I had a talk about Custer. We thought he had been repulsed and was unable to join us, and that we ought to move that night, as we then had fewer casualties than we were likely to have later."

McDougall: "I did not converse much during the 25th and 26th, except with Captain Godfrey. During the night of the 25th the conclusion was that Custer had met with the same crowd and they were either following him or else he had gone to General Terry. We based it on the fact that we had heard firing down there, and all the Indians had come back after us, and I thought perhaps he had retreated to General Terry and they had come back to finish us . . . I had no idea Custer's command had been destroyed. It was no more reasonable to suppose they were than ourselves—supposed our positions were about similar."

Varnum: "I don't think there was any idea or thought that he was in the fix he was. The command felt in doubt—wondering if he were corraled as we were, or had been driven away to Terry —but that he was wiped out—there was no such thought. I had no such idea."

Mathey: "The general impression was that Custer was surrounded and in the same fix as we were, and that he could not leave his wounded."

Sergeant Culbertson: "I don't think anyone had any impression that General Custer was having any more trouble than we were . . . It was the general belief among the men that General Custer had been wounded and could not come to us just as we could not go to him."

As the men worked at their entrenchments and wondered what had become of Custer they could hardly avoid speculating about what was in store for themselves. That problem was also on the mind of Major Reno. His order to entrench implied that the issue was to be fought out here on the hill. It was given early in the evening, probably immediately after the firing ceased, and indicated his intentions while he was still his normal self and thinking like a soldier.

And this brings us to a subject we would rather side-step than discuss. But it has already entered the inflamed controversy between the partisans of Custer on the one hand and those of Reno on the other. It has been asserted that Reno made the flat proposal on the evening of the 25th that the command abandon its position, leave all the wounded who could not ride, and flee to the base camp on the Powder River. We shall, therefore, present the essential facts as far as we have been able to ascertain them and state what they seem to us to mean.

Did Reno make such a proposal, and if so, to whom? It is certain that the wounded believed on the 26th that a proposal to abandon them was, or had been under consideration. Colonel Gibbon, in referring to this in his article in the *Catholic Quarterly Review*, said: "Poor fellows! An impression had, in some way, gained footing amongst them during the long weary hours of the fight on the 26th that, to save the balance of the command, they were to be abandoned."

Benteen in a letter to Godfrey dated January 3, 1886, said: "Don't you think Reno has been sufficiently damned before the country that it can be afforded to leave out in the article the proposition from him to saddle up and leave the field of the

Little Big Horn on the first night of the fight? Don't think I would do it, but that he did so propose, there is no manner of doubt. 'But the greatest of these is Charity.'"

On January 6, 1892, in answering some questions asked by Theodore Goldin, Benteen said; "Ans. to 3rd query, is this,—I expect Godfrey to say in his article that Reno recommended the abandonment of the wounded in the night of the 25th, and of 'skipping off' with those who could ride, as he did to me, but I killed that proposition in the bud; the Court of Inquiry on Reno knew there was something kept back by me, but they did not know how to get it out by questioning, as I gave them no chance to do so; and Reno's attorney was 'posted' thereon."

Captain Moylan, writing to Godfrey January 17, 1892, said: "Of his (Reno's) personal conduct in the bottoms or subsequently on the hill the less said the better. If what Colonel Benteen told me at Meade in 1883 was true, and I know of no reason to doubt it, then Reno ought to have been shot."

At a dinner of the Order of Indian Wars, January 20, 1930, General J. Nicholson said Benteen had told him the same story, and at another dinner of the same order on February 20, 1937, General Jefferson R. Kean said he also had this story from Benteen.

In a letter to J. A. Shoemaker of Billings, Montana, March 2, 1926, Godfrey related that Benteen started to tell him of this incident on June 28 while they were on their way to Custer field to bury the dead, but that before he could do so someone rode up near them and Benteen said "I can't tell you now." It was not until 1881 when they were on a fishing trip near Point Pleasant, New Jersey, that they found themselves alone, and then Benteen told him of Reno's proposal.

This would seem to leave no room for doubt that Benteen made the statement as claimed, not only once but a number of times to different persons and over a period extending from 1881 to 1892. It is possible that Reno did not word his proposal as bluntly as Benteen represented it, but its substance was essentially the same, or how account for the idea Gibbon found current among the wounded when he arrived on the 27th?

How shall we explain this incident? No amount of special pleading or gloss can clear Reno if we assume he was his normal self when he made the proposal. Indeed, knowing Benteen as he must have known him, would he not have known also what his reaction would be? We believe so.

Nor is this the only difficulty. It is safe to assume that Benteen would have rejected the proposal even had it not involved the abandonment of the wounded. For, if it was feared that they could not hold their entrenched position, the best available, how could they hope to survive after they had left it and were back on the trail? They now knew the aggressive temper of the Indians and their overwhelming numbers. If the troops fled it was certain they would be pursued by at least as large a force as had just attacked them. At this time of year and in this latitude there is a scant six hours of full darkness. Part of this brief period had already passed when the proposal was made. Many of the horses had been killed or wounded, and all that remained were weak from hunger, thirst and marching. Even had there still been horses to mount all the men, which is doubtful, they could not have moved faster than a walk without risking the loss of many horses from exhaustion. In any case the packtrain could not have moved faster than that. It was all it had been able to do during the day, and the mules were now weaker than they were when they started in the morning. The packtrain, unless they abandoned this also, would have set the pace for the whole command.

In addition to this there was the task of unscrambling the packs and re-tieing them on the mules, and all the rest of it. It would have been a difficult and time-consuming job in the daytime to reorganize the command for the march. It would have been next to impossible to do so in the dark, in the available time, and make anything more than a mob of it. And meanwhile the Indian scouts left to observe the command during the night, would have detected the preparations for flight and notified the warriors in the camps. Before the command could have gotten more than a mile or two on the way the warriors would have been at their heels, and by daylight they would have been ringed by fire from behind every ridge, knoll, and bush, as well as from the ravines and depressions along the narrow valley of Reno Creek. In a few minutes the packtrain would have been a shambles, many of the mules killed and the rest stampeding wildly, taking with them whatever they were carrying. Remembering that of Reno's original command "G" Troop had been completely shattered and the morale of "M" and "A", badly shaken, how long would it have been before the whole command disintegrated into a panic-stricken rabble. Every soldier who knew anything about Indian fighting would have foreseen this, and there was not the slightest chance that Benteen would fail to grasp it instantly.

A short move to a selected position could have been made during the night, but an attempt to flee out of reach of these Indians under the existing circumstances was something so utterly wild that no experienced soldier would have undertaken it, and Major Reno, when in full possession of his faculties, was not lacking in tactical skill or the intelligence to analyze the simple military problem confronting him, namely to remain in his entrenchments and keep the Indians at bay until they were driven off by Gibbon or withdrew of their own choice. At the Court of Inquiry Reno said that in this had been his only hope and that he had so explained it to the men on the line to induce them to do their best where they were.

Our analysis, then, leads us to the conclusion that Major Reno was not "in full possession of his faculties" when he made his shocking proposal involving the abandonment of all wounded who could not ride. We believe that the explanation is to be found in the testimony of the two civilian packers, B. F. Churchill and John Frett, who came to the packs around 10 o'clock in the evening of the 25th in search of blankets and something to eat. Before they could secure either they came across Reno. Frett, who had been in the service as a soldier for over three years some time before, saluted and said "Good evening, sir." Reno then asked them what they wanted and they told him they had come to get something to eat. Reno asked further if the mules were tied. It sounded like "tight" to Frett, who nevertheless answered "yes." When Reno repeated the question Frett, puzzled, asked "What do you mean by "tight?" Reno, furious, it seems, because his condition had been detected, replied "tight, God damn you," and slapped Frett across the face, while whisky from a bottle in his other hand spattered over both Frett and Churchill. Then he seized a carbine and told Frett he would shoot him if he found him among the packs again, a strange threat to make against a man who had been engaged for the very purpose of assisting in taking care of the packs. When Reno was on the stand he made a very unsatisfactory explanation of this incident. He merely said that he thought the man had no business there and that Frett had somehow angered him. The Recorder did not press him, quite possibly because he saw that whatever Reno's condition may have been at 10 o'clock at night it had no effect on the course of events.

We have already shown that no rations were distributed on the evening of the 25th, and that McDougall went to the packs to get some hardtack for his men. Mathey, who had charge of the packtrain, made no complaint of the conduct of either troopers or packers. On the contrary, he said he did not think anyone would have interfered if he saw someone taking rations, and as far as the record shows, no one except Reno did interfere other than for the purpose of getting the men back on the line.

The truth is that before Churchill and Frett testified none of the officers had as much as mentioned stealing and looting, or made any criticism of the men coming to the packs to get something to eat. But when the testimony of the two packers showed that Reno had been guilty of striking a man without apparent justification and had been accused of drunkenness, Benteen was recalled to pull him out of his "tight" place. He did so effectively by scoffing at the idea that Reno could have been drunk, and leaving the impression that a goodly portion of the men in the command were no better than a pack of common thieves and looters. We shall see later that he found some use for them when he himself was in a "tight" place of a different sort.

We have found no evidence that Major Reno was, at this time of his life, an exceptionally hard drinker. It is well known, however, that he was of the type of drinkers who become quarrelsome and violent when under the influence of liquor long before they betray pronounced physical symptoms of intoxication. McDougall, in effect, called attention to this fact when Mr. Gilbert pressed him to be more positive in his statements concerning Reno's sobriety, saying that some men can conceal the first stages of intoxication, leaving the impression that he thought Reno may have been to some extent under the influence of liquor. This is, we believe, very near the mark. Reno was not exactly "drunk" as that term is ordinarily understood, but he was far enough along to be muddled somewhat in his thinking and judgment.

It is well known that certain drugs, among them alcohol, have the effect of deadening our more recently acquired characteristics, such as our finer moral perceptions, leaving the victim a prey to his blind primordial urges common to saint and sinner alike, and self-preservation is one of the strongest of these urges. Nothing more need to be said to understand the incident we have been discussing.

The confirmed Reno-hater will make a mountain of this. In actual fact it was of little or no importance whether Reno was sober or drunk at this time of night, aside from the injustice done to the two packers. He had already given the necessary orders for defense and was about to lie down to get a few hours of sleep, giving his orderly, Davern, instructions to waken him at midnight. The chances of a serious attack by the Indians before daylight were practically nil as long as the command made no move to escape. Colonel W. A. Graham, in a letter to the late W. A. Falconer of Bismarck, North Dakota, put the common sense evaluation of the incident into two short sentences: "What difference did it make if Reno was as drunk as a boiled owl during the night? No one claims he was drunk while they were fighting."

Closely connected with this subject is the fact that Benteen had virtually taken command from the moment he arrived on the hill, and Reno had tacitly acquiesced in the usurpation. This was humiliating for Reno, but it did not show poor judgment, for the command was in a desperate situation, and if anyone was to come out of it with his hair on the best leadership was not too good. And Reno knew, as did all the rest of the officers and many of the enlisted men, that Captain Benteen was by far the best soldier present. It was, therefore, far from stupid on the part of Reno to permit Benteen to supervise the actual fighting. There was nothing in this contrary to regulations and it did not, in itself, cast any reflections on Reno. But it would have been better if he had formally designated Benteen as the tactical officer in command of the skirmish line. Or so, at least, it seems to the writer who is not a soldier.

While the men worked at their entrenchments the Indians provided them with a kind of entertainment which, if unpleasant, had the virtue of adding zest to their labors. From under the light of huge bonfires came the sounds of a frenzied celebration, the beat of tom-toms, screechings, wild firing of guns, and even the sound of a captured trumpet which some red-skinned musical (?) genius had somehow managed to manipulate, raising momentarily a vain hope that the random notes healded the approach of Custer. Eyes wearied by long, anxious peering into the darkness, finally registered the wished-for sight, dim, shadowy columns of marching troops coming to the rescue. Fortunately they knew not then that their commander and comrades lay stark and cold on the field they had looked down on only a few hours before while many of them were still fighting desperately in a battle they knew would end in their own destruction.

Meanwhile Benteen, who had already passed two successive nights without sleep, remained awake and watchful, while his men slept on the line beside their weapons, since they were not entrenching. When he went to visit his sentries he found them asleep. He tried to prod them to their feet with the toe of his boot, but they preferred sleep with kicks to wakefulness without kicks. They were too far gone to be dependable, so he and Gibson took over for the rest of the night.

It was probably at the first glow of light on the northeastern horizon that the warriors began to leave their camps to surround the command for the second time, and more completely than they had done the evening before. By the time it was light enough to see they had arrived in force sufficient to pour a very heavy fire into the position. It did not do a great deal of damage except to the horses and mules in the corral and Benteen's men lying along the high southern rim of the "saucer" where they presented a perfect target at long range for the warriors across the position to the north and northeast. There can be little doubt that it was this fire rather than that from the front that caused the heavy casualties and accounted for the difficulty Benteen experienced in keeping his men on the line. This is suggested by what Benteen himself said as well as by the official casualty list of Company H, showing 11 wounded and 3 killed, a ratio of nearly 4 wounded to 1 killed. K had 3 wounded and 5 killed, D 2 wounded and 4 killed, B 2 wounded, 2 killed. This comparison suggests strongly that most of Benteen's men reported wounded had been hit by spent, or nearly spent, bullets.

By the time the firing started Benteen had about reached the limit of his endurance unless he could somehow secure a few minutes of sleep. He went over his line, and finding everything satisfactory, left it in charge of Lieutenant Gibson, then laid down on the hillside behind his men. This slope was fast becoming the hottest spot in the whole position. Almost before he could close his eyes a bullet struck the heel of his boot. Another kicked up the dust under his armpit; but, like the sentries he had tried to prod into wakefulness not long before, he, too, refused to stir. He thought he got his "forty winks" of sleep before a sergeant awakened him to tell him that Gibson was having a "regular monkey and parrot time of it." He experienced a fearful urge to say something naughty to that sergeant, but passed up the pleasure to attend to still more urgent business. "Down I ran," he says, "and through and through the packtrain, getting together some 15 to 16 soldiers and packers, making them carry up some sacks of bacon, boxes of hard bread, packsaddles and materials of that kind,—quite a sufficiency to build a respectable breastworks, which, after propping up as well as we could, I turned over with the "Falstaffian crowd," to 'Gib,' my First Lieutenant, telling him to hold the fort notwithstanding what might become of us; then I walked along the front of my troop and told them I was getting mad, and I wanted them to charge down the ravines with me when I gave the yell; then each to yell as if provided with a thousand throats; the Chinese act was sufficiently good for me if it would work, but I hadn't so much real trust in its efficacy; however, when the throttles of the 'Haters' were given full play and we dashed into the unsuspecting savages who were amusing themselves by throwing clods of dirt, arrows by hand, and otherwise, for simply pure cussedness, among us, to say 'twas a surprise to them, is mild form—for they somersaulted and vaulted as so many trained acrobats, having no order in getting down those ravines, but quickly getting; de'il take the hindmost."

This was the charge that opened the way for the water carriers through the ravine the head of which came close to Benteen's line near the point where it curved back northward. As the account shows, it was from the head of this ravine, or from a point a little above it, that the Indians threw dirt and arrows on the troops.

Having secured the ravine Benteen sent word to Reno and asked for camp kettles. These were brought by men who had volunteered for the dangerous undertaking of actually getting the water. To protect them while they were crossing the narrow strip of open ground between the bluffs and the river and while dipping up the water, men were stationed on the edge of the bluffs. Across the river there was some timber or brush, and into this these men sent a steady stream of bullets. No harm came to the water carriers from this source; but from under the shelter of the bluffs some Indians fired upon the carriers, wounding a number of them and killing J. J. Tanner of Troop M.

They did not get all the water they wanted or needed, but enough for the wounded and a few others, it is said.

When Benteen made the charge down the ravine he left on the line, as far as we can determine, only the "Falstaffian crowd" behind the hastily constructed breastworks. The Indians seem to have taken advantage of this by crawling up closer and in great numbers; for, soon after the line was reestablished on the return of the men there was an incipient panic noted by Edgerly who said: "At one time there was a break in Benteen's line and the men were, I thought, rushing back where I was." This panic, however, was checked and the line restored, and then Benteen crossed over and stood near Edgerly who heard him say to Major Reno: "We have charged the Indians from our side and driven them out. They are coming to our left and you ought to drive them out." Reno replied: " 'If you can see them, give the command to charge'. Benteen said: "Alright, ready boys; now charge and give them hell'."

It is only fair to say here that Benteen, from his high position where his line stood, could see far better what was in the broken ground in front of Reno than could Reno himself.

Reno and several other officers went out in this charge, among them Edgerly, Varnum, Hare and Weir, Varnum receiving a slight flesh wound in each leg below the knee. The Indians made no pretense of meeting the charge but scrambled out of the way as fast as they could. Reno ordered the troops back after they had gone 40 to 50 yards. Aside from Varnum no one seems to have received a scratch.

As is well known, the officers who testified at the Court of Inquiry did not tell all they knew, and Edgerly's account of this incident was rather discreet. Benteen, who preceded him on the stand, had been even more discreet. Godfrey, who followed Edgerly, was less reticent. He said: "When Captain Benteen came over and said we would have to drive the Indians from our front because they were firing over on the rear of his line, he had to repeat the request several times to Major Reno before the charge was ordered." On re-direct examination he said: "He (Reno) hesitated some time when Benteen told him the Indians must be driven out, and it was not until Benteen told him that unless they were, they would come in on us, that Reno told him 'Alright, to give the command'."

This detail is not brought out to suggest that Reno was a coward. On direct question Godfrey denied that Reno's hesitation indicated cowardice. It was, however, one of many indications that Benteen rather than Reno was the actual leader in defense of the whole position.

At the time this charge was made there was strong pressure on the lines all around, and the fire was very heavy. We believe that before Benteen left here he asked for reinforcements, and by dint of insistence induced Reno to send him Company M, or most of it. A few men may have been left at the head of the ravine facing M to check any attempt of the Indians to crawl up through the gap in the line after the troop had withdrawn. Indians making such an attempt would have been caught in a crossfire in the open as they crawled up a long slope out of a deep ravine. Eight or ten men could easily have checked them if posted at the head of the ravine.

The posting of some of the M Company men here and the transfer of the rest may account for the confusion in regard to the position of M in the line. Until it was sent to Benteen it had stood on the left of K. Since Benteen's men had necessarily stood at wide intervals because of the extent of ground they were holding and were badly thinned by casualties, their line was undoubtedly shortened by closing up toward the left, and M deployed in the gap thus created between B and H.

There is not much more to tell of the fight. The charge we have just discussed was made around 10 o'clock. Soon after that the fire of the Indians slackened greatly but did not at any time cease entirely. Benteen finally secured some spades and constructed three redoubts on his line. At 2 o'clock the Indians made a final, determined effort to overrun the position, but were met by a steady fire and driven back, not, however, before some of them in McDougall's front had come close enough to Benteen's men to reach them with arrows in an annoying cross-fire. Under Benteen's order McDougall made a charge to drive them out, but received so heavy a fire in his rear and right flank that he ordered his men back after going only about 60 yards.

About 3 o'clock the fight was virtually over. A few warriors with long-range guns remained, perhaps with the object of holding the attention of the troops while the village was being dismantled preparatory to flight. Below the bluffs, near the river, a few others for a time guarded the approach to the water. The rest were withdrawn in large groups by signals given at intervals by a warrior stationed in the valley, according to DeRudio who, with O'Neil, was still in hiding along the river.

It was, perhaps, an hour before sunset when observers on the Hill saw an astonishing and welcome sight. From behind a smoke screen over the nearer side of the valley emerged the head of an immense column of humans and animals. Both in size and order it resembled a large division of troops on the march, covering a space a half mile wide and two to three miles in length. As the troops on the Hill looked down on this great concourse of men and animals, they gave their departing enemies three cheers, no doubt out of an overpowering sense of relief and the thought:

"Well, they saw all they wanted of us," for they did not know then that Terry and Gibbon were at that moment on the march only 9 to 10 miles down the valley, confronted by a strong rear guard of warriors as they neared the present site of Crow Agency, where they camped for the night within sight of some of the dead on Custer field.

As Gibbon's scouts and flankers were making contact with the warriors in their front, Reno's men watched the sinister column as, far up the valley of the Little Big Horn, it faded out in the darkness like an evil dream.

The stench from the dead men and animals had now become so offensive that the command was withdrawn to the slope on the west. We have not been able to obtain a clear idea of the manner in which it was disposed in the new position. We know, however, that Benteen retained part of his old line in the rim of the "saucer," very obviously because from this point he could sweep the whole of their old position with his fire if the Indians returned to the attack. The lines of the rest were formed along the ravines down the slope toward the river north of Benteen. It may be assumed, perhaps, that they also left some of their men to support Benteen's cross-fire in case of renewed conflict.

That night the dead were buried, some of them in the rifle-pits, it is said. Also, they finally recovered the body of Lieutenant Hodgson and buried it the next morning. McDougall, on being recalled to the stand, said: "On the night of the 26th, I took Privates Ryan and Moore of my company, and got Lieutenant Hodgson's body. We carried it up to our breastwork and kept it there until the next morning. After sewing him up in a blanket, we proceeded to a little knoll between my position and the works on the hill and these two men and myself dug his grave and buried him."

CHAPTER 8

Terry and Gibbon March to the Battlefield

June 21 to 27

THE Montana column, in camp four miles below the mouth of the Rosebud, pulled stakes at 9:45 on the morning of June 21 and started for the mouth of the Big Horn 64 miles away. Gibbon and Brisbin remained with Terry for the conference on the *Far West* and to see Custer off at noon the next day. After the Review they returned to the boat with General Terry, Gibbon not to leave it again until the morning of the 26th because of a severe attack of illness on the night of the 23rd to the 24th. A high wind delayed the departure of the boat until 4 o'clock. It did not overtake the command until 4:30 A. M. of the 24th a mile below Fort Pease where the infantry were in camp for the night. An hour and a half later it arrived opposite the camp of the cavalry two miles below the mouth of the Big Horn. Orders were at once given to prepare to march with eight days' rations to be carried on packmules, except for Captain Kirtland with his company of infantry to be left in charge of the camp containing the wagon train and other heavy equipment.

At 11 o'clock 12 Crow scouts were sent up Tullock's Creek with orders to "proceed until they found a Sioux village or a recent trail"—a rather large order. Had it been obeyed these Crows would not have seen the command again until about noon of the 26th, and perhaps not even then. They returned just before dark, "whooping down the valley," and reported finding one buffalo recently wounded with arrows. Another uncomplimentary entry in Bradley's Journal!

The transfer of the command to the south bank of the Yellowstone began about noon and was accomplished in five trips by the boat. By 5:30 all were across and in camp for the night just above the mouth of Tullock's Creek about 4 miles from Fort Pease. The next morning they started up the Creek at 5:45,

141

Lieutenant McClernand acting as guide. But after going a little over 3 miles Terry, on the advice of Muggins Taylor, decided to mount the divide to the right and follow it to the Little Big Horn. This was a mistake, for, as Gibbon wrote after the end of the campaign, Taylor was a frontiersman who had lived mostly in the small towns of the west and did not know the terrain in question, as the command soon discovered. Ravines from both the Big Horn and Tullock's cut the divide in many places, some of them a hundred feet or more in depth. To get the Gatling guns across the worst of them it was necessary to let them down the precipitous sides by hand, using a number of lariats tied end to end. There was no water here, and soon after noon the infantry were not only tired but suffering from thirst as well.

Meanwhile Bradley had scouted up Tullock's for about 9 miles and then halted to see if the command was following him. After a considerable wait a squad of cavalry came up and informed him of the change of route, whereupon he cut across to the right and soon rejoined the command. He found it "involved in a labyrinth of bald hills and deep, precipitous ravines completely destitute of water." Terry now sent him to a high ridge 8 miles to the front and left, in the hope that he would be able to see the Little Big Horn and possibly an Indian camp. But when he climbed this ridge he saw that another several miles distant completely obstructed the view in the direction of the Little Big Horn, and as he had been ordered not to go beyond the first ridge, he returned, coming up with the infantry just as they were going into camp for the night at 6:50, about 25 miles from the Yellowstone by the way they had come.

The cavalry, because of the necessity of finding water, had finally struck out for the Big Horn. They reached it about 4 o'clock, and after watering their horses and sending a detachment loaded with filled canteens back to the infantry, mounted a very steep ridge just beyond which they came to a meadow studded with large cottonwoods, a beautiful camp ground they were not to enjoy for the night, as they had hoped to do. Here they waited for Terry to come up and started to make coffee and fry some bacon. But when Terry arrived around 4:30 he appeared to be greatly worried and wanted to push on with the cavalry, though it had just begun to rain and the night threatened to be wet and dark. The trumpet blared "Boots and Saddles," the hungry troopers threw their half-fried bacon on the ground and were off again at 5:45 for one of the most weird night-marches in history. The infantry, too exhausted and foot-sore to go on, went into camp at 6:50 where the cavalry had halted, or very near this place.

When Bradley reached the Infantry he learned that the Crow scouts he had sent up Tullock's in the morning ahead of his own detachment, had returned and reported having seen smoke in the direction of the Little Big Horn, which was thought to indicate the presence of a Sioux village; that the cavalry and battery of Gatling guns had gone on, and that he was to follow them. When he overtook them he learned that they were being guided by cavalry officers, and since their knowledge of the country was "far from profound," the column found itself confronted by one obstacle after another. There is some evidence in his Journal that the campaign was beginning to tell on Bradley's nerves. His "dig" at the cavalry officers was undeserved, and he knew it. He knew that either McClernand or Captain Ball could have gone to the Little Big Horn almost blindfolded, daylight or dark, had it been left to them, for they had come down Tullock's Creek less than two months before. But he could not well blame General Terry who had been the innocent victim of a man who pretended to a knowledge he did not possess.

The march during the day had been difficult and exhausting to men and animals alike. It became positively nightmarish after the rain and darkness set in. With the ground slippery and everything more than a few yards distant blotted out, the column wriggled along blindly like a gigantic earthworm, alternately stretching and contracting and always in danger of losing its tail or a segment along its squirming sides. There was fear that it might disintegrate altogether, leaving only scattered groups lost in the endless mazes of ridges and ravines, in which there is no order here. It is the edge of the "Bad Lands" and like them in general contour, a "geological delirium," to use Mr. Van de Water's aptly descriptive term.

Nothing serious, however, happened until about 11 o'clock when the cry went up: "The battery is missing!" The column was halted and the trumpet blown repeatedly. But as no response came Terry sent Captain Hughes to find the lost sheep. But Hughes could find no trace of it. Lieutenant Schofield, who had gone on a similar mission, was equally unsuccessful. Nevertheless the search and hallooing went on until the battery was located and set right. It was about a mile out of place.

Not long after the battery had been retrieved the command received its greatest shock of the night. As the column was going down slope on the crest of a hogback the head of it suddenly came to the brink of a precipice along the base of which swept the waters of the Big Horn 150 feet below. For some minutes General Terry and those about him sat on their horses and looked at the water gleaming dimly below and the black abysses to right and left, ravines whose precipitous sides and gloomy depths were only slightly less appalling than the precipice in front. The ridge was too narrow for countermarching, and any movement whatsoever was a creepy business. The cavalry guides seemed to be at the end of their wits, and Terry "appeared undecided and irresolute." Finally Bradley suggested to Terry that they accept the guidance of one of his Crow scouts, Little Face, an old man who had roamed this country as a boy and claimed he had been on this hogback before. The suggestion was accepted, the column "dragged up by the tail," and in a few minutes they were following their new guide to a little valley with water and grass in it. The men dismounted and lay down to sleep, holding their horses by the reins. An "A" tent was set up for Terry. Brisbin and Captain Ball crawled under the raised end of a fallen cottonwood and likewise went to sleep. They had covered 12 miles since starting at 5:45, and it was now around midnight.

But the command was not all here. Tyler, with one troop of cavalry, had been lost from the column, when or where we are not told. He had picked his own way through the darkness and was seen at daylight some distance away watering his horses. Low with his battery of Gatlings also was missing at first, but like Tyler, got in on his own resources.

What a merry time this weary, bedraggled and scattered command might have experienced if the "wild man" Terry had sent up the Rosebud four and a half days before had gone up into Wyoming around the head of the Wolf Mountains and then down the Little Big Horn, as Major Brisbin insisted the "insufferable ass" should have done, instead of marching straight on the Indian village and putting an end to the preparations then being made there to move to the mouth of the Little Big Horn in the afternoon of the 25th! For we are now dealing with the morning of the 26th, and at the time Brisbin was crawling out from under his fallen cottonwood and wiping the sleep from his eyes the overmarched and foot-sore infantry, perhaps 180 men, were still 12 miles down the Big Horn, with about an even chance that the whole Indian horde would have been in his front just over a ridge, had not the "wild man" interfered with their plans the day before.

Around 11 o'clock Gibbon, still far from well, arrived a little ahead of the infantry and received back his command from General Terry. They then started to pick their way down into the valley of the Little Big Horn but soon halted again to await the arrival of Bradley who had been sent ahead early in the morning and was now seen approaching. Bradley had come upon three Indians who had fled across the Big Horn losing some articles the Crows recognized as belonging to some of their tribesmen who had been sent with Custer. Through means of signals mutual identification was made and a parley held across the river. The fleeing Crows, Goes Ahead, White-Man-Runs-Him, and Hairy Moccasins, told a terrible story of defeat and death, of the complete destruction of Custer and his battalion and the probability of the destruction of the rest as well. This Little Face, through Barny Bravo, reported to Bradley who now came to repeat it to General Terry. In his Journal Bradley wrote: "I therefore rode back until I met the command, which was halted just before I came up, and narrated to the General the ghastly details as I had received them from Little Face. He was surrounded by his staff and accompanied by General Gibbon, who had that morning joined, and for a moment there were blank faces and silent tongues, and no doubt heavy hearts in the group just as there had been among the auditors of Little Face at its rehearsal by him. But presently the voice of doubt was raised, the story was sneered at, such a catastrophe it was asserted was wholly improbable, nay impossible; if a battle had been fought, which was condescendingly admitted might have happened, then Custer was victorious, and these three Crows were dastards who had fled without awaiting the result and told this story to excuse their cowardice. General Terry took no part in these criticisms, but sat on his horse silent and thoughtful, biting his lower lip and looking at me as though he by no means shared in the wholesale scepticism of the flippant members of his staff.

While this scepticism was not universal it was nevertheless quite general, for such was the belief of both Gibbon and his engineer officer, McClernand,[48] the former writing "for I do not suppose there was a man in the column who entertained for a moment the idea that there were Indians enough in the country to defeat, much less annihilate, the fine regiment of cavalry Custer had under his command."

This blanket statement did not apply to the Crow scouts, who could not be induced to rejoin Bradley still in advance with his twelve mounted infantry. Angrily Gibbon ordered them to the rear, an order they obeyed with suspicious alacrity, he thought. After getting to the rear of the column they fled back to their agencies, their interpreter, Bravo, with them.

The command now entered the valley of the Little Big Horn up which a heavy smoke was observed in the distance. After crossing the river they halted to make dinner and to give the weary infantry, which had already marched 19 miles since leaving their camp at 5 o'clock, a rest.

It was now 2 o'clock, or later, and still the smoke continued to rise in their front about 12 miles away. Was Custer burning the village, as the guides had said, or were the Indians burning the grass, as the fleeing Crows had insisted? While they were halted here Bostwick and Taylor were sent with messages for Custer, the former over the hills east of the river, the latter over the bench to the west. Bostwick returned not long after the march had been resumed and reported the country ahead full of Indians. A little later Taylor brought back a similar report.

The command moved on again at 5 o'clock, infantry in the center with the Gatlings close in the rear, cavalry on the right, Bradley on the left and slightly in advance.

Toward evening a few Indians were seen on the bench three or four miles away to the right and front. Lieutenant Roe with his troop of cavalry was sent there to investigate and to act as guard of the right flank with instructions not to pass from sight of the main column. When he mounted the bench he found hundreds of Indians in his front, some only a few hundred yards away, the main body about two miles off in his front. One group of these Indians was clad in dark suits (cavalry uniforms), carried a guidon and went through evolutions similar to those of a cavalry troop. A sergeant sent in advance was fired on, but no disposition was shown to bring on a serious action here, the nearer Indians withdrawing to the main body farther back as the troop advanced. Before Roe left the bench he saw far up the valley beyond the Indians in his front, a vast body of humans and animals moving southward—the main body of Indians withdrawing from the fight against Reno. On the hills across the valley he saw also some dark objects looking like buffalos lying down—some of Custer's dead horses.

As Bradley on the left of the column near the river advanced with his twelve mounted infantry he picked up 12 to 15 Indian ponies and sent them back to the command. Later, as it was getting dark, he approached a grove of trees with heavy underbrush into which he saw a number of Indians entering as he neared it. He believed it to be an ambush but felt it to be his duty to go on, his will and soldier's pride forcing his rebellious flesh to obey. It is worth observing here that Bradley was one of the truly brave who possess the moral courage to admit being frightened in the face of great danger. He and his command were saved in this case by the timely arrival of an order to return to the command. A little over a year later, at the Battle of the Big Hole, he faced such a situation again, and this time no order came. He entered the thicket and was shot dead in his tracks.

Colonel Gibbon's summary of the march from 5 to 8 o'clock in the afternoon gives us a clear picture of what developed in their front as they advanced, as well as an accurate description of the topography. Incidentally it also contains a suggestion of the manner in which the Indians in the village and the warriors around Reno were kept informed of the movements of the troops, reporting their numbers and warning them that among them were many of the dreaded "walking soldiers."

"After we had proceeded several miles," wrote Gibbon, "some stray ponies were picked up by the advanced guard, which were evidently strays from the Indian camp. On our left, the stream bordered with timber and brush wood, and some distance on our right the valley was bounded by low rolling hills. In our front the stream after cutting into the bluffs crossed the valley from right to left (west to east), the timber shutting out the view beyond, save above its top appeared a sharp mountain peak on the edge of which could now and then be indistinctly made out a few moving figures, and just beyond this peak the smoke appeared to have its origin. Up to this time no Indians had been seen, but shortly after one of our couriers came riding in from the front, and reported that in attempting to reach Custer's command he had run into a number of Indians in the hills, and was unable to proceed further. A company of cavalry was now thrown out to the hills on our right, and the column pushed forward as rapidly as the men could march, the infantry responding with alacrity and almost keeping up in pace with the horses. Small scattered bands now began to make their appearance on top of the hills up the river where the latter began to deflect its course northward, and as it grew dark more of them could be seen in the distance.

The "sharp mountain peak" mentioned by Gibbon is the highest point on the Weir ridges about a mile and a third from Reno Hill and is the one perfect receiving point for signals to be transmitted to the camps and the warriors around Reno. The best point from which to have observed the advance of Gibbon is the high ridge near Crow Agency, and suggestively enough it was upon this ridge the main body of warriors confronting Lieutenant Roe was stationed. From here signals could have been flashed directly to the high peak on the Weir ridges about 4 miles away.

"As night closed around us," continues Gibbon, "the command was halted and bivouaced in the open prairie; the scouting parties were called in, who reported seeing quite a large number of Indians on the distant hills, but in the gathering darkness nothing could be plainly made out. After watering and grazing the animals they were all carefully picketed inside the command formed in a square, guards established just outside, and the tired men sank to rest eight miles from the brave little band of fellow soldiers, which, unknown to us, was watching and waiting on the bleak bluffs of the river above."

The next morning they made a very early start, especially Bradley who was sent across the river to the hills on which the brown objects had been seen the evening before. The rest moved to the right around the loop in the river which had up to then obscured the view of the ground on which the Indian camps had stood. The first thing that attracted their attention after rounding the loop were two tepees about two miles up the valley, which, when they came to them, were found to contain 8 dead warriors, the first conclusive evidence that a fight had occurred. More sinister objects picked out of the litter near the tepees were a pair of bloody drawers with the name "Sturgis" on them, and a buckskin[49] coat with a bullet hole in it, recognized as having belonged to Lieutenant Porter of Troop I.

While they were at these tepees a messenger arrived from Bradley who reported the finding of several dead horses in a ravine. A little later Gibbon noticed a number of dark objects on a hill (Reno Hill) beyond the sharp peak which were finally identified as human beings but whether red or white could not be determined at once. About the same time three horsemen[50] were observed watching the command from Weir Peak. Some of the cavalry in advance now moved forward rapidly, and the three horsemen moved cautiously nearer and were finally seen to communicate with a staff officer sent forward by Gibbon. A few minutes later this officer came galloping back and reported that the three horsemen were scouts from Reno's command, and that they had said the Seventh Cavalry had been cut to pieces, and that Major Reno with a remnant was fortified on the bluffs.

This was the first word of the disaster coming from the living still on the field of action. But the dead had already spoken through Lieutenant Bradley, who had come up while they were watching the three horsemen, and in a trembling voice reported to Terry that he had found 196 bodies among the hills across the river.

Terry and Gibbon, at the head of the main column, now moved on toward the loop in the river opposite the present Garryowen station and were met by Lieutenants Wallace and Hare with their orderlies. Describing the meeting, Gibbon wrote: "Hands were clasped almost in silence, but we questioned eagerly with our eyes, and one of the first things they uttered was 'Is General Custer with you?' On being told that we had not seen him, they gave us hurriedly an account of the operations of the past two days, and the facts began to dawn on us. No one of the party which accompanied General Custer when the command was divided, about noon on the 25th, had been seen by the survivors, and our inference was that they were all, or nearly all, lying up in the hills where the scouting party had found the dead bodies."

Terry now accompanied Wallace and Hare who led him to Reno's entrenchments on the slope just west of the position on which he had made his stand during the fighting, while Gibbon brought his command into the river loop just below the point where Reno had crossed in retreat, and made camp.

The scene that followed Terry's arrival was one never to be forgotten by anyone who made a part of it. Wild cheering and choking sobs of relief until the grave look on the General's face brought a sudden, frozen silence. Terry raised his hand for attention and began to speak, tears coursing down his face into his gray beard, his voice all but strangled by an overpowering emotion as he told them what he had found among the hills a few miles downstream. So, that was it! Custer had not deserted them. Wholly unexpected the news came as a stunning blow to all of them, but it must have struck with special force those who had on the evening of the 25th damned Custer for running away to Terry and Gibbon, as they had supposed, leaving the greater part of his command to the Indians who swarmed about them in numbers seemingy numberless. We can well imagine that, as John Burkman put it: "some of 'em was sobbin' out loud. Some of 'em looked funny, their faces so white and twisted, the tears tricklin' down their cheeks, makin' white streaks through the powder black and dirt."[51]

CHAPTER 9

General Custer Rides into Legend

His March from the Lone Tepee
to Custer Hill. 2:20 to 4:40

WE NOW come to the most difficult chapter in the whole story of the battle of the Little Big Horn, a chapter concerned with events for the most part shrouded in mysteries in which are rooted a goodly share of the heated controveries that have bedeviled the study of our subject from the very beginning. It covers the passage of Custer and his five troops, "C," "E," "F," "I" and "L," from the Lone Tepee four and a half miles from the river, to the battlefield, a distance of 11 miles, more or less, by the route we believe he followed. He left the tepee around 2:20 and reached the hill on which he died, about 4:40, according to our timing of his movements.

Our narrative here necessitates a long and tedious analysis involving some repetitions to bring the picture into focus as Custer must have seen it at the time he sent Reno to pursue a body of Indians supposed to be fleeing down the valley of the Little Big Horn.

It has been surmised by some writers that Benteen's scout was not intended as a scout at all, but as a maneuver to bring him into the valley above the Indian village for the purpose of attack. There is nothing in the orders given Benteen, as far as the record shows, to justify such a conception. All Custer's movements up to this point indicate that he was in doubt concerning the location and dispositions of the Indians in the valley. Benteen's move was part of the reconnaissance the regiment was making from the Divide on. Benteen might run into Indians while engaged in this, and he was supposed to attack them if he did. Custer assumed the same for himself and Reno. We repeat here what has already been stated several times, that not until the Indians had been definitely located could there have been anything that can be called a plan of battle. Moreover, standard battle tactics were all but useless against such nimble and versatile fighters as these Plains Indians. Unless surprised and cornered they simply would not stay put to accommodate such tactics. The Indians, because of their superior mobility, held the initiative when out in the open, and thus compelled the troops to accommodate their tactics to those of the enemy. This usually left little room for more than the barest outline in the form of a plan. The line officer would have to plan as the fighting progressed, which is always true to some extent, but was especially so in Indian warfare. To a large extent it was this fact that determined Custer to move against the Indian village without reference to possible odds in order to reduce the extent of ground over which the warriors could maneuver. In other words, he tried to force the warriors to follow more nearly the tactics of the troops by compelling them to defend a fixed position. In this he largely succeeded, and had he not been deceived by appearances, and had he acted less pre- cipitately throughout after making actual contact, there is good ground in the evidence for thinking that no very great losses would have been incurred, though the Indians would have escaped.

The subject of the present chapter sets an exacting task for the historian; for, after Custer had passed the high ridges we have called "Weir Point," no white man except his orderly trumpeter, John Martin, saw him or any of his men alive except those who rode with him.[52] From this point on the history of the five troops must be reconstructed from the numerous, conflicting Indian stories, Custer's two orders, the route he followed, the firing heard, the nature of the terrain and the distribution of the dead men and horses on the battle field, the whole checked carefully against time and distance.

One very useful key to our method was supplied by the late W. M. Camp, in his field notes bought by R. S. Ellison (deceased 1945) and now presumably in possession of Mrs. Ellison. "It is amusing," he wrote, "to read the accounts of some writers who, ignorant of the facts, have sought to show how Custer, when he ordered Reno forward, intended Benteen to swing around to the left and come into the valley behind Reno. When Custer ordered Reno forward, neither he nor Reno, nor Benteen were aware of the existence of a village. No one in the command had as yet seen a single tepee except the lone one where they now were, which gave Custer the impression that the Sioux had pulled off the village, until he came out on the bluffs, and even then he did not see it all."

That the deception was such as Camp supposed is confirmed by Lieutenant DeRudio. Testifying at the Court of Inquiry, he said: "Pretty soon we came to a vacated village where there was a tepee with some dead Indians inside. The impression was that the Indians had left that village not long before."

In a preceding chapter we noted that Custer had struck a very heavy and fresh trail after resuming his march at 5 P. M. on the 24th. Whether or not he knew that this fresh trail was not made by the same body of Indians whose trail he had been following up to this point, we have been unable to determine. In any case, when at the Lone Tepee he could not have known that the Indians who, as he supposed, had "pulled off" the village, were now camped in one place to which the few warriors he had flushed were assumed to be fleeing. As to that he knew no more then than he knew when he sent Benteen to learn whether or not there were Indians up the valley. Dust in the valley at this time was taken as evidence that the village he thought he had all but surprised at the place he then was, was now continuing its flight in the valley. But if this was the main body of the enemy, it did not seem reasonable to suppose that they had not massed their warriors in his front to delay pursuit in the rough ground east of the river, for that was standard Indian practice. So, at least, any soldier experienced in Indian warfare would have reasoned, and as Custer actually seems to have done.[53]

This granted, the order to Reno becomes understandable. Otherwise Custer, who had up to this time been outstandingly successful as a commander both during the Civil War and later in his Indian campaigns in the south, had suddenly become an incompetent who could send 125 men, plus a few Indian scouts and civilians, to charge possibly 3000 warriors who were, man for man, as good or better than were the troops.

When the scientists, including the historians, comes in his analysis to anything as improbable as this he more than suspects that he is on the wrong trail, and starts over again in search of something less repugnant to reason and common sense.

The three objective facts upon which Custer based his action were all misread. The village had not been "pulled off" "not long before," but exactly a week before, though that fact was obscured by the fresh trail. The warriors he had flushed here were not a part of the village. They were the warriors of a small band of Cheyennes on their way to their tribesmen in the camps and did not flee to the village directly.⁵⁴ They fled down the trail for only a short distance and then turned northward to rejoin their non-combatants. The dust in the valley was not made by fleeing Indians. It was kicked up by the ponies being rushed into camp by the herdboys.

Just as Reno was leaving under an order that promised him support by "the whole outfit," Lieutenant Varnum, who had been scouting on the left of the column, rode up to Custer and reported that from a high point to the south he had seen a large body of Indians downstream in the valley. This did not seem to alarm Custer, for he proceeded rather slowly down the trail after receiving the report, then turned to the right after passing the headland between the main channel of Reno creek and a small tributary coming in from the northeast. Crossing the tongue of land between the two channels, he stopped for about ten minutes to water his horses, according to John Martin. This done, and again according to Martin, he quickened his pace and rode about 300 yards "straight ahead," before again turning to the right.

Martin's testimony was so confused, contradictory, and in many cases so at variance with known facts and the testimony of more coherent witnesses that both Recorder Lee and Mr. Gilbert, Reno's counsel, soon threw up their hands and dismissed him; and Colonel W. A. Graham nearly fifty years later, had no better luck with him. Nevertheless there is here an intriguing detail, Martin's statement that Custer rode straight ahead for about 300 yards after completing the watering of the horses, before he turned to the right again. Adjutant Cooke and Captain Keogh who had gone down to the river with Reno at a fast gait and had started back when Reno had nearly completed reforming his column after crossing, were about due at the place where Custer turned to the right, and the message brought by Cooke that the Indians were swarming up in great numbers against Reno may well have alarmed Custer and caused him to rush up to the top of the bluffs at almost charging speed to gain a point from which he could determine definitely what confronted him. This is, of course, conjecture; but if the reader will consult the map of the area involved he will see that it is in full accord with all the known facts. Things do not just happen. There is always a cause or reason for them. Custer had some reason for what he did after Reno had left, and the above conjecture supplies the only reason we have been able to conceive. It may be wrong for all that; but science, including history, advances from the known to the unknown and new knowledge via analysis and hypotheses. With this word of caution to the reader and a plea for patience, we proceed in our effort to find at least a plausible explanation for Custer's march from the Lone Tepee into the mists and legend.

It may be assumed, we think, that if the reader were in position to do so he would ask questions about as follows:

1. Why did Custer send Reno to make an all-out attack with his small force?

Answer. He believed the Indians were in wild flight and would not turn to do serious fighting. In any case he, Custer, would come into the fight as soon as Reno's attack had caused the Indians to show their hand. That is one of the things a vanguard attack is supposed to do.

2. In what way did he intend to support Reno when he gave the order?

Answer. We do not know, but unless otherwise stated in the order, the usual assumption is that the support will come from the rear. This, however, would depend on circumstances, especially on the position of the enemy and on the nature of his reaction to the attack of the advance guard.

3. Can you explain more definitely what you mean by that?

Answer. A flank attack is often more effective support than an attack in actual conjunction with the advance guard, and can sometimes be delivered so near the advance guard as to make possible a rally of the two forces in a single unit should that become desirable. Custer's first turn to the right, after receiving Varnum's report, seems to indicate that he had something of this kind in mind. In this case the support would have been given in less time than support from the rear.

4. What information, if any, did Custer receive after Reno left that could have caused him to decide on a flank attack?

Answer. The report of Varnum that he had seen a large body of Indians downstream in the valley. This proved definitely that the Indians supposed to be fleeing as suggested by the dust in the valley, were going downstream, and that Reno would, therefore, also go downstream. By heading toward Reno's line of advance he would be in action much sooner than by following his trail.

5. What indication is there in Custer's action that he at any time contemplated this kind of support?

Answer. His turning to the right after passing the headland, as already explained.

6. Why, then, did he not make such an attack?

Answer. Because he received the report of Cooke that the Indians were rushing up against Reno in heavy force. This was probably at the point where he turned still farther to the right about 300 yards from his watering place.

7. But did not that report indicate that Reno might be in need of support?

Answer. Yes, certainly, eventually.

8. Then why did he abandon his apparent intention to support Reno, by turning to the right?

Answer. Because he suspected that he had committed a grave tactical error in sending Reno to attack; that the evidence on which that order was predicated did not mean what it had appeared to mean. He was greatly alarmed by the report because it suggested that his scouts might, after all, have been right in their insistence that a village of unprecedented size was located a little downstream from where he then was. The report of Varnum had confirmed the scouts at least in part, and that of Cooke pointed to the same conclusion even more forcibly.

9. But would not that make it all the more necessary to go to the support of Reno?

Answer. Yes. But not necessarily at once. For Reno's force, if small, was still too large for the Indians to attempt to rush and destroy in hand-to-hand combat. The Indians used such tactics only in ambush or on extremely small bodies of troops. If Reno used discretion he would be able to hold out for a considerable time. Custer, therefore, had some time to inform himself definitely of the real situation and decide what was best to be done.

10. Then did he not definitely abandon his intention to give Reno some kind of support?

Answer. No. But he found he could not give it in the manner expected and as originally intended. Actually he created a diversion, rather belatedly it is true, but nevertheless in time to relieve the pressure on Reno, which probably saved the rest of the regiment from destruction before its scattered elements could be assembled for defense.

We learn from Sergeant Kanipe and Trumpeter Martin that Custer seemed to be in a great hurry after he turned northward, and went up the slope at a furious gallop, a distance of two miles more or less. When he halted many of the horses were so excited that they were all but out of control. Somewhere during this horse-killing ride two of the poor brutes reached the end of their endurance and were left behind along with their riders. The command was halted about 700 yards north of the knoll on which the Reno monument now stands, or about opposite the point where the Hodgson marker stood until recently.

Leaving his command halted, Custer, accompanied by Cooke and several others, rode westward to near the brink of the bluff for his first view of the village. He was seen here by DeRudio down in the valley with Reno, and by the Crow scouts who had been riding on the left of the column and were opposite the rear of it when it halted. One of these Crows, Goes-Ahead, is reported as saying: "As Custer swung off the trail after Reno left to cross the upper ford, there was an Arikara scout and three Crows with him. Custer rode to the edge of the high bank and looked over to the place where Reno's men were, as though planning his next move. When they (the Crows) had arrived at about the point where Hodgson's headstone was later placed, the three Crows saw the soldiers under Reno dismounting in front of the Dakota camp and they thought the enemy were 'too many'."

Taking this in connection with the further statement by Goes-Ahead that "close to where Reno and Benteen later in the day were attacked by the Dakotas, on the ridge above the river, the three crows were left behind," and Kanipe's statement that when the command halted Reno was seen charging down the valley, we have the exact picture in time. What Goes-Ahead means is that when the column halted the Crows were on Reno Hill and from there saw Custer go to the edge of the bluff, while they kept going, and that by the time they had gone the 700 yards, more or less, to opposite the position of Hodgson's marker, they saw Reno's men dismounting. This would indicate that Custer reached the edge of the bluff three or four minutes before Reno dismounted, which in the general time-sequences as we have worked them out, would be about 3:05. The reader will understand that this is only an estimate; for the last time the official timekeeper, Lieutenant Wallace, looked at his watch it was 2:00 o'clock when Custer was about a mile above the Lone Tepee. Everything after this was guess-work. But by constantly checking time against distance it is possible to keep spatial relationships approximately in order, which is the important fact rather than the sidereal or clock-time.

The instant Custer came to the edge of the bluff and looked upon the Indian village he knew that the order to Reno was a serious blunder. He might salve his conscience somewhat in the knowledge that this order had been given in good faith and was tactically correct for the circumstances as he had believed them to be. Still, it could have been but small comfort when he saw Reno approach the huge village nearly two miles in length, with only 112 enlisted men. If he followed his orders and plunged headlong into the swirling mass of enemies, how far would he get before his charge bogged down through the losses in both men and horses? And once brought to a standstill, how long before the survivors would be rushed and wiped out? Ten or fifteen minutes, perhaps. But why speculate? Destruction was certain if he charged into the village, as all in the command who later testified declared emphatically.

There were three or four minutes of dreadful suspense for the little group on the bluff as they watched Reno approach the river loop beyond which lay the great village. Would he turn to the left and pass its farthest point more than a mile and a half away to the west? If he did not a mother's son of them would they ever see again except, perhaps, as mutilated corpses. The suspense ended as the line of horsemen suddenly slithered to a halt, dismounted and went into action. In spite of the long, fast run down the valley and the presence of a large number of recruits, the thing was rather smartly done, according to DeRudio; and Custer, looking down on the scene from an elevation of 300 feet, expressed his appreciation with a cheer and a wave of his hat, an act of approval which neither Major Reno nor anyone else in his command except DeRudio saw, as far as is known, though parts of Custer's command were seen in motion near his point by both Varnum and Gerard a few minutes later.

The fear of what might be true which, as we believe, had led Custer to abandon his apparent intention to give Reno direct support and brought him to the top of the bluffs at a horse-killing pace, had now been justified.

But what was to be done now? The cautious, routine soldier would, in all probability, have recalled Reno instantly by trumpet, sent a company or two to the river and lined up the rest at the brink of the bluff to protect his crossing, and then fallen back on Benteen and the packs. Such a move would have betrayed his weakness and relieved the warriors of all fear of flank and rear attacks. They outnumbered the whole regiment five or six times, and would have swarmed after the retreating detachment from the very beginning. The regiment would have been halted in the valley of Reno Creek flanked by a maze of ravines, ridges and hills and offering a terrain perfectly suited to the Indian style of fighting, but next to impossible for cavalry. Crook, with about two and a half times Custer's force and fewer Indians to deal with, had faced just such a situation a week before on the upper Rosebud and had thought it prudent to withdraw after the warriors had broken contact with him; which, as the evidence seems to indicate, he would not have done had it been possible to pursue and fight the warriors in open ground.

But what could have been worse that what Custer actually did, the critic may ask. Here he was with a fourth of his regiment down in the valley unsupported, with hundreds of warriors fast encircling them. Benteen was an hour's march back on the trail, and the packtrain about twice that distance. And what does Custer do? He deliberately leaves Reno in the lurch and rushes four miles downstream evidently with the wild idea of attacking the village in the flank or rear! Sheer madness! The act of a fool, as Sitting Bull said, it is reported.

So it would have been had he made such an attack. But he did not attack when he had the opportunity to do so, and hence there is no basis for the assumption other than the fact that he continued his march downstream. On the other hand, all that he did or ordered done from this time on is wholly inconsistent with such an assumption.

Since the surface indications here do not make sense we must look deeper to discover Custer's plan of action as he was now hammering it out. If we start with the assumption, or working thesis that he realized the enemy was too strong to risk a definitive action, and that it was necessary to play for time until Gibbon came up, everything he did and ordered done after seeing the village, becomes clear and consistent. Having reached this conclusion he worked out the details as he rode along.

After leaving his lookout on the bluff he rode on for perhaps a quarter of a mile thinking over the situation and then sent Sergeant Kanipe to the packtrain with an order for it to come on "straight across country." A little farther on he came to the two high ridges now officially designated as Weir Point. The ravine down which the column was marching turns to the right at this point. Here he halted again and with his orderly, Martin and several others rode to the top of one of these ridges, probably the one nearest the river, and made another observation of the village. From this point he could see all, or very nearly all the camps he had not been able to see from his first observation point. Since he was in search of a good defensive position in which to reassemble the regiment and await the arrival of Gibbon, we must assume that while on this high point he scanned the ground downstream near the valley. If he did so he could hardly have failed to note the relatively high mass of land jutting into the valley about a mile below the lowest camp. This would be the ideal place for his purpose provided it contained a good defensive position; for, from this point he could push into the level valley easily because it offered very little opportunity for the warriors to dispute his passage. Once in the flat, open valley the troops would have had two pro- nounced advantages over the warriors, first in the fact that the carbine decidedly outranged all but a negligible number of the Indian weapons, and second, the valley offered an opportunity to use the mounted charge the Indians never dared to face head-on. Unfortunately the direction of the secondary slopes of this mass of land made it impossible to determine positively whether or not it contained a satisfactory defensive position. We shall see in a moment that there is some reason for thinking that he was not satisfied on this point. To make a serious mistake in this matter could easily lead to disastrous consequences. It was worth at least a few hundred yards extra marching to settle the doubt, if possible, and we believe that the detour we shall later de- scribe was made partly, at least, for this purpose.

Up to this point we have depended solely on analysis and constructive reasoning to discover Custer's plan of action. There is, however, one piece of oral evidence completely confirming our major thesis. This is in the field notes of the late W. M. Camp and reads as follows: "The remark of Bouyer to Curley, that Custer was *seeking a high point to await the arrival of the other troops;* and Bouyer's remark that he did not think they would come, having probably been 'scared out,' shows that Custer had probably been waiting for Benteen, and watching for the result of Reno's battle."

When we received this passage from the Camp notes from Mr. Ellison our researches on this part of our subject had been virtually completed and a first rough draft of the narrative sub- mitted to other students for criticism. It can, therefore, be easily imagined that this flat statement purporting to have come from Custer himself was rather startling. It would be entirely human for us to assume that this positively settles the matter. Unfortunately human nature is not always scientific, wherefore we are forced to content ourselves with the statement that this story belongs in a category of evidence the historian is inclined to accept as probably substantially true, for reasons which will appear in a moment in connection with a general criticism of the Camp material.

The Crow scouts, including Bouyer, had passed along the high bluffs just above the valley, while Custer had turned northeastward at Weir Point. They were still here at the time Custer reached a point in Medicine Tail Coulee about a mile from the river where there was an irregular open space or flat created by erosion and consequent drift brought down by several branches coming down from opposite directions.

From their position on the bluffs Bouyer and Curley saw Reno retreat, and Bouyer signalled the fact to Custer, after which they rode down and joined him. This, also, is a story Curley told Camp. It tallies rather closely with our timing of the movements of Custer and Reno, which is, for us at least, a point in favor of credence.

From this as well as from the time Custer's presence north of the Coulee was discovered by some of the warriors who had followed Reno to the bluffs, it would seem that he halted on this flat for fifteen to twenty minutes. He might have done this to let the hard-driven horses catch their breath, or because he was in doubt about something and was thinking it over; or, finally, to give the rest of the regiment time to shorten the distance between himself and them, before taking the final, dangerous plunge in search of a position on which to make his stand. Now that he knew that Reno had fled to the bluffs where he would soon receive reinforcements, there was less need of haste in creating a diversion. He knew that as soon as he, Custer, mounted the high ground north of the Coulee he would be discovered and that then the warriors would swarm up against him. Summed up logically, this meant that action would now be quickly transferred from the upper to the lower end of the village; for the rush of the warriors northward to meet the new threat would be followed by the rush of the troops down Custer's trail. His orders to McDougall and Benteen showed that he did not want them to go into the valley in support of Reno, but to move as fast as possible downstream east of the river for a rally of the whole regiment somewhere below the village.

To an experienced soldier on the ground all this must have

been routine stuff hardly requiring conscious rationalization to spell out its meaning. They all knew that Custer had gone northward east of the river. They heard his firing and saw the warriors rushing downstream both in the valley and along the bluffs east of the river. Nor is there any doubt in our own mind that all concerned understood clearly that Custer was trying to rally the whole regiment somewhere downstream. We have shown in a preceding chapter how Reno and Benteen tried to carry out Custer's intention and why their attempt failed.

Coming back now to Weir Point, when Custer had completed his observations he dashed back to the head of his column and went on again at a fast gait down the immense ravine that empties into Medicine Tail Coulee about two miles directly east of the Middle Ford. After going about 300 yards[55] he sent Martin with the much-discussed order to Benteen: "Benteen, come on, big village, be quick, bring packs. W. W. Cooke. P. S. Bring packs."

When Benteen received this order around 4 o'clock two miles, more or less, from the river, he hardly knew what to make of it; for, less than 15 minutes before this Sergeant Kanipe had brought him an order which, though it was not intended for him, called for the packtrain to hurry forward straight across country. We have already discussed this in the chapter on Benteen's scout; but something went wrong with this, making it necessary to continue our dry analysis of the evidence in an attempt to discover what it was.

In the first place, was this written order worded exactly as Custer had given it? It is known that Cooke was very careful in all matters pertaining to his duties as adjutant. And that very quality of faithfulness to duty may have led to a fatal mistake in this instance. We are dependent here entirely on Martin's conflicting stories. In his testimony at the Court of Inquiry he said that Custer gave the order directly to Cooke. In a later account he said Custer turned to him, Martin, and called out: "I want you to take a message to Captain Benteen. Ride as fast as you can and tell him to hurry. Tell him it's a big village, and I want him to be quick, and to bring the ammunition packs."

Now, it may be perfectly safe to entrust a brief and simple order containing only one or two items, to an experienced soldier who understands clearly the language in which that order is given. It was anything but safe to give such an order in English to an Italian who was little more than a boy, had been in the country only about a year and understood English only imperfectly. This Cooke would have grasped instantly and his intervention came as a matter of course, if the order was given as above related. As Martin turned his horse to go Cooke shouted; "Wait, orderly, I will give you a message." Both pulled aside out of the way of the column and Cooke hurriedly scribbled the order as it was received by Benteen.

The significant thing to note here is that in the Martin statement at the Court of Inquiry the order called specifically for the *ammunition* packs, not for the whole packtrain to which an order to hurry forward had been sent just before the command reached Weir Point.

Here every rational consideration leads us to think that the account Martin gave to Colonel Graham expresses the truth rather than the one he gave to the Court of Inquiry, except the omission of the word "ammunition" by Cooke, as we believe.

If we accept this, then Cooke either did not hear the word "ammunition" or, in his haste, failed to get it on paper, his mind running too far ahead of his pencil. The probability, however, is that he failed to hear it. He was undoubtedly riding on the left of Custer, the usual position for the adjutant, and Custer had turned partly in his saddle—to the right, naturally—to shout the order to Martin who was a few yards behind him. In the noise made by the feet of their own horses and by the fast-riding column behind them, it must have been difficult to catch every word of a speaker whose face was turned away.

Whatever may be the truth about this, there can be little doubt that Custer wanted the ammunition, but not because he was then in need of it, or expected soon to be, as has been supposed. He had not yet fired a shot and was, at the moment, actually riding away from the village. Even had he intended to attack by way of the Middle Ford, he still had about three miles to go by the route to which he was now committed. Meanwhile Reno had been firing heavily for at least 15 minutes, and would be completely out of ammunition in about 45 minutes more of firing, as the record shows; for his men fired, on the average, at the rate of about 100 rounds per hour. The fact that this order left Reno seemingly entirely out of the picture in the matter of the reserve ammunition, is in itself an indication that he did not expect him to remain to fight it out where he was; for it is absurd to assume that he intended deliberately to sacrifice him and his command. That is what such an assumption amounts to.

There is no rational way out of this except to assume that Custer wanted the ammunition safe at the rallying-point of the regiment where it would probably be badly needed before the fighting was over. He expected Reno to flee to the bluffs when he should find it necessary to do so, or when he saw Benteen on his own, Custer's trail. He had not recalled him when he saw him go into action because, since the Indians had been alerted, he must be left there to pinch-hit for the regiment until those back on the trail had come up. Then he could join them and go on with them to the point of assembly—that is, to the defensive position Custer would by that time have chosen. This was a nasty item in the plan, but there was no help for it after the mistake of sending him had been made.

Had the order said definitely "Bring ammunition packs," Benteen would have known at once what to do. The 24,000 rounds of carbine ammunition had been packed on the strongest and most reliable mules capable of going much faster than the weakest animals in the train which set the pace for the rest. Apparently Custer was resigned to the possible loss of the packtrain. He saw that it might not be possible to get it through. The loss would result in serious inconvenience, but would not be fatal if the ammunition was saved. It could not be defended against any considerable body of warriors while it was on the march; but the 130 men in charge of it would probably be able to take care of themselves if Custer's demonstration at the lower end of the village came in time to divert the attention of the warriors from what was still back on the trail. There is ample evidence that it did come in time to save Reno's command from annihilation and the whole from serious molestation until after Custer had been destroyed.

This bungled order to Benteen shouted from the back of his galloping "Vic" with such blythe disregard of the necessary precautions, was, in effect, Custer's farewell to the best soldier in his regiment, one whose friendship he had desired in vain but whom he knew he could trust. Nor was that trust misplaced; for in spite of all the bitter criticisms levelled at Benteen, and all the long-winded explanations seeking to show why it could not have been done, we assert our conviction that it would have been attempted and in all probability successfully, had that order come to him worded as Martin says it was worded by Custer when he gave it to him originally. With this order dispatched, Custer passed into legend. Except for a hasty backward glance by Martin no white man, except those who perished with him, ever saw him or any of his men alive again, as far as is known, though the crop of "sole survivors" threatens to exceed the number of men in the battalion![56]

As far as the direct evidence is concerned we have to depend from here on on the Indian accounts which, for the most part, reflect the theories and preconceptions of the white questioners rather than the knowledge of those they questioned. What we make of this will depend largely on the degree of our own emotional detachment relative to the nature of the varied conclusions that may be drawn from this huge mass of conflicting stories.

It is in this problem of conflicting evidence that the historian undergoes his severest test, and it is doubtful that anyone ever has or will come out of it with a grade of 100%.

A working thesis is an absolute necessity for the historian. It is to him what the probe is to the surgeon. But he must not become so enamored of it that he cannot modify it or discard it altogether when the evidence demands it. And above all he must avoid the blinding tendency of his thesis, the unconscious tendency to overlook everything that does not lie directly in its path. In other words, he must not make "blinders" of his thesis.

The field notes of Mr. Camp, some of which we are using here, illustrate this perfectly. It is quite evident that Mr. Camp came to his researches in the field already fully convinced that Custer had attacked at the ford, that the Indians he questioned detected this and answered his questions accordingly.[57] He says that he took great pains to avoid "leading questions," and we have no doubt that he was entirely sincere in giving us this assurance. Nevertheless, when Standing Bear told him that Custer's men did not fire into the village but passed from Medicine Tail straight across to the battlefield ridge, he tried repeatedly, but without success, to induce him to change this statement. And when he tried by indirect leading to elicit from Curley a statement showing Custer had attacked at the ford, he drew another blank, if not something worse than a blank. Because we have here a good illustration of the pitfalls to be avoided, we quote the incident exactly as it appears in the excerpt received from Mr. Ellison.

"On another note Camp asked Curley, when he and Bouyer on Bouyer Hill saw Custer's command up Medicine Tail, was it standing still or coming down the coulee?, and noted, "It was coming.""

On another note, he asked Curley when he and Bouyer went from bluff down into Medicine Tail Coulee, did Custer remain there any length of time? with notation: "No, kept going right on."

On another note Camp asked Curley, in retreating from the river, what was the formation, column or skirmish line? What officer did he see on this retreat, and where was he, in front or rear? What was Custer doing down at river and how long did he wait down there? with the notation on the last question: "No time at all."

Can we not see Curley staring at Camp nonplussed, as if to say "Why, what are you talking about?" He could understand what Camp meant about Custer coming down the coulee and halting in it, but he knew nothing about a "skirmish," a "retreat" or a "wait," simply because none of these things were in the factual picture in his mind, and so he ignored them in his reply. Years later he told a fellow tribesman, Russell White Bear, what we believe to be the truth. In a letter to Mr. Dustin in 1938 White Bear said that Curley had told him that when Custer left Medicine Tail he turned to the right, but sent the Gray Horse Troop down the coulee toward the river.

The question may be asked: "Why do you select the exceptions rather than the rule, the three or four statements inconsistent with the great bulk of the rest?" Precisely because they *are* exceptional as not being the product of Camp's "leading," something of the truth that got through in spite of the suggestions in the nature of the questions betraying what was expected or desired.

In a general way this Camp material is typical of the great mass of Indian accounts. In sharp contrast to this are the accounts Dr. Thomas B. Marquis secured from the Cheyennes whose camp stood almost directly opposite the mouth of Medicine Tail Coulee. In them there is very little that is vague or obscure. There is a total absence of rhetoric and oral dramatization. There is an abundance of drama reminding us of Xenophon and Thucydides. Marquis had known these Cheyennes for years and was on the friendliest terms with them; and it is quite clear that they understood that he wanted them to tell him the truth however unpalatable some of it might be. As a rule their specific, objective facts are localized in both time and space and can, therefore, be checked on the ground. We have checked some of them on Custer field and found them in every instance to be exact.

All the Cheyennes consulted by Dr. Marquis over a period of years, stated positively and without hesitation, that Custer was not at any time in Medicine Tail Coulee or nearer the ford than where the bodies of his men were found. When they first saw him he was on a ridge about two miles east of the river. Three Cheyennes and several Sioux raced their ponies up there and fired a few long-distance shots at the troops.

This is, in part, born out by Mrs. Spotted Horn Bull and her husband who told Godfrey that Custer was never near the ford, and Godfrey himself said that on the day of the burials he and his orderly, Pennwell, rode to the ridge east of the field and saw there a trail made by shod horses, which did not impress him then because, like all the rest, he was then obsessed with the officers' "working thesis," or natural assumption that Custer's object had been to attack the village in the flank or rear. At the Court of Inquiry less than two years after the battle, all the officers questioned on this point replied either non-committally or said there was no evidence of a fight here, Benteen remarking that if there had been a fight there must have been some casualties in both men and horses, but since no bodies of either were found he did not believe there had been a fight here. In fact the only evidence presented that Custer had passed here were the tracks of two shod horses and the body of Sergeant Butler 600 yards or more northeast of the ford. Neither fact signifies anything to the point in question, for under and around the body of Butler were found many empty cartridge cases showing that he had fought here alone.⁵⁸ As to the tracks of two shod horses, if they had been part of a trail made by a body of cavalry, the Indian ponies would have trampled them out with the rest.

Recorder Lee said in his *Summation:* "Leaving out mere matter of opinion, it appears to me from all the testimony that General Custer never attempted a crossing at ford "B". He must have gone around the head of the ravine, and evidently sought to attack the village lower down." The ravine referred to was, of course, Medicine Tail Coulee.

This is what the Cheyennes believed because Custer had not come down far enough for them to see him in the coulee; and Marquis, basing his opinion on what they had told him, traced Custer's route on his map accordingly.

When Benteen, who denied on the stand that Custer had been at the ford, was asked how near he might have come to it, he replied: "Three furlongs (660 yards) I should say."

Some pages back we said Custer had halted on a flat in Medicine Tail about a mile from the river, and later quoted Curley as having told Russell White Bear that Custer, when he left here, turned to the right and sent the Gray Horse down the coulee.

We believe that the statement by Benteen to the Court of Inquiry and the one by Curley to White Bear tie in and are mutually confirmatory; for, when Benteen with part of his company went to examine the Custer Battlefield on the 27th, he went down what he called the "gorge" up which the warriors had swarmed on the evening of the 25th. He then believed that Custer had gone down this gorge to Medicine Tail, but later changed his mind and told the Court of Inquiry that he thought Custer had gone "east of the second divide and not to the river at all;" which is to say he had turned to the right at Weir Point, as Martin and Goes-Ahead said. The gorge enters Medicine Tail at the flat about a mile from the ford, on which we believe Custer halted for some time, and where Bouyer and Curley must have rejoined him, unless in this also the Camp notes are unreliable.

It is not difficult to follow Benteen's mental process here. Although he had gone down the gorge in the belief that he was on Custer's trail he had found no signs of a trail here and reasoned that the Indian ponies had trampled it out. Since the warriors had come up Medicine Tail to get to the mouth of the gorge, Custer's trail had been obliterated there also. But if Custer had left the coulee before reaching the ford, to go to the battlefield, the shod horses would have left a plain mark on the north cutbank as they climbed out. The cut bank was too high for some distance below the flat for horses to climb without great difficulty, if at all. Farther down it would not have been difficult to get out if the bank was then as it is at present.

Now, remembering that Curley said Custer sent the Gray Horse down the coulee, and knowing that it certainly did not go to the ford, it must have left the coulee at some point between the flat and the river. If it did, where did it go? Where, if not to the ridge a half mile north of the coulee where Mr. Blummer years ago found many empty cartridge cases and other material showing that troops had passed here and fired on Indians between them and the coulee. Later Colonel Nye, R. G. Cartwright and Captain Luce have found more cases, in all, several hundred. Since Custer had turned to the right with his four remaining companies, it could not have been he who had this skirmish here, which, in any case, could hardly have taken place if the Gray Horse had passed to Custer battlefield by going between the ridge and the river, for if it had the warriors would have stopped to dispose of it before going on to Custer. Moreover, it is absurd to suppose that the Gray Horse was sent on a wholly pointless venture at the ford or to pass to the battlefield by this route.

Remembering further that Benteen said he thought Custer might have come to within about 660 yards of the river, he must have had some evidence in mind leading him to this conclusion. What evidence could he have had other than the scratched-up cutbank where the Gray Horse scrambled out to go to the ridge where the evidence of a skirmish was found? When he passed down the coulee he must have been on the alert for a trail leading out of the coulee to the battlefield; but if he did see it it did not impress him at the time because, like Godfrey who saw the trail east of the field, he was obsessed by the working thesis that Custer must have gone to the ford to attack. As to the actual fighting, Benteen worked out his own guess within a week after the event and described it in a letter to his wife dated July 4. We quote this part of his letter exactly as it stands in the copy we received from Captain Luce:

"From that point (Weir Point. C. K.) Cooke sent the note to me by Martin, which I have quoted on 1st page. I suppose after the five companies had closed up somewhat Custer started down for the village, all throats bursting themselves with cheering (So says Martin). He had 3½ to 4 miles to go before he got to the ford—as the village was on the plain on opposite side to Custer's column to cross at all, is a moot question, but I am of the opinion that nearly—if not all of the five companies got into the village—but were driven out immediately—flying in great disorder and crossing by two fords instead of the one by which they had entered. "E" Co. going by the left (Note by C. K.: he means the ford at the mouth of the deep ravine running up to the battle-field almost directly north in which 18-20 bodies of "E" Troop were found) and "F", "I" and "L" by the same one they crossed. What became of "C" Co., no one knows—they must have charged them below the village, gotten away—or have been killed in the bluffs on the village side of the stream—as very few of "C" Co. horses have been found. . . . After the Indians had driven them across, it was a regular buffalo hunt for them and not a man escaped. We buried 203 of the bodies of Custer's command the second day after the fight—The bodies were as recognizable as if they were in life."

Several questions are now clamoring for answers. Why did Custer halt so long on the flat in Medicine Tail, 15 to 20 minutes? Camp said it was half to three-quarters of an hour, which we think too long because it is out of line with the time Custer's firing was heard by Reno's men on the hill and by Gerard in the valley. Camp also said "Bouyer did a lot of talking to Custer when he joined him and kept talking while they were riding side by side."

Why did Custer turn to the right, and where did he go?

Why did he send the Gray Horse down the coulee toward the ford?

As to the first question, we may ask another: What could Bouyer and Custer have been talking about so much if not about the defensive position Custer was still seeking? When they left the flat in search of that position they were still talking. Both knew that as soon as they came out on the ridges they would be seen and that swarms of warriors would come out against them. This meant that serious action was close at hand, and still no position such as his plan called for. He could guess that he would have to hold that position at least an hour before reinforcements arrived. That was a long time for his small command unless the position was a good one or the warriors were disinclined to risk much. The risks were great enough at best, and it was worth a few minutes' delay to let his horses catch their breath while he questioned Bouyer carefully about the general topography toward the northwest, and in particular about the land mass about a mile below the ford, the *perfect location* he could not have failed to note while he was on Weir Point. But from Weir Point all the minor features of this small plateau are shut off by the ridge the Indians called Greasy Grass Hill, or ridge. Also the distance of three miles was too great for him to obtain anything more than a very general impression of the topography of the place even had the view not been shut off by the intervening ridge.

There were only two ways of settling the doubts. One was to go there with his whole command, taking the chance that nothing would be found that could serve. Failure in this case could easily lead to destruction, for, as Lieutenant Hare pointed out at the Court of Inquiry, mounted action was impossible or useless on this kind of ground, and the warriors could easily have eluded any number of charges and at the same time continued firing on the troops. This is the sense or meaning of what he said. The alternative was to go to some high point or ridge from which he could look down upon the whole area likely to become involved in the coming action. Just such a ridge is the high one about a mile east of the field. From the flat in the coulee this ridge stood out invitingly, towering high above all the ground toward the west.

In our opinion Custer passed over this ridge and thoroughly examined the terrain in question, while the Gray Horse went down the coulee until it found a point where it could scramble over the cut bank, and then started out for the ridge about a half mile north of the coulee to the 3400 elevation marked on the Geological Survey, and waited there while Custer passed along and made his observations. We have been over this farther ridge several times and can say positively that from there the details of Custer field stand out clear and sharp. Both the Calhoun position on the east end and that of Custer at the Hill can be clearly seen. Either of them could have been held for hours by the Custer battalion alone and both of them together by the whole regiment, with the sloping plain between absolutely untenable by an enemy not entrenched.

But even if Custer had been satisfied by his observations from Weir Point that a satisfactory defensive position existed on the ground that became his battlefield, it is probable that he would still have sent the Gray Horse over the nearer ridge while he passed over the other, for he was now setting the stage for a double holding action in which maneuvering and bluffing are expedients always used when possible. The chief desideratum of such an action is time—time wasted for the enemy and gained for the expected reinforcements, in this case Terry and Gibbon eventually and more urgently for the other detachments of his own regiment. As we see it the move by the Gray Horse was designed to worry the Indians about a threatened attack by way of the Middle Ford, a part of the bluff he was now making. By taking the rest of his battalion farther north he created speculation, doubt and hesitation until he turned toward the river, clearly indicating that he intended to attack from down the valley. This double move delayed the concentration of the warriors for a good half hour and incidentally brought them toward the river and down the valley away from his own trail and thus out of the way of the other detachments now presumably rushing forward at all possible speed to rejoin him.[59]

While Custer was passing over the eastern ridge the Gray Horse, dismounted and deployed as skirmishers, moved slowly along the lower ridge downward toward the deep ravine sometimes called "North Medicine Tail," the horse holders behind them and completely sheltered by the crest of the ridge. When Custer approached the point of the ravine toward which the Gray Horse was moving he fired down the ravine to drive back the warriors who had ridden up here from the ford to take part in the fight against the Gray Horse. It was about this time that Varnum on Reno Hill, on hearing a sudden burst of heavy firing, exclaimed: "Jesus Christ, Wallace, hear that? And that?" This heavy fire cleared the way for the Gray Horse to cross the ravine to rejoin Custer, and then the whole battalion rode up the slope to the Calhoun position and on to the end of the battleridge at Custer Hill, and halted.[60]

Did this maneuver accomplish what Custer had expected of it? We believe that it did, as the following account by a very intelligent and accurate eye-witness seems to show—Mrs. Spotted Horn Bull, who was at the ford while the troops passed from Medicine Tail Coulee to Custer Hill, and then seems to have gone downstream to nearly opposite the battlefield.

"Our chiefs and young men," she said, "rode quickly down to the end of the village opposite the hill upon which there now stands the great stone put up by the whites where Long Hair fell. Between that hill and the soldiers was a ravine which started from the river opposite the camp of the Sans Arcs (North Medicine Tail), and ran all around the butte. To get to the butte Long Hair must cross the ravine; but from where he was riding with his soldiers, he could not see into the ravine nor down to the bank of the river. The warriors of my people, of all the bands, the Sans Arcs, the Cheyennes, the Brule, the Minniconjous, the Oglala, the Blackfeet, all had joined with the Uncpapa on our side of the Greasy Grass and opposite the opening of the ravine. Soon I saw a number of the Cheyennes ride into the river, then some young men of my band (Uncpapa), then others, until there were hundreds of warriors in the river and running up the ravine. When some hundreds had passed the river and gone into the ravine, the others who were left, still a very great number, moved back from the river and waited for the attack."[61]

A little farther along in her account she said: "I saw Crazy Horse lead the Cheyennes into the water and up the ravine; Crow King and the Hunkpapas went after them." This was, of course, downstream opposite the battlefield, and the "ravine" in this case is the one which runs up to the battleridge from the northwest. The warriors to whom she refers here were those who had "moved back from the river and waited"—waited to see from which direction Custer would strike. She does not mention any firing by Custer or any halt before he reached the hill. This may be simply an omission, or it may be because she was at one of several points near the ford from which the skirmish ridge cannot be seen, and so missed this part altogether. According to Goes-Ahead, one of the three Crows who went along the river bluffs to near Medicine Tail, the troops who did the firing on the skirmish ridge were dismounted and "standing behind the line," behind the crest of the ridge, he meant, no doubt, for there is where the cartridge cases have been found.

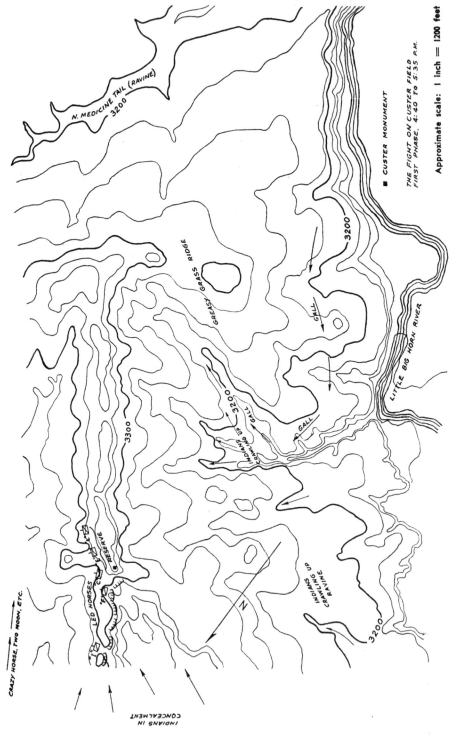

CRAZY HORSE, TWO MOON, ETC.

INDIANS IN
CONCEALMENT

N. MEDICINE TAIL (RAVINE)
3200

GREASY GRASS RIDGE

3200

INDIANS UP
CRAWLING GALL

GALL

GALL

3300

LED HORSES

RESERVE

TWO

INDIANS UP
CRAWLING
RAVINE

3200

LITTLE BIG HORN RIVER

3200

N

■ CUSTER MONUMENT

THE FIGHT ON CUSTER FIELD
FIRST PHASE, 4:40 TO 5:35 P.M.

Approximate scale: 1 inch = 1200 feet

CHAPTER 10

The Action on Custer Field

Explanatory Remarks

IF we wish to describe a battle intelligibly we must begin at the beginning and follow the action step by step to the end. Among civilized nations battles are fought by troops organized in definite units whose formations and manner of movement are known. The Custer battalion was composed of five troops or companies each commanded by two commissioned officers assisted by a number of sergeants and corporals. A troop might act as a unit or as two or more separate platoons. The basic unit in all evolutions was the set of fours, except in actual fighting in skirmish line where the individual was left more or less free though not at liberty to break the battle formation. Under no circumstances, except stark panic or the death of every commissioned and non-commissioned officer, would either the larger or smaller units scatter or wander about aimlessly. When they went anywhere they did so for a reason and under orders. In the course of action they might be crowded back or rush forward without specific orders, but they would continue to act as a unit, not as a rabble. Knowing these facts it is usually possible to reconstruct an action by a study of the manner in which the bodies of the slain are distributed over the field. No description can be satisfactory in which the various units appear from nowhere, are left in a certain place and the bodies of their members later found elsewhere. Time sequences and spatial relationships must be made clear and kept so throughout. This is something almost entirely missing in every description of the Custer battle we have read. The reason for this is to be found in the vagueness and inconsistencies of the evidence at hand.

In writing this chapter we have kept all these things constantly in mind. We do not flatter ourselves with the belief that all our constructions are true in detail. We hope that others will discover any mistakes we may have made and correct them. On the other hand we make no

apology for using the direct remains as the best material
we have for the study of the battle. It is a method long
established among historians, who invariably use such
material whenever it is available as a check on the notor-
iously tricky oral evidence. In this instance, however, there
is a difficulty in the fact that the actual remains are no
longer in evidence. The headstones, or markers, on the
field do not represent the exact truth, thanks to irresponsible official action almost unbelievably stupid in placing markers haphazardly where no bodies were found.
Further reference to this will be made at the appropriate place in this chapter.

About the time Custer with his whole battalion was moving
up the slope toward the Calhoun position the warriors who had
ridden downstream, as described by Mrs. Spotted Horn Bull, were
crossing the river west of the battlefield to spread out on the plain
southwest of Custer Hill and in the deep, irregular depression to
the west and northwest. Others, including Crazy Horse and Two
Moon, passed farther on into the ravine that runs up to the
battleridge at a sharp angle and breaks into two branches at the
Calhoun position, with a short spur continuing on toward the
battleridge near the place where the first platoon of Troop I
(Keogh) was destroyed. Still others crossed the river at the ford
at the mouth of the deep ravine running about straight north to
the battlefield where it breaks into many branches over the whole
space between the battleridge and Greasy Grass Ridge, or hill,
as the Indians called it.

The warriors who had come up the deep ravine from the
Middle Ford and those who had been sniping with the Gray
Horse Troop on the ridge, drifted westward and also came to the
field by way of this ravine. A few were still coming from this direction when Wooden Leg crossed the Middle Ford after returning
from the Reno fight. When he arrived on the field the whole
battalion was still together on the ridge with only a little long-
distance sniping going on. Kate Bighead, who came to the field
about the same time, tells the same story in substance. She also
crossed at the Middle Ford, and, riding northward over the open
ground, passed near, or over the Calhoun position near which
she saw a few warriors but evidently no troops. From here she
passed down the ravine north of the battleridge, looking for her
nephew, Noisy Walking, among the warriors now making their
way up this ravine. Not finding him, she circled around westward,
coming finally to Greasy Grass Ridge to a point about south of

Custer Hill, or a little east of south. And still no fighting except the slow, almost harmless sniping, though the deep gulch and ravines between her and Custer Hill were now crowded with warriors, largely Cheyennes and Ogalalas. A few others had crawled over Greasy Grass Ridge a little farther east and concealed themselves in minor depressions, in the grass and behind clumps of sage brush.

Some of these movements were within plain sight of Custer as he rode on toward the little knoll at the end of the ridge, for, while the troops probably kept to the even slope to the right, Custer himself would naturally ride over the crest of the ridge to be able to see what the warriors were doing. The ridge is too narrow in places for a column of fours to pass over without considerable trouble for the outside files. The greater part of the Indian movement was, however, out of sight in the deep ravines and in the valley behind the bluffs; and it is certain that those who entered the ravine north of the ridge had not gotten up far enough for Custer to see them as he passed, as will become evident later.

It should be stated here definitely that Custer took his whole battalion down to the west end of the ridge while these movements were taking place, and that the action began here, not on the east end of the ridge. This was made quite clear by Mrs. Spotted Horn Bull in her account given to McLaughlin at the Spotted Tail Agency in 1909, from which we have quoted in the preceding chapter. Quoting still further from this account: "But the sun was no longer overhead when the warwhoop of the Sioux sounded from the river bottom and the ravines surrounding the *hill* at the *end* of the ridge where Long Hair had taken his stand. Then the men of the Sioux nation led by Crow King, Hump, Crazy Horse and many other great chiefs, rose up on all sides of the *hill,* and the last we could see from our side of the river was a great number of gray horses. The smoke of the shooting and the dust of the horses shut out the hill, and the soldiers fired many shots, but the Sioux shot straight and the soldier fell dead." [61(a)]

This tells us that when she saw this Mrs. Bull was across the river at a point from which she could look up the comparatively open slope northeastward toward Custer Hill. The Gray Horse Troop crossed her line of vision as it came down from the Hill to take position in the skirmish line the markers show stood here at one stage of the fighting. Mrs. Bull was an Uncpapa Sioux

whose intelligence, frankness and truthfulness impressed Godfrey
no less than it did McLaughlin; and what she says here is fully
confirmed by other witnesses, among them another Indian woman,
either a Cheyenne or an Ogalala who was just as intelligent,
truthful and accurate in her descriptions, and in a much better
position to see the Gray Horse Troop and what happened to it.
We shall come to that later. Here it is necessary to complete the
account of the initial movements of the warriors to block Custer's
way to the village.

While Crazy Horse, Two Moon and others were crawling up
the north ravine "Gall . . . rode along the bench by the river
to where Long Hair had stopped with his men," said Mrs. Bull.
In this statement she corrects a long-standing misconception concerning the route by which Gall came to the field and his position after he arrived. According to Godfrey, Gall came up the
dry run, or deep ravine sometimes called North Medicine Tail
which runs up from the Middle Ford in a north-northeast direction and passes about a third of a mile east of the Calhoun
position. From what Mrs. Bull says it is clear that he came to
the field by the same deep ravine south of the Hill that most of
the others used; but finding the ground here already crowded with
warriors he turned up the first branch north of Greasy Grass
Ridge and followed it to the east end of the battlefield where it
breaks into a number of branches leading up to the angle in the
ridge and to the east wing of it. Here he remained concealed
until the troops were driven within reach, at first a few members
of the Gray Horse and later Calhoun's men.

As Custer was riding along the ridge he could see down to
the southwest, in the little valley already mentioned several times,
and on the small plateau on which the National Military Cemetery
was later established, a large number of mounted warriors riding
back and forth "putting on a show" but evincing no inclination
to attack. To the west and northwest of the Hill the ground is
much broken up by a deep, irregular ravine which splits up into
numerous branches as it approaches the ridge, forming many
pockets and hillocks. It afforded perfect cover for hundreds of
warriors and is the only place from which a mass attack on the
Hill could be launched without crossing a long stretch of open
ground. Directly opposite this is a low, flat spur of the main
battleridge running several hundred yards northwestward. Back
of this to the east across a deep, narrow valley is a second ridge

This photograph, taken about 1926 from the western slope of the Custer battle ridge, shows markers of Troops "C" and "E"; the terrain sloping down to the river; and the gullies which concealed those Indians who attacked from the south and west.

nearly parallel with this spur. This ends in a headland about 160 yards from the main ridge.

When Custer arrived on the Hill he must have noticed at once this danger spot to the northwest and ordered Keogh and Yates to deploy their troops, "I" and "F" respectively, on this spur to check any move the warriors might make from this direction. These troops fired a few rounds from the saddle, then dismounted and engaged in a slow exchange of shots with the enemy, part of it directed against the warriors in the open to the southwest. Their horses were, of course, led a few paces to the rear where the ridge protected them from the enemy fire. The three remaining companies were held in reserve close at hand north of the main ridge.

The Cheyennes say that this sniping continued for about an hour and a half before the serious fighting began. They admitted, however, that this was only a guess by the old men of the tribe. But if they included in this the light skirmish with the Gray Horse Troop from near Medicine Tail, it agrees very closely with our own time table and the constructions based on it. The skirmish near Medicine Tail began around 4:15. Custer arrived on the Hill around 4:40, leaving 25 minutes of skirmishing before he got there. This agrees with the testimony of Gerard, who said the skirmishing along the line of march lasted for 20 to 25 minutes. This indicates that there were 65 minutes of light skirmishing at the Hill before the serious fighting began, according to the Cheyenne accounts. This brings us to 5:45, about 15 minutes after Weir's troop appeared on Weir Point, which was the signal for Custer to make his dispositions to facilitate the passage to Custer Hill for the rest of the regiment now presumably on their way and making all possible haste to join him, Benteen in the lead with the reserve ammunition. The Cheyennes say further that this skirmish did little damage to either side. One of their warriors was wounded so seriously that he died several days after the battle; and it is probable that Captain Yates and Lieutenant Reily were either wounded or killed, for they were not with their command where it was later destroyed. Two moon, in his interview with Hamlin Garland in 1898, spoke of an officer being killed as all the troops were "bunched" together on the Hill just before they started back eastward along the north side of the ridge. In other words, just as Keogh and Yates were coming off the line to re-form for the march. He said he had heard that this officer was General Custer. It could have been Custer or anyone of the

5 or 6 officers whose bodies were found behind the breastworks
of dead horses at the Hill. No one knows when Custer was killed.
In our narrative however, we assume that he was not killed at
this time.

For about an hour after his arrival, then, everything seemed
to go as Custer must have desired. Actually the situation was
not as favorable as it appeared to be. His maneuver to bring the
warriors downstream along the river and away from his trail had
succeeded as well or better than he could have expected; and as
far as he could see he was holding them there while he was resting his horses and incurring small loss. Better still, the warriors
were showing a marked disinclination to come to close quarters.
But now, at 5:15, or a little later, he saw what he must have
been waiting to see for some time—a troop of cavalry on one of
the Weir Ridges about three miles away as the crow flies. The
chances are that he took it to be one of the three troops of
Benteen's battalion, as it actually was, though he could not
have known that it had come there without orders if not in
defiance of orders. Benteen and McDougall were the only officers
who had received special orders to hurry forward on his trail, and
since McDougall was acting as guard of the packtrain, he knew it
could not be he whose troop he saw. It was, therefore, Benteen with
the reserve ammunition. As stated in the preceding chapter, he
may have seen Benteen's battalion as it was approaching Reno Hill
while he, Custer, was on the high ridge a mile or so east of the
battlefield. That was more than an hour ago, more than enough
for Benteen to reach Weir Point.

This construction has been challenged on the ground that,
since the troops on Weir Point could not see Custer, Custer could
not have seen them. We might reply that a well-known law of
optics rules out any such blanket statement. As an illustration
we may say that a hunter in his "blind" can see the ducks over
his decoys, but the ducks cannot see him. There was, of course,
considerable dust and smoke at this time, especially where the
mounted warriors were still milling around southwest of the Hill,
and also where the two troops were firing northwest of the Hill.
The day was sultry, cloudless and windless, or nearly so, as both
the Indians and the officers whose statements we have, say.
What little movement of air there was, was from north to south,
as Gerard remembered it from the drift of the smoke where Reno
had fought in the valley, and where the Indians had fired the
grass after the retreat of the troops.

But Custer's men may have been in the eastern end of the dust and smoke and invisible to the troops on Weir Point. Those who were doing the firing were lying down and hard to see in any case, and the rest were in the low ground north of the ridge where they would not have stood out prominently, and if partly obscured by smoke and dust, were easily overlooked. But anyone a little east of the Hill would have had a clear view of Weir Point *at this* time. Fifteen to twenty minutes later it would have been an entirely different story, though it is nearly certain that at any time glimpses of Weir Point could have been obtained through the rifts in the murk.

If the situation up to this time was substantially as we have described it we are forced to the conclusion that what Custer now did can be explained only on the assumption that he had seen Weir's troop on the high ridge and thought that Benteen was there with his whole battalion. Any other construction makes his action incomprehensible. For he now sent troops "C" and "E" to form a skirmish line from near the Hill to near Greasy Grass Ridge bordering the south of the field and a half mile from the Hill, "E" in the lead.

The whole line was completely outside his defensive position. Nor was any part of it posted for defense or a standing fight, or any attempt made to take advantage of the small facilities the ground offered for such a fight. On the contrary, it stood partly in a shallow, narrow valley and along the western slope of a low, flat ridge, partly on a small flat, the whole faced by hillocks, knolls and ravines to the west where hundreds of warriors had concealed themselves, many of them undoubtedly within bowshot of the line. The situation in the rear of the line also was anything but satisfactory from the defensive point of view. But in spite of all this it is improbable that a serious disaster would have occurred here had not Lieutenant Sturgis who commanded Troop "E" dismounted his men and left them standing holding their horses by the reins, good evidence that no immediate action was expected here. Further evidence for this construction is the fact that neither Tom Custer nor Smith had gone down with their commands, as far as the evidence shows. Their bodies were found in the Custer group behind the dead horses. Had immediate action been expected it would have been decidedly a point of honor for them to be with their men. The troops were carefully posted by Harrington and Sturgis, the latter only a year out of West Point. Tom Custer and Smith had evidently remained behind for final

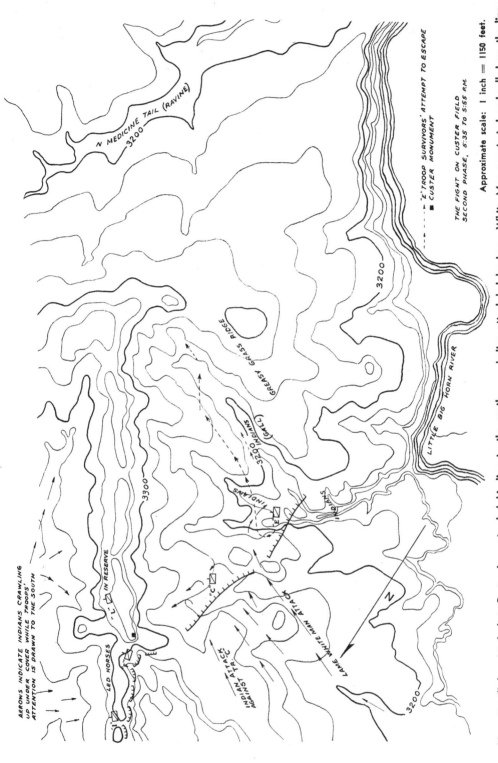

ARROWS INDICATE INDIANS CRAWLING
UP UNDER COVER WHILE TROOPS'
ATTENTION IS DRAWN TO THE SOUTH

LED HORSES

"C" IN RESERVE

3300

3200 INDIANS
(GALL)

INDIANS

"E"

"C"

INDIAN ATTACK
AGAINST

LAME WHITE MAN ATTACK

N

3200

N MEDICINE TAIL (RAVINE)
3200

GREASY GRASS RIDGE

3200

LITTLE BIG HORN RIVER

- - - - - "E" TROOP SURVIVORS' ATTEMPT TO ESCAPE
■ CUSTER MONUMENT

THE FIGHT ON CUSTER FIELD
SECOND PHASE, 5:35 TO 5:55 P.M.

Approximate scale: 1 inch = 1150 feet.

Here it will be noted that Custer has extended his line to the south   Indian attack led by Lame White Man penetrated and rolled up the line, orders when the time came for the line to go into action; which suggests several other things, namely that this action depended on what the warriors in its front did, and what the supposed Benteen did; for the troops must have been sent down the instant Weir was seen on the high ridge.

But the serious mistake made by Lieutenant Sturgis would probably not have mattered had it been really Benteen who was seen on Weir Point ready to hurry forward as soon as he had located Custer; for in that case the dismounted warriors facing the line, and those in the rear also, would almost certainly have rushed to their ponies they had left in the gulch and ravines, instead of attacking. And it is not too far fetched to suggest that General Custer had counted on this; for, while he certainly did not know the actual situation, he must have more than suspected that there were at least some warriors in this ground so exactly suited to their tactics, but did not believe they were there in sufficient numbers to risk attacking. If the Curley story quoted in footnote No. 64 is true, it would seem probable that Bouyer attempted to persuade the two Custers not to send the troops because of the danger of an ambush by overwhelming numbers —about 20 to 1, according to Kate Bighead who from her position on Greasy Grass Ridge looked down on them from the rear and could thus form some estimate of their numbers.

Whatever the detailed reasons may have been, the purpose of the line was undoubtedly to facilitate the passage of Benteen either by holding back the warriors or closing in on their rear if they left to oppose Benteen. Calhoun's Troop "L" was still in reserve and could have been thrown in to take care of anything developing south of the Hill while this maneuver was being carried out.

We have tried to explain the reason for the south skirmish line, and in so doing have gotten somewhat ahead of the objective facts. These facts, in their essential outlines are no longer in doubt. Many Indian accounts contain fragmentary portions of them. Several of the Cheyenne accounts, especially those of Kate Bighead and Wooden Leg, make some things quite clear when applied to the distribution of the markers here and elsewhere. McClernand's article in the Cavalry Journal for January, 1927, contains a few key-facts, and the testimony of the officers at the Reno Court of Inquiry contains others.

From the analysis of this material a clear picture emerges. Among the Indian accounts that of Kate Bighead is the clearest

up to a certain point. It will be remembered that she had come
to the field in search of her nephew, and after nearly circling it,
had stopped on Greasy Grass Ridge south of the field. She remained
here on her pony watching the sniping action that had begun
before she arrived. Finally she saw a body of troops on the ridge
mount their horses and come galloping down the Coulee almost
directly toward her. Though she does not mention the color of
the horses, we do know that it was the Gray Horse Troop seen by
Mrs. Spotted Horn Bull from across the river, as already related.
She saw the troops deploy, dismount and stand by their horses
holding them by the bridle. While the troops were coming down
the warriors directly in their front scampered back down the
ravine, as did most of those on their flanks. Some of them, however, remained with their chiefs, and as the troops made no further move, these chiefs began calling to their warriors to return. Hundreds of them did so, until, as she thought, there
must have been about twenty warriors to every soldier there.
Among the chiefs in front of the line was Lame White Man, a
Southern Cheyenne regarded by many as the leading war chief
of the tribe. He had been so long with the Northern Cheyennes
that he had been accepted as one of them. When he was ready
to strike he shouted to his warriors "Come on, we can kill them
all." This is Wooden Leg's wording of the order to charge.
Kate Big Head words it differently, but she was too far away
to have heard it clearly. Wooden Leg was among the warriors
on this part of the field and probably heard it, though he took no
prominent part in the fighting, since has father had asked him
not to expose himself to great danger, the family honor and
duty not requiring it. That had already been fully taken care of
by his part in the Reno fight and by his older brother, who had
gone out against Custer before Wooden Leg returned. Wooden
Leg also saw the troops come down from the ridge, about 40
men, he said, but seems not to have seen the other troop. Kate
Bighead seems to have seen at least part of it.

At this call call from Lame White Man the warriors in both
front and rear of the troops rose up and for a moment just
stood and looked as the horses plunged about, broke loose and
ran away to the river.

This is all these two excellent witnesses would tell Dr. Marquis
about the few minutes of deadly fighting here. Not a word about
the ghastly mess found in the ravine behind the line, or the short
exchange of shots where the left of "C" was turned, and where

The battlefield visualized during the second phase of Custer's fight. The nearest marker is within a few feet of the deep gulch used as base of attack by the Indian hordes. Custer's command post located as shown by the monument on the sky line, left of center. The break in the line of markers (center of photo) is where Lame White Man pierced the skirmish line, killed 18 to 24 "E" troopers and lost his own life.

View of same part of the battlefield, taken from Custer's battle ridge, and showing the ground beyond the gulch where the extreme left of Troop "E" stood. Greasy Grass Ridge in the left background.

the Indians must have incurred the greater part of their admittedly heavy loss. Instead of going on with the description of the actual fighting, they told him a fairy tale to account for the 50 bodies more or less that were found where the line had stood and to the east of it. Both tell about the same story, namely that after the horses had run away the troopers began killing themselves and each other. When the warriors rushed in all, or nearly all, were dead! Nevertheless, in another part of his story Wooden Leg says that the Indian loss here was greater than on any other part of the field. Also, an unidentified Sioux told Colonel J. W. Pope in 1877 while he was visiting the field with a small party, including two Indians who had been in the fight, that a troop standing "well forward, making an angle with the other troops on Custer ridge.........made a considerable fight and that nearly all the Indians killed fell at this fight; (estimated loss of 30 to 40); that this troop was soon driven back to the position where it was overwhelmed with the whole command; that when nearly all the command had been killed a few ran down to get shelter in the timber or ravines." This very obviously refers to the south skirmish line, for the markers show nothing else to which it could refer.

Fortunately the distribution of the markers, the finding of nearly a platoon of the Gray Horse men lying close together in the ravine back of the line, Lame White Man among them, the break in the line of markers, nearly opposite these bodies, taken together, tell a good part of the story. All this proves quite conclusively that Lame White Man and his warriors struck the Gray Horse near the point where it closed up with "C" Troop, broke it, tumbled into the ravine after the troopers and crushed them by sheer weight of numbers.

But this is not the whole of the story. The markers show that the warriors facing "C" Troop on the left of Lame White Man, also attacked and inflicted heavy casualties, but failed, apparently to shatter the line. The evidence indicates that "C" had not dismounted and that some of its men tried to stem the rush against the helpless Gray Horse. Both Godfrey and McClernand say that some bodies of "C" were found among those of the Gray Horse. Since McClernand found no dead horses where the Gray Horse line had stood, he suggested that the men here had been ordered to turn loose their horses. But he saw some dead horses to the left—that is, toward Custer Hill. "Those near Custer Hill killed theirs in a circle about 30 feet in diameter," he says.

It is extremely doubtful that any of the Gray Horse men escaped to the Hill; and we do not know how many of "C" Troop were killed on the line; for it is nearly certain that some of the markers for this troop were set up at random to account for some of the supposed "missing men," as was done for the Custer group, where not over 42 bodies were found but where there now are 52 markers. Somewhere between 20 and 27 markers were thus planted for phantom troopers, nearly all of them in the south line or at the Hill. Elsewhere the number of markers corresponds closely to the number of men reported for each troop. The mischief of this thoughtless action cannot now be undone, except perhaps in a few instances, so that we are left to long range guessing in places where otherwise a reasonable degree of accuracy might have been attained. Our guess is that Troop "C" lost about 12 men before getting back to the Hill. The basis for this guess will appear later.

The general outline of the fighting in the south line seems clear enough. Some of the details are not so clear. We have enough evidence, however, to attain strong probability in some of the details and considerable plausibility on the rest.

Where, for instance, were the bodies of the Gray Horse Troop found in the deep ravine, variously estimated at 18 to 28 in number?[62] Benteen said they were 50 to 75 yards from the river, a statement so far out of even remote plausibility that it may be safely ignored. Moylan said they were about three quarters of a mile from the river, and Hare that they were in skirmish line about 300 yards from Custer Hill. Fortunately a statement by McClernand makes it possible to locate them exactly by referring it to the terrain. He said they were slightly in front of the line and to the right of it. His account shows that he thought the line had faced east, and that it did not extend southward clear to the ravine, or the bodies could not have been to the right of the line. This reveals a significant fact about the markers there today. There are now twelve directly back, or west of where he says the bodies lay in the ravine. Since he studied this line carefully before the bodies had been buried, he could hardly have overlooked these twelve had they been there. The markers are almost as carefully aligned as men in skirmish line on the parade ground, and extend northward from the ravine some 60 to 70 yards. They stand in a shallow watercourse just east of an elongated and fairly high knoll behind which Lame White

Man must have collected his warriors. The charge, however, was not made over the top of this knoll, but around the north end, so that the men behind the knoll were by-passed. It is certain that men had stood there, for the line extended well across the ravine. Five men were killed south of it, two of them in line with those across the ravine to the north, and one of these two right on the south bank. Why, then, were there no bodies behind the knoll, and why are there 12 markers there now? Because the men who had stood here fled after Lame White Man had passed them, leaving the ground immediately north of them clear, or relatively clear, of warriors, while the warriors farther north were rolling up the flank of "C" Troop against the south end of the ridge there. Then how shall we explain the 12 markers where these men had stood? Before we try to answer that question, let us ask another. Where were the bodies buried that were found in the ravine? Certainly not where they were found,⁶⁸ for the first heavy storm would have washed them out and down the gulch. There are no markers where they were found, though there are now two farther up the ravine where it is wide and shallow with a hard bottom and a comparatively low grade or fall.

Considering all the facts we believe that it is not stretching credulity too far to say that these bodies in the ravine were carried out and buried where the 12 markers now stand in their nice parade—ground order—far too nice to represent men killed in a fight here.

What became of the men who left the line where the 12 markers now stand? If we assume that our description of the fighting up to this point is substantially correct, this question is easily answered. They started northward as soon as Lame White Man had passed and was busy killing the men he had followed into the ravine, and tried to shoot their way through to the Hill. The warriors in their front were now facing the rolled-up left of "C" Troop and were thus taken in the flank and rear by this small band, the exact number of which we do not know. There may have been 15 or more, for those who escaped from the line south of the ravine must have joined them, and some of them were, in all probability, mounted. Their attack must have come as something of a surprise and in any case materially lessened the pressure on this part of "C" Troop at a critical moment. But they did not get through, and they probably lost heavily before they fled after emptying their pistols, for there are a number of scattered markers where this action would have taken place under the deductions we are making. Their pistols empty, too closely pressed to reload, the ground north, west and south swarming with warriors, the remnant of the little band, approximately 8 or 9 in number, broke eastward across the ravine a little above the point where at this moment Lame White Man must have been completing the butchery of a third or more of the troop, and started up a small "draw" leading to the level slope beyond. Before they got out of the draw one of their number was killed. About 200 yards farther on they lost another man. Seve ty-five yards more a third man went down. One hundred and forty-three yards beyond they came to a deep steep-sided ravine just where it splits into two branches. Plunging through it they left o e man whose marker now stands on the low tongue of land betw n the two branches. One man, probably because he was a littl behind the rest and warned of what was in the ravine, turned to the left and ran, or rode northeastward, blundered near the west branch of the ravine after going about 180 yards and was then killed. The four men who had gotten across the deep ravine, or gulch, turned slightly to the right and ran or rode on. One hundred and fifteen yards from where they had crossed they lost another man. Here they veered to the left, away from the dangerous, shallow ravine on their right. Too late! Anoth r casualty in the next 34 yards, and still another in the next 26 yards. Only one man left now. He ran for 152 yards up the slope toward the east wing of the battle ridge, and there to all appearance ended the career of the famous Gray Horse Troop, except for the 7 men in the packtrain and its commander, First Lieutenant Algernon E. Smith, who had remained with Custer at the hill. It is possible that one or two mounted men of this small band broke through Gall's scattered warriors here, but were followed by mounted warriors and killed before they got very far; for in several Indian accounts we are told that one man on a white horse got through and was outdistancing his pursuers when he suddenly drew his pistol and killed himself. Also in later years the skeletons of several men were found in this neighborhood not far from the battlefield fence. But these skeletons may represent men among Calhoun's horse-holders surprised on the east wing of the battleridge a half hour later.[64]

Returning to the skirmish line, the distribution of the markers south of the ravine is suggestive. Two of them are in line with those on the north side, one of them standing right on the edge of the high bank. Two others are off to the west close together and within a few feet of the bank. The instant impression is that these men were scouts sent to learn the character of the ground over which the troops would have to pass in the action to follow, and that they were shot from across the ravine. The fifth man was killed a hundred yards or more from here as he was approaching a small draw leading out from the main ravine, or gulch, as it is here. It is an arresting fact that all over the field markers are found at the heads of ravines and their minor branches we have called "draws."

The results, then, of this preparatory move to facilitate Benteen's passage from Weir Point on Custer Hill, was the loss of the Gray Horse Troop and approximately a third of Troop "C," 50 men, more or less, and leaving 50 carbines and the same number of revolvers in the hands of the warriors together with nearly the full supply of ammunition carried by these troops. In addition there must have been a heavy loss in morale among the surviving troops and a corresponding gain in this respect among the warriors who now became more aggressive, though they did not repeat the costly venture of charging the troops to fight it out at close quarters in the open. What was Custer to do now? About a fourth of his battalion had been wiped out. What remained of it could not defend the position very long against the concealed, crawling advance of the warriors. Even if every man was placed on the skirmish line they could not cover the position and save the horses. Two gaps, one on the southeast, the other to the north would have to be left that would have invited a rush and a quick finish after the warriors had crawled up close enough and in sufficient numbers. Benteen forestalled two such rushes on the 26th where the situation was much more favorable for the troops. If a single troop could have been held in reserve these gaps would not have been particularly dangerous, for the warriors would not have faced a countercharge while the line remained intact. They made no attempt to do so at Reno Hill, though here the charges were made by the line, not by reserves.

What Custer now did shows that he knew he could not hold out indefinitely unless he received reinforcements. What reason had he to expect such reinforcements in time to save him if he remained where he was? The troops he had seen on Weir Point had disappeared 15 to 20 minutes before and were presumably on his trail somewhere up Medicine Tail Coulee, and about this time troops again appeared on Weir Point and in much greater

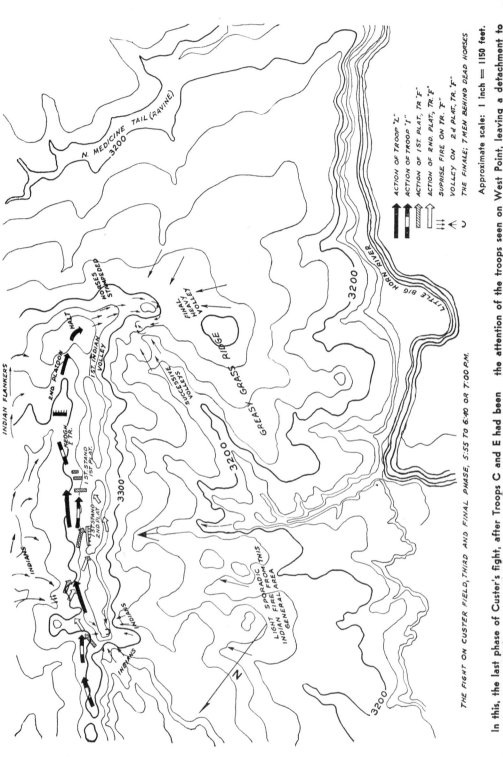

N. MEDICINE TAIL (RAVINE)
— 3200

INDIAN FLANKERS

HORSES
STAMPEDE

HALT

2ND PLATOON

1ST INDIAN
VOLLEY

FINAL
HEAVY
VOLLEY

KEOGH
I TR.

I ST. STAND
1ST PLAT.

1ST STAND
1ST PLAT

1ST STAND
2ND PLAT

GREASY GRASS RIDGE

SUCCESSIVE
VOLLEYS

INDIANS

INDIANS

INDIANS

LIGHT SPORADIC
FIRE FROM THIS
INDIAN GENERAL
AREA

3300

3200

3200

N

LITTLE BIG HORN RIVER

3200

ACTION OF TROOP "L"
ACTION OF TROOP "I"
ACTION OF 1ST. PLAT., TR "F"
ACTION OF 2ND. PLAT., TR."F"
SURPRISE FIRE ON TR."F"
VOLLEY ON 2d PLAT., TR. "F."
THE FINALE; 7 MEN BEHIND DEAD HORSES

Approximate scale: 1 inch = 1150 feet.

THE FIGHT ON CUSTER FIELD, THIRD AND FINAL PHASE, 5:55 TO 6:40 OR 7:00 P.M.

In this, the last phase of Custer's fight, after Troops C and E had been   the attention of the troops seen on West Point, leaving a detachment to

strength than before—three full troops, in fact. But again they
halted. Why did they hesitate? Perhaps they could not see him.
There was now a good deal of dust and smoke where he was
fighting. Did he, perhaps, see the slight flutter of the guidon
Benteen had planted on one of the highest points to attract his
attention? If so, what did it mean to him, if not that they intended
to stand where they were and expected him to join them, or
were for some reason in doubt as to their further movements?
Not very reasonable, considering the orders he had sent back,
unless they really did not know where he was or how desperately
he needed them. Unless, then, he fled, leaving his wounded, he
must somehow show them where he was and do what he could
to help them over the three intervening miles. With only 150 men
he could not carry off his wounded in the presence of possibly 2000
warriors now exultant over the defeat of Reno and the destruction of the south line. But neither could he abandon the wounded.
Some troops must remain to protect them until the rest of the
regiment arrived. The only remaining alternative was to use
the three troops still intact, "F," "I" and "L," to make contact
with those on Weir Point and return with them to the defensive
position on the Hill.

This might have succeeded had the facts at this stage of
the action been such as Custer believed them to be. Though he
must have felt that the situation had become extremely grave,
the chances of success were still in his favor when calculated on
the basis of past experience in Indian warfare. There seemed
little question that the three troops he was sending out to make
contact with those on Weir Point could do so and return. The
real question was: could the small band left to protect the
wounded hold out until rescued? The Wagon Box fight, Beecher
Island, and numerous other encounters, proved that well armed
men behind breastworks could hold out for a long time against
Indian warriors regardless of their number.

Both distribution of the markers and some fairly clear oral
accounts indicate what was done to carry out Custer's decision.
We have already cited McClernan as saying that the men in the
south line who stood nearest the Hill had killed their horses
for breastworks. It was these men, therefore, who formed the bulk
of the group of about 40 who remained to defend the wounded.
The number given in the different accounts vary from less than
30 to 42. The latter figure, given by Godfrey, is probably an

actual count made at the time and may, we believe, be accepted as correct. There is also the letter of Colonel Pope to Godfrey in 1877, citing the statement of an unidentified warrior saying that one troop had stood for some time at an angle with the rest, but was driven back to the Hill and overwhelmed with the rest. Finally there is the story Two Moon told Hamlin Garland in 1898. He said that after a long time of fighting only about a hundred men remained and stood on the hill "all bunched together." He saw these men ride away toward the river, led by a man in buckskin shirt (Keogh) at the head of "maybe so, forty men (Keogh's Troop "I," about 36 enlisted men)." Two Moon was north of the main ridge and took part in the fighting there, and what he says here is exactly what he could have seen if our general construction is correct; for the three troops that were riding away numbered a little over a hundred men—116, to be exact, if no allowance is made for possible casualties in "F" and "I" during their long sniping action. The Custer group below the cutbank Two Moon could not have seen.

This gives us the essentials of the picture. Putting the pieces together, we may say that when "C" Troop fled back to the Hill, possibly covered by Calhoun's men firing over the heads of the fugitives as they came near enough to make this safe, they rallied below the cutback under the protection of this fire and turned to check the rush of the warriors.

Custer now undoubtedly had "Officers' Call" sounded, and after a brief, hurried consultation, reached a decision, explained his plan and issued his orders. First he ordered Tom Custer to form the breastwork of dead horses, while "F" and "I" still held their line, and had all the wounded brought within the protecting semicircle. That done, he ordered the rest, under the command of Captain Keogh, to march with all possible speed over the level slope along the north side of the battleridge to show themselves on the high Calhoun position then still outside of the area of dust and smoke, and do everything possible to attract the attention of the troops on Weir Point—fire volleys in their direction, if necessary by the three companies simultaneously.[65] This would have awakened the Seven Sleepers on Weir Point, had they been there, though they might not have been heard by the two self-proclaimed deaf men, Reno and Benteen. As it was the slightly hard-of-hearing Godfrey heard the much lighter firing more than a half mile farther back, and Sergeant Windolph, sole surviving member of the Seventh Cavalry who had a part in the fight, remembers to this day that he heard it. But had they all been "stone deaf" they could at least have seen the cloud of smoke from the explosion of over a hundred heavy charges of black powder. Nor does it seem that it would have been difficult to communicate by signal, using a cavalry guidon for the purpose if nothing larger was available. A half hour later those on Weir Point clearly distinguished individual horsemen riding around and shooting at something on the ground, something much harder to make out than a brightly colored guidon waved by a man on horseback. In short, there was nothing extraordinary in Custer's assumption that it was practicable to inform the troops on Weir Point of his position, and that he wanted them to "come on." Similar situations often develop in warfare and the expedients here described have been used for ages—trumpets, smoke, mirrors, firing, and above all the flags used in the signal corps of today.

But the position of the warriors was not what Custer had evidently supposed it to be. Clearly he was unaware of their presence in the ravine north of the battleridge. They had been there for a long time now, and while the fighting south of the Hill was absorbing the attention of all the troops, they had, under the lead of Crazy Horse, Two Moon and others, crawled out under cover of the hill and ridge lying parallel to the north wing of the battleridge and up a long curving branch leading out of the main ravine to the head of this second ridge. They were favored also by the heavy clumps of sage growing here in the characteristic dark-gray soil in which this plant especially thrives. They were now within easy range of the troops, and the fact that they did not strike betrays their extreme caution and dread of a mounted charge. Their ponies were far down to the northwest. If they had been caught here in a mounted charge their casualties would have been appalling. When they saw the three troops start away from the Hill they must have guessed that they were fleeing the field, and their action shows that they were willing to let them escape rather than take the consequences of a head-on collision. It was a seemingly trivial circumstance that gave them the opportunity to spring a double surprise which eliminated most of the risk. This circumstance was the premature move of Calhoun.

If Calhoun (Troop "L") had waited until the other troops were ready it is probable that no attack would have been made.

Calhoun's troop had not been in action unless, as already related it had fired a few rounds over the heads of Tom Custer's men as they retreated to the Hill and while they were preparing the breastwork. As soon as this was completed Calhoun was ready to march. But troops "F" and "I" on the north wing of the ridge naturally held their ground until all who were to remain were in position for defense. It is evident from what happened that as these troops came off the line Calhoun turned his troop around and started off. He was several hundred yards on his way before the men of "F" and "I" could secure their mounts, form in column and follow, Keogh in the lead at the head of his own troop.

The warriors let Calhoun pass. He headed straight for the ravine which parallels the battleridge from a point a little over a quarter of a mile from Custer Hill. It lay there peaceful under the afternoon sun with no sign of an enemy in it. The warriors had not entered it because they would have been seen by the first trooper who looked in that direction. It was directly in Calhoun's line of march, and troops riding in it could not be seen by the warriors south of the ridge, which was an important consideration.

What followed Calhoun's entrance into this ravine was as natural and inevitable as the fall of a stone that has been tossed into the air. Although we have not a single word from an eye-witness concerning the fight of this troop, except for its closing incidents, the story in its main outlines can be read from the markers as easily as we read print, provided we first banish from our minds all preconceived ideas not soundly based on established facts. We must see clearly with the mind's eye the three troops ride away eastward from the Hill, Calhoun several hundred yards in advance, Keogh (Troop "I") in the center and behind him Troop "F" minus its commissioned officers, Captain Yates and Lieutenant Reily. We must also clearly visualize the position of the warriors and keep in mind the fact that the troops did not know of their presence here or anything as to their numbers. They knew that the ground to the west, southwest and south of Custer Hill was crowded with warriors; and since they wanted to escape detection as long as possible, they retreated back of the ridge and well down the slope.

The storm broke suddenly and without warning, in the form of two volleys in quick succession. Just as the last of Calhoun's

Taken from near spot where Keogh's body was found.
Shows the east slope of the battle ridge with the ravine (clearly defined in center beyond the markers) from which the Indian attack surprised and routed Keogh's and Calhoun's troops.

View of the north of the field from Calhoun's marker.
Looking down the "Calhoun Ravine" from near Calhoun marker. Gives a general idea of the main battle ridge seen from the Calhoun position.

men were slithering their horses down the steep embankment the warriors concealed in the turn of the ravine to the left opened fire. An instant later another and heavier volley crashed into the flank of Troop "F" as it was passing the end of the ridge and ravine northeast of Custer Hill. It was this second volley that sealed the fate of Calhoun by halting Keogh who would otherwise have extricated him by taking the warriors in flank and rear, giving him time to re-establish order in his command and restore contact with the rest. This will become fully apparent as we go along.

The first volley dropped one "L" trooper at the foot of the embankment. The horses of several others plunged violently to the right up the short ravine toward the battleridge. Two men were killed here before they could get out of the steep-sided pocket in which they were trapped. The rest were carried in confusion straight ahead up the ravine eastward, but got their horses under sufficient control to halt after going about 50 yards, for it is at this point we find the first markers, except for those already mentioned. A quick decision was now evidently made to dismount the rear platoon, the horses being turned over to the first platoon which then rode up the ravine out of range. This turned out to be a mistake, and it may have been done out of absolute necessity to check the pursuit of the warriors, which was difficult for men on frantic horses that could not be faced about or gotten into order in the confined space. Perhaps the fact that Crittenden, who commanded this platoon, was an infantry officer, may, in part, account for this. If he was inexperienced in commanding cavalry, this was a severe test.

The warriors followed the troops into the ravine and rushed after them, dropped to the ground and began their slow, crawling advance when the latter dismounted. They held a pronounced advantage in having the sun at their backs, giving them maximum visibility of their target, while the troops were partially blinded by the low-hanging sun. Even if the sun was obscured by clouds a decided disparity would have existed, as every man who has fired a rifle knows. The troopers took advantage of whatever protection and opportunity for concealment the vegetation and eroded surface at the base of the slopes offered, as the position of the markers show. As they were crowded back they left their dead scattered up the ravine for about a hundred and fifty yards. Counting the three already mentioned, there are

14 markers, the last five part-way up the north slope. From there on no markers are found for 110 yards. Then, in the flat amphitheaterlike depression northeast of the turn in the battleridge, we come to 12 more, among them those for Calhoun and Crittenden. Two stand in the angle across the ridge—the angle made by the turn in the ridge. Some distance to the southeast across the east wing is another, quite isolated. Farther south, on the crest of the ridge, or near it, are the bulk of the first platoon.

The break of 110 yards in the line of markers is to be explained by the intervention of Lieutenant Porter in bringing up Troop "I," posting it so that the first platoon stood massed above the entrance to the ravine. This placed it squarely in the rear of the warriors Calhoun and Crittenden were fighting, compelling them to seek cover and putting them out of the fight. This made it possible for Calhoun to withdraw most of the men to meet a new danger. This danger came from a flanking movement the warriors had begun some time before. They saw that Calhoun, in trying to save his horses, had put half of his troop out of the fight. When the rear platoon dismounted it contained not over 20 men several of whom may have been already wounded. They could hold the narrow front comprised in the width of the ravine, and nothing more. The first platoon could not help in any way as long as it was employed in holding the horses. Attempting to remount the second platoon as long as it was under fire was too risky, for the warriors were too close and might have rushed them before the shift could be completed. If, from the first, the men had been able to manage their horses and keep some kind of formation Calhoun would, no doubt, have ridden out of range after the first volley, reformed, then turned and charged, breaking his way out of the trap. The ground is rough here but not impossible for cavalry action. As it was, he pinned his hopes on quick assistance from the other troops, for he must have known that his position in the ravine would become untenable in a comparatively short time, for the ravine is of the open type without cutbanks, leaving his men exposed on both flanks.

There were at first not many warriors on this part of the field, but more were constantly coming up the ravine from the northwest. Since only a comparatively few could find cover in front of the troops the later arrivals left the main ravine farther back beyond the turn, and crawled up eastward north of the ridge which forms one side of the ravine in which Calhoun was fighting. This move Calhoun could not see unless he went to the top of the ridge in question, but it was undoubtedly observed by Keogh and Porter who may have warned him by signal or trumpet. It was one reason for bringing up Troop "I" which, from its new position could fire on these flankers as they left the ravine and before they could get behind the ridge. If Calhoun's position had not been so precarious Troop "I" would have gone to support "F" more effectively than it did.

Relieved of the pressure on his rear Calhoun with about ten men rushed up the ravine to face this new danger. Meanwhile the first platoon had either been fired on by these flankers or had in some way become aware of their presence north of the ridge opposite their position, and had moved to the right out of range. They halted on the east wing of the battleridge, not knowing that Gall and his warriors lay concealed in the ravines running up to the ridge from the west and southwest, and that others were posted in the low ground to the south beyond the tip of the ridge. The attention of the horseholders was naturally centered on the fighting to the northeast of them, part of which they could see.

Within less than ten minutes, probably, from the time Calhoun and Crittenden arrived in the open space at the upper end of the ravine where the horseholders had first stationed themselves, the fighting on this part of the field was over. Gall and his warriors had been here for some time, and it may be taken for granted that they had occupied the ravines clear up to the low cutbanks in which they ended, as others had done toward Custer Hill. They undoubtedly sprang their surprise as soon as the horseholders had halted and turned their attention back to the fighting, as they would do instinctively. Delaying the attack would only have increased the chances of discovery and make complete success less certain.

General Godfrey speaks of this incident and the destruction of the rest of Calhoun's men as Gall had explained it to him during a reunion of participants on the tenth anniversary of the battle, 1886. Either Gall's memory betrayed him or Godfrey misunderstood him. For Gall is represented as having come up the ravine which runs northeastward from the Middle Ford and passes about a third of a mile east of the Calhoun position opposite which Custer is said to have dismounted Keogh's and Calhoun's troops and sent them on "double time" to take position on the east end of the battleridge, leaving their horses and horseholders in the ravine where Gall surprised and destroyed them. But no bodies of either men or horses were found here. The bodies of the horseholders and of some of the horses were found on the east wing of the battleridge. We have already quoted Mrs. Spotted Horn Bull showing that Gall rode along the bench near the river, not up the eastern ravine as indicated on Godfrey's map.

If one studies the U. S. G. S. Survey map and notes that the markers for the horseholders are on the east wing of the battle-ridge, he will require little, if any oral description to visualize what happened. He will also note that these horseholders were, under Godfrey's conception, between Calhoun's own skirmish line and the warriors coming up from the south—a complete absurdity. He will also note that there is not a single marker on the ridge where Keogh's and Calhoun's lines are said to have stood; that Calhoun's skirmishers were killed in the ravine behind the ridge, and that Keogh's whole troop was destroyed while it stood in column of platoons well down the slope north of the ridge. All this is so absolutely irreconcilable with Godfrey's conception that no further discussion of it would seem to be necessary.

The markers representing Calhoun's first platoon, the horse-holders, are strung along the whole length of the wing of the ridge. Many of them stand opposite the cutbanks at the head of the ravines. Both facts seem to us significant. It is perfectly certain that the men did not spread out in this long line when they halted here. The explanation is, we think, that they had halted not far south of the turn in the ridge. It was as far as they needed to go to be safe from the flankers. They were first fired on from the northwest by those of Gall's men who were far up in the ravine that ends in the angle of the ridge. This fire and the yelling stampeded the horses southward along the ridge. As they passed the heads of the ravines they received successive volleys each of which registered in the bodies found there. As the last of them were about to plunge down the end of the ridge a very heavy volley on the slope of it dropped 6 men close together. The horses of the rest veered frantically to the right and rear. As they neared a ravine a shower of bullets and arrows wiped them out.

While the horseholders were being carried southward and killed the warriors had gone up the ravine that leads to the angle made by the turn in the ridge until, by standing erect, they could see and fire on the remnant of the second platoon engaged with the flanking force to the north and northeast. There are only 12 markers here, including the two for Calhoun and Crittenden. At the Court of Inquiry Captain Moylan, Calhoun's brother-in-law, said that the men here had stood in regular skirmish-line order; and this is probably the way they were originally posted. But it is not the way they fell, if the markers there now were correctly placed. According to the markers some of the men faced about and left the line to confront Gall's warriors when they were fired on from the rear. Moylan, however, may have based his statement on the line of shells found lying at regular intervals. Around the body of one man he counted 28 empty cases. This suggests a stand of perhaps 10 minutes.

In Godfrey's account of the battle it is said that Gall's warriors, mounted and afoot, finally rushed over Calhoun and then over Keogh. This may be true of the last man or two; for the position of at least one of the markers gives the impression that the man had started to bolt northeastward over the ridge in his front, and it may be true of the few men left farther down the ravine. It is not true of Keogh, as we shall see later.

It is not possible to determine exactly how long the Calhoun action lasted. The reader who accepts the description of it here given as approximately correct, will probably agree that it could not have been less than 20 minutes. From the very clear and circumstantial story by Kate Bighead it would seem that at least a half hour elapsed between the end of the fight in the south line and the killing of the horseholders. This is based on the estimate of the time she spent in riding about and in watching the fighting at Custer Hill. She seems to have remained on Greasy Grass Ridge for a few minutes after Troop "E" had been destroyed, for the Indians had begun to pick up their wounded and take them to the camps when she left it. She saw one of these wounded on a pony being led from the field. She rode after him thinking it was her nephew, Noisy Walking. But Noisy Walking was lying in the gulch south of the Hill, mortally wounded and helpless. She did not find him until the battle was over, after a Cheyenne warrior had told her where he was. She returned then to the scene of the fight she had witnessed where the warriors, having secured the guns and pistols of the dead troopers, had begun the attack on Custer Hill. She does not seem to have seen Custer shoot his horses, for she does not mention it. This was probably done while she was away to the south looking at the wounded Sioux she had mistaken for her nephew. She mentions watching Calf Trail Woman, an Amazon actually taking part in the fighting at long range, fire many shots with her muzzle-loader revolver. Then a young Cheyenne warrior lost his pony. She called to him and Calf Trail Woman that the women had plenty of good horses, meaning the captured cavalry horses. She saw Calf Trail Woman take the warrior on her pony to go and get one of these horses.

But the fighting against Custer seemed dull. A good part of it was rather long-distance firing at troops enveloped in a pall of smoke created by the heavy charges of black powder from more than thirty carbines closely grouped against the cutbank. There was only a slight stir of air southward, leaving the dust and smoke hanging nearly motionless in the air. Gibbon's men, many miles away to the north, saw a column of smoke over the valley of the Little Big Horn during the afternoon. It is immaterial whether this was the smoke of battle or that of grass fires. The point is that if there had been anything more than a slight stir of air the smoke would have been dissipated and too close to the ground to have been seen by Gibbon's men 25 to 30 miles away.

Things seeming comparatively slow and dull around Custer Hill, Kate Bighead looked about for something more exciting. The fearful racket north of the ridge, slowly drifting eastward, presaged a climax there soon. We may suppose that it was the sudden appearance of the horseholders on the east wing of the ridge that first attracted her attention in that direction. She knew that Gall's warriors were in the ravines there, for she could hardly have failed to see them while she was stationed on Greasy Grass Ridge south of the field. Something was certain to happen there within the next few minutes. "I started to go around the east end of the soldier ridge," she says. "Just then I saw lots of Indians running toward the end of the ridge." That is to say, the horses were being stampeded southward toward the tip of the ridge and the warriors in the ravines there, after firing into the jumbled mass, got up and ran after them. "Pretty soon I saw that all the white men there were dead and the warriors were among them getting their guns," she continues, "I did not see how they were killed, but I think they must have killed themselves."

Two things are to be noted here. She says she did not see how the men were killed. In other words, she saw no fighting. This is easily understood if our description of the fighting is correct, for Gall's warriors fired while lying down in the heads of the ravines where she could not have seen them from where she then was in the low ground south, or southeast of Custer Hill. After the warriors came out onto the higher ground near the ridge or on it, she could see them. Again if it be true that the appearance of the horseholders on the ridge caused her to ride there, it confirms our statement that the attack came very soon after the men halted there.

While "L" Troop was thus being destroyed by attacks from three directions, Troop "F," the "Bandbox Troop," as the regiment had dubbed it because it "never had a buckle unshined or a boot unpolished," was making a magnificent fight on the north slope of the ridge. It had ridden close on the heels of Keogh with Troop "I" which the warriors had permitted to pass undisturbed, as they had Calhoun. But as "F" came squarely opposite their position behind the head of the ridge and the ravine below it, they opened fire, knocking over 4 troopers. The startled horses, some of them certainly wounded and with arrows dangling from their flanks and hindquarters, plunged wildly forward and to the right.

We said some pages back that this volley came an instant after the one against Calhoun. How do we know this? The answer is very obvious if we have in mind a clear picture of the situation at this moment. For, if the volley against "F" had come before Calhoun entered the ravine farther east, he would have been warned. He would have halted and not gone into the ravine at all, but waited to see what was to be done after the unexpected attack. On the other hand, if this volley had not followed immediately after that against Calhoun, Keogh would have spurred forward against the warriors in Calhoun's rear, a move urgently called for to give Calhoun time to restore order in his troop before being called on to fight. That he did not make so obvious a move proves that something was happening elsewhere that called for his intervention even more urgently. His own troop, if it received any of the fire at all, was not seriously harmed. There are no markers on or near the place it must have been at the time of the volley. His men are all accounted for on or near the spot where they made their final stand, still in column of platoons showing that they had been held in reserve ready to be flung at any point where a mounted charge could be made to advantage. It was not under heavy attack until near the close. The Indians in the ravine here were concentrating on Troop "F." Those in the ravine opposite

Troop "I" were hurrying after Calhoun. Toward the close the ravine here was empty, or nearly so of warriors, as is shown by the fact that one man, evidently in blind panic, broke away, crossed the ravine and ran northeastward, killing himself with his revolver as he was mounting the higher ground there.[66] If there had been any considerable number of warriors in the ravine here firing on the troop he would not have run in this direction or succeeded in crossing the ravine. There were some warriors crawling through the grass to his right after he crossed, but they were facing away from him intent on flanking Calhoun.

This double attack forced Keogh to make a choice. Common sense urged him to take his three troops off the field pell-mell at least as far as the high Calhoun position, restore order in "F" and "L" and signal the troops on Weir Point. Had he done this his own loss would have been small; for the warriors were afoot and would not have risked attacking the three troops acting as a unit and mounted. But he knew that this meant, in all probability, the quick destruction of Custer who had not anticipated a serious attack from the north. He had posted only 7 men behind dead horses to protect the rear of his position below the cutbank, which suggests that he believed the troops on Weir Point would come down on the gallop the instant they definitely discovered his position: which is to say, when Keogh came into sight on the Calhoun position where they could not have failed to see so large a body of mounted troops while the ground was still clear of the horde of old men and boys on their ponies, which was the case a half hour or less after the decision had been made. Keogh knew also that if he could bring the three troops back to the Hill substantially intact they would still have some chance of escaping destruction provided they unhesitatingly made the necessary sacrifice of horses, which Custer had been unwilling to do before he knew the full extent of his danger.

In the face of this situation Keogh threw his orders overboard and prepared to fight his way back. This would have been easy enough for his own troop and Troop "F." Troop "I" was still intact and ready to be flung into line to strike in any direction. Had it charged back past Troop "F," now reorganizing by platoons near the ridge, the latter would have followed in the wake of the charge and reached the Hill without any fighting at all. The warriors would not have faced the charge, as every cavalry officer knew. This was not because they lacked courage, but because they possessed too much sense to fight at such a disadvantage when it could be avoided.

What prevented such a move was the critical situation of Calhoun, in whose troop, as already suggested, there was evidently too much disorder or difficulty with the horses to get it into shape to fight mounted and as a single unit. In sending forward his own troop to clear the way for Calhoun to rejoin him Keogh was forced to meet the brunt of the Indian attack with only the orphaned Troop "F" which had already lost at least 5 men of the less than 40 with which it had left the Hill. He might at once have ordered Lieutenant Porter to undertake a vigorous offensive against the relatively small number of warriors fighting Calhoun at this time, and effect a quick rescue; but this would have left "F" without any support at all and exposed to the danger of being rushed before it could pull itself together for a stand. Troop "I" was undoubtedly held for a while where it first halted after the attack, to give "F" time to reorganize. As soon as "F" was lined up and firing "I" was naturally sent to assist Calhoun, as already described. We do not know when and how it lost its horses. We do know that the men were not mounted toward the close of the fighting here.

In stampeding toward the right as a result of the volley into their flank the two platoons of "F" were carried toward the ridge on diverging lines. The rear platoon came to a stand at the base of the ridge with its left up near the crest. The 8 markers here indicate that the men formed up in an orderly manner.

The leading platoon halted about 160 yards farther east some distance north of the ridge. It is altogether probable that Troop "I" also veered to the right and forward so that when it halted it stood near this platoon. To complete the picture of the situation at this moment we must see Calhoun and Crittenden in the ravine to the east dismounting their disordered rear platoon and turning to engage the Indians rushing up the ravine in pursuit while the first platoon moves eastward with the horses to the depression opposite the turn of the ridge to the south.

The leading role had now passed from Custer to Keogh, Irish soldier of fortune, former Papal guard at the Vatican and a veteran of our Civil War. The manner in which he played his part filled the warriors who saw him with a profound and lasting admiration though they knew neither his name nor his rank. It was not Captain French, as has been supposed, but Captain Keogh to whom the Sioux chief of the Council Lodge, Red Horse, referred when he

said in 1881: "Among the soldiers was an officer who rode a horse
with four white feet. The Sioux have for a long time fought many
brave men of different people, but the Sioux say that this officer
was the bravest man they ever fought. I don't know if this was
General Custer or not. Many Sioux men I hear talking say that
it was. I saw this officer many times but did not see his body. It
has been told me that he was killed by a Santee Indian, who took
his horse. This officer wore a large-brimmed hat and a deerskin
coat. This officer saved the lives of many soldiers by turning his
horse and covering their retreat. Sioux say that this officer was the
bravest man they ever fought."[67]

Our other witness of Keogh's exploits is Two Moon who, at
the time of the battle, was one of the nine Little Chiefs of the Fox
Warriors, and the Cheyennes' prize liar. It is fortunate for the historian that, when interviewed by Hamlin Garland in 1898, age
had cast its blight on the exuberant fancy of the chief and forced
him to lean heavily on the prosaic crutch of truth, otherwise Mr.
Garland might have been just one more victim of his creative
faculties. There was a long list of them, according to his fellow
tribesman, Wooden Leg.

Two Moon was in the fight here with Crazy Horse and other
chiefs. He noted an officer in buckskin shirt who was evidently in
command of all the troops on this part of the field. This officer
was so ubiquitous and so astonishing in his activities that to Two
Moon he seemed to be the chief subject of interest in the fight.
"The shooting was quick, quick, pop, pop, pop, very fast," he says.
"Some of the soldiers were down on their knees, some standing.
Officers all in front. The smoke was like a great cloud, and everywhere the Sioux went the dust rose like smoke. We circled round
and round him—like water swirling round a rock. We shoot, we
ride fast, we shoot again. Soldiers drop and horses fall on them.
Soldiers in line drop, but one man rides up and down the line—
all the time shouting. He rode a sorrel horse with a white face
and white forelegs. I don't know who he was. He was a brave man."

"Indians keep swirling round and round and the soldiers
killed only a few. Many soldiers fell. At last all horses killed but
five. Once in a while some man would break out and run toward
the river, but he would fall. At last about a hundred men and five
horses stood on the hill all bunched together. All along a bugler
kept blowing his commands. He was very brave too. Then a chief
was killed. I hear it was Long Hair. I don't know, and then the five

horsemen and the bunch of men, maybe so forty men, started toward the river. The man on the sorrel horse led them, shouting all the time. He wore a buckskin shirt and long black mustache. He fought hard with a big knife. His men were all covered with white dust."

Thus out of the jumbled memories of an old man come the outlines of a picture analysis had forced on us long before the story was read. If we arrange the objective facts in their proper sequence we see the three troops "all bunched together on the Hill" just before they started to ride away eastward north of the ridge. Then we see Keogh place himself at the head of his troop, his men, about 40 in number, "all covered with white dust" which had settled on their uniforms as they lay for nearly an hour on the north wing of the ridge sniping with Indians to the west and southwest. They are all mounted now, but the old chief accepted his mind-pictures as they came, haphazardly, as did nearly all other Indians whose accounts we have. The fighting he describes could have taken place only after these troops had left the Hill, and they lost their horses in this fighting, for there were only a little over a hundred men in the three troops to begin with. But there had been an hour's fighting elsewhere, which may have confused him. What we may accept here as undoubted fact is that toward the end of the fighting only a few of the troops still had their horses. The nature of the fighting would suggest this, and there is direct evidence from the Cheyennes to this effect. It is about what Captain Benteen thought after going over the field to determine how the battle was fought, saying that the men had probably turned loose their horses in the course of the fighting.

If we possessed only Two Moon's account of the fighting north of the ridge and no knowledge of the terrain; if there were no markers showing where the men fell, we would conclude that the Indians fought mounted here, "swirled all round him shooting fast." But remembering that the Indians largely disregarded temporal sequences in telling their stories, we have only to assume that Two Moon referred to their fast riding in coming to the field. The "swirling" came later, at first on the outskirts of the fighting, closing in as the fire dwindled and one group after another of the troops were wiped out, until the whole field swarmed not only with warriors but with hundreds of old men and boys as well.

Coming back now to the orderly description of the action, we find that Keogh left his own troop in command of Porter and turned to the spot of the greatest immediate danger, the momentarily shattered Troop "F" in the leadership of which he was to distinguish himself as the "bravest man the Sioux ever fought."

The Indians were to find the pretty birds of Troop "F" unexpectedly tough. In spite of the surprise and the large quota of recruits among them, they did what only the very best troops are supposed to be able to do—reorganize under fire in the presence of an overwhelming enemy. Whether or not they could have done it without the inspiring action of Keogh in "turning his horse and covering their retreat" must obviously remain an unanswered question.

The rear platoon of "F," after coming to a halt as noted, formed a line with its left resting against the ridge. How long the men stood here it is impossible to say. They left 8—possibly only 7—of their number on the spot when, as it would seem, a sudden forward surge of the Indians once more caused their horses to become unmanageable, and they were carried over the ridge directly toward the head of a ravine. A heavy volley by Indians concealed here dropped 4 men. The horses recoiled to the left and toward the ridge, and as the few remaining members of the platoon were in all probability trying to reach the leading platoon, they rode eastward. As they were mounting the ridge to cross over to the first platoon 4 more men were killed, undoubtedly by a volley from Indians concealed in the head of another ravine here. There is another marker on the south slope of the ridge about 40 yards farther east which may represent the last man of the platoon.

The first platoon, as we have said, came to a halt about 160 yards east of the second platoon and faced about. There are 10 markers here, five closely grouped, the rest scattered. Fifty yards farther east it made a second stand on and behind a little cross-ridge only a few feet above the general level of the slope. Here there are 8 markers in pairs and nearly in line. Thirty yards farther east are 3 markers, and 13 yards beyond these are 2 more, evidently the last of the troop, 29 yards from the rear platoon of Troop "I".

Captain Keogh remained with Troop "F" to the end. He went down under the rush of stampeding horses near the last five surviving members of the troop. This is suggested in the narrative of Wooden Leg who was at this moment on the second ridge—the one bordering Calhoun's position on the north—just to the northeast of Keogh's troop. He had fired twice on the men here and then ceased firing because Indians were all around the men and so close to them that he feared he might hit them instead of the soldiers. A Waist and Skirt Indian came to him here and told him he had been watching a certain man who appeared to be telling all the rest what to do and that he must, therefore, be the chief of the soldiers. He started to point out this man, but just then a band of stampeding horses ran over the soldiers jostling them and knocking them down, and stirring up a cloud of dust. When the dust had settled the "chief" had disappeared. This could hardly have been any other than Keogh, the same "chief" who had so impressed both Two Moon and Red Horse, for the only other commissioned officer present was Lieutenant Porter who was certainly with his own troop "I."

Further interesting evidence is to be found in a photograph made a year after the battle and showing the marker put up for Keogh when his body was removed. Two or three yards to the southeast of the marker is the skeleton of a horse, the only one visible in the picture. From the topography it is possible to locate this marker accurately. It stood a few yards west of the second platoon of "I," and about the same distance from the last men of "F". The skeleton of the horse and its position suggest that Keogh was still mounted when he was bowled over by the stampeding horses. These horses almost certainly belonged to "F" and "I". When released they had naturally crossed the ridge to get away from the fighting, and were now turned back by Gall's warriors and the crowd of noncombatants after Calhoun's troop had been wiped out. They were, therefore, coming from the southeast, and when Keogh's horse was run over it naturally threw its rider toward the northwest as it went down. Apparently neither man nor horse rose again.

Keogh's body was found unmutilated. Why it was spared is anyone's guess. The second Mrs. McGillycuddy says in her book, *McGillycuddy: Agent,* page 78, "Captain Keogh's body was not mutilated for two reasons—the Indians knew and liked him well, and they found around his neck, when he was stripped, a silver charm, the *Agnus Dei,* which they looked upon as a holy charm." Her authority for this statement was Crazy Horse between whom and her husband a mutual respect and friendship had sprung up during the brief period they knew each other at Fort Robinson before the latter was killed there.

It was nearly over now on this part of the field. Troop "I" had moved forward in column after Keogh left, and had come to a halt on the bench with its leading platoon six or seven yards from the entrance to the eastern extension of the ravine, the point where Calhoun had entered it not long before. The object of this move has already been explained. It remained here in column of platoons until the end. Until Troops "F" and "L" had been disposed of it seems to have received little attention from the Indians. The ravine to the north had been emptied of warriors going in pursuit of Calhoun. The rest were engaged with Troop "F" and the troops with Custer at the Hill. But as soon as Troops "F" and "L" were out of the way the warriors converged on Troop "I" from every direction. In Godfrey's account of the battle we are given to understand that it was chiefly Gall and his men, mounted and afoot, who swept over this troop in a frenzied charge. Wooden Leg and Kate Bighead, the one on the ridge just to the northeast, the other behind a knoll a hundred yards or so to the southeast, both looking down on what took place here, saw nothing of this charge. Kate Bighead had easily followed the Indians as they crowded back along both sides of the ridge after finishing with Calhoun, and she saw the men of Troop "I" still alive but without horses. Both she and Wooden Leg say that they were closely surrounded by warriors creeping through the grass, and that they all killed themselves or killed each other.

We have seen that as soon as Troop "E" had been destroyed and "C" driven back to the Hill, the Indians engaged here had seized the weapons and ammunition of the dead troopers and opened fire from this direction. Concerning the fight of the Custer group at the foot of the Hill we know little more from any eyewitness worthy of credence other than what has already been told. Kate Bighead saw part of this after she returned from the wounded warrior who was being taken to camp. From what she says we gain the impression that the fighting here was not exciting. It was an exchange of shots mostly at comparatively long range, much as had been the fighting for the first hour or so when only troops "F" and "I" were engaged. The warriors could not approach the Hill closely from this direction without exposing themselves more than an Indian likes to do. There was not much cover within good range south of the Hill, and the close-packed Custer group was too formidable to invite a charge. When they had charged the thin line a few minutes before they had learned how costly was this kind of fighting. They could see, moreover, that there was no need for them to take much risk, for Custer had placed his men on a steep incline where the dead horses gave but slight protection to them.[88] At the lower part of the semi-circle or ellipse, there was some protection, but farther up the men were exposed along either side because they were above the horses lower down and could be

"Custer's Last Stand." The two headstones to the right, near the fence corner, are believed by the author to be spurious, set up without good reason after 1896.

The Battle ridge from near Custer Monument. Note Weir Point in central background. (Edith Kuhlman 1935).

shot by Indians delivering an enfilading fire. Besides this the position was menaced by a low ridge about 60 yards to the southwest. As long as "F" and "I" had stood on the north wing of the main ridge the Indians could not occupy or hold this ridge because the fire of these troops could sweep the farther side of it. But when these troops were withdrawn they could easily crawl up behind it from the southwest. All the men along the east segment of the semi-circle made a perfect target for the warriors on this ridge, especially so for the bowmen who could shoot their arrows in a moderately high curve without exposing themselves at all, once they had the range. Those who used guns, however, were exposed to the fire of the 7 men behind dead horses on top of the Hill[69] until the latter were forced to give their attention to the warriors crawling up from the north and northeast.

There was no charge on Custer Hill, nothing of the heart-stirring action characteristic of desperate hand-to-hand fighting, such as the painters and some writers have represented it. The men here caught a fleeting glimpse of the head of an Indian, saw a puff of smoke and at this they fired virtually random shots because there was not time to take aim before the target vanished. And since the Indian was an expert and the cavalryman a novice in this kind of fighting, it was an entirely one-sided affair, as, indeed, it was for the most part all over the field; for the Indians pursued the same tactics throughout. Nowhere did the cavalry find an opportunity to fight in the one way in which they unquestionably outmatched the Indian, the mounted charge, in which they could come to close quarters, forcing the Indians to stand erect and face the superior weapons and organization of the cavalry.

The indications are that when the warriors, after destroying "F" and "I," streamed westward to take part in the closing scene of the battle, the guns in the group below the cutbank were already silent. There remained 7 men behind dead horses on top of the Hill directly above the Custer group. From behind these dead horses the sharp bark of the carbine still issued defiantly. From the north and northeast the warriors, like great lizards, came slithering up the incline, their heads popping in and out of the grass as they advanced, a veritable sea of them. There were hundreds of heads constantly in sight, said Kate Bighead, who was then on the main ridge some distance to the east. Wooden Leg, after Keogh's men had been killed, left his place on the ridge northeast of them and rode westward until he arrived opposite Custer Hill, left his pony in the ravine there and crawled up after the warriors who had gone up this way while the fighting with "F" and "I" was still in progress. When he approached those in advance the nearest warriors were only a few yards from the dead horses. He caught glimpses of the men, but they were too fleeting to permit him to take aim, so he just fired at the horses. A Sioux in war-bonnet, one of the few who wore this regalia during the battle, was half the length of a lariat rope ahead of him, raising his head to fire and then ducking again. Finally, as his head was up, a bullet struck him squarely in the middle of the forehead. His limbs twitched convulsively for a moment. Then the body went limp and lay still. A Cheyenne boy, close behind the unfortunate Sioux, seeing the sight, ran away terrified down the slope, missing the much-coveted "coup blow."

At last the shots ceased to come from behind the dead horses. The Indians near them ran forward, shouting to those farther back that all the soldiers were dead. To their surprise 7 men jumped up and ran away toward the river, getting over the cut-bank before any of them could be killed. Both Wooden Leg and Kate Bighead saw these men run away, but the ridge shut them from sight of the former at once and he saw nothing further of them, but heard later that they had killed themselves. Kate Bighead could see them until they disappeared in the smoke and dust with hundreds of Cheyennes and Sioux after them, but she did not see what became of them. She also heard that they had killed themselves.

When the warriors cried out that all the soldiers were dead the crowd of old men and boys who had gathered on the ridges toward the close of the battle rode wildly onto the field, and an indescribable scene followed. Wooden Leg said that it "looked like a thousand dogs might look if all of them were mixed together in a fight;" and Kate Bighead said that when she stopped at the Custer group the dust was so thick that it nearly choked her. There is no doubt that the ground around Custer, especially immediately to the west of where he fell, was badly torn up so as to give the impression that a desperate struggle had taken place here. The shod horses of troops "C" and "E" had passed here in going down to form the skirmish line, and when the horses were later led back and shot for breastworks, the ground was again trampled. This was followed by a milling horde of Indians both mounted and afoot. The trampled condition of the ground is, therefore, no evidence of the character of the fighting here.

It is almost certain that not a single Indian came within good pistol range of the Custer group until after the men on top of the Hill had run away. As long as they held their ground no Indian could approach the Hill from the south to plunder without running the risk of being speedily killed. After these men had fled the warriors who had been fighting them crowded around Curter's forlorn hope in which no sign of life was at first apparent. One officer, however, was not dead. As if coming out of a swoon he raised himself on his left elbow and looked around in bewilderment, still clutching his revolver. The Indians, believing the man to have come back from the dead, drew back frightened; but one Sioux, less superstitious than the rest, wrenched the revolver from his hand and shot him through the head with it, after which others beat and stabbed him. Wooden Leg placed the muzzle of his captured carbine against the head of a dead trooper and pulled the trigger. He noticed the long sideburns of Adjutant Cooke and scalped one side of them. The body of Tom Custer was horribly mutilated—scalped, the abdomen ripped open, the skull crushed and shot full of arrows; but the story that Rain-in-the-Face had cut out his heart and eaten it is just another of the innumerable pieces of lurid fiction that clutter up the material we have to deal with in the study of our subject.

And so ends our story of the action on Custer field, save for a brief discussion concerning Custer's personal part in it. Where was he during the two hours or more of the fighting? When and where was he killed? Did he kill himself?

The writer does not know of any evidence permitting a definite answer to any of these questions. The rational assumption is that he remained at the Hill because it formed the chief bastion of his defensive position. Under the constructions presented in this chapter there were only two incidents that might have caused him to leave it temporarily. He may have gone down with Tom Custer to rally the troops in the south line. There is, in fact, an Indian story saying that two men in buckskin rode down from the Hill, were shot from their horses, but that their bodies were not found later after the Indians had secured possession of the ground. We know that both General Custer and his brother Tom were wearing buckskin coats on this campaign, and it may be assumed, we think, that Tom started to go to his troop the instant the Indians launched their attack, and that General Custer may have gone with him. It is because both of them *ought* to have done this that we are inclined to take this story seriously without necessarily inferring that one of the men in question was General Custer. If the story is substantially true, it is possible that one of the men was Lieutenant Sturgis, and Tom Custer the other, that the two met about where "C" and "E" joined flanks, and tried to do something to rescue the men farther south. A good many "C" Troop men were found mixed with those of "E" on this part of the line.

The other incident was the surprise attack on Troop "F" northeast of the Hill. If Custer was not killed on the south line he may have ridden out here to do what he could to restore order; but in our opinion Keogh attended to that before Custer could have done so, though it is true that Red Horse said that the officer who distinguished himself here rode a sorrel horse with four white feet. But Two Moon, who unquestionably refers to Keogh also said that this officer's horse had four white feet. In neither case is the description exact. Custer's mare, Vic, had only three white feet, and Comanche, Keogh's mount, had no white feet at all, and was a "claybank," not a sorrel.

In any case Custer seems to have been on the ridge and mounted some distance to the east, but we do not know why or when; for McClernand says that he saw a dead horse on the ridge 100-150 feet east of the Hill, and was told it was the horse Custer had ridden on the day of the battle. The way the horse had fallen gave him the impression that it was running westward when it was killed.[70]

Did Custer kill himself? And why was his body not mutilated?

Custer was shot through the temple and left breast, both wounds fatal. From this it is argued that he could not have committed suicide. The conclusion does not follow from the premise; for he could have shot himself in the breast and been shot through the temple by the Indians after he was dead. It was a common practice of the Indians to shoot bullets and arrows into their dead enemies.

Most of the Indians said that they did not know when Custer was killed or who killed him; that they did not know he was there, or that the man in buckskin was the commander of the troops. The Cheyennes bluntly call all stories to the contrary pure fabrications motivated by a desire to attract attention or credit for themselves. The warriors did not know why his body escaped mutilation. There were other bodies not hacked up, stripped or scalped, and there may have been no special reason for sparing the body of Custer, as far as the Indians in general were concerned. So argued Wooden Leg and the Cheyennes consulted by Dr. Marquis—all except Kate Bighead who gives us a plausible explanation for the condition in which Custer's body was found, with a glimpse into the heart of an Indian betraying a touch of sentiment of which few of us think them capable. Custer lay with his arms outspread across the bodies of two other men, his face undistorted by pain or any sign of horror such as marred the features of many others. As Lieutenant Bradley wrote, he seemed as one who had gone peacefully to sleep and pleasant dreams.

Now, it is at once apparent that he had not fallen in this way, for, since the bodies were stripped they had all been pulled about so that one resting across another must have been moved after the one under it had been stripped. Moreover, Custer's wounds had evidently been cleansed of blood and an effort made to close them, since several persons who saw the body failed to observe them. Who then, had taken the trouble to do that for a fallen enemy? Certainly not any of the warriors. What is probably an approximately true answer to this question is given us by Kate Bighead as follows:

"I may have seen Custer at the time of the battle, or after he was killed. I do not know, as I did not know then of his being there. All our old warriors say the same—none of them knew of his being there until they learned of it afterward at the soldier forts or the agencies, or from Indians coming from the agencies.

"But I learned something more about him from our people in Oklahoma. Two of the Southern Cheyenne women who had been in our camp at the Little Big Horn told of having been on the battlefield soon after the fighting ended. They saw Custer lying dead there. They had known him in the south. While they were looking at him some Sioux men came and were about to cut up his body. The Cheyenne women, thinking of Me-o-tze, made signs: 'he is a relative of ours', but telling nothing more about him. So the Sioux men cut off only one joint of a finger. The women then pushed the point of a sewing-awl into each of his ears, into his head. This was done to improve his hearing, as it seemed he had not heard what our chiefs told him when he smoked the peace pipe with them. They told him then that if ever afterward he should break that peace promise and fight the Cheyennes the Everywhere Spirit surely would cause him to be killed.

"Through almost sixty years, many a time I have thought of Hi-es-tzie as the handsome man I saw in the south. And I often have wondered if, when I was riding among the dead where he was lying, my pony may have kicked dirt on his body."[71]

Appendix I

NOTES

1. **Four** such paintings have been reproduced in the *Kansas Historical Quarterly*, vol. XIV, No. 4, November, 1946, by Dr. Robert Taft, professor of chemistry, University of Kansas, Lawrence, Kansas. This study, excellently documented, is part of a series on "The Pictorial History of the West," and is intensely interesting to every student of Western history, if our own reactions are any guide. The numbers are, we believe, available in reprints. P. 6

2. Our interpretation of Benteen's statement that he counted only 2 dead Indian ponies on Custer field has been questioned by Colonel Graham and the late W. J. Ghent. Mr. Ghent did not present any evidence to support his criticism made in a letter to the late Mr. W. A. Falconer of Bismarck, North Dakota. He contented himself with a lofty "pooh! pooh!" of the Cheyennes, Dr. Marquis, Benteen and the present writer. There is, therefore, no need to refute this Olympian. It is a different matter when it comes to a student of the quality of Colonel Graham who quoted Generals Godfrey and Edgerly as having told him that they had seen a number of dead ponies near Custer Hill. Here there is no question of bias or good faith. It is, however, notorious that, while Godfrey was one of the clearest and least evasive witnesses at the Court of Inquiry, his memory in later years was so faulty that little reliance could be placed in it. Years of thinking, speculating and reconstructing had insensibly so intermingled the mind-pictures of direct observation with those constructed by the imagination that he could no longer distinguish the one from the other. There is no need to be astonished at this; for this confusion takes place in a greater or less degree in the minds of all of us, and is taken account of in all courts of law. It was, therefore, true of General Edgerly also. But Captain Benteen spoke under oath and less than three years after the event. Moreover, he had examined the field with the express object of determining how the battle was fought; and the number and distribution of the dead horses and ponies, like that of the dead troopers, were important pieces of evidence. He used the word "counted," implying that the number was significant, not an indefinite term such as "noted," "saw" or the like, neutral terms reporting something idly observed in passing.

Aside from the two witnesses cited in the text, accounts with the objectivity of a Thucydides and approaching the clarity of a surveyor's map as to spatial relationships, there is the general statement by Dr. Grinnell based on what the Cheyennes had told him. "The Indians state positively," says Grinnell, "that they did not kill the troops by charging into them, but by shooting them from behind the hills. The final charge was not made until the troops in the main body had fallen, though of course, many soldiers were still on foot scattered down toward the river. When all the troops on the Hill had fallen, the Indians gave a loud shout and charged up the ridge." This is, in substance, the same as the stories by Wooden Leg and Kate Bighead published by Dr. Marquis. A great shout, *after* the Custer group at the Hill had been wiped out, and *then* the rush of old men, boys and the scattered warriors who had been on the outskirts of the fighting who were *mounted* and, therefore, in condition to make what the Indians called a "charge."

It is true that there are many Indian accounts picturing Custer as having been wiped out in a mass charge by mounted warriors, and that writers like Byrne, Van DeWater, and McLaughlin have so represented it. How did this conception arise? There would seem to be little reason to doubt that it arose chiefly from the white man's misunderstanding of what the Indian meant by a "charge." If we read these accounts attentively we soon discover that to the Indian a charge meant simply wild riding in the direction of the enemy or circling around him. Unless the enemy was extremely weak and could be bowled over in the first shock of meeting, these charges were never driven home. The charges of the Cheyennes against Forsyth's small force of about 50 men on Beacher Island, are usually represented as unparalleled in Indian warfare; but every one of these charges petered out before it came to the desperate hand-to-hand fighting in which a real charge ends. Dr. Grinnell says that the Cheyennes "lost heart" when the decisive moment arrived and passed the island, part of them on one side and part on the other. P. 7

3. For the detailed facts in this disgraceful affair see the excellent little book by E. A. Brininstool; *Crazy Horse, the Invincible Ogalalla Sioux Chief.* Wetzel Publishing Co., Inc. Los Angeles, Calif. P. 13

4. The itinerary of the scout was kept by Lieutenant Sturgis and may have been on his person when he was killed. In any case it has not been found, as far as the present writer knows. We have followed the account of the marches given by Dr. DeWolf in a letter to his wife dated "Yellowstone, Mouth of the Rosebud, June 21, '76." After correcting a rather obvious slip of the pen, the total mileage comes to 265. It seems to us altogether probable that he received the daily milages directly from Sturgis. His letter indicates that he was well liked by the officers and was on friendly hobnobbing terms with several of them. P. 21

5. Colonel Robert P. Hughes. *The Campaign against the Sioux in 1876.* Journal of the Military Service Institution of the United States. Vol. XVIII, No. LXXIX. P. 28

6. Letter of W. W. Carland to W. A. Falconer of Bismarck, N. D. Oct. 27, 1930. W. W. Carland was the son of the Lieutenant Carland mentioned in the text. He served as herder on the march from Fort Lincoln, and was later with Captain Baker's company on the boat. P. 28

7. The same. Also Hanson, *Conquest of the Missouri.* P. 28

8. A term used in a letter by an officer who served in the 9th Cavalry with Brisbin. P. 28

9. Letter of Major Brisbin to Captain Godfrey, Jan. 1, 1892. P. 28

10. According to Brisbin Custer's answer was, "The Seventh can handle anything it meets." The answer given in the text is from Terry's confidential dispatch of July 2. The wording here makes it hard to believe that anyone except Terry himself made the offer. Hughes says: "It is certain, on Terry's authority, that *at the conference* (italics ours) he offered, if Custer so desired, to modify his plan and give him all the cavalry, but he objected and it was not done."

216

There is another serious difficulty in Brisbin's story. Gibbon's command had started up the north bank of the Yellowstone at 9:45 that morning and camped for the night on the Great Porcupine 17 miles from Custer's camp. Custer started at noon the next day. It would have been necessary for Brisbin to ride through the night, bring back his cavalry, organize a packtrain, draw rations and ammunitions, and be ferried across the river, all in about 15 hours. It could, perhaps, have been done in this time; or, if not, Custer's departure might have been delayed long enough for Brisbin to get ready. But why this fumbling? Have we to do here with a bit of time-juggling by both Hughes and Brisbin to plant a solicitude in Terry's mind which was not there at this time? There is much of this kind of juggling all through the Hughes article, as anyone can easily discover for himself if he will read the evidence with an open mind. There is no question whatever that the offer was made; but was it made belatedly out of fear that the "wild man" would blunder into grief? Or was it because of a tardy appraisal of the fact implied in the order and openly admitted by both Terry and Gibbon, that Custer was almost certain to make contact with the Indians long before Gibbon could do so, and that in consequence he would be compelled to herd them, perhaps for several days? Could he do that with so small a force as the Seventh Cavalry? There were four lines of escape from the valley of the Little Big Horn, namely, the main trail by which they had come, the Indian Creek-Sioux Pass route, the one past the head of the Rosebud, and straight south to the Big Horn Mountains. Since the Indians held the inside line Custer, if he was to make certain that they would not escape by one or more of these routes, would have been forced to leave a detachment near enough to all of them to meet them and drive them back before they could cross the Rosebud. This spelled nonsense; and it would still have been nonsense if Gibbon's four troops of cavalry had been added to Custer's twelve. Every experienced Indian fighter knew that success in this case would depend more on chance than on anything else; and in our opinion, General Terry, as well as Gibbon and Custer, was fully aware of this. The one chance no one had considered or even imagined, was that there might be a serious disaster, as Gibbon, in effect, put it a year after the campaign. The fear of disaster was an after-the-event invention. This is a fundamental fact we must understand before we can hope to understand much of anything about Terry's plan and orders. Because that fact was deliberately obscured we have such hopeless muddles as the one Brisbin presents to us here. We shall meet others stemming from the same motives, as we go along. P. 28

11. Hanson, Joseph Mills. *The Conquest of the Missouri.* Murray Hill Books, Inc. Second Edition, page 261.

The "sabers" must be excused as poetic license. Private William C. Slaper of Troop "M" wrote: "At the Powder River, our wagons were all sent back. Our sabers also were boxed and returned; no one, not even an officer, retaining this weapon." Brininstool, E. A., *A. Trooper with Custer.* The Hunter-Trapper-Trader Co. Vol. I. page 25. P. 31

12. The following table showing the movements of the Indians with the approximate dates of their various camps from the time they arrived on the Rosebud to June 26, is here given for the convenience of the reader: P. 35

Camp 1. May 23 or 24 to 29.
Camp 2. May 30.
Camp 3. May 31.
Camp 4. June 1 to 6.
Camp 5. June 7 to 10. Sundance.
Camp 6. June 11. Within about 10 miles of Davis Creek.

Camp 7. June 12 to 14. Cheyennes south end, directly opposite Davis Creek.
Camp 8. June 15. Near Divide.
Camp 9. June 16 to 18. At forks of Reno Creek.
Camp 10. June 18 to 24. In valley east of LBH just south of Busby road.
Camp 11. June 24 to 25. Where Custer found them.
Camp 12. 25 to 26. Just below campsite of 25th.

13. Bourke, Captain John G. *With Crook on the Border.* Pages 300-301. Compare with pages 34-38 of our chapter 2. The two accounts tally except in the number of horses drowned—4, instead of all of one company. P. 38

14. Much has been made of Custer's failure to scout the upper Tullocks region as he marched up the Rosebud, and of his neglect in not sending a messenger to Terry with a report of what he had found there.

The truth is that Terry seems to have been poorly informed as to what this would have involved. A look at the map will show that the upper Tullocks could not have been examined by the usual flankers of the command as they marched along. It would have been necessary to organize an independent scouting party and start it at least a day before the march began, if the courier, Herendeen, was to get to Terry before he broke camp at 5:45 on the morning of the 25th, as he was expected to do. This scouting party would have been compelled to follow the Rosebud to near Busby and then cross over to the head of Tullocks to make observations and then return to report to Custer. If it had tried to reach its objective by going in a direct line from the mouth of the Rosebud it would have had to cross an endless succession of ravines and ridges, making progress extremely slow and exhausting the horses to the point of unfitness by the time they got to Custer's camp on the evening of the 24th.

Brisbin, in his letter to Godfrey in 1892 shows that he thought the command would cross the Tullocks on its march. Perhaps we have here the source of Terry's misconception of the nature of the task imposed.

In the same letter Brisbin said also that "Herendeen did report to Custer when you reached Tullock, and said: 'General, this is Tullock, and here is where I am to leave you to go down it to the other command.' Custer was riding on his horse at the time and Herendeen rode up beside him. Custer gave Herendeen no answer, but heard him and looked at him. Herendeen kept near Custer for some time, expecting to be called and be dispatched down the Tullock to us, but seeing he was not wanted, he fell back, nor did Custer ever speak to him again, though he knew Herendeen was there to go down the Tullock and communicate with us, by Terry's orders, and in this Custer disobeyed distinctly the Department Commander's wishes and orders."

We do not know upon whose authority Brisbin made these statements, but here is what Herendeen himself said in a letter to the *New York Herald*, January 22, 1878.

"On the morning of the 24th we broke camp at 5 o'clock and continued following the trail up the stream. Soon after starting Custer, who was in advance with Bouyer, called me to him and told me to get ready, he thought he would send me and Charlie Reynolds to the head of Tullock's Fork to take a look. I told the General it was not time yet, as we were travelling in the direction of the head of Tullock, and I could only follow his trail. I called Bouyer, who was a little ahead back and asked him if I was not correct in my statement to the General, and he said 'Yes'; further up on Rosebud we would come opposite a gap, and then we could cut across and strike the Tullock in about fifteen miles." Custer said "Alright; I could wait."

This makes sense. Evidently Custer knew from the beginning that nothing could be done about the Tullocks until he got well up along the Rosebud; which explains why his scouts paid no especial attention to the right, a fact upon which his critics have based the charge that he had intended all along to "cut loose" from Terry. But he may not have known that he would still be 15 miles from the Tullocks when he reached a point 5 to 6 miles below the site of Busby, a point they would not reach until about 6 o'clock. If he did know he would also have known that Herendeen could not make the scout and return to him until after midnight, with a horse that had already made over 50 miles that day and could, therefore, not be expected to make the 50 miles through the night, partly over very rough ground, to Terry's camp. The fact that he intended to send Reynolds also rather suggests that he knew Herendeen could not be sent until the next day if he returned to report, and that he was to go directly to Terry, while Reynolds returned and reported to Custer.

One thing is entirely clear: on the morning of the 24th Custer intended to send Herendeen and Reynolds to examine the upper Tullocks. Why, in the end, he sent no one at all is a matter of speculation. Perhaps the whole matter was driven from his mind by the discovery of the fresh, heavy trail. P. 44

15. We have already mentioned the small band of Cheyennes under Little Wolf who saw Custer go into camp on the evening of the 24th. Had Custer continued up the Rosebud on the 25th they would have reported his presence here about the middle of the afternoon of that day. They seem to have moved about parallel with him just across the divide between Reno Creek and the heads of the numerous branches of Tullock's Creek. The warriors Sergeant Curtis found at the package of hardbread were scouts from this band, and the small body of Indians flushed at the Lone Tepee undoubtedly consisted of the full warrior force of this band acting as guards for the non-combatants. Custer's rapid advance cut them off from the camps for the time being. They remained in the hills to the east until the Custer fight was over and then entered the village near the camp of the Sans Arcs. See Marquis, *A Warrior who Fought Custer*, pp. 248-250. P. 50

16. Hughes' statement on this point is as follows: "It should be borne in mind that these operations were directed against a village community; that the fighting force of this community could not leave their village to attack one of the approaching columns without abandoning their wives, children, and property an easy prey to the other."

Strange reasoning! But any port in a storm.

The only way this village differed from other Indian villages was in its size. It was no more nailed down than were other villages which were continually eluding the troops unless they were surprised in their winter quarters, or in dawn attacks.

If the Indians discovered the two columns of troops, as the Hughes argument assumes, and they wanted to attack one of them, the non-combatants would have pulled stakes and fled from the one that was free to attack, Gibbon's, in this case. As Gibbon wrote in the *Catholic Quarterly*: "The Indians can always, in summer, avoid a single column, or select their own time for meeting it." If, then, Custer had continued up the Rosebud on the 25th, in the afternoon of which the Indians would have learned of his presence here, the whole warrior force could have fallen on him on the morning of the 26th, as they had done when Crook threatened them from this direction. Then, even if Gibbon had known exactly where he was, he could not have reached him until late on the 28th. That would have left Custer to fight for three days with only 150 rounds of ammunition. The Indians had received heavy reinforcements during the interval, but Crook, with more than twice Custer's force and after only one day of fighting, thought it prudent to return to his base partly because of the serious depletion of his ammunition. Meanwhile the non-combatants would have escaped up the valley of the Little Big Horn, taking all their property with them, as they actually did on the approach of Gibbon.

That this argument of Hughes is a mere subterfuge designed to mislead the uninformed or careless reader is proved by what he says in another part of this article where he admits that Custer should have been on the morning of the 26th where he actually was on the morning of the 25th. But, since he repeatedly insists that Custer should have continued up the Rosebud on the 25th, how was he to get back to strike on the morning of the 26th? On that morning he would have been more than 50 miles from the Indian village, and out of the fight until about the middle of the forenoon of the 27th, or about the time Terry arrived on Reno Hill!

We are not, at present, prepared to charge Colonel Hughes with conscious bad faith in the wider sense of that term. He may have believed that Custer deliberately disobeyed both the letter and spirit of his instructions. But the method and spirit of his arguments are not those of the historian seeking the truth. Introduction of irrelevancies to prejudice the reader in advance; mis-statements of fact in official documents it is clear he had before him while writing; and even the truncating of a sentence from such documents to make it imply exactly the opposite of what the sentence as a whole implies, condemn the article as a partisan product. The sentence from the report of Wallace to which we refer reads as follows: "Custer determined to cross the divide that night (24th-25th), conceal the command, the next day find out the locality of the village, and attack the following morning at daylight." But Hughes quotes only: "Custer determined to cross the divide that night," leaving the reader to infer that he decided on the evening of the 24th to attack on the 25th in order to gather all the glory himself, as Hughes insists was the object in following the trail across the divide. Had he quoted the sentence in full he would have destroyed his whole case, for, as stated above, he admits that Custer should have been in position to attack on the morning of the 26th. This he was forced to admit because of the known fact that on this day Gibbon would approach the village from the north. P. 50

17. Both Wooden Leg and Kate Bighead said that in the Custer fight the bow had served better than the rifle, and explained how it was used effectively against both men and horses with little risk to the bowmen. P. 51

18. The American *Catholic Quarterly* Review, Vol. 2.
We note also that when Reno moved to join Custer on the evening of the 25th, it required three of the six platoons in his battalion to carry the wounded, though he had left in the valley all those who could not ride their horses after being hit. And after the fighting ceased that evening an idea prevailed among the officers that the reason Custer had not rejoined them was that he might not be able to move on account of his wounded. P. 51

19. Testimony of Lieutenant DeRudio. P. 52

20. Libby, C. G. *Arikara Narrative*. North Dakota Historical Collection, Vol. 6. Bismarck, North Dakota, 1920. See Story by Young Hawk. Colonel Graham writes that the scouts set the tepee a-fire. *Story of the Little Big Horn*, p. 30.
Some of the Indians were still driving ponies downstream both in the valley and on the benchlands when Reno was crossing. See testimony of Hare and Dr. Porter. Even so they left a number of ponies near the river below the ford. Some of the Arikara left the column to capture them. All of this goes to show how complete was the surprise of the attack. P. 52

21. For these facts concerning the march see our chapter on Benteen's scout to the left. P. 53

22. Testimony of Fred Gerard, interpreter for the Arikara. P. 54

23. If the line had been deployed as indicated by Godfrey most of the men in it would have been able to see the greater part of the village; but it is clear from the testimony that they saw little or nothing of it. Hare, who was 200 yards from the left of the line, saw only 400-500 tepees, and these must have included those of the Blackfeet, which stood farthest westward from the river.

There may have been Indians in the farther ravine, the one directly opposite the Uncpapa camp standing in the first loop downstream from the Garryowen loop. But the officers who testified on the point said that the nearest Indian camp was 800 to 1000 yards away. P. 55

24. Fred Dustin, in *The Custer Tragedy*, chapter XXI, has an excellent analysis showing where each of these scouts was during the battle and what he was doing. It was an extremely difficult piece of work and is, in all probability, final as to essentials. P. 62

25. The line could not have been brought in "round the horses," which were in the timber at the right of the line *before* it was faced about. As we shall see in a moment, Varnum brought in the horses behind the line *after* it faced about.

Reno's statement that he told Hodgson to bring in the line is misleading, though not intentionally so. The truth is that while Reno was with the detachment of "G" Company on the bench Moylan became alarmed over the situation in the rear of the line, and called to Reno across the clearing to come and see for himself how things stood. Reno did so and then himself ordered the line into the edge of the timber. Then why did he say he had told Hodgson to call in the line? Because he had actually told him to do so.

What happened is as follows, and we give the details here partly because it clears up some of the obscurities in the movements of Varnum. Varnum, hearing the shout: "G" Company is going to charge!" rode down on the bench, intending to take part in the charge; but Reno asked him instead (since there was no question of a charge) to go back to the line, see how things stood, and come back and report. On his way Varnum met Hodgson in the clearing. Hodgson was coming to Reno to report as he had been ordered to do. But he thought his horse had been hit and asked Varnum to look at it. Varnum agreed to do so after he had gone to the line and come back, while Hodgson went on to Reno. They met again in the clearing a few minutes later and Varnum started to look at the horse. While about this Moylan came to the edge of the high bank and shouted to Reno, practically over the heads of Varnum and Hodgson. Hearing the shout and seeing Reno go to Moylan, they understood there was no need for them to do anything further. P. 63

26. Brininstool, E. A. *A Trooper with Custer*. The Frontier Series, Vol. I. The Hunter-Trader-Trapper Co., Columbus, Ohio. 1926. P. 64

27. Brininstool, E. A. *A Trooper with Custer*. pp. 30-31. Account by William C. Slaper of Company "M". P. 67

28. Gerard and Reynolds seem to have remained near their horses until near the time the order was given for the men to mount and then went through the edge of the timber along the farther side, toward the extreme left of the line to the "brow of the hill" so often mentioned in Gerard's

testimony. They had secured their horses and left before Herendeen returned from his position in the tip of the line of timber. Their movements are timed also by the testimony of Sergeant Culbertson who said he came to the "brow of the hill" with 3 men, presumably of "A" Company, and fired 3 or 4 shots before they heard the cry "Charge! Charge." In running for their horses one of the men was wounded and they left him. This was probably the man Moylan said was wounded as the command went out. In any case Gerard and Reynolds reached the brow of the hill only a minute or two after Culbertson had left it. Although this had now become a very dangerous spot they loitered here until A and M went out, Reynolds remaining mounted in spite of Gerard's suggestion that he ought to dismount in order to lessen the chances of being hit. At the moment the troops left the two were some distance apart and Indians got in between them. Reynolds then started out to overtake the troops, apparently by going along the farther side of the line of timber, which we know now contained a good many Indians. The impression left by Gerard's account is that he did not get very far before he was hit. In falling he lost his rifle and as he struck the ground was dragged some, how far we are not told.

The headstone for Reynolds now stands over 200 yards west by north from the point where, according to Gerard, he was hit. Gerard's account seems, in this particular, to agree with an account by Dr. Porter in possession of Mr. Dustin. In this account Dr. Porter said that while he was attending a wounded trooper (Private Henry Klotzbucher, as the context shows) Reynolds called to him that the Indians were firing directly at him and was killed an instant later. The only difference between the two accounts is that, according to Gerard, Reynolds was mounted and riding to overtake the troops, whereas according to Porter, he was standing in the brush. It will be noted, however, that in timing the two accounts tally to a dot. Klotzbucher was hit in the volley that killed Bloody Knife, a minute or two before "A" and "M" went out on the gallop. P. 68

29. In a narrative of undetermined date, by General Winfield Scott Edgerly, a copy of which was received by the writer from Captain E. S. Luce, we find the following: Speaking of the retreat from the Valley, which Reno called a "charge," Edgerly said "This was very aptly called by Captain French 'the sauve qui peut movement.'" P. 75

30. The second clause in this sentence does not appear in the Official Record. In his incomplete story written, it is believed, in 1891 or 1892, Benteen said that he was ordered to a line of bluffs "about 2 miles away," which is near the fact, if one may judge from the view obtained from the Crow's nest. P. 82

31. Testimony of Lieutenant Edgerly. P. 83

32. Testimony of Captain McDougall. It is rather surprising that neither Lieutenant Mathey who was in charge of the packs, nor Captain McDougall commanding the guard, mentions seeing Benteen. P. 83

33. While we have no direct statement on the subject, inferences drawn from the testimony of McDougall and Mathey are to the effect that the pack-train was close-up at the time the command started from the Divide. P. 83

34. Lieutenant Gibson, in a letter to George L. Yates dated April 28, 1915, said: "Benteen asked Reno where Custer was, and when told said: 'Well, let us make a junction with him as soon as possible.' This I know, for I heard it."

In this letter Gibson said also that Benteen followed Custer's, not Reno's trail, a point concerning which there has been considerable doubt, though the impression gained from the accounts of Godfrey and Edgerly is in accord with Gibson's statement.

We are indebted to Captain E. S. Luce for a copy of this letter now in the collection for the Custer Battlefield Museum. P. 84

35. These distances have since been re-checked by Captain Luce by going over the ground with a Chevrolet and a Ford truck, accompanied by Colonel Frank R. Olin, U. S. Army, Fort Francis E. Warren. Both trucks recorded the distances exactly the same as the Dodge sedan.

Several years after these checks were made some doubt was expressed concerning our identification of the morass. Might not Benteen have referred to a place in the creek about a half mile farther down stream, it was asked. In answer to this it may be urged: Why choose a place 4½ miles from the Divide when Benteen said is was 4 miles? But what would seem to be decisive is the identification made by John Burkman, Custer's personal orderly, who was in the packtrain on June 25th. Years ago he and the late I. D. O'Donnell retraced the march of the regiment, and O'Donnell, on our trip in 1939, said that Burkman positively identified the spot 4 miles from the Divide as the place in which some of the pack-mules had mired down: P. 87

36. Copies of these letters were furnished the writer by Captain Luce. P. 89

Writing to Theodore Goldin February 24, 1892, Benteen began his letter with "I have been on a slight 'jag,'" and then turned to a subject that seems to have rested heavily on his mind since that fatal afternoon of June 25, nearly sixteen years before. "If I had carried out to the letter the last order brought to me from General Custer by the Sergeant Major of the regiment, which was to the effect that, if from the farthest line of bluffs which we then saw I could not see the valley—no particular valley specified—to keep on until I came to a valley (or, perhaps *the* valley) (The bracket is Benteen's) to pitch into anything I might come across, *and notify them at once*. (Italics ours). Now. I don't know how much further I should have had to go in the direction I was headed to have found the valley of the Little Big Horn River, but think that perhaps six or seven miles would have brought me to it."

It is well known that the Demon Rum is sometimes the friend of Truth, especially where the sensitive and troubled conscience of a strong moral character is involved! And yet how very little there had been in his conduct throughout for which he had reason to reproach himself. No carelessness, no wilful negligence, and certainly no treachery. An oversight, perhaps, while on his scout, and a mistake in reading the meaning of what he saw on Custer field while he was at Weir Point, part of which, we believe, he later suspected if he did not know it as a fact.

It is those of high moral worth, not the morally dull, who harbor the tormenting internal conflicts. One such conflict must have been Benteen's as a result of his espousing the cause of the North against his own people. The popular clamor against him in connection with the Battle of the Little Big Horn added another to reinforce the first.

The real Benteen is not to be found in the cock-and-bull stories he told at the Court of Inquiry, nor in his numerous quarrels, the result of his aggressive, not to say provocative attitude in the face of the world generally. It would not be too difficult to portray the real Benteen behind the unattractive facade, but there is no space for that here since it is not essential to our analysis. P. 89

37. In the fragment already referred to, Benteen wrote: "John Martin, the trumpeter bringing this dispatch, was a thick-headed Italian, just about as much cut out for a cavalryman as he was for a king." P. 94

38. The following is from Benteen's testimony as given in the *Chicago Times*. P. 95

Question. Was there anything in the orders you received from General Custer when you started from his column, or afterwards, that induced you to believe that you were not to join or come up with the main column in the event of your not finding any Indians?

Answer. I do not believe the General would have told me that. He would have known that I would come up.

Q. I wish you to state whether a reasonable interpretation of the orders you received would be that you should go "valley-hunting *ad infinitum*" without reference to a separation from his column?

A. I might have gone 20 miles in a straight line without finding a valley. Still I was to go to the first valley, and, if I found no Indians, to go to the next, and no interpretation at all. At least I had to go to the second valley. I don't know what stream is next west of that.

Q. You stated that your orders were to go "*valley-hunting ad infinitum*": Do you mean that that was the order, or your conclusion or opinion of it?

A. That is the way I want my answer to appear. That is the way I understood it. I understood it was rather a senseless order. We were on the main trail of the Indians. There were plenty of them on that trail. We had passed immense villages the preceding days. It was scarcely worth while to hunt up a few more Indians. We knew there were 8,000 to 10,000 on that trail, and I think it was well enough to stick to that.

Q. What do you mean by 8,000 to 10,000 Indians—women and children, or that many warriors?

A. General Crook had fought these Indians seven days before we did. He saw enough of them to let them alone. I am giving you now an idea of the numbers. He had a larger force than we had. He remained from the 17th of June to the 15th of August in the same place for reinforcements. He did not think it prudent to go after them. I knew there was a large force, and knew it at the time, but why I was sent to the left I did not know. It was not my business to reason why. I went.

* * * * * * *

Q. What valley did you go to?
A. I did not go to any valley.
Q. Did you come to the valley of the Little Big Horn?
A. No sir, to the ford A and did not see the river until I got there.
Q. At the time General Custer gave you the order to move to the left, could he have known enough about these successive bluffs and the formation of the country to give you special and detailed instructions so as to regulate your every movement?
A. I do not think he could, and I do not think he thought it necessary.
Q. Then the matter was left to your discretion? A. Yes.
Q. Was your bearing to the right to strike the main trail a compliance with the spirit of the instructions General Custer had given you?
A. Scarcely a compliance.
Q. Did you consider it a violation of your instructions?
A. I must state that I did.
Q. Could either yourself or General Custer have known at the time what was behind the second line of bluffs without sending someone to ascertain?
A. He could have found out by following the trail he was on.

The above extracts are only a small sample of Benteen's evasions all through his testimony, but they are sufficient to justify his boast years later that the Court of Inquiry did not know how to get the truth out of him. In a letter dated June 16, 1892, to Theodore Goldin, he wrote: 'The Court of Inquiry knew there was something kept back by me, but they did not know how to get it out of me by questioning, as I gave them no chance to do so; and Reno's attorney was 'posted thereon.' This was by way of elucidation of a passage in a letter of January 22 in which he had said: "Had I not been quite ill when I made the first report I should have had more to say than I said in it; but as to the queries before the Court of Inquiry, there I would answer as I did then, and shield Reno quite as much as I did then, and this simply from the fact that there were a lot of harpies after him,— Godfrey not the smallest of the lot."

39. There is nothing new in what I am saying here. In the following passage from Recorder Lee's *Summation* the same thing is said in more diplomatic language, in connection with Reno's retreat to the bluffs. The indicated caution should be observed in the use of the testimony throughout.

"It is but natural, however, that almost every officer and soldier who survived the disastrous move from the timber to the hill would, in his own mind, by imperceptible degrees, ultimately arrive at a conclusion that after all it was the best thing to do, and results which could not be foreseen at the time may have been taken into consideration to excuse or palliate. *Esprit du corps* is a strong inducement to participants to do this, notwithstanding they may have no responsibility in the matter. There is necessarily in the minds of participants a sort of community of interest, and most certainly their judgments and opinions cannot remain absolutely impartial. Especially is this liable to be the case after a long lapse of time, when many things are forgotten, and opinions become insensibly modified." P. 97

40. The following is taken from Godfrey's article as reprinted in the *Montana Historical Contributions*, Vol. 9.

"Looking toward Custer's field, on a hill two miles away we saw a large assemblage. At first our command did not appear to attract their attention, although there was some commotion among those near our position. We heard occasional shots most of which seemed to be a great distance off, beyond the large group on the hill. While watching this group, the conclusion was arrived at that Custer had been repulsed and the firing heard was the parting shots of the rear guard. The firing ceased, the groups dispersed, clouds of dust arose from all parts of the field, and the horsemen converged toward our position. The command was dismounted to fight on foot."

The last sentence fixes the time the firing ceased on Custer field. It was a little before the troops on Weir Point started back to Reno Hill, and after Benteen and Reno had left. The "hill" mentioned is what the Indians called "Greasy Grass Ridge," or hill which borders Custer field on the south, and shuts off part of it from the view of anyone on Weir Point. P. 108

41. In his Report dated July 5, 1876, Reno said: "We now thought of Custer, of whom nothing had been seen or heard since the firing ceased in his direction about 6 o'clock P. M."

Gerard said in his testimony: "Ten or fifteen minutes after Reno left the timber (which is to say, about 4:15) I heard firing to the left of where he was." (This was the firing by the Gray Horse Troop. according to my constructions as set forth in Chapter 9). Gerard continued; "There was a continuous scattered fire all the time, until it got down where Custer's battlefield was, and then it became heavy————But the firing along the line of march lasted twenty or twenty-five minutes. The heavy firing on Custer field lasted about two hours."

According to Gerard, then, the firing by Custer's men lasted for two hours and twenty minutes, or a little longer, which agrees with what the officers had told Lieutenant Maguire right after the battle—two to three hours. Gerard, not under pressure to avoid certain conclusions, was here saying what the officers had said at a time when the event was fresh in their minds and when they, likewise, still felt free to report facts as they believed them to be.

It was admitted at the Court of Inquiry that firing was still going on on Custer field when the troops arrived on Weir Point; but they made a distinction between firing indicating fighting and firing not indicating fighting. This distinction, dubious under the circumstances, gained plausibility from the known fact that Indians often fired their guns aimlessly. A known fact was thus reduced to the expression of an opinion about a fact. An opinion may be questioned, but it is difficult to disprove the good faith of the person expressing the opinion. But after the man seeking vindication had been long in his grave, Lieutenant Hare told Mr. Camp (Feb. 7, 1910), that when he was with Weir in advance on the high ridge the Indians were thick on Custer field and firing, and that he then thought Custer was fighting them. I can find nothing in his testimony indicating that he had drawn such a sapient conclusion from the evidence while it was impinging on both his sight and his hearing.

When Godfrey was asked what he saw while they were on Weir Point, he replied: "I saw a lot of Indians down the river. They seemed to be tending down the river. From the faint firing I heard, I supposed General Custer had been repulsed, and that they were watching him." (*Chicago Times Record*.) Compare with preceding Footnote. P. 109

42. We have no further information concerning the fate of this man; nor is there any marker for him where he fell. It is fairly certain that neither Edgerly nor anyone else went back for him; for, when Edgerly overtook Captain Weir he told him about the man and the promise he had made him. Weir replied that he was sorry, but that they could not stop to take care of him. This was immediately after they had passed Godfrey who deployed his troop a moment later and drove the Indians back over the high ridge and gave Edgerly the chance to make good his promise. Why did he not take the chance? He could have sent back a sergeant with a set of fours to pick him up under cover of Godfrey's fire. No officer with any feeling at all would have failed to make the effort unless there was a compelling reason forbidding it. As he left it at the Court of Inquiry Edgerly's account is absurd; for if he could not pick up the man when he told him he would come back for him, what chance was there to bring him out at all? He made this promise *before* Godfrey had provided the opportunity to fulfil it. It was so delicate a matter that neither Recorder Lee nor Mr. Gilbert risked a question on it.

Were both Weir and Edgerly cowards or wholly devoid of human feeling? Since there is no ground for either assumption, the only explanation of their conduct I can see is that they both feared the troop would disintegrate in panic if they tried to halt it to send back for the wounded man. That Weir believed this danger had existed is clearly implied in his coming to Godfrey after the firing ceased that evening and thanking him for having saved his troop from disaster. Both French and Edgerly had used poor psychology in starting out, the former at a gallop, the latter at a trot; for, as the late Prof. William James said in his *Principles of Psychology*, we do not run because we are frightened. We are frightened because we run, an overstatement of a truth the military folks understand very well even if they do not always remember it in time to avoid unnecessary trouble. Godfrey demonstrated that truth when, with only 22 men on the line he kept them in order, slowly retreating as they fired, in spite of the fact that they had just seen two troops in what was nearly, if not quite, a panic flight. But Godfrey had not made the mistake of starting out at a gallop.

The testimony of Edgerly in connection with his retreat gives us, incidentally, another indication that at the time of the conference just before Benteen and Reno turned back toward Reno Hill, there was no thought in anyone's mind that the Indians were then attacking in force or that they would do so for some time; for Edgerly said he "overtook" Weir. Since Weir had been at the conference he knew it had been decided to turn back and so had started to follow Benteen in whose battalion he was serving, leaving Edgerly in command of his troop as he usually did. But had there been a serious engagement in progress at this time, or the certainty of such an engagement within the next five or ten minutes, would he have left his lieutenant to attend to the dangerous business? Especially if, as represented by Hare and others, Weir and French had been ordered to cover the retreat of the rest? And who were the "rest"? Wallace with his 7 men had already left, so that only Godfrey remained, and as the event proved, there was no need for anyone to cover his retreat. It is my understanding that had Weir received such an order it would, under the circumstances as represented in the testimony, have been definitely a point of honor for him to be with his troop—if not something more than a point of honor. P. 116

43. Unpublished narrative written not long after the Battle of Wounded Knee, Dec. 29, 1890. Copy furnished by Captain E. S. Luce.
At the Court of Inquiry Benteen was asked; "Was there an opening in the line?" He replied: "There was an opening toward the river. The line was in the shape of a horseshoe, with one point longer than the other, and the short point turned in at right angles a little; the long line was my position." P. 125

44. Godfrey said: "I was not assigned a position; my men were mixed in with those of B, M, G, and D." P. 125

45. Benteen gave the positions of the troops as follows: A, G, D, B, M, K, and H; Godfrey: A. D. K. M. G, B, and H.
The accounts of the officers given at the Court of Inquiry, taken as a whole, show clearly that when the line had been straightened out after the fighting ceased on the evening of the 25th, the troops stood in the following order: A, G, D, K, M, B, and H. They remained in this order until M was sent to reinforce Benteen and posted between B and H, with possibly a few of the M men remaining on the immediate left of K. The final order then was A, G, D, K, B, M, H. P. 126

46. F. F. Churchill, a civilian packer, testified: "We went out to find our own kitchen, or mess. We thought we could not find it because everything was piled up together—officers' kits, companies' kits and everything piled together without regard to whom they belonged." P. 127

47. McDougall: "During the night of the 25th I told my men to take their butcher knives and tincups—we had no axes—and throw up more dirt and make a kind of barricade for their heads, so the Indians could not see our heads. We had no breastworks. I received no order from Major Reno or his adjutant." P. 128

48. See McClernand in the *Cavalry Journal* for January, 1927. What McClernand says of some of the members of Terry's staff is about the same in tone and substance as the quotation we have given from Bradley's *Journal*. P. 145

49. The account in the text is taken from Gibbon's article in the *Catholic Quarterly Review*. McClernand in his article in the *Cavalry Journal* does not mention the bloody drawers, and says that the buckskin shirt with the two bullet holes was marked with the name "Sturgis." The tepees stood on the ground where the camps had been on the 25th and the troops, in going to them, had marched over the campsites of the 26th apparently without being aware of it. P. 148

50. Fred Dustin has, we believe, correctly identified these horsemen as two Ree scouts and the interpreter, Fred Gerard. P. 148

51. Glendolin Damon Wagner in *Old Neutriment*. P. 150

52. This is the general belief among students of our subject, and we let it stand, though it is probable that Fred Gerard from his position in the timber after Reno had fled to the bluffs, saw some of Custer's men, at least dimly, as they passed over or near the Calhoun position on their way to Custer Hill. It would have been possible if the sun was shining brightly at the time, though the distance was nearly three miles. P. 152

53. Sheridan, in his report to General Sherman, made the same point. P. 153

54. It is true that we have no direct evidence identifying this band of warriors or their mission here. It seems to be tacitly assumed that they were scouts from the camps, and that when they were flushed by the troops they ran "like devils" to alert the village. But there are several reasons for doubting this construction. In the first place we know positively that the village was not alerted in this way. Moreover they did not act the part. Would scouts on the lookout for enemies on the trail of their people have been caught virtually asleep until the troops were almost upon them, when it was of the utmost importance to report their coming at the earliest moment possible? Had they been watching the trail for this purpose they could not have failed to see the column or its dust a mile or more up the trail. In our opinion they were scouts from Little Wolf's band of Cheyennes we have mentioned elsewhere as going to the village on Custer's right just over the divide between Reno Creek and the heads of the branches of Tullock's Creek. This was the special hunting ground of the Cheyennes, and they knew every foot of it. It was necessary for Little Wolf to be extremely careful, and he knew that between the Little Big Horn and the rough ground that concealed his movements as he advanced there was a mile or more of comparatively open ground he must cross to get to the village. If he was caught here he was lost. He, therefore, needed scouts in front of Custer to observe his movements and keep him informed. Should Custer turn north when he came opposite this open ground, as he actually did, it was necessary for Little Wolf to be informed of it before he exposed himself. This meant that the scouts in front of Custer must not get so far head of him as to run the risk of being cut off; which explains why they *seemed* to have been caught asleep. When they saw Custer turn north they seem to have sent messengers to Little Wolf while the rest deliberately exposed themselves to lead Custer on while they keep out of range. We think it probable that they were the Indians Sergeant Kanipe said were ahead of the troops when they halted while Custer went to view the camps from the high point northwest of Reno Hill.

In a maneuver of this kind the Cheyennes had, perhaps, no peer among the Plains Indians. It was their proficiency in this respect that caused them to be selected to lead the tribes on the march during the months preceding the battle. P. 154

55. We have accepted his statement at the Court of Inquiry because it is the only one that checks reasonably close in the matter of time and distance. He started with the message around 3:25 and reached Benteen at 4:00, or a few minutes later. Benteen was then on Custer's trail a little above the point where the latter had stopped to water his horses, according to Martin, which checks closely with Benteen's account. This point was a little over two miles from the river, according to Benteen. From Martin's starting point to Reno Hill is a good mile and a half, and from Reno Hill to where he met Benteen is probably two and a half miles, more or less, a total of about 4 miles, calling for a gait of between 7 and 8 miles an hour. This, considering the roughness of the terrain, was a fast gait, especially for a tired horse which was hit by an Indian bullet somewhere along the route.

In another account Martin said he went with Custer all the way down to Medicine Tail Coulee, and in still another that he went with Custer to within a short distance of the ford. In neither of these cases would it have been possible for him to get back to Benteen by 4:00 o'clock. P. 162

56. Some time after the present chapter had been completed we became convinced that a trooper named Frank Finkel, member of Company "C", did escape from the fight. For the benefit of any reader interested in the details of this case, we append the following brief statement.

Frank Finkel's own story was first reluctantly told before the Kiwanis Club of Dayton, Washington, in 1921. It was later discussed in the *Walla Walla Bulletin* in connection with a letter of Mrs. Billmeyer, Mr. Finkel's second wife, and again in 1937 in the *Oshkosh Northwestern*, Oshkosh, Wisconsin. Finally it appeared in the *Billings Gazette*, June 23, 1947, under the name of Kathryn Wright.

In 1949, at the request of Mrs. Billmeyer, we made an analysis of all the material in her possession, and found that the facts given by Mr. Finkel concerning the manner of his escape from the field and the nature of the terrain he came to after his pursuers gave up the chase, are in entire harmony with what we now know, and more especially so with the nature of the action of Company "C", of which nothing was known by historians in 1921, when Finkel told his story. Our manuscript, 17 pages of standard double-spaced typing, together with added comments by Mrs. Billmeyer, is now in the Oshkosh Museum, Oshkosh, Wisconsin, placed there by Mrs. Billmeyer herself for the use of any historian who may wish to make further research; for there are still a number of unanswered questions and a line of approach that has not as yet been followed. P. 165

57. This is not to be taken as a general criticism of Mr. Camp's work. In view of the fact that the excerpts we have from Mr. Ellison are only an infinitesmal part of the great mass of his notes, such a criticism would be absurd. What we mean to say is that his working thesis here caused him to ask the wrong kind of questions, questions that mystified the Indian witnesses who, like all primitive people, tended to fit their replies to what they felt was desired. His belief that Custer had attacked at the ford was not his only mistake. He also held the erroneous idea that all the Indian camps except that of the Uncpapas had stood below the ford. It is not strange, therefore, that he should have believed that, after being repulsed at the ford Custer formed a line extending from the site of the Butler marker to the tip of the east wing of the battleridge, a distance of nearly a half mile, where according to Mr. Ellison's reading, "C" Troop, or a part of it, was destroyed, while the

229

rest, beset front, flank and rear, passed to Custer Hill via the Calhoun position and across the south part of the field.

We should remember, however, that nearly all constructions made in field notes are merely tentative, made to serve the memory and as an aid to the imagination when the complete general synthesis is being worked out. Even the few excerpts we have show quite clearly that Mr. Camp possessed an excellent imagination as well as an unusual capacity for taking pains to obtain grass-root details, both prime requisites for the making of a good historian. What conclusions of a general nature, if any, he came to before his untimely death in 1925, is unknown to the present writer. The field notes bought by Mr. Ellison are only a part, and probably only a minor part, of Mr. Camp's notes. Moreover, others had already gone through the material and taken their pick of it. It is, therefore, altogether probable that the student of our subject who succeeds in gaining access to the whole will be fortunate indeed. P. 165

58. Two theories have been advanced to account for the presence here of the body of Sergeant James Butler. General Godfrey suggested that he may have been sent by Custer as a messenger to Reno. The other theory is that he was a casualty in a general engagement here and was left to the mercy of the Indians as the troops fled northward.

We cannot accept either of these views; and more especially not the second; for, if there had been a major action here a number of other bodies would certainly have been found in this locality. None, however, were found. The empty cases indicating a light skirmish, found by Mr. Blummer, Professor Cartwright, Colonel Nye, and more recently by Captain Luce, were several hundred yards east and northeast of the spot where Butler was found.

The iron stake discovered by Captain Luce in 1948 undoubtedly marks the place where Butler was forced to make his stand. No one seems to know who drove the stake. It may have been done by the Geological Survey in 1891 or some time later; for the point is marked on its contour map about 750 yards east by north of the Middle Ford.

But what is extraordinarily interesting in connection with this discovery of the grave site of Sergeant Butler is the finding, also by Captain Luce, of a line of three cartridge cases extending northwestward for 75 to 100 yards toward the south tip of the east wing of the Battle Ridge where the last of Calhoun's horseholders were killed. On the same line and about 300 yards from the iron stake, was found a horseshoe especially designed to correct a faulty gait. Captain Luce sent this horseshoe to Colonel Nye for expert study. The conclusion reached is that the shoe dates from the period of the Custer battle; that the horse was a blooded animal and that the special knowledge and expert workmanship required to forge the shoe made it too expensive to justify its use except for an unusually valuable horse.

Was the horse which lost this shoe Butler's mount? The shoe was certainly not dropped by an Indian pony. And it would have been something bordering on the miraculous had some other horse than Butler's lost this kind of shoe in this particular place over which Butler must have ridden just before he was set afoot. For, while it is true that only three cases were found between the shoe and the iron stake, it is improbable that all that were fired over the 75-100 yards were found. But even the three cases recovered are more than could have been fired from the back of a horse which, under any plausible construction, must have been going under its maximum speed. The obvious deduction is that the man who fired the shots was afoot, standing still to fire and running while reloading, until he was either headed off or wounded and forced to stop though he continued to fire for a long time, as is proved by the many empty cases found around and under his body.

Two further intriguing facts are to be noted here. If we look southward over this line of cases and the iron stake we find the Weir Ridges, a scant mile and a half away, directly in our line of vision, the ridges at this time occupied by virtually the full striking force of the Reno and Benteen commands combined, and engaged in a very light skirmish with Indians 600 to 800 yards in their front. And if we look down this same line in the opposite direction we see two branches of North Medicine Tail, one starting from the tip of the battleridge just mentioned, the other beginning about where the horseshoe was found, the two entering North Medicine Tail from opposite directions and at about the same point, both serving as at least a partial protection against fire from the flanks of anyone riding in them.

James Butler was the First Sergeant of Calhoun's Troop "L" whose horse-holders—in this case the whole first platoon—were killed on the east wing of the Battleridge. The other platoon was fighting in the ravine nearby to the north, and both Calhoun and Crittenden were with it, leaving only a duty sergeant to command the first platoon with the horses. About the time this platoon moved to the east wing of the ridge Calhoun's situation was becoming desperate (See our description of the Calhoun action in the next chapter), and it would have been necessary to bring it into the fight soon in one way or other, mounted or dismounted, had the troop not been suddenly overwhelmed a few minutes later by the attack of Gall. Butler was a good soldier with 22 years of service behind him. On the march the position of the first sergeant is at the rear of the column. But they were not marching now, and he was not needed as a non-commissioned officer with the platoon doing the fighting. But a good soldier was needed by the first platoon. Therefore I think he was sent by Calhoun to take charge of it. In any case he must have been with it when Gall's warriors stampeded the horses along the ridge, away from the dismounted men. The distribution of the markers shows that nearly half— ten men—were killed on the very tip of the ridge, 6 on the higher part and 4 on the west slope nearby, carried there when the horses recoiled from the volley in front by warriors on the steep slope of the tip of the ridge. Butler, with no horses to hold, plunged down through the warriors before they could reload, into the ravine mentioned above as beginning at this point. There was nothing else for him to do unless he chose to be killed to no purpose; for he could not return to Calhoun because the warriors had swarmed in between to plunder, as Kate Bighead saw them do as she was approaching. He may have received a shower of arrows as he broke through and been fired at before he was out of range. But after going same distance he was at least partly protected from the flank fire of Indians that may have been in position to deliver such a fire. He was doomed when his horse, because of the loose shoe, stumbled, threw its rider and ran away. We do not know what became of the horse. It evidently was not killed here, for no dead horses were reported as found here, nor any skeletons found in later years, as far as the writer knows.

But why not assume, as did General Godfrey, that Butler was sent by Custer? In the first place, as Captain Luce has pointed out, first sergeants are not sent, as a rule, because they are needed with their commands, and a duty sergeant can carry a message as well as can a first sergeant. To this may be added that, after Custer had arrived on the field the warriors in large numbers were crossing the ford and covered the long, open slope to Greasy Grass Ridge so that no messenger with any sense would have ridden by the way Butler took, if he had any choice. He would have gone farther east, as Butler would have done had he been sent by Custer, for in that case he could have chosen his route. As it was the only chance he had lay in the speed of his blooded horse. P. 167

231

59. If Custer did pass over this high ridge and looked back over his trail he could hardly have failed to see Benteen who was at this time nearing Reno Hill. The battalion must have left Medicine Tail a little after 4 o'clock, for Gerard heard the firing ten or fifteen minutes after Reno left the timber, which was around 4 o'clock. The Gray Horse was fired on soon after it left the coulee on its way to the ridge. It had gone perhaps a half mile, including the distance it had passed down the coulee, before the Indians discovered them and got near enough to open fire. Custer had about the same distance, or a little farther, to go to reach the south end of the high ridge. The length of this ridge is 1020 steps, or approximately 1000 yards, and Custer probably was on it from about 4:10 to 4:20. From the north end of this ridge to the point in North Medicine Tail opposite the end of the skirmish ridge is a little over 1020 yards. Allowing another 10 minutes for Custer to traverse this distance, we have 4:30 as the time he fired those volleys down the ravine, driving the Indians back, as White Bull says he did. (See also Note 60, following.)

But what data or key-facts have we to justify this fixing of a whole series of points in time, when Wallace's official record, made on the spot, ends at 2 P. M.? How do we know when Reno left the timber and when Benteen joined them? Our timing here is wholly out of line with nearly everything that has been published on the subject, and the testimony of the officers is so conflicting that little can be made of it directly. This places a heavy burden of proof on our shoulders, forcing us again to analysis and constructive reasoning. For the most part we have to depend on the firing heard and the distances involved. Fortunately Godfrey has left us a key-fact that enables us to carry the timing on from 2 P. M. He says he found in his notebook the entry "4:20" made while they were on Reno Hill before they started to go to Weir Point, but that for many years he could not recall what it signified. Finally, however, he became definitely convinced that it stood for the time Benteen joined Reno. Since long before seeing this statement we had fixed the time of this event at 4:25, we are strongly inclined to believe that Godfrey's memory finally caught up with the fact!

Since several officers testified that Benteen arrived 10 to 15 minutes after Reno reached the hill we are fairly safe in saying that the latter arrived about 4:10 to 4:15; which in turn, tells us that he must have left the timber around 4. The distance between the timber and the place he halted on the bluffs is approximately a mile and a half along the route he followed. On a good road and horses in good marching condition that distance could have been covered in 7 to 8 minutes. But there was a river to cross and a long, hard climb, so that 10 to 15 minutes is probably somewhere near the fact. This brings the beginning of the light skirmish fire heard by Gerard to 4:10 to 4:15. He said it lasted 20 to 25 minutes. We have already checked the time of the volleys by the time Benteen arrived on the Hill, showing that they were fired about 4:30. This, it will be noted, places the light skirmish between 4:10 and 4:30.

We do not pretend that every one of these points in time is exact to the minute. We believe, however, that they are near enough to the reality to justify our constructions which are partly based on them. For the time checks the same from the story by Kate Bighead who left the camp of the Minniconjous as Reno was crossing the river in retreat, or a few minutes after 4:00. Her own camp was about a mile away, and as she approached it she saw Custer on the ridge to the east exchanging shots with the warriors. She was badly frightened and ran as fast as she could. She must, therefore, have reached her camp around 4:20. P. 172

232

60. This heavy firing was reported also by Godfrey, Hare, Edgerly, Davern and Herendeen, who said either that it occurred immediately after Benteen arrived, or gave data from which it is closely apparent that they heard it at this time.

But a light skirmish had been going on for 20 to 25 minutes before this burst of heavy firing variously described as "volleys," "heavy firing," or as "a sort of crash, crash," as Varnum put it. This important fact is found only in the very enlightening testimony of Gerard who, it will be remembered, returned to the timber after attempting to overtake Troops "A" and "M" which led in the retreat to the bluffs. "Ten to fifteen minutes after Reno left the timber I heard heavy firing on the left of where I was," he said. "It was on my right, and on the right bank. I could see the Indians going up the ravines on that side, and the firing was as if they were shooting at passing troops. I had seen troops back of that. There was a continuous scattered fire all the time until it got down below where Custer's battlefield was, and then it became heavy. There was a skirmish fire all the way from where I first heard it."

But the firing along the line of march lasted twenty to twenty-five minutes. The heavy firing at Custer field lasted about two hours.

Asked in re-direct examination how long after the general engagement the heavy firing on Reno Hill began, he replied that it was probably about a half hour. We have shown in Chapter 6 that the fight on Reno Hill did not begin until well past 7 o'clock, and possibly not until nearly 8.

This thins the mist into which the Custer battalion vanished after Trumpeter Martin saw it for the last time as he turned in his saddle about an hour before. For the reader unfamiliar with the topography this must still leave only a very imperfect and dim picture. Perhaps we can make it a little clearer by going somewhat more into detail.

In the first place it is to be especially noted that these scattered shots over a period of 20 to 25 minutes were *along the line of march*. In other words, from near Medicine Tail Coulee to the little knoll with a 3400 elevation and from there on down to North Medicine. There was, therefore, no serious engagement here amounting to a defeat for Custer, as is held by some students. Consequently Custer did not flee from here in a desperate search for a defensive position. Neither dead men nor dead horses were found here, though from the Calhoun position a dead sheep or even a dead dog would probably have been noted by the burial squads on the 28th, had they been there, to say nothing of Godfrey and his orderly, Pennwell, who rode to this ridge while the burials were being made. All he later reported as having seen there were the tracks of shod horses. So light, indeed, had been the firing there that it was not heard by anyone on Reno Hill, as far as the record shows.

The first firing heard on Reno Hill were those ragged volleys which we believe were fired down North Medicine Trail by Custer's four remaining troops as they neared the point in the ravine toward which the dismounted skirmishers of the Gray Horse Troop were now moving while continuing their fire. According to a nephew of Sitting Bull, White Bull of the Sans Arcs, Custer did not cross the ravine. Stanley Vestal, in the Blue Book Magazine for September, 1933, reports him as saying: "Most of Custer's five troops of cavalry had passed the *head* of the ravine by the time White Bull was near enough to shoot at the soldiers. From where he was the soldiers seemed to form four groups of mounted men heading northwest along the ridge. He was shooting at the group in the rear." Here Vestal added in parenthesis: "Lieutenant James Calhoun's Command."

233

If we are to make sense of this we must assume that by "group" White Bull meant "troop." In fact Vestal seems to suggest as much when he identifies the rear group as having been Troop L. All through the article we find it difficult, or impossible, to determine whether the language is that of White Bull or Vestal.

What is of interest here is that when White Bull came closer to the troops he saw only "four groups of mounted men" instead of five "groups" mentioned earlier in the account. One of the five groups was evidently not mounted now. We suggest that the missing fifth group was the Gray Horse dismounted and in skirmish line and moving down to cross the ravine to rejoin Custer, who had passed the *head* of the ravine a good thousand yards farther up, near the western tip of the farther ridge shown on the Geological Survey. It was in the "rear" of the column after it had crossed the ravine and the united command was moving up the slope of the Calhoun position. Then, since the enemy had turned his back, White Bull followed, as was the custom of the Indian warriors, and then it was the "rear group" he was shooting at.

Earlier in his account White Bull is represented as having said: "As he advanced, he saw Custer's five troops trotting along the bluffs parallel to the river."

These troops, then, could not have been on the nearer ridge, for we know positively that those who passed here were not trotting as they came down. They were dismounted and in skirmish line, firing at Indians between them and South Medicine Tail.

Godfrey, relying on what Gall had shown and told him while they were on the field in 1886, traces Custer's course along this farther ridge, as can be seen by consulting his map accompanying his article in the *Century* magazine. In this article he says: "Not long after the Indians began to show a strong force in Custer's front, Custer turned his column to the left and advanced in the direction of the village (confirmed below by White Shield) to a place now marked as a spring, halted at the junction of the two ravines below it."

This spring was *above* the junction of the two ravines, so that Custer could not have come over the skirmish ridge which is just *below* the junction. The volleys down the ravine must, therefore, have been fired as they neared the point where the skirmish ridge ends against the ravine—North Medicine Tail. The other ravine in question runs along the north side of the skirmish ridge, as shown on the Geological Survey.

When White Bull said "most of Custer's men had passed the head of the ravine," he meant the four mounted troops with Custer, for they were riding straight toward him and when they halted filled the ravine with flying lead, which made them a prominent item in his memory and blanketed the fifth "group" to his right and front, which he probably could not see here if he was in the ravine, though he knew it was there. It became the "rear group" after it had crossed the ravine and re-joined the column, and then he fired at it simply because it was the nearest to him.

The account by White Shield, as reported by Grinnell in *The Fighting Cheyennes,* (Charles Scribner's Sons), agrees in general with that of White Bull and, in part, clarifies it. It clearly implies that the Custer battalion was not marching as a unit in its passage from South Medicine Tail to the point in North Medicine Tail where Godfrey says it halted. It rather suggests, however, that the troop coming over the skirmish ridge was not the Gray Horse which, according to White Shield, was at the head of the column that passed over the farther ridge and headed straight down North Medicine Tail toward the Middle Ford. It halted and dismounted at the point where the column turned to the right to go to the battlefield, after delivering a very heavy fire against the Indians in the ravine. The rest of the column also dismounted here, he says, but apparently was not brought into position to fire.

In order that the reader may draw his own conclusions we here reproduce the part of White Shield's story dealing with the point in hand. As will be noted, it is not all direct quotation from White Shield; but Mr. Grinnell did a better job of reporting than did Mr. Vestal in the case of White Bull.

"When White Shield, hurrying back from his fishing ,reached the camp his mother had already secured his horse and was waiting for him. He began to dress, and while doing this he saw Custer's troops in seven groups approaching the river. Some Sioux and Cheyennes had already seen them, and some men who were in the camp crossed the river at the ford to meet Custer. White Shield overtook a group of four Cheyennes, among whom were Roan Bear, Bobtail Horse, and Calf. Mad Wolf—probably Mad Hearted Wolf, often called Rabid Wolf, but actually meaning Wolf that has no sense—was riding with White Shield. He was one of the bravest and wisest men in the tribe. As they rode along he said to White Shield: "No one must charge on the soldiers now; they are too many." As the Cheyennes rode out of the river toward the troops, who were still at a distance, the soldiers were following five Sioux who were running from them. They gradually circled away from in front of the soldiers and the troops did not follow them, but kept toward the river. *The troops were headed straight for the ford* (Italics ours) about a half mile above the battlefield, and White Shield and the other Cheyennes believed that Custer was about to cross the river and get into the camp. The troops were getting near them, but suddenly before the troops reached the river the Gray Horse Company halted and dismounted, and all who were following them, as far as could be seen, also stopped and dismounted."

"White Shield rode off to the left and down the river while Bobtail Horse, Calf, and two or three others who were with them stopped close to the river, and under cover of a low ridge began to shoot at the soldiers. The five Sioux whom the troops had at first seemed to be pursuing, now joined Calf and Bobtail Horse, and the ten Indians were shooting at the soldiers as fast as they could. About the time the soldiers halted one man was killed. Now more Sioux and Cheyennes began to gather, the Indians crossing the river and stringing up the gulch (North Medicine Tail) like ants rushing out of a hill. The two troops of cavalry (probably the two separate platoons of the troop that had come over the nearest ridge—White Shield says there were seven groups altogether) that had come nearest to Bobtail Horse fell back to the side of a little knoll (the 3400 elevation marked on the Geological Survey) and stopped there. Yellow Nose charged close up to them alone. The troops remained there only a few moments. Crowded back, they crossed a deep gulch (North Medicine Tail) and climbed the hill on the other side (The Calhoun hill, or knoll) going toward where the monument now stands, where by this time the Gray Horse had stopped."

In the careful work now being done under the direction of Captain Luce it has been shown that some troops left South Medicine Tail, evidently by way of a ravine leading up to the plateau from a point about a half mile from the ford. It is, therefore, an intriguing fact that when Benteen was asked at the Court of Inquiry how near Custer may have come to the ford, he replied "about three furlongs"—660 yards—which is to say, about 200 yards below the mouth of this ravine. The first shells were on slopes 100 feet above the level of Medicine Tail, most of them east of the ravine. Only one was found west of it, though more were probably fired here. This suggests that the troop was moving in two separate platoons as it left Medicine Tail. On the east side a line of cases extends straight north to the 3300 level, where it ~onnects with another line extending nearly east and west. Here the two

235

platoons seem to have lined up together in close order, turned and fired with-out dismounting, probably, and then went on to the 3400 knoll, as explained by White Shield. At the knoll they dismounted and deployed in skirmish line just north of the crest of the ridge leading to North Medicine Tail, and began their slow movement downward, as the empty cases there show.

White Shield distinguishes these troops from the rest by saying they came the nearest to Bobtail Horse and his party. It is obvious from this line of shells and those nearer South Medicine Tail, that it was not these troops who were "headed straight for the ford." It was the column farther north coming down North Medicine Tail that constituted the real menace in the opinion of the warriors. But it was the single troop which had come so near the ford that had first alerted the Indians and brought them swarming out of the camps. In our opinion this troop was sent here as a feint, a bluff to mystify the warriors, keep them guessing as long as possible to prevent their con-centration.

It is possible that the maneuvering of this troop gave rise to the theory that Custer with his whole batttalion fought a major action here from which he fled blindly in search of a tenable defensive position. P. 172

61-61(a). *My Friend the Indian*, by James McLaughlin; Houghton Mifflin Company, Boston and New York. Pps. 172 and 177.

62. It should be explained that the ravine here has, in one respect at least, changed greatly since the time of the battle. At the point where it crossed the line it is now a very deep and steep-sided gulch difficult for a man a-foot to cross and wholly impossible for horses. The top soil in the bottom of the ravine is a firm clay covered with grass and, therefore, strongly resistant to erosion. Immediately under this is a loose, ash-like layer some 15 to 20 feet deep and easily carried away during a heavy shower. The result is that the head of the gulch is a perpendicular cut-bank which crumbles more or less with every run-off so that its location constantly moves upward in the ravine. Today it is some 30 to 40 yards above the place where the skirmish line stood.

On the other hand, it is probable that at the time of the battle the sides of the ravine upstream from the gulch were steeper than they are today. This is suggested by what some of the officers said about marks of hands and feet on the side of the ravine suggesting attempts on the part of the men to climb out. But it could not have been a deep gulch as it is farther down, for in that case it would hardly have been possible for Curley to have seen the fight from his position on the Calhoun knoll.

It may be said further that, in general, the sides of the ravines and the heads of them, were steeper in 1876 than they are now, and offered consider-ably more cover for the warriors than they would today. Vegetation was heavier then than it is now, its roots protecting the surface soil on the banks more or less from erosion, while the soil below the roots washed away rela-tively much faster, thus creating steep sides more like breastworks for the warriors than are the sloping sides. This, taken in connection with the taller grasses and the other vegetation, accounts largely for the ability of the warriors to partially encircle the troops as closely as they did without being discovered. This is a very important fact to be constantly kept in mind while studying the action on Custer field. There is no doubt as to the fact; for William White, a member of Gibbon's packtrain, remembered it when he saw the field again on becoming superintendent of the Cemetery, and mentioned it to Dr. Marquis. It is well known all over this western area that the taller grasses were destroyed by over-grazing, resulting in a heavier run-off during rains, with the further result that the other vegetation was more or less thinned out or stunted through the decrease in the amount of moisture retained in the soil after rains. P. 186

63. Several years after this was written we received from Colonel Graham a copy of a letter by McDougall in which he said he had been in charge of the burial of the bodies of the men of the Gray Horse Troop, but that those in the ravine had presented such a revolting sight that the members of the burial squad had soon become too nauseated to continue the work in the usual manner. They therefore merely shovelled earth on them from the banks of the ravine. We learned also that Theodore Goldin had mentioned the same fact in a letter to Mr. Dustin.

We must, therefore, conclude that the remains of these men were taken up during the re-burials in 1877 and removed to the line, as stated in the text.

In a letter to the writer dated August 22, 1946, Mr. Brininstool tells of a visit to the field in 1913 in which he may have been on the point of securing some details of the fighting here that would have definitely cleared up some things at which we can now only guess.

"We went over the field in September, 1913," he says, "with Curley and a young agency employee named Squires. . . . We found a lot of bullets and empty shells that day. Curley had stated before we left the agency that he wanted to take us to a depression where he said he saw about 12 soldiers fighting as he left the field."

Unfortunately, before they got down to discuss the fighting here, Mr. Squires began teasing Curley for not having shown them something extraordinary, violently offending him, causing him to mount his pony and ride back to the agency in high dudgeon.

By referring to footnote No. 64, it will be deduced that Curley had taken them to the ravine in which he had seen the fighting of which he had spoken to Mr. Camp on July 19, 1910.

A plague on Mr. Squires' mis-timed levity! Here they were actually on the place where Curley had certainly seen the fighting, explain it as we may. What details and clues might he not have given had they discussed the fighting on the spot and at length!

Twelve men seen fighting in this ravine. No markers there today. But 12 markers in a neat line nearby where McClernand had seen no bodies in spite of his close study of the skirmish line! P. 187

64. To the reader who has never been on the battlefield or seen the widely dispersed bits of evidence which, taken as a whole, all point to the same conclusion, our constructions here may seem like something pulled down from the blue sky. What follows should help to give them substance. More could be presented.

In the Camp field notes there is a thought-provoking passage dealing with an interview he had with Curley July 19, 1910. As copied for us by Mr. R. S. Ellison, the note reads as follows, the words in parentheses being our own.

"Curley got out at four markers at extreme southeast. (The four markers on the Calhoun position farthest east.) While here the Indians were killing soldiers by Finley and all soldiers were halted here. Sioux were on all sides shooting. Soldiers were dismounted and leading their horses and firing at Sioux as best they could. Sioux were all along on Custer ridge. (He probably meant the low ridge of the Hill. He had just ridden eastward on or along the main ridge, which he could not have done had the Sioux been there.) Miltch Bouyer said 'You had better leave now for we will all be cleaned out.' Bouyer had just been talking with Custer and Custer's brother (Tom) and then he came and told me this. When I rode out there were no Sioux in front . . . I took up the coulee to the head of the distant ridge." That is to say

237

that from the four markers he went down to North Medicine Tail and followed it up to the head of the eastern ridge where Custer had come down. Before he left this ridge he saw the destruction of the Gray Horse Troop, as will appear presently.

To be noted first is that Curley repeatedly denied when questioned by Bradley after the troops had returned to Fort Pease, that he was in the fight or inside the Indian encirclement.

Is this necessarily inconsistent with what he told Camp? We do not think so. The Cheyennes said that the long opening skirmish did not amount to much. The real fighting began soon after the south line had been established. At that time the troops were not encircled. "No Sioux in front," as Curley said. The opening skirmish had been so insignificant that he did not consider it at all when answering questions; and in any case he had taken no part in it. His mind was obsessed, overwhelmed by the terrible things that happened later, as his state of mind when he reached the steamer at the mouth of the Little Big Horn shows.

An intriguing part of the story is that Bouyer seems to have attempted to dissuade Custer from sending the troops down south of the Hill, no doubt because he feared an ambush. This is suggested by his coming at once to Curley to tell him he had better leave because they would "all be cleaned out."

By the time Curley got to the four markers about a half mile from Custer Hill the fighting had begun. Incidentally he confirms the statement of Kate Bighead that the troops dismounted and held their horses by the reins. There are several other Indian accounts in which the same fact is noted.

"Finley," in the Camp notes, refers to the position in which the body of Sergeant Finley was found, according to Camp's information or belief. It was one of the bodies across the ravine where the extreme left of "E" had stood on that part of Greasy Grasss ridge north of the first branch of the main ravine. When Camp asked Curley if any of the troops had gone to this place he replied; "Yes, 10 or 15, probably guides or flankers." In other words, men sent to scout the ground over which the troops would have to pass when ordered forward to support the advance of Benteen should he come straight acrosss and the Indians left to oppose him.

There seems to be no escape from the conclusion that Curley saw most of the fight in the south line from start to finish, from some high point to the east close enough to see some of the details, as well as the shooting of the horses at Custer Hill. He probably could not see much of "C" Troop before it crossed the ridge in its rear as it fled back to the Hill. His reference in four separate stories is always to the Gray Horse Troop, especially to a terrible fight he saw in a ravine, the memory of which seems to have clung to him like a nightmare during his long, solitary ride from the battlefield by the round-about way of Fort Pease to the *Far West* at the mouth of the Little Big Horn, where he arrived around noon of the 27th, according to Hanson, on the 28th according to the record kept by the engineer of the boat, as Captain Luce informs us. Here, while his mind was still afire from what he had seen, he told his first story of the fight. There being no interpreter on the boat, he was only vaguely understood. The general impression he left was that Custer had been surrounded and the entire Seventh Cavalrv destroyed. The only clear details his listeners received, according to Mr. Hanson, (*Conquest of the Missouri,* p. 277, Second Edition) are that some of them (the troops) had used their horses for breastworks, and that a remnant of one troop, "E," under First Lieutenant A. E. Smith, had tried to cut its way out, but was utterly destroyed.

On pages 185-188 of the present chapter we have tried to describe the attempt of this remnant of Troop "E" to escape. When the first draft of the chapter was written some time in 1936, about a year after we had begun our study, we had not heard of Mr. Hanson and his book, nor have we at any time found the suggestion that the 9 headstones along the line over which this remnant fled, represent men of "E" Troop fleeing from the field. On the contrary, as far as they have entered the discussion at all they are represented as coming to the field from the southeast. In 1938, in company with the then Superintendent of the National Cemtery, and one other, a long-time student of the subject, we started from the position of the skirmish line and followed the string of markers eastward while we made our own explanation of it. We received a fish-eyed stare for our pains—and nothing else.

As far as we know the only intelligible attempt ever made to account for these isolated bodies along this line is that of Lieutenant Maguire who, however, admitted that it was a speculation based solely on the tracks of two shod horses from the ford to the southeast corner of the battlefield, and here there was no question of "E" Troop in particular, but of "C," "E," and "L," all going west, not east. We have pointed out elsewhere that these two tracks cannot possibly be used as evidence to support the construction.

The thing to which we wish to call attention here is this: If no one had guessed that these headstones represent an attempt of a remnant of "E" Troop to escape, how did Hanson know it unless Curley did report this at the boat? Curley could not have visited the field after the fight, to discover the bodies here, and he may or may not have known that the Gray Horse was officially designated as Troop "E." But he could recognize the white horses, and see the men and horses as they came out of the ravine and rushed eastward down the open slope of the ridge on their left, if he was, as he has said in several of his stories, on the high ridge east of the field. The fact that the horses were white identified the troop for his listeners, as the Gray Horse commanded by Lieutenant Algernon E. Smith.

So deeply had the fight in the ravine impressed itself in the mind of Curley that he referred to it on at least three later occasions, and it probably remained with him vividly for the rest of his life. No matter how many fantastic stories we find ascribed to him, most of them irreconcilable among themselves, this story about the fight in the ravine remained substantially the same for at least 37 years. The second story that comes into consideration here appeared in the Army and Navy Journal for August 5, 1876, a copy of which we received from Colonel W. A. Graham along with other material that helped to fill some lacunae in our evidence. In this we find: "He, Curley, says that as he rode off he saw, when nearly a mile away from the battlefield, a dozen or more soldiers in a ravine fighting with Sioux all around them. He thinks all were killed, as they were outnumbered five to one, and apparently dismounted." The third reference we have to this is the story given to Mr. Camp in 1910, as related above. The fourth is reported in the letter of Mr. Brininstool discussed in another footnote. This meeting, it will be noted, occurred in 1913, 37 years after the battle and ten years before Curley's death. P. 188

65. General Hawkins in one of his letters to us said flatly that the troops north of the battleridge, when called on to fight, were marching away from Custer Hill, not toward it as is generally assumed. He did not elaborate other than to say that he did not know *why* they were doing so, thus neither accepting nor rejecting our own constructions. It is significant, however, that he was certain they were on the march, not in skirmish line anywhere along the ridge. He rejected the latter idea as too absurd for serious consideration. It is equally certain that they were not in skirmish line on the slope of the ridge and facing north when they became involved in fighting. The leading platoon of "F" Troop did make two stands in skirmish formation, but in both cases the line stood perpendicular to the ridge. The rear platoon made

239

one stand in skirmish line 160 yards from the first platoon. "I" Troop was never deployed at all, and the rear platoon of "L" fought in the bottom of an open ravine and left no evidence of a line except for about 10 men on the extreme east of the position, and the bodies of the leading platoon, along with some of the horses, were scattered along the whole length of the east wing of the ridge.

Reduced, then, to the inescapable conclusion that these troops were marching away, the question at once confronts us: Where were they going? Were they fleeing the field altogether, leaving Custer with the wounded and less than a single troop, to the Indians?

There seems to be only one alternative to this conclusion—the one we have adopted for which there is considerable positive evidence. There is no such evidence for the other alternative, as far as we are aware. P. 192

66. Wooden Leg saw this man run away and what happened to him. He was on and near the west end of the ridge that flanked Calhoun's position on the north and only a hundred yards or so away. The headstone for this man, standing alone and so far from all others, seems to arouse the interest and imagination of many visitors who happen to notice it. And small wonder. P. 202

67. It has been generally supposed that Red Horse referred to Captain French, not Captain Keogh. There are several reasons for the different view expressed in the text. One is that French's first Sergeant, John Ryan, said French rode a white, not a sorrel, horse. Another is that Red Horse said the man in question was killed. We know that French was not. We know, also, from a detailed study of the fighting in the valley where French commanded Troop "M," that the only time the exploits mentioned could have taken place was after the troops had left their position in the timber. This would have to be under the supposition that he was not at the head of his troop during the wild flight to the river. This is, indeed, what he claimed in a letter addressed to the wife of Dr. A. H. Cooke of Chicago, some time in June, 1881, in which he assumed that Red Horse referred to him. But Sergeant Ryan, in his long article of June 25, 1923, in the Billings Gazette, Billings, Montana, makes no mention of anything of the kind, though elsewhere throughout he more or less heroizes his captain. And the testimony of Sergeant Culbertson at the Reno Court of Inquiry makes it clear that French was across the river while the troops were still crossing. (See the incident as described in Chapter 4).

In support of his claim French referred to the testimony given at Fort Lincoln in January 1879. A court martial had dismissed him from the army, a sentence later commuted to suspension and loss of pay. Not having seen the record of this court martial, and not knowing the date it was held, we cannot say whether or not he referred to the testimony given there. The Reno Court of Inquiry was held in Chicago, January to February, 1879, so he could hardly have referred to this. Moreover there is nothing in the testimony before this court remotely resembling his claim, though there is nothing in it actually discreditable to him. P. 204

68. This story of the Cheyennes about the 7 men on top of the Hill is the clearest and most detailed we have and the only one, as far as we know, that describes the actual fighting they did and just how they were driven out. The bare fact that at the close of the fighting a few men ran away toward the river is confirmed by the unidentified Sioux we quoted elsewhere in the present chapter. Further confirmation and added details are given by Chief White Bull of the Sans Arcs, part of whose story we recounted in the preceding chapter. It is particularly interesting when compared with Colonel

Gibbon's account of his visit to the field the day after the burials to which we are coming in a moment.

Said White Bull: "All this time White Bull was between the river and the soldiers on the hill. The few remaining troopers seemed to despair of holding their position on the hilltop. Ten of them jumped up and came down the ravine toward White Bull, shooting all the time. Two soldiers were in the lead, one of them wounded and bleeding from the mouth. White Bull and a Cheyenne waited for them. When they came near he shot one; the Cheyenne shot the other . . . The remaining soldiers kept on coming, forcing White Bull out of the ravine onto the ridge. White Bull snatched up the soldier's gun and started up the hill. Suddenly he stumbled and fell."

He had been hit on the ankle by a spent ball and was out of the fight.

This ravine is quite obviously the one by which Gibbon and his party came to Custer Hill and in which they found the body of Mark Kellogg, and a little farther on where the "open grassy valley" narrows and takes on the character of a ravine, the body of a trooper, both overlooked by the burial squads of the day before because they had not gone this far out from the skirmish line. Are the bones of these two still lying here partly covered by drift and the thick covering of grass? No one seems to know. The marker for Kellogg now stands in the group of three nearest to Custer Hill on the northeast.

"On the very top (of Custer Hill) are four or five dead horses, swollen, putrid, and offensive, their stiffened limbs sticking out straight from their bodies," wrote Gibbon. What horses, if not those behind which the 7 men had lain and fought until their comrades all over the field were down and their own ammunition exhausted or reduced to a few rounds reserved for what they would meet in their dash for cover? P. 208

69. When Lieutenant-Colonel W. V. Sheridan was on the stand at the Court of Inquiry Mr. Gilbert asked him: What was the character of the place where General Custer's body was found? He replied: "It was a little to one side of the top of the ridge which was wide enough to drive a wagon along. It was not a good place for defense." P. 209

70. Curiously enough James T. Gatchell told Frazier and Robert Hunt that a half dozen Cheyenne warriors had pointed out to him the exact spot where Custer's body was found on the east slope of the battleridge a hundred feet or more from where the monument now stands. Only one said it was lying on the west slope. The terms should, of course, be "northeast" and "southwest" respectively, since the ridge runs southeastward from the Hill. But these Cheyennes cast doubt upon this story by telling several others which do not ring true. They said that the Cheyennes' chiefs and headmen guarded the body of Custer from mutilation in order to show that they, the Cheyennes, had killed Custer, their great enemy, and that three of the Cheyennes had made the first coups on his body. They denied that he or any of his men had committed suicide, and reported correctly that he had been shot in the temple and left breast. They are exactly the kind of stories which Wooden Leg warned his friend, Dr. Marquis, were told by persons who wanted to gain credit or fame for themselves. Underlying all such stories is the necessary assumption that the Indians knew Custer was in command of the troops and recognized him during the fighting, which is extremely improbable. His long, yellow hair by which some might have recognized him had been cut off before he started out on the expedition. A half dozen or more wore buckskin coats, so that he could not have been identified by his dress. *I Fought with Custer,* by Frazier and Robert Hunt; Charles Scribner's Sons. New York, (chapter 9). P. 212

241

71. We have accepted this account as the most plausible because it is in harmony with the known circumstances, and the only one that accounts for the appearance of Custer's body as reported by Lieutenant Bradley and others, among them Charles Windolph who stood beside it while Benteen fashioned a piece of wood for a marker into which he pushed an empty shell containing a slip of paper with Custer's name on it.

It was not the fairies who laid him here all "clean and bright" as a mortician might have done. Only someone with some kind of sentimental interest in him would have done that. P. 213.

Appendix II

Findings of the court of inquiry, convened at Major Reno's request, which sat in Chicago during the month of January, 1879, were published by the War Department as follows:

General Orders ⎫   Headquarters of the Army,
          ⎬   Adjutant General's Office,
No. 17.   ⎭   Washington, March 11, 1879.

1. The Court of Inquiry of which Colonel John H. King, 9th Infantry, is President, instituted by direction of the President, in Special Orders No. 255, Headquarters of the Army, Adjutant General's Office, November 25, 1878, on the application of Major Marcus A. Reno, 7th Cavalry, for the purpose of inquiring into Major Reno's conduct at the battle of the Little Big Horn River, on the 25th and 26th days of June, 1876, has reported the following facts and opinions, viz:

FIRST. On the morning of the 25th of June 1876, the 7th Cavalry, Lieutenant Colonel G. A. Custer commanding, operating against the hostile Indians in Montana Territory, near the Little Big Horn River, was divided into four battalions, two of which were commanded by Colonel Custer in person, with the exception of one company in charge of the pack-train; one by Major Reno and one by Captain Benteen. This division took place from about twelve (12) to fifteen (15) miles from the scene of the battle or battles afterwards fought. The column under Captain Benteen received orders to move to the left for an indefinite distance (to the first and second valleys) hunting Indians, with orders to charge any it might meet with. The battalion under Major Reno received orders to draw out of the column, and doing so marched parallel (with) and only a short distance from, the column commanded by Colonel Custer.

SECOND. About three or four miles from what afterwards was found to be the Little Big Horn River, where the fighting took place, Major Reno received orders to move forward as rapidly as he thought prudent, until coming up with the Indians, who were reported fleeing, he would charge them and drive everything before him, and would receive the support of the column under Colonel Custer.

THIRD. In obedience to the orders given by Colonel Custer, Captain Benteen marched to the left (south), at an angle of about forty-five degrees, but, meeting an impracticable country, was forced by it to march more to his right than the angle above indicated and nearer approaching a parallel route to that trail followed by the rest of the command.

FOURTH. Major Reno, in obedience to the orders given him, moved on at a fast trot on the main Indian trail until reaching the Little Big Horn River, which he forded, and halted for a few minutes to re-form his battalion.

243

After re-forming, he marched the battalion forward towards the Indian village, down stream or in a northerly direction, two companies in line of battle and one in support, until about half way to the point where he finally halted, when he brought the company in reserve forward to the line of battle, continuing the movement at a fast trot or gallop until after passing over a distance of about two miles, when he halted and dismounted to fight on foot at a point of timber upon which the right flank of his battalion rested. After fighting in this formation for less than half an hour, the Indians passing to his left rear and appearing in his front, the skirmish line was withdrawn to the timber, and the fight continued for a short time—half an hour or forty-five minutes in all—when the command, or nearly all of it, was mounted, formed, and, at a rapid gait, was withdrawn to a hill on the opposite side of the river. In this movement one officer and about sixteen soldiers and citizens were left in the woods, besides one wounded man or more, two citizens and thirteen soldiers rejoining the command afterwards. In this retreat Major Reno's battalion lost some twenty-nine men in killed and wounded, and three officers, including Doctor De Wolf, killed.

FIFTH. In the meantime Captain Benteen, having carried out, as far as was practicable, the spirit of his orders, turned in the direction of the route taken by the remainder of the regiment, and reaching the trail, followed it to near the crossing of the Little Big Horn, reaching there about the same time Reno's command was crossing the river in retreat lower down, and finally joined his battalion with that of Reno, on the hill. Forty minutes or one hour later the pack-train, which had been left behind on the trail by the rapid movement of the command and the delays incident to its march, joined the united command, which then consisted of seven companies, together with about thirty (30) or thirty-five (35) men belonging to the companies under Colonel Custer.

SIXTH. After detaching Benteen's columns Colonel Custer moved with his immediate command, on the trail followed by Reno, to a point within about one mile of the river, where he diverged to the right (or northward), following the general direction of the river to a point about four miles below that (afterward taken by Major Reno) where he and his command were destroyed by the hostiles. The last living witness of this march, Trumpeter Martin, left Colonel Custer's command when it was about two miles distant from the field where it afterwards met its fate. There is nothing more in evidence as to this command, save that firing was heard proceeding from its direction from about the time Reno retreated from the field to the time the pack-train was approaching the position on the hill. All firing which indicated fighting was concluded before the final preparations (were made) in Major Reno's command for the movement which was afterwards attempted.

SEVENTH. After the distribution of ammunition and a proper provision for the wounded men, Major Reno's entire command moved down the river in the direction it was thought Custer's column had taken, and in which it was known General Terry's command was to be found. This movement was carried sufficiently far to discover that its continuance would imperil the entire command, upon which it returned to the position formerly occupied, and made a successful resistance till succor reached it. The defense of the position on the hill was a heroic one against fearful odds.

The conduct of the officers throughout was excellent, and while subordinates, in some instances, did more for the safety of the command by brilliant displays of courage than did Major Reno, there was nothing in his conduct which requires animadversion from this Court.

OPINION

It is the conclusion of this Court, in view of all the facts in evidence, that no further proceedings are necessary in this case, and it expresses this opinion in compliance with the concluding clause of the order convening the Court.

II. The proceedings and opinion of the Court of Inquiry in the foregoing case of Major Marcus A. Reno, 7th Cavalry, are approved by order of the President.

III. By direction of the Secretary of War, the Court of Inquiry of which Colonel John H. King, 9th Infantry, is President is hereby dissolved.

By command of General Sherman:

E. D. TOWNSEND,
Adjutant General.

OFFICIAL.

245

Bibliography

(MAJOR SOURCES ONLY)

Bourke, Capt. John H., *With Crook On the Border*, Chas. Scribner's Sons.

Brininstool, E. A., *A Trooper With Custer*, The Hunter-Trader-Trapper Co.

Dustin, Fred, *The Custer Tragedy*.

Fougera, Katherine G., *With Custer's Cavalry*, Caxton Printers, Ltd.

Graham, Colonel W. A., U. S. A. Ret., *The Story Of The Little Big Horn*, Military Service Publishing Co.

Grinnell, George B., *The Fighting Cheyennes*, Chas. Scribner's Sons.

Godfrey, *Montana Historical Contributions*, Volume 9.

Hanson, Joseph Mills, *The Conquest of the Missouri*, Murray-Hill Books, Inc.

Hughes, Colonel Robert P., *The Campaign Against The Sioux In 1876*, Journal of the Military Institution of the U. S.

Hunt, Frazier and Robert, *I Fought With Custer*, Chas. Scribner's Sons.

Libby, O. G., *The Arikara Narrative Of The Campaign Against The Hostile Dakotas*, North Dakota Historical Commission.

Luce, Capt. E. S., U. S. A. Ret., *Keogh, Comanche and Custer*.

Marquis, Dr. Thomas B., *A Warrior Who Fought Custer*, Caxton Printers, Ltd., Caldwell, Idaho.

McLaughlin, James, *My Friend The Indian*, Houghton, Mifflin Co.

Schultz, James W., *William Jackson, Indian Scout*, Houghton Mifflin Co.

Van de Water, Frederic F., *Glory Hunter*, Bobbs, Merrill Co.

Wagner, Glendolin Damon, *Old Neutriment*, Miss Ruth Hill, 1934.

PERIODICALS

Army and Navy Journal
Billings Gazette
Blue Book Magazine
Cavalry Journal
Century Magazine
Chicago Daily News
Chicago Times
Helena Herald

Journal of the Military Institution of the United States
Kansas Historical Quarterly
Miles City Journal
New York Herald
Oshkosh Northwestern
The American Catholic Quarterly Review, Volume 2.
Walla Walla Bulletin

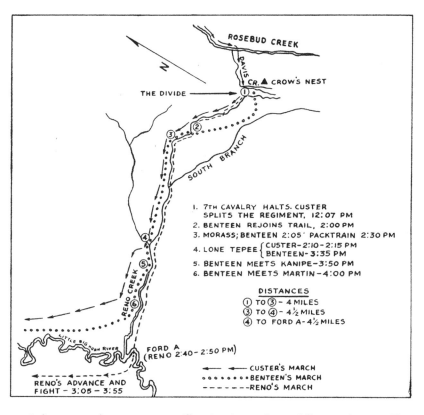

ROSEBUD CREEK

DAVIS CR. ▲ CROW'S NEST

THE DIVIDE ⟶ ①

SOUTH BRANCH

RENO CREEK

LITTLE BIG HORN RIVER

FORD A
(RENO 2:40 - 2:50 PM)

RENO'S ADVANCE AND
FIGHT - 3:05 - 3:55

1. 7TH CAVALRY HALTS. CUSTER
   SPLITS THE REGIMENT, 12:07 PM
2. BENTEEN REJOINS TRAIL, 2:00 PM
3. MORASS; BENTEEN 2:05' PACKTRAIN 2:30 PM
4. LONE TEPEE { CUSTER-2:10-2:15 PM
                BENTEEN-3:35 PM
5. BENTEEN MEETS KANIPE-3:50 PM
6. BENTEEN MEETS MARTIN-4:00 PM

DISTANCES
① TO ③ - 4 MILES
③ TO ④ - 4½ MILES
④ TO FORD A - 4½ MILES

⟵ ⟵ CUSTER'S MARCH
○○○○○○○○BENTEEN'S MARCH
------RENO'S MARCH

Reference to these two maps will assist the reader in following the text. The small map above shows the 12 to 15 mile march of the three battalions of Custer's 7th Cavalry from "The Divide" westward along Reno Creek to the battle area, which is depicted on the contour map to the left.

All important terrain features are noted, as well as the key time and space factors which play an important part in the author's reconstruction of the events preceding and during the several battles.

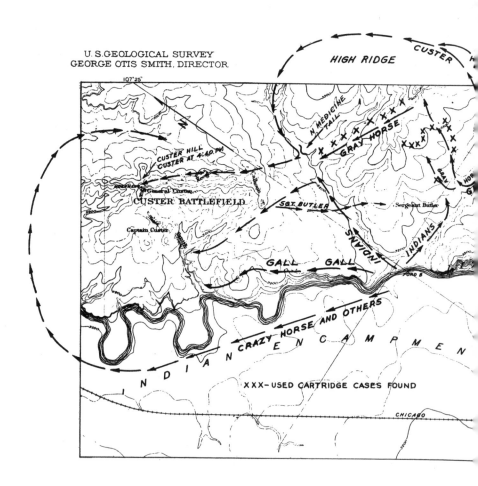

HIGH RIDGE

CUSTER

N. MEDICINE TAIL

GRAY HORSE

CUSTER HILL
CUSTER AT 4:40 P.M.

General Custer

CUSTER BATTLEFIELD

Captain Custer

SGT. BUTLER

Sergeant Butler

INDIANS

GALL   GALL

CRAZY HORSE AND OTHERS

INDIAN ENCAMPMEN

XXX—USED CARTRIDGE CASES FOUND

CHICAGO

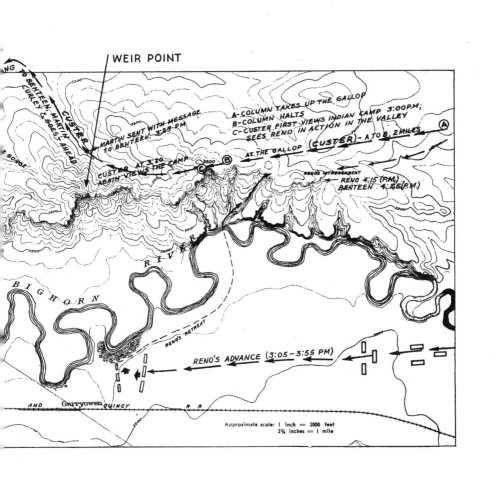

WEIR POINT

A-COLUMN TAKES UP THE GALLOP
B-COLUMN HALTS
C-CUSTER FIRST VIEWS INDIAN CAMP 3:00 P.M;
SEES RENO IN ACTION IN THE VALLEY

AT THE GALLOP (CUSTER) - A TO B, 2 MILES

MARTIN SENT WITH MESSAGE
TO BENTEEN, 3:25 PM

CUSTER AT 3:20
AGAIN VIEWS THE CAMP

RENO'S INTRENCHMENT
RENO 4:15 (P.M.)
BENTEEN 4:26 (P.M.)

RIVER

BIG HORN

RENO'S RETREAT

RENO'S ADVANCE (3:05-3:55 PM)

AND Garryowen QUINCY R.R.

Approximate scale: 1 inch = 2000 feet
2¾ inches = 1 mile

ORGANIZATION AND STRENGTH TABLE OF GENERAL CUSTER'S 7TH U.S. CAVALRY, JUNE 25, 1876

On June 25, 1876, about 12:00 noon, on the slopes of the low Divide between the valleys of the Rosebud and Little Big Horn Rivers, in the State of Montana, the Seventh U.S. Cavalry, Lieutenant Colonel George A. Custer commanding, was halted while Custer split his Regiment temporarily into three combat groups and a pack-train, in furtherance of his reconnaissance-in-force mission, to locate and pin down the Indians reported to be assembling in unknown strength.

The four separate elements of the command, with the names, rank and unit assignments of the officers; the fate in store for each; and the strength of each troop as represented on the pre-battle rosters* of the regiment, are shown in the following table, which the reader will discover is of vital interest for orientation purposes, as the tragic events in the narrative unfold.

* Custer may have made oral transfers and reassignments at the Divide; if so, no record exists.

NAME	RANK	BATTLE ASSIGNMENT	FATE OF OFFICER	BATTLE STRENGTH PRESENT June 25, 1876		KILLED June 25-26 NUMBER		WOUNDED NUMBER All ranks	REMARKS
				Officer	Enlisted	Officer	Enlisted		
HEADQUARTERS and HQ. DETACHMENT									
George A. Custer (Brevet Major General)	Lieut. Colonel	Comdg. Officer	K	2	30	2	16	..	K—Killed
William W. Cooke (Brevet Lieut. Colonel)	1st Lieut.	Adjutant	K	..	..	..	..	..	M—Missing and unidentified, presumed killed
THE CUSTER BATTALION									S—Survived
Thomas W. Custer	Captain	Troop "C"	K	2	60	2	36	4	Normally asg'd to:
Henry M. Harrington	2d Lieut.	Troop "C"	M	..	..	..	..	..	[1] Troop "A"
Algernon E. Smith	1st Lieut.	Troop "E"[1]	K	2	53	2	37	2	[2] Troop "M"
James G. Sturgis	2d Lieut.	Troop "E"[2]	M	..	..	..	..	..	[3] Troop "C"
George W. Yates	Captain	Troop "F"	K	1	61	1	36	None	[4] Atch'd from 20th Infantry
Myles W. Keogh (Brevet Lieut. Colonel)	Captain	Troop "I"	K	2	49	2	36	2	[5] Strength of 280 men was reduced to approx. 214 before reaching Custer Field, by details to
James E. Porter	1st Lieut.	Troop "I"	M	..	..	..	..	..	
James Calhoun	1st Lieut.	Troop "L"[3]	K	2	57	2	44	2	
John J. Crittenden	2d Lieut.	Troop "L"[4]	K	..	..	..	..	..	
Dr. G. E. Lord		Asst. Surgeon—attached	K	..	..	1	..	..	
William Van W. Reily	2d Lieut.	Unassigned	K	..	..	1	..	..	
TOTAL BATTALION				9	280[5]	11	189	10	

Name	Rank	Command						
Frank M. Gibson	1st Lieut.	Troop "K"	S				5	6
Edward S. Godfrey	Captain	Troop "K"	S	2		41	11	29
TOTAL BATTALION				5	1	136[6]		
THE RENO BATTALION								
Marcus A. Reno (Brevet Colonel)	Maj. Comdg.	Troops "A," "G," "M"	S	2	1			
Benjamin H. Hodgson	2d Lieut.	Adjutant[7]						
Myles Moylan	Captain	Troop "A"	K	2		47	8	14
Chas. C. DeRudio	1st Lieut.	Troop "A"	S					
Donald McIntosh	1st Lieut.	Troop "G"	K	2		44	13	2
George D. Wallace	Captain	Troop "G"[8]	S					
Thomas B. French	Captain	Troop "M"	S	1		55	12	10
H. R. Porter	Surgeon		S	1				
J. M. DeWolf	Acting Surgeon		K	1				
Chas. A. Varnum	2d Lieut.	Comdg. Indian Scouts[9]	S	1				
Luther R. Hare	2d Lieut.	Comdg. Indian Scouts[10]	S	1				
Attached								
George Herendeen	Civilian	Courier	S					
Charley Reynolds	Civilian	White Scout	K					
Fred Gerard	Civilian	Interpreter	S					
Isaiah Dorman	Civilian	Interpreter	S			19 Indian Scouts[11]		
TOTAL BATTALION				11	3	146[12]	33	26
THE PACK TRAIN								
Thos. M. McDougall	Captain	Comdg.[13]	S	2	None			
Edward G. Mathey	1st Lieut.	2d in command[14]	S					
TOTAL TRAIN				2		45[15] (84)[16]		
TOTAL STRENGTH OF REGIMENT	29 officers and 637 enlisted men[17]			2	(129)	14	233	65

[6] Normally asg'd to: Troop "B"
[7] Troop "B"
[8] Acting Engineer officer, normally asg'd to Troop "G"
[9] Normally asg'd to: Troop "A"
[10] Troop "K"
[11] 6 Scouts left to forage for Indian ponies
[12] Actual strength, about 112 after details to Pack Train and other losses.
[13] Normally asg'd to: Troop "B"
[14] Troop "M"
[15] Troop "B"
[16] Men in charge of Troop packs, 1 NCO and 6 privates from each of 12 troops, 6 civilian packers
[17] Excl. of scouts & civilians

Author's Note: The strength figures shown in the above tabulation were taken from appendices D and E to the book, *Keogh, Comanche and Custer,* by Captain E. S. Luce, U.S. Army (ret.) with the permission of the author.

Inclosure to LEGEND INTO HISTORY, by Charles Kuhlman; The Stackpole Company, Harrisburg, Penna., Publishers.

Index

This index is designed as a guide to the names of the men—White and Indian—who were the dramatis personnae of this stirring narrative. The events before, during and after the Battle of the Little Big Horn are keyed to these people, so that reference to them will lead the reader to a description of what happened.

However, the names of the *principal* characters thread so continuously through the narrative that it would be only confusing to catalogue them. The index, therefore, does not include the names of General George Armstrong Custer, Major Marcus A. Reno, and Captain Frederick W. Benteen. For the same reason the index does not include the names of the various Indian tribes, Custer Field and its environs, the Seventh Cavalry, or the rivers which focus the action: Yellowstone, Big Horn, Little Big Horn, Tongue, Rosebud and their tributaries.

Did Custer
Disobey Orders

at the
Battle of the
Little Big Horn?

A Study by
DR. CHARLES KUHLMAN
Author of
LEGEND INTO HISTORY

THE STACKPOLE COMPANY
HARRISBURG, PENNSYLVANIA

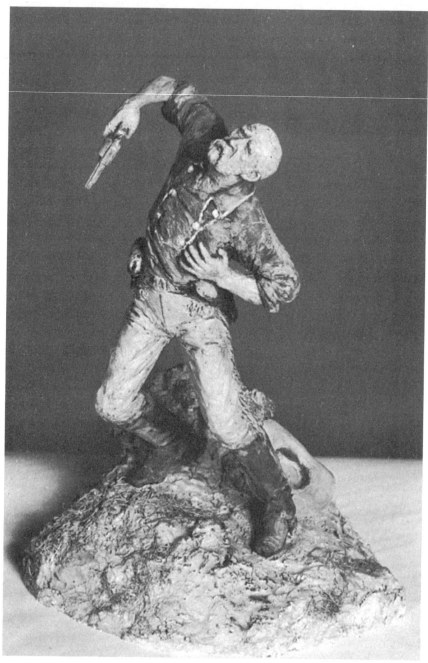

From THE CUSTER MYTH © W. A. Graham
The Passing of the Yellow Hair.

Foreword

IN HIS STORY of the "Little Big Horn" Colonel W. A. Graham said that our treatment of the Indians is a "black, disgraceful page in our history."

This is equally true of the Reconstruction period after the Civil War, which represents the lowest ebb in every type of skulduggery in our history, a situation with which the personally honest Grant was unable to cope, encompassed as he was by the saurian-minded corruptionists he mistook for friends; men who dropped him, penniless, when they had no further use for him, leaving him to carry on as best he might after having rebuffed his true friends who had sought to stem the rush downward into Avernus.

The tradership graft of General Belknap, which has received so much attention in connection with Custer, was a picayunish affair compared with the misdeeds of the rest of the gangs, loosely headed by General Babcock, who was for eight years Grant's private secretary.

Out of the whole unsavory mess only three men who figure prominently in our study came out clean: Secretary of State Hamilton Fish; the General of the Army, Sherman; and the stormy petrel, Lieutenant Colonel George Armstrong Custer, U. S. Army.

A series of disastrous mistakes in the life of a man who has served his country with signal distinction does not necessarily damn him for all time in the eyes of his countrymen or the world.

And was there not also "Appomattox" where he appeared as truly great?

And yet, after all that can be said in extenuation of Grant's association with the vultures in human form who swarmed around him, there still remains his unjust treatment of Custer who was doing his best to clean out a shameful graft that vitally affected the welfare of the people under his care. I do not believe that President Grant was in any way connected with this. But his brother, Orville, certainly was,

259

for he admitted it under oath. And there was the President's crudity in refusing to receive Custer in the purely formal, but obligatory, ceremony of "leave-taking," followed by the order of arrest and suspension from command based, ostensibly, solely on this omission. The fact that Custer had tried at least three times to "see him" before leaving Washington was brushed aside.

All this constituted a disgraceful misuse of power, recognized as such by General Terry who exploded the whole case against Custer in a single short paragraph.

Acknowledgments

ALTHOUGH THE RESPONSIBILITY for the constructions in the present study rests entirely with me, a good part of the evidence on which they are based has been contributed by others. One of the victims of this kind of sponging is the publisher to whom I am especially indebted for the clarifications of some troublesome technicalities involving what seemed to be, at the time of the battle, a partial overlapping of the War Department and the duties of General of the Army·Sherman. It is worth remembering that in this connection Sherman and Custer were fighting in the same cause, namely to protect the occupants of the army posts as far as they could against the extortions of the parasitic horde General Belknap loosed on them. Among these bandits was President Grant's brother Orville, who had admitted in his testimony that he had received $1,000, a fact repeated by Custer before the Clymer Committee. This must have infuriated Grant who had, by this time, clearly lost his self-control.

Lieutenant James S. Hutchins is another careful student of Custeriana to whom I am greatly indebted for sending me the data in General Stanley's *Memoires* dealing with the expedition of 1873. Copies of these *Memoires* are now about as scarce as hen's teeth. Fortunately for me Mr. Hutchins has a copy from which he extracted everything of consequence in connection with Custer's arrest and his difficulties throughout the campaign, and sent it to me *gratis,* together with a down-to-earth discussion of the details of what might be called "Rules and Regulations" in an army on campaign. This, taken with Custer's letters to his wife, published by Miss Marguerite Merrington, opens the way to a complete debunking of the narratives so far published in connection with the question of "Disobedience."

Other contributors who have helped to fill out the picture are:
Dr. Lawrence Frost,
Major E. S. Luce, retired,

Don Russell of the Chicago Daily News,
Dr. Norman McLean of the Department of English, University of Chicago,
Lieutenant Colonel Alvin Bielefeld.

And, finally, there is a long overdue "Thank you" for the uniformly highly favorable reviews of *Legend into History* by both the military students, retired and active, and civilians specializing in the subject. This was wholly unexpected, but it is the real "pay" for the many hours of climbing up the steep and crumbling surfaces of hillsides often while the thermometer stood in the high nineties and sometimes past the century mark down in the ravines. But I was not always alone in those trips, and credit is due to the many who at one time or other played a part in the evolution of this thesis.

And so, at last

VALEDICTORY.

The Main Argument
on Disobedience

IT WAS UNFORTUNATE for General Terry, an able and conscientious soldier with a good record in the Civil War, that in this campaign he was surrounded by a staff composed in part of irresponsible sycophants. It was, perhaps, even more unfortunate that his personal aide and chief of staff was Colonel Robert P. Hughes, who, if he was not a sycophant, seems nevertheless to have believed that, to save the military reputation of his brother-in-law, it was necessary to destroy that of Custer. Still worse, perhaps, was it that he relied on Captain Benteen for his information on Custer's marches instead of consulting Lieutenant Wallace, the official itinerist of the marches; for, as every student of our subject knows, Benteen habitually exaggerated, especially if his exaggerations tended to damage the reputation or prestige of persons he disliked with or without cause. Anyone who doubts this needs only to read his correspondence with Theodore Goldin to be convinced.

The point under consideration here is the thinly veiled charge in Terry's confidential dispatch of July 2 that Custer had disobeyed his orders by resorting to forced marches and in following the Indian trail across the Divide as soon as he came to it, and as a result struck the Indian village on the 25th instead of the 26th of June, the day Gibbon was expected to reach the mouth of the Little Big Horn. But, as will appear in a moment, the charge could not be made to stick on the basis of the actual distances marched as shown by Wallace's record.

For the convenience of the reader I here reproduce that part of Terry's dispatch concerned directly or indirectly with the subject of disobedience.

I think I owe it to myself to put you more fully in possession of the facts of the late operations. While at the mouth of the Rosebud I submitted my plan to Genl. Gibbon and to General Custer. They approved it heartily. It was that Custer with his whole regiment should move up the Rosebud till he should meet a trail which Reno had discovered a few days before, but that he should not follow it directly to the Little Big Horn; that he should send scouts over it and keep his main force further to the south so as to prevent the Indians from slipping in between himself and the mountains. He was to examine the headwaters of Tullock's creek as he passed it and send me word of what he found there. A scout was furnished him for the purpose of crossing the country to me. We calculated it would take Gibbon's column until the 26th to reach the mouth of the Little Big Horn and that the wide sweep which I proposed Custer should make would require so much time that Gibbon would be able to cooperate with him in attacking any Indians that might be found on that stream. I asked Custer how long his marches would be. He said they would be at first about thirty miles a day. Measurements were made and calculations based on that rate of progress. I talked with him about his strength and at one time suggested that perhaps it would be well for me to take Gibbon's cavalry and go with him. To this suggestion he replied that without reference to the command he would prefer his own regiment alone. As a homogeneous body, as much could be done with it as with the two combined and he expressed the utmost confidence that he had all the force that he could need, and I shared his confidence. The plan adopted was the only one that promised to bring the Infantry into action and I desired to make sure of things by getting up every available man. I offered Custer the battery of gatling guns but he declined it saying that it might embarrass him: that he was strong enough without it. The movements proposed for Genl. Gibbon's column were carried out to the letter and had the attack been deferred until it was up I cannot doubt that we should have been successful. The Indians had evidently nerved themselves for a stand, but as I learned from Capt. Benteen, on the twenty-second the Cavalry marched twelve miles; on the twenty-third, thirty-five miles; from five A. M. till eight on the twenty-fourth, forty-five miles and then after night ten miles further, then after resting but without unsaddling twenty-three miles to the battlefield. The proposed route was not taken but as soon as the trail was struck it was followed. I cannot learn that any examination of Tullock's Creek was made. I do not tell you this to cast any reflections upon Custer. For whatever errors he may have committed he has paid the penalty, and you cannot regret his loss more than I do, but I feel my plan must have been successful had it been carried out, and I desire you to know the facts. In the action itself, so far as I can make out, Custer acted under a misapprehension. He thought, I am sure, that the Indians were running. For fear that they might get away he attacked without getting all his men up and divided his command so that they were beaten in detail.

Since one of the main charges against Custer is that he resorted to forced marches in order to strike the Indian village before Gibbon could come up to participate in the attack, it is necessary to call attention to the fact that Terry relied on Benteen's report of the daily marches, which, it will be noted, made a total of 102 miles, including the night march of 10 miles, as against the 76 miles as reported by Lieutenant Wallace, the official itinerist of the march, making the differ-

ence between the two accounts 26 miles. This is about a fair day's march, and just about right for accusing Custer of disobedience. Was this merely a mistake or a deliberate falsification on the part of Benteen? The mileage given by Wallace corresponds closely to the distance given on the modern road maps.

As the confidential dispatch shows, the rate of march agreed on was about 30 miles a day, which would have been 75 miles in the two and a half days from noon on the 22nd to the evening of the 24th, or five miles more than he actually did march.

Whether or not this exaggeration on the part of Benteen was due merely to a long-standing habit, a deliberate falsehood, or an honest mistake, we do not know. In any case it was the source of a good deal of unhappiness for General Terry for the rest of his days.

These fictitious 26 miles may well have looked suspicious to Terry, and it may be taken for granted, I think, that Hughes and all the rest of the staff did all they could to confirm him in his suspicion that Custer had crowded the pace beyond what had been understood. They certainly did so in the evening when Terry read them his dispatch to Sheridan, all of them clamoring loudly for inclusion of a statement that the disaster was due to disobedience on the part of Custer, a demand Terry rejected by saying that he himself would accept responsibility for what had happened. This was a generous thing to do and at the same time a serious mistake because there had not been time either for himself or for the men half dead from fatigue and loss of sleep to think clearly enough to recall vital details and to put them together into a coherent picture. We have, for instance, found nothing to show that anyone at the time noticed the all-important fact that the Indians were 40 to 50 or more miles further downstream than they were believed to be, at the time the attack was made, and what this had to do with Custer's action in following the trail. Certainly Terry did not see it at the time or any other time before he sent his Confidential Dispatch.

It was the failure to correct the *ante hoc* deductions by the use of the *post hoc* evidence supplied by direct observation that caused most of the confusion and the consequent charges and counter-charges. Added to this were the grossly exaggerated distances marched by Custer dinned into the ears of Terry, who does not seem to have checked them against the official record of Wallace, whose special duty it was to keep track of the marches. But this failure on the part of Terry is easily understandable and as easily excused; for he had many other things to attend to. Not so Colonel Hughes twenty years later, when he had the Wallace record before him as he worked. But if he could not quote Wallace correctly in the interest of his objectives he could misquote him by mutilating one of his (Wallace's) sentences in such a way as to make it imply the exact opposite of what the sentence as a whole implies. The sentence in question reads as follows: "General Custer determined to cross the Divide that night (24-25) to conceal the command, the next day find out the locality of the village and attack the following morning at daylight. The "next morning" was the 26th, the day Hughes says Custer should have been in position to attack. He was forced to admit that because it was notorious that Gibbon was expected to enter the valley of the Little Big Horn on the 26th.

So here he was at a dead end, completely stymied by the official record which showed that Custer had followed the only practical course that could possibly bring about the combined attack Terry had hoped for. There was nothing wrong with Wallace's record. The modern survey shows that it was very nearly correct. There was no way out of this for Hughes except by some type of deception, the use of some device that would blind the reader to Custer's real intention; and it must be admitted that in this choice he was as clever in expedients as he was short of intellectual rectitude, to put it mildly. For what he quoted from Wallace was perfectly true as far as it went: "Custer determined to cross the Divide that night." The trouble with it is that it did not go far enough, for it left the reader to infer that Custer had intended to continue on to the river and attack on the morning of the 25th, a day too soon for Gibbon to be in position to participate in the battle. Had he not cut the sentence where he did the reader would not have been deceived, but would have seen that Custer had intended as early as the evening of the 24th to attack on the morning of the 26th instead of the 25th as the mutilation of the sentence makes Wallace say. Here we seem to have a case perfectly illustrating the old saw that a half truth can be a contemptible lie in effect.

Closely connected with the distortion we have just discussed is

another misstatement about distances that is belied not only by the report of Wallace but also by the map Terry used on this campaign and printed by Hughes in his article. To prove that Custer was not anyway "nearly in contact with the enemy" on the evening of the 24th and was, therefore, not justified by his orders to use discretion, he says further that Custer had not, on the evening of the 24th, discovered any facts that had not been known at the time the order was made out.

Both of these statements are untrue, and if Hughes did not know they were so it is not because they were a deep secret. All he needed to do to inform himself was to read the Wallace report which he had at hand while he was writing.

As to the distance from Custer's camp on the evening of the 24th to the Indian village, this was on the map Terry used during the campaign and was reprinted in the article under discussion. Hughes says the distance was 40 miles. The measurement on the map shows 23 miles, and on the modern survey it is 22 miles, both measurements straight line. By the trail the distance was several miles more.

Why this exaggeration? Why, if not to bolster the false charge that Custer was not nearly in contact with the enemy at the time he decided to follow the trail across the divide instead of continuing his march up the Rosebud, as Hughes claims he should have done. But since he claims also that Custer should have been in position to attack on the morning of the 26th, we are puzzled to understand how he could have marched up the Rosebud on the 25th and gotten back to strike the Indians on the morning of the 26th, especially since, according to Hughes, the distance from the Rosebud to the Little Big Horn was 40 miles. Assuming that he had made thirty miles in the wrong direction on the 25th, he would have been something like 70 miles from the Indian village on the morning of the 26th, if he countermarched the 30 miles.

This is positively the dizziest thing I have come across in my more than sixty years of nonprofessional study of warfare; and it strikes me that this comic opera idea of Colonel Hughes can be fairly taken as the measure of the straits to which he was put in his endeavor to build up a plausible case against Custer. It certainly was a poor compliment to his readers, not all of whom were morons; nor is it suggested here that Hughes was such. It is not his intelligence but his method and motives that are under consideration.

There is another instance of a similar if not quite as gaudy a hue as the above. In order to make out a case for Terry it was necessary to find enough warriors to condemn Custer for attacking before Gibbon came up. On the other hand there must not be so many as to lay him, Terry, open to criticism for having divided his command. He must

267

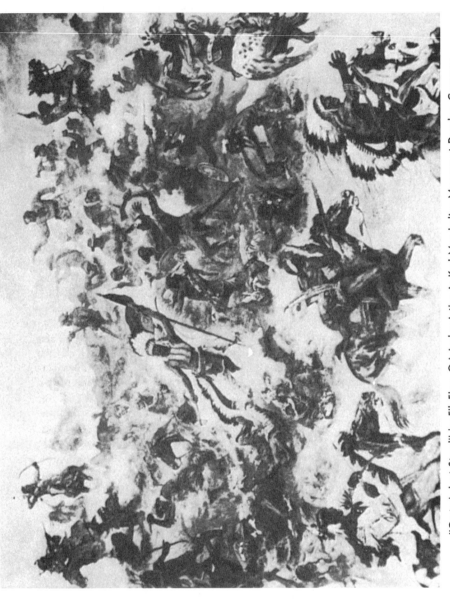

"Custer's Last Stand" by Elk Eber. Original painting in Karl May Indian Museum at Dresden, Germany.

find the golden mean which, unfortunately, did not exist ready-made in any estimates at hand. On page 32 of *Legend into History* I gave an example of how Hughes worked to get what he thought he needed, and I can do no better than to repeat here what I said there. The remarks ascribed to Custer were addressed to his officers assembled in his tent on the evening of June 22. The quote: "In his letter to the Herald he (Custer) said that the camp Reno had discovered contained 380 lodges. Godfrey says that on this evening Custer remarked that the Reno report indicated a warrior force of 1,000, but that from his own study of the report of the commissioner of Indian Affairs on the number of Indians usually absent from the agencies, they might find as many as 1,500 but not more than that; a statement Colonel Hughes, for his own *ex parte* objectives, distorts into "According to Godfrey, Custer himself stated in terms that they would have to face three times that number," thus turning an *improbable maximum into an absolute minimum*. Hughes was using the estimates of 500 to 800 given in General Fry's "Comments," published with Godfrey's article in the *Century Magazine*. This makes Custer say that they would *have* to meet 1500 to 2400 warriors. The object of this distortion was, of course, to point up Custer's supposed rashness as contrasted with Terry's caution."

The point to which I want to call the reader's attention is not that Hughes was wrong in his estimate of the number of warriors. It is his distortion of Godfrey's estimate the reader should note because it is a characteristic running through the whole of his article. As a matter of fact the 2400 figure is probably about as near the truth as we shall ever get.

From this point in his narrative Hughes goes on to the scene on the Crow's Nest on the morning of the 25th to prove that Custer was aware of the unprecedented size of the Indian village; from which we are to infer that Custer was very rash in attacking on the 25th; and as he says a little farther on in his narrative, he purposely attacked a day too soon for no other reason than the glory he hoped to reap from a victory gained without assistance from Gibbon.

That this construction is pure moonshine will become apparent as we go along. What Hughes should have said here is that Terry and Gibbon would be in great danger of destruction if the Indians discovered their approach before Custer was within striking distance of the village. Also that the size of the warrior force threatened both Custer and Gibbon, for the warriors could strike in either direction on ground unsuitable for cavalry action and perfect for the Indian style of fighting.

And here was the place in his narrative to call the attention of the reader to the fact that, instead of the Indians being at the headwaters of the Tongue and the Rosebud as had been supposed, they actually were within about 15 miles of the mouth of the Little Big Horn. But had Hughes done this many readers would have made the necessary re-orientation and understood the nonsense involved in a march up the Rosebud on the 25th, and the smoke-screen created by Hughes would have been dissipated and Custer's clear reasoning made apparent.

And here is another piece of transparent jugglery. "As the question of the number of warriors in the hostile camps has been raised" says

Photograph of Sitting Bull. Photo by D. F. Barry.

Hughes, "it may not be amiss to recall an incident that took place on the hill on which Reno took refuge within a few minutes after Terry's arrival. He and some of the officers of his staff were surrounded by a group of officers of the 7th Cavalry amongst whom were Major Reno, Colonel Benteen, Colonel Weir and Major Moylan—all officers of long and varied experience in the Army. General Terry put the direct question to them: 'What is your estimate of the number of Indian warriors?' The replies pivoted around the figure 1500, and I can recall Colonel

Benteen's reply almost verbatim, which was as follows: 'I have been accustomed to seeing divisions of cavalry during the war, and from my observations I would say that there were from fifteen to eighteen hundred warriors.' No one in the group at that time put his estimate above 1800."

Seven days after this incident on Reno Hill Benteen wrote a letter to his wife in which he said, *"Three thousand warriors were there."* And General Terry, in his dispatch to Sheridan written on the day he received these estimates, said, "Major Reno and Captain Benteen, both of whom are officers of great experience, accustomed to see masses of mounted men, estimate the number of Indians at not less than twenty-five hundred. Other officers think the number was greater than this."

And Major Reno in his Report of July 6th estimated the number as at least 2500.

If Colonel Hughes had intended to inform his readers instead of deceiving them, why did he not quote the figures given in Terry's dispatch of the 27th containing the estimates obtained from the officers only a few hours before the dispatch was written instead of pretending to cite them from memory twenty years after the event?

The following quotation may be regarded as nearly a final summary of both fact and construction as Hughes saw it, or pretended to see it, and offers us a new departure for further analysis.

Custer's discretion to deviate from them (his orders) might be exercised: First: If the condition of things was found to be essentially different from what Terry believed it to be when he issued his orders. Second: if Custer should see *sufficient reason* for departing from them.

All the evidence known to exist points conclusively to one fact: that in no particular was the conditions of things, as anticipated by Terry, when making the order, in any way different from the condition found by Custer up to the point when the direction taken by the Indians' trail was definitely ascertained. At this point, personal examination demonstrated that the conditions actually existed that Terry had so clearly anticipated, namely: It was found (as it appeared to Terry, "almost certain it would be found"), that the trail turned towards the Little Big Horn. Hence there was nothing in this that warranted any deviation from the order. We thus logically arrive at the second case, that there must be "sufficient reason."

Did it exist?

We look in vain in any narrative of the events, we apply in vain to anyone having knowledge of the controlling facts, for any reason for departing from the order at this point. Still less is there a scintilla of evidence of any "sufficient reason" for such a deviation from the order as to completely change Terry's plan, and, as the event showed, make the plan impossible.

Exactly what was found to be true, Terry had anticipated would be found to be true! And in that event Custer was left in no doubt what Terry intended he should do, and with no discretion to do otherwise than as ordered— "still proceed southward, perhaps as far as the headwaters of the Tongue," and, at this critical point, exactly what Terry did not want done, was done,

and instead of "still continuing southward," the trail of the Indians was followed directly to the village, and with such extraordinary haste that there can be no reasonable doubt that Custer had deliberately formed the purpose to follow the trail and attack the village upon reaching it, regardless of where Gibbon's column might be, and without considering that force as a factor in the action!

Well, that certainly ought to finish Custer! It certainly did so in the minds of the innocent readers who believed that Colonel Hughes was writing in good faith, as did the present writer until he was alerted by certain passages that did not square with known facts, especially distances and terrain. Full disillusionment, however, was a long and sometimes an unpleasant process because he had regarded Colonel Hughes as a high-minded officer defending a friend and relative as a matter of right or justice. This was a natural and fine thing to do provided that he first ascertained the facts and presented them correctly. Had he done this he would have discovered that there was no real ground for serious criticism of anyone in command. He was doubly obliged to do this because the man whose reputation he tried to blast was no longer in position to defend himself against unjust criticism involving the grossest kind of distortions and flat falsehoods.

So now, wearily we resume the task of probing into the dark corners of a mind obsessed with the idea that the military reputation of his brother-in-law could not be kept clean without besmirching the reputation of a man who had voluntarily taken a desperate chance in an attempt to save a situation arising from a failure in reconnaissance no one with command responsibility had thought practical or necessary. To repeat, and with all possible emphasis; Hughes was not telling the truth in saying that Custer had found things exactly as Terry had predicted, and his trick in cutting a sentence in the report of Wallace, explained some pages back, proves that he *knew* he was not telling the truth. And he was equally at fault in saying that when Custer decided to follow the trail across the Divide he was not in pos?sesion of any new evidence to justify his departure from the letter of his orders. The evidence was in the report of Wallace, the official itinerist of the march, a document with which Hughes was familiar. This, then, was the place to look for evidence; and had he looked here he would not have looked "in vain," as the following quotation from the Wallace report will make plain.

> June 24, 1876—The command moved at 5 A. M. this morning. After we had been on the march about an hour, our Crow scouts came in and reported fresh signs of Indians, but in no great numbers. After a short consultation, General Custer, with an escort of two companies, moved out in advance, the remainder of the command following at a distance of about half a mile—At 1 P. M. the command halted, scouts were sent ahead, and the men made coffee. The scouts got back about 4, and reported fresh camps at the forks of the Rosebud. Everything indicated that the Indians were *not over thirty miles away.* (Emphasis our own.) At 5 P. M. the command moved out; crossed to the left bank of the Rosebud; passed through several large camps; the trail was now fresh, and the *whole valley scratched up by the trailing lodgepoles.* At 7 P. M. we camped on the right bank of the Rosebud. Scouts were sent ahead to see which branch of the stream the Indians had followed . . . About 9 P. M. the scouts returned and reported that the Indians had crossed the divide to the Little Big Horn river. General Custer determined to cross the divide that night, *to conceal the command, the next day find out the locality of the village, and attack the following morning at daylight.*

Colonel Hughes could have found substantially the same evidence in a statement given by George Herendeen to the New York *Herald* early in July, 1876, and also in a letter given to the same paper, dated July 22, 1878. Add to this Benteen's assertion made at the Reno Court of Inquiry in 1879, that 8,000 to 10,000 indians had passed over the trail, and it seems to me that Custer had "sufficient reason" to ignore the phantom Indians at the "headwaters of the Tongue and the Little Big Horn," when the fresh trail proved that there were plenty of flesh-and-blood Indians not over 30 miles ahead and on their way across the Divide or already on the Little Big Horn, who were likely to run into Gibbon, or Gibbon into them, while Custer was expected to be around no matter when or where anything like this happened.

It is generally assumed that you cannot "turn a grindstone both ways at the same time." Then why assume, as the Custer critics do, that Custer could march his regiment both ways at the same time?

There are none so blind as those who' *will* not see.

The weakness of Hughes' case is apparent from the desperate expedients to which he resorted to make his case.

Let us now state clearly the more important assumptions in Terry's mind that can be clearly inferred from the order and the clarifications in a dispatch to Sheridan made out a few hours before the conference on the *Far West* quoted, in part, below. He was confident that Custer could take care of himself without assistance from Gibbon. The measures he advised Custer to take to guard against escape of the Indians necessarily implied that he anticipated the possibility of fighting before

Gibbon could arrive on the scene of action. As conceived in the order a collision might occur as far up as the head of the Rosebud or the Tongue, eighty miles or more from where it did occur. This construction is buttressed by the dispatch alluded to above, which runs as follows: "Custer will go up the Rosebud with his whole regiment, thence to the headwaters of the Little Horn, thence down the Little Horn."

This dispatch ended with the following significant words: "I only hope that *one* (emphasis our own) of the two columns will find the Indians. I go personally with Gibbon."

According to Colonel Charles Francis Bates these words are in every copy of the dispatch on file in the War Department, but have never appeared in any history of the battle!

Why were these sentences omitted if not to conceal the fact that before the battle there was no fear in Terry's mind that either Custer or Gibbon might come to grief if they encountered the Indians while the two columns were out of supporting distance of each other. So well was this understood that Lieutenant Bradley, Gibbon's scout commander, wrote in his diary on the evening of June 21st, after the conference on the *Far West:* "Though it is Terry's expectation that we will arrive in the neighborhood of the Sioux village about the same time and assist each other in the attack, it is understood that if Custer arrives first he is at liberty to attack if he deems prudent."

And Gibbon wrote soon after the campaign: "For I do not suppose there was a man in the column (his own) who entertained for a moment the idea that there were Indians enough in the country to defeat, much less annihilate, the fine regiment Custer had under his command."

So Colonel Gibbon *post hoc,* which did not deter him from writing Terry in a letter dated November 6, 1876: "Except so far as to draw profit from past experience it is perhaps useless to speculate as to what might have been the result had your plan, as originally agreed on, been carried out. But I cannot help reflecting that in that case my column, supposing the Indians' camp to have remained where it was when Custer struck it, would have been the first to reach it, that with our infantry and gatling guns we should have been able to take care of ourselves, even though numbering only about two thirds of Custer's force, and that with six hundred cavalry in the neighborhood, led as only Custer could lead it, the result to the Indians would have been quite different from what it was."

Yes, if the Indians had remained where Custer struck them. But we know positively that they would not have remained there if Custer had not attacked them on the 25th. For we have it from both the Cheyennes and the Sioux that some of the women had begun to take down their tepees preparatory to moving down to the mouth of the

Sitting Bull Receiving The Message "We Have Killed Them All." From an original painting in the Karl May Indian Museum, Dresden, Germany.

Little Big Horn, but abandoned these activities when they saw Reno's battalion coming down the valley.

This means that if Custer had delayed his attack until the 26th Terry and Gibbon would have run into the Indians on the morning of the 26th. Had the Indians discovered the cavalry early in the morning the command would have been in no shape to meet an attack. Gibbon was still on the *Far West* miles downstream and did not reach Terry

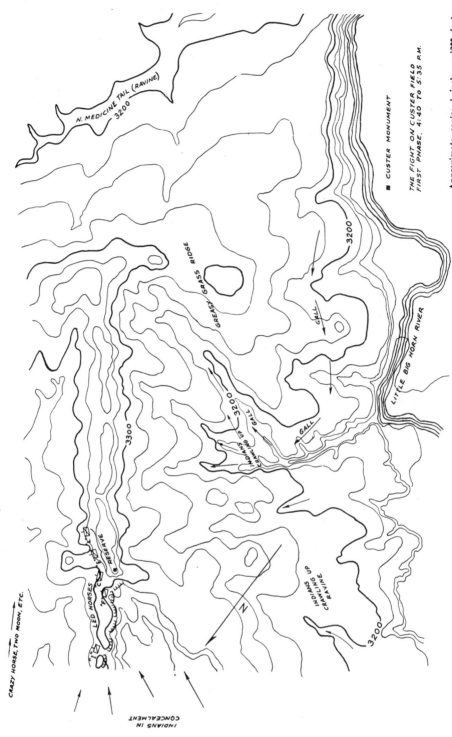

CRAZY HORSE, TWO MOON, ETC.

INDIANS IN
CONCEALMENT

LED HORSES

RESERVE

3300

INDIANS UP
CRAWLING
RAVINE

3200

N

INDIANS UP 3200
CRAWLING GALL

GALL

GREASY GRASS RIDGE

GALL

3200

N. MEDICINE TAIL (RAVINE)
3200

LITTLE BIG HORN RIVER

CUSTER MONUMENT

THE FIGHT ON CUSTER FIELD
FIRST PHASE, 4:40 TO 5:35 P.M.

Approximate scale: 1 inch = 1200 feet

Map shows the battle-ridge with Custer's troops in a position of readiness, two troops on the line covering the balance in reserve. The Indians, on foot, their ponies concealed in ravines, are crawling cautiously up the ravines from the west and north and the cavalry until nearly noon. At dawn the infantry was 12 miles downstream.

A little farther along in our narrative we shall give General Hugh Scott's appraisal of this subject.

In another part of the same letter Gibbon said, "Knowing what we do now, and what an effect a fresh trail seemed to have upon him (Custer), perhaps we were expecting too much to anticipate a forbearance on his part which would have rendered co-operation on his part practicable."

A "mournful might-have-been"? Perhaps. But we wonder who would have mourned had Custer used the "forbearance" Gibbon thought he should have used. With equal justice—or injustice—we might call attention to the "forbearance" of Reno and Benteen while Custer was being wiped out. A little more of the Custer "recklessness" might not have come amiss here.

There may have been some excuse for Gibbon at this early date; for in all probability he did not have many of the facts Hughes had twenty years later. Also it would be fair to assume that Gibbon was actuated, in part at least, by a desire to give what comfort he could to Terry, who was profoundly shaken by the disaster, as was evident when he faced the survivors on Reno Hill.

And now we come to a decisive fact which has never, to my knowledge, been clearly set forth. This is the radical shift in the basic conception of the strategy outlined in the order and clearly explained in Terry's dispatch to Sheridan quoted above. All the evidence that has come to light to this day shows beyond the shadow of a doubt that there was no fear in the minds of Terry, Custer, and Gibbon that either of the two columns might be defeated if attacked while out of supporting distance of each other, as might easily have happened, as far as anyone knew at the time, almost anywhere along the line of march from Custer's camp on the evening of the 24th to the site of the battle, a distance of 134 miles more or less. And the fact that it did so happen is the proof of this contention. The order itself, as well as the dispatch to Sheridan, shows the real fear was that the Indians might escape past Custer's left flank, before he could reach the headwaters of the Tongue to block their way eastward into the Bad Lands. If an encounter had taken place in this area how in the name of all that is rational could Gibbon have come up in time for the fighting?

Eight days before the battle Crook, with a much larger force than Terry's, had suffered a strategic defeat by what was probably less than half the number of warriors Terry had to deal with.

It cannot be too often repeated that Custer's real mission was to so maneuver as to prevent the escape of the Indians wherever he

277

might find them. The attempt to corner them was a secondary consideration, a thing to be attempted if it could be managed. This plan has been ridiculed in certain quarters; but it was heartily approved by both Custer and Gibbon when Terry explained it to them. And as a matter of fact Custer came very near bringing about just that kind of attack, as I have explained it in *Legend into History* (The Stackpole Company, 1951), not being aware at that time that General Hugh Scott had reasoned much the same as I did to show why it failed. His account was printed in an unidentified newspaper and was reprinted by Colonel Graham in his fine work, *The Custer Myth* (Stackpole Company, 1953), and since the article seems to have been overlooked generally, I think it should be advertised as widely as possible, I here reproduce the more important part of it. Part of it seems to have been taken from Dr. Marquis' *A Warrior who Fought Custer.*

> "I have never held a brief for either Custer or Reno," wrote General Scott, "and I disliked the latter intensely. But I do not like to see either of them censured unjustly. Custer was told in his orders to move toward Tongue River, on the flank of the Indians. It is well known that an Indian has no flanks any more than a bird. If Custer had demonstrated his attack in the open, the Indians, if ready to fight, would have overwhelmed him. If not they would have run away toward Terry, whose command was mostly infantry, and the mounted Indians could have passed all around in plain sight and escaped, as they did when Terry came up.
>
> "How it was expected of foot soldiers to catch Indians was always a puzzle to me. Unless they were overwhelmingly strong they would scatter like quail and disappear, and that was just what Custer feared they would do. And if he allowed them to escape under the orders he had received—putting the whole thing up to his own judgment—he could have expected no mercy.
>
> "As it was Custer had not intended to attack until the 26th, at which time Terry and Gibbon would have reached the mouth of the Little Big Horn River. But his hand was forced by the Cheyenne, Little Wolf, to whose party Custer's attention was called from the Crow's Nest on the divide between the Rosebud and the Little Big Horn, and who saw Custer and his command. Moreover an Indian had been seen back on the trail.
>
> "Custer had intended to hide on the divide and attack at daylight on the 26th, but he had a right to feel that he had been discovered by those Indians. If he did not attack before they gave the alarm the Indians would have escaped, for which he would have to answer to a court-martial. He hurried down to prevent their escape."

To the student who has no axe to grind nothing more would seem to be needed to convince him that the charge of disobedience is false; that the discretion enjoined upon Custer had been intelligently exercised. Whether or not Hughes knew of the role played by Little Wolf we do not know. But it may be confidently assumed that, had he known it, he would not have mentioned it in his article. Nor have we up to date found the Little Wolf incident mentioned in any narrative by a Custer critic. And if they ever do mention it we may with equal confidence assume that Custer's statement that he had not, at the time he started to follow the trail across the divide, intended to attack on the 25th, was a deliberate lie invented to conceal his real purpose.

The answer to such a contention is found in the narrative of Red Star, one of the Arikara scouts who had carried Varnum's message to Custer in the night camp. His statement as to Custer's intention is as follows:

> Then the scouts sat down, and one of the Crow scouts, Big Belly (Half-Yellow-Face), leader of the Crow scouts, got up and asked Custer what he thought of the Dakota camp he had seen. Custer said: "This camp has not seen our army, none of their scouts have seen us." Big Belly replied: "You say we have not been seen. These Sioux we have seen at the foot of the hill, two going one way, and four the other, are good scouts, they have seen the smoke of our camp." Custer said, speaking *angrily* (Emphasis our own) "I say again we have not been seen. That camp has not seen us. I am going ahead to carry out what I think. I want to wait until it is dark and then we will march; we will place our army around the Sioux camp." Big Belly replied: "That plan is bad; it should not be carried out." Custer said: "I have said what I propose to do. I want to wait until it is dark and then go ahead with my plan."
>
> Red Star as he sat listening first thought that Custer's plan was good. The Crow scout insisted that the Dakota scout had already seen the army and would report its coming and that they would attack Custer's army. They wanted him to attack at once, that day, and capture the horses of the Dakotas and leave them unable to move rapidly; Custer replied: "Yes, it shall be done as you say."

Since we are now at the crucial point on the question of disobedience it is necessary to set straight the details as far as the available evidence permits. How shall we explain Custer's angry reply to Half-Yellow-Face and his quick change in conceding, in effect that he

279

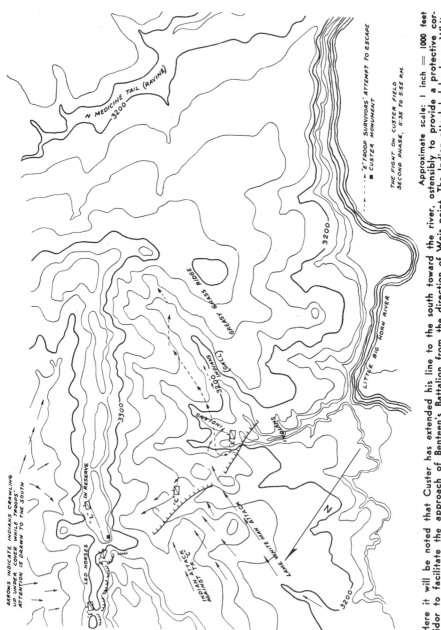

ARROWS INDICATE INDIANS CRAWLING
UP UNDER COVER WHILE TROOPS'
ATTENTION IS DRAWN TO THE SOUTH

LED HORSES

"L" IN RESERVE

3300

3300

INDIAN ATTACK
AGAINST "I"

LAME WHITE MAN ATTACK

"C"

INDIANS

"I"

"F"

320 INDIANS (SKFL)

GREASY GRASS RIDGE

MEDICINE TAIL (RAVINE)
3200

3200

3200

LITTLE BIG HORN RIVER

N

– – – "E" TROOP SURVIVORS' ATTEMPT TO ESCAPE
■ CUSTER MONUMENT

THE FIGHT ON CUSTER FIELD
SECOND PHASE, 5:35 TO 5:55 P.M.

Approximate scale: 1 inch = 1000 feet

Here it will be noted that Custer has extended his line to the south toward the river, ostensibly to provide a protective corridor to facilitate the approach of Benteen's Battalion from the direction of Weir point. The Indian attack led by Lame White Man penetrated and rolled up the line, at one blow putting 40% of Custer's force out of action.

was right? One guess might be that his outbreak was merely a spontaneous expression of disappointment, and his quick reversal due to what had passed between them on the night march, as recounted by Gerard in his testimony at the Reno Court of Inquiry. In this testimony Gerard said that Custer, at about 11 P. M., had ordered him to take Bloody Knife and Half-Yellow-Face and ride with him, Custer, at the head of the column as guides. During a short halt on this march Custer asked Gerard how many Indians they would have to fight, and Gerard replied that there would be no less than 2500. Then Custer asked Bloody Knife and Half-Yellow-Face if they could cross the divide before daylight, and was told that they could not. Then Custer asked if they could cross the divide after daylight without being discovered by the Indians, and again received a negative answer. Finally Custer asked where there was some timber in which they could conceal the command. Before Gerard could give his answer the Recorder cut him off by saying that he need not repeat the conversation with Custer.

It would seem then that by the time Custer started back to his command he was nearly, if not fully, convinced that scouts from the camps had discovered his presence and that they would hurry back to the village and spread the alarm; which might mean a hard fight in the rough ground east of the river while the noncombatants fled and scattered. This was an old story with which the army was thoroughly familiar. It would be either this or a fight to the finish for him and his command, or for Gibbon if the Indians fled downstream. The heavy trail he was following and the sharp warning from his Indian scouts were ominous signs. It did not require a military genius to perceive that the sooner he got down to the level valley and nearer to Gibbon the less would be the chances for appalling losses or actual defeat; and it will not be argued by anyone who knew Custer's past that he was slow in analysing any situation that confronted him. He understood instantly that whatever else might happen he must not become involved in a pitched battle on ground made to order for Indians and next to impossible for cavalry.

But whatever doubts Custer may have felt during the short ride back to the camp, the report of Sergeant Curtiss that he had found several Indians at a package lost during the night march, seems to have been decisive.

But it is not true, as Hughes argued, that this was what Custer wanted in order to strike the village before Gibbon could come up. On the contrary he was dismayed by the apparent necessity of attacking at once, as is proved by his angry reply to Half-Yellow-Face who insisted that the command had been discovered, and that he must attack at once or be himself attacked. It is proved also by the questions he put to Half-Yellow-Face on the night march, and the entry in the record of Wallace, misquoted by Hughes to misrepresent Custer's real intentions.

What Hughes wrote in this connection is, in plain words, that Custer lied to conceal his supposed guilty intention of disobeying his orders for the express purpose of gaining all the glory to be reaped from a brilliant victory without assistance from Gibbon, who would appear before the world as a laggard to be laughed at.

Although what has been said up to this point should convince the unbiased reader, there yet remains a talking point in Custer's failure to examine the upper Tullocks area and send a messenger through to Terry with a report of what was found there. Hughes goes so far as to say that the reason no messenger was sent is that he did not want Gibbon to have any part in the fighting.

That this charge was wholly false is easily proved, as I have shown in *Legend into History*, page 44 and footnote 14. The evidence is in a letter of George Herendeen to the New York *Herald* and is dated January 22, 1876. In this letter Herendeen says that on the morning of the 24th not long after the march had been resumed, Custer told him he was going to send him and Charlie Reynolds to examine the upper Tullocks. To this Herendeen replied that it was not time yet, that he could only follow the troops until they came near the head of Tullocks. He called to Mitch Bouyer, who was a little ahead, who confirmed what he, Herendeen, had said; and added that farther up they would come to a break in the bluffs and that they could then get to the head of Tullocks in about 15 miles. Custer said all right, they could wait. Why, in the end, he sent no one we do not know positively. It may be suggested, however, that the subject slipped from his mind when he struck the heavy fresh trail about the time they came opposite the break in the bluffs six miles more or less below the site of the present Busby some time between five and six o'clock, as near as we can determine today. It is impossible to say how far it was from this point to Terry's camp on Tullocks Creek. A very rough guess would be, taking account of the nature of the terrain, that it was somewhere near 50 miles. About half of this

282

would have to be covered in a very dark night—which is to say, at a walk. The command that night made only about six miles in something like three hours, or two miles per hour. Herendeen would have had to make six to seven per hour to reach Terry's camp by midnight, the time Hughes says he would have had to arrive to be in time for Gibbon to cooperate in the fighting.

For this Hughes argues that Custer deliberately neglected to send Herendeen in order to keep Terry and Gibbon out of the fight! For, if Herendeen had been sent Gibbon could have hurried up Tullocks Creek and arrived on the battlefield by the afternoon of the 25th, instead of going over the divide between Tullocks and the Big Horn.

But whether or not it would have been possible for Herendeen to have reached Terry and Gibbon in time for them to take part in the action is not the real question here. The question is Custer's *intention*—a question of motives, not of deeds. The letter of Herendeen shows conclusively that on the morning of the 24th Custer intended to send Herendeen and Reynolds to examine the upper Tullocks region. The fact that he included Reynolds suggests that he knew that Herendeen would not have time to return to report before going on to Terry and that Reynolds was to report in his stead.

But be all this as it may, his orders left Custer free to change his mind if he saw "sufficient reason" to do so, Hughes to the contrary.

Hughes and other Custer critics insist that this clause about the Tullocks is an imperative. But it does not say positively that Custer shall send a messenger. What it *does* say is that he shall *endeavor* to send one; which clearly implies that Custer might find it impracticable to do so. Both Edgerly and Godfrey said it would have been nonsense to send a messenger after the command was on the main trail of the Indians.

Summing it up: The argument over this subject is a mere quibble.

Finally, if Hughes was speaking his real conviction when he wrote that Custer had found, as he reached the point where the trail left the Rosebud, everything to be "exactly as Terry predicted that they would be found to be," he must have known also that the Indian village was where it was found to be on the 25th; and since he had a fairly accurate map of the region in question and also knew Custer's rate of march (since this had been checked before Custer left the mouth of the Rosebud) he needed no messenger to tell him that Custer would be within striking distance of the enemy on that date, and that he would have to strike to prevent the escape of the Indians up the Little Big Horn.

If in this construction I am simply feeding Hughes his own unpalatable fodder, so much the worse for him.

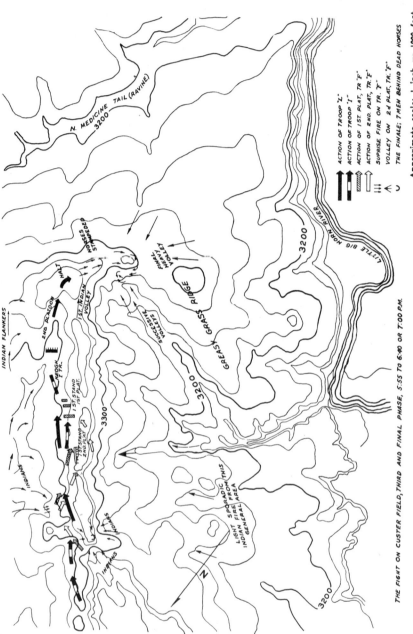

THE FIGHT ON CUSTER FIELD, THIRD AND FINAL PHASE, 5:55 TO 6:40 OR 7:00 P.M.

ACTION OF TROOP "L".
ACTION OF TROOP "I".
ACTION OF 1ST PLAT, TR "F".
ACTION OF 2ND. PLAT., TR "E".
SURPISE FIRE ON TR. "F".
VOLLEY ON 2d PLAT, TR. "F".
THE FINALE; 7 MEN BEHIND DEAD HORSES

Approximate scale: 1 inch = 1000 feet

In this, the last phase of Custer's fight, after Troops C and E had been put out of action, Captain Keogh, in command of troops L, I and F, moved out mounted, by Custer's order, along the battleridge to attract the attention of the troops seen on Weir Point, leaving a detachment to protect the wounded and hold the command post.

Much more could be written on our subject by going farther afield. But a mere piling of Osa on Pelion does not get us anywhere; for it is not the mass but the character of the evidence that counts.

And now, except for a brief discussion of the thought-provoking attitude of General Terry, we have come to the end of our story, the telling of which has been both a difficult and a rather distastful job.

Did General Terry really believe that Custer disobeyed his orders? Our own conclusion is that he did so believe until after he had gone through his papers on returning to his office in St. Paul. For it is clear from his confidential dispatch that he had not noted the all-important fact that the Indian village was only a few miles down-stream from the point where the trail struck the river, whereas he had carried in his mind the belief that it was near the headwaters of the Little Big Horn and the Tongue. This misconception evidently stuck in his mind while he was still on the ground. The same confusion still persists in the minds of many students of the battle, and no amount of explanation seems to clear it up.

But when Terry came to the report of Wallace, and with his maps before him, he must have received a shock, especially if he used pins, as General Hawkins did in his study of the battle. For here was the truth in plain black and white. As a lawyer Terry had been trained in clear and logical thinking, and could not have missed the significance of the facts recorded by Wallace concerning the marches and the sinister discoveries made on the 24th as they neared the fresh trail across the divide.

This report proved that Custer had not resorted to forced marches. Second: that he had not intended to attack until daylight on the 26th. A third decisive fact was that his own Indian scouts insisted that scouts from the hostile camps had already discovered his approach and would report it to the camps, and strongly urged him to attack at once rather than wait to be attacked.

This meant that the Indians would either run or stand to fight. Custer's orders were to prevent their escape. Since there was some doubt as to the distribution of the camps along the river, he sent Benteen to the left and front to learn whether or not there were camps upstream from the point where the rising smoke indicated the presence of a large village some distance downstream from where the trail entered the valley of the Little Big Horn.

The facts in the Wallace report showed clearly that Custer had, on the evening of the 24th, planned to do exactly what Terry had expected him to do; namely so maneuved as to bring about a simultaneous attack by the two columns as nearly as this could be managed.

On the face of it this is what Terry should have announced publicly as soon as he discovered the facts. Had he promptly and

CONTOUR MAP OF CUSTER BATTLEFIELD

Approximate scale, 1 inch = 2625 feet

CONTOUR INTERVAL, 25'

A: Custer Hill
A-B: Battle Ridge
C-D: Calhoun Ridge
E-F: Greasy Grass Ridge
G-H: N. Medicine Tail

I: "I" & "L" Led Horses
J: Crazy Horse Crossed
K: Gray Horse Ambushed
L: "C" & "F" Routed
M: "I" Destroyed

N-O-P-Q: Crazy Horse Strikes
R-S-T-U: Gall's Attack
V-W-X: Lame White Man's Attack
Y: Sergeant Butler

This is a reproduction of the U. S. Geological Survey map of the battlefield, upon which the Author has (a) superimposed the movements of the Indian warriors who played decisive roles in the destruction of Custer's Battalion; and (b) spotted the principal terrain features and the actual locations where the several troops of the 7th Cavalry are presumed to have been overwhelmed.

Careful study of the various elevations, contour intervals, (25 feet between lines), ravines and ridge lines will result in a more rewarding appreciation of the Hoskin's painting (end papers).

It will be noted that the above map extends beyond North Medicine Tail to the south, while the painting itself limits its foreground to Calhoun Ridge (the observer facing north).

286

definitely exonerated Custer of the false charges of disobedience, accompanied by a clear statement explaining the manner in which all concerned with command responsibility had been deceived both as to the location and the numbers of the enemy, he would have been applauded by every intelligent and fair-minded person in the country.

Then why did he not make such a statement?

We do not know. We can, however, make a plausible guess based on an article in the New York *Herald*, part of which was reproduced in the Army and Navy Journal in its issue of September 16, 1876. In this we find:

> The New York Herald has interviewed the President at Long Beach, and reports as follows: "Correspondent: Was not Custer's massacre a disgraceful defeat of our troops?
>
> "The President: (with an expression of manifest and keenly felt regret) I regard Custer's massacre as a sacrifice of troops, brought on by Custer himself, that was wholly unnecessary—wholly unnecessary. He was not to have made the attack before effecting the junction with Terry and Gibbon. He was notified to meet them on the 26th, but instead of marching slowly, as his orders required in order to effect the junction on the 26th, he enters upon a forced march of 83 (!) miles in 24 hours and thus has to meet the Indians alone."

The voice is the voice of Terry through his Confidential Dispatch; but the hand is the hand of Benteen whose vitriolic hatred of Custer did not die at the graveside. When, in going over the field, he came to the body of Custer he expressed his satisfaction in the indecent exclamation: "There he lies, G-d d-n him. He will never fight any more." He had already poisoned Terry's mind with his exaggerated distances marched, which by the time the news reached Washington, had grown to 83 miles in 24 hours. The fact is that the greatest distance marched in any given 24 hours was 35 miles, and the whole distance from the Rosebud to the battlefield was, according to Godfrey, 113 miles—which is not far from the truth. There is little doubt in my own mind that, after Terry had returned to his office and had put the record of the campaign in order, he discovered Benteen's exaggerations, as he must have done after reading Wallace's itinerary in which the intentions of Custer were recorded; he saw his

own mistake and realized that Custer was forced to attack or leave Terry and Gibbon in the lurch, exposing them and their command to probable destruction; for we know positively today that the Indians would have been near the mouth of the Little Big Horn on the morning of the 26th where Terry and Gibbon would have run into them soon after resuming the march with the cavalry while the infantry were still 12 miles down on the Big Horn.

But if Terry had made his findings public? . . . Oh well—let us not speculate about what the President would have said. We have no maledictions to heap on his head. He was himself a victim of abuse and slander. If in this instance he struck back blindly and unjustly it can be understood and forgiven. Peace to his Manes!

And so General Terry spent the rest of his life trying to carry water on both shoulders, a fate he had not deserved and which was, apparently in part at least, a product of his own decent nature.

And finally, what of Custer, one of the best cavalry officers our army ever possessed? Thanks in part, at least, to his detractors, his has become in the minds of millions of his countrymen.
"One of the few, the immortal names
That were not born to die."

Did Custer Disobey General Terry's Orders

A study of the article by Colonel Robert P. Hughes
in the Military Service Institution
of the United States, January 1896.

THE CONTROVERSIAL ORDER.

Camp at the mouth of the Rosebud River,
Montana Territory, June 22, 1876.

Lieutenant-Colonel Custer,
7th Cavalry.

Colonel:

The Brigadier-General Commanding directs that, as soon as your command can be made ready for the march, you will proceed up the Rosebud in pursuit of the Indians whose trail was discovered by Major Reno a few days since. It is, of course, impossible to give you any definite instructions in regard to this movement, and were it not impossible to do so, the Department Commander places too much confidence in your zeal, energy and ability to impose on you precise orders which might hamper your action when nearly in contact with the enemy. He will, however, indicate to you his own views of what your action should be, and he desires that you should conform to them unless you shall see sufficient reason for departing from them. He thinks you should proceed up the Rosebud until you ascertain definitely the direction in which the trail above spoken of leads. Should it be found (as it appears almost certain it will be found) to turn to the Little Big Horn, he thinks you should still proceed southward perhaps as far as the headwaters of the Tongue, and then turn toward the Little Big Horn, feeling constantly, however, to your left, so as to preclude the possibility of the escape to the south or southeast by passing around your left flank. The column of Colonel Gibbon is now in motion for the mouth of the Big Horn. As soon as it reaches that point it will cross the Yellowstone and move up at least as far as the forks of the Big and Little Horn. Of course its future movements must be controlled by circumstances as they arise, but it is hoped that the Indians, if upon the Little Horn, may be so nearly inclosed by the two columns that their escape will be impossible.

The Department Commander desires that on your way up the Rosebud you should thoroughly examine the upper part of Tullock's Creek, and that you should endeavor to send a scout through to Colonel Gibbon's column, with information of the results of your examination. The lower part of the Creek will be examined by a detachment of Colonel Gibbon's command. The supply steamer will be pushed up the Big Horn as far as the forks if the river be navigable for that distance, and the Department Commander, who will accompany the column of Colonel Gibbon, desires you to report to him there not later than the expiration of the time for which your troops are rationed, unless in the meantime you receive further orders.

E. W. Smith, Captain 18th

Infantry.

Acting Assistant Adjutant General.

About 130 hours after this order was delivered to Custer, General Terry was reading his dispatch of June 27th to Sheridan, to the members of his staff in Gibbon's Camp. As he finished a clamor arose demanding that a statement should be included accusing Custer of disobedience. Terry waved the demand aside with the statement that he himself would accept responsibility for what had happened, a resolution to which he adhered apparently to the end of his life. What he actually did believe after he had more fully informed himself may never be known; for his personal papers seem to have been destroyed. We shall make a reasoned guess at it near the close of our study. As Terry left it we have a noble gesture, a vicarious atonement that cannot satisfy anyone; for a pardon cannot wash out guilt. It merely remits punishment.

Although the above instructions to Custer have been called an "order," technically they should be called a "Letter of Advice." A skilled dialectician, in analysing these instructions, would inevitably

This portrait, said to be the last Custer had made, was engraved on steel and used as the frontispiece of Whittaker's "Life of General Custer," which was published late in 1876. His hair was even shorter than shown in this portrait at the time of the battle, as he had it cropped short with clippers before starting from Fort Lincoln on his last campaign.

come to the conclusion that the only imperatives in them are that Custer shall proceed up the Rosebud in pursuit of the Indians and that he shall be guided by his own judgment as to the means adopted to attain the objects sought.

This dialectic answer to the charge of disobedience was brilliantly set forth in a letter dated September 1, 1904, written to Dr. Cyrus Townsend Brady by Colonel Jacob L. Greene who had acted as Adjutant General on Custer's staff from the time the latter was promoted to the rank of Brigadier General, and remained with him in this capacity until he was mustered out of the service in 1866. We quote from this letter as follows: "In other words, the charge of disobedience can never be proved. The proof does not exist. The evidence of the case forever lacks the principal whose one and only definite order was to take his regiment and go in pursuit of the Indians whose trail was discovered by Major Reno a few days since. They were the objectives; they were to be located and their escape prevented. That was Custer's task. All details were left, and necessarily left, to his discretion. All else in the order of June 22nd contain merely the 'views' of the commander to be followed 'unless you shall see sufficient reason for departing from them'."

The argument that Custer disobeyed this order seems to resolve itself into two forms. One is trying to read into the order a precision and a peremptory character which is not there and which no ingenuity can put there, and to empty it of a discretion which is there and is absolute; the other is assuming or asserting that Custer departed from General Terry's views without "sufficient reasons." And this argument rests in part upon the imputation to Custer of a motive and intent which was evil throughout, and in part upon what his critics in the light of a later knowledge and the vain regrets of hindsight think he ought to have done, and all in utter ignorance of Custer's own views of the conditions in which, when he met them, he was to find his own reasons for whatever he did or did not do. Under that order it was Custer's views of the conditions when he confronted them that were to govern his actions, whether they contravened General Terry's views or not. If, in the presence of the actual conditions, in the light

of his great experience and knowledge of handling Indians, he deemed it wise to follow the trail, knowing it would reach them, and deeming that so to locate them would be the best way to prevent their escape, then he obeyed that order just as exactly as if, thinking otherwise, he had gone scouting southward where they were not, and where neither Terry nor he expected them to be.

To charge disobedience is to say that he willfully and with a wrong motive and intent did that which his own military judgment forbade; for it was his own military judgment, right or wrong, that was to govern his own actions under the terms of the order. *The quality of the judgment does not touch the question of disobedience.* (Italics our own). If he disobeyed that order, it was by going contrary to his own judgment. That was the only way he could disobey it.

From the point of view of formal logic this is quite obviously conclusive.

The case of the Custer critics being lost on logical grounds, their only apparent recourse was to call Custer's good faith in question, asserting that he had been positively forbidden to follow the Indian trail across the Divide. Custer, they say, was "glory-hunting"; that he did not want Gibbon to have any part in the anticipated battle. Their arguments have a superficial plausibility which Custer himself supplied before the expedition left Fort Lincoln. Instead of ascertaining the conditions confronting Custer they either ignored them or, like Hughes, distorted them.

The point involved here was clearly and forcibly stated by an expert in this field, the late Colonel W. A. Graham, as a caution for readers of the Hughes article reprinted in the fourth edition of his "Story of the Little Big Horn," which reads as follows: "Readers should remember that to every controversial question there are two sides, and that between wilful disobedience of orders and justifiable disregard of instructions there yawns a gulf both wide and deep. That Custer did disregard Terry's instructions seems reasonably clear; whether he was justified in doing so is a question that will bear examination. The commander on the scene is entitled to the benefit of every doubt, if there be room for doubt; and particularly is this true when neither he, nor any other who may have known his reasons, survived to present them."

Our chief problem then is to determine whether or not Custer found the facts to be so far out of line with the assumed facts in the order as to justify the use of discretion.

This sends us right back to the objective data, namely, distances, the number and location of the Indians, and the terrain involved in the operations.

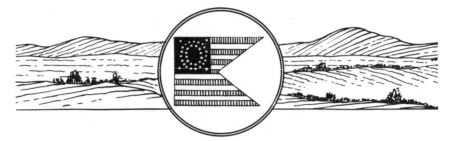

But these decisive factors Colonel Hughes and those who follow his line of argument ignore, distort or deliberately falsify. It can be truthfully said that this article of Hughes, which is the basis of our study, has served for nearly sixty years as the main arsenal from which the critics of Custer have drawn their chief weapons and ammunition. The author was a brother-in-law of General Terry and was, at the time of the battle, serving as his personal aide and chief of staff. Under these circumstances a natural bias, a strong impulse to shield General Terry as much as possible is understandable. But it does not justify a long-drawn-out innuendo followed by the grossest kind of distortions and what amounts to the falsification of official documents such as we shall come to in the course of our study.

The object of all this was obviously the establishment of a *prima facie* case of guilt in the minds of his readers. Such a procedure is, we believe, the rule in the courts of law. It cannot be used by the historian without incurring the gravest risk of going astray because there is no judge or opposing counsel to question his reasoning and his evaluation of the evidence. In spite of this obvious risk Colonel Hughes devoted about a third of his article to his *prima facie* case. But about all he could find that is really pertinent to our inquiry is a statement by Colonel Ludlow that Custer had told him soon after he had been restored to the command of his regiment (not to the command of the expedition) that he intended to "cut loose" from General Terry during the summer; that he had "got away with Stanley and would be able to swing clear of Terry."

Colonel Hughes explained that "Colonel Ludlow had just been ordered to Philadelphia and his position on the staff was taken by Lieutenant Maguire. It thus happened that the above-mentioned announcement of the intention did not come to the knowledge of Terry until his return to St. Paul the last of September, and until then Colonel Ludlow was not called upon to remember the exact words which Custer used, and, while these exact words may have faded from his memory, the idea conveyed to him was still perfectly clear and was given by him as above quoted, in a letter to General Terry. All of

294

these officers (Colonel Farquhar—General Ruggles—and General Card) agree as to the character of the remark made by Custer to Ludlow as given within a few hours after it was made."

It is, then, not claimed definitely that Custer used the exact expression "got away with Stanley" and "swing clear of Terry." We have a general *idea* but nothing specific as to what that idea involved. We shall come back to that in a moment. Here it has to be said that, on the face of it, this looks very bad indeed; and there is one piece of evidence that Custer was aware of it, as the following incident plainly shows though there are two ways of reading it.

Quoting Mrs. Custer's letter to Colonel Greene: "A day before the expedition started, General Terry was in our house alone with Autie (the General's pet name.) A's thoughts were calm, deliberate, and solemn. He had been terribly hurt in Washington. General Terry had applied for him to command the expedition. He was returned to his regiment because General Terry had applied for him. I know that he (Custer) felt tenderly and affectionately toward him. On that day he hunted me out in the house and brought me into the living-room, not telling me why. He shut the door, and very seriously and impressively said: 'General Terry, a man usually means what he says when he brings his wife to listen to his statements. I want to say that reports are circulating that I do not want to go out to the campaign under you. (I suppose that he meant, having been given the command before, he was unwilling to be a subordinate), but I want you to know that I do want to go and serve under you, not only that I value you as a soldier, but as a friend and man.' The exact words were the strangest kind of declaration that he wished him to know he wanted to serve under him."

Mrs. Custer here describes correctly Custer's real attitude toward Terry. The reason she had found it strange is not far to seek. He evidently had not told her of his unconsidered and ill-advised remarks to Ludlow which, as he must have realized, might cause him serious trouble because of the slurs he seemed to cast on both Terry and Stanley; and the fact that he had not told her is pretty good evidence that he knew that he had laid himself open to fresh trouble; that one or more of the four officers to whom he had made these remarks would "tattle" (as we know they intended to do, and did do

295

after Terry's return to St. Paul) and then the fat would be in the fire. What could he do about it?

There is an old military dictum that the best defensive is a prompt and vigorous offensive, and it may be that Custer was acting on this principle, though it is possible that such reports actually were in circulation; for a week or more had passed since he and Terry had left St. Paul; time enough for rumors to have reached Bismarck and Fort Lincoln.

There is nothing in Mrs. Custer's letter to Colonel Greene, as far as it is reproduced here, to show what, if any, answer Terry made to Custer's protestations of loyalty or what were his reactions to the cryptic element in Custer's statement. The only evidence we have indicating what Terry thought of Custer's state of mind on the point in question here is a passage in Major Brisbin's much-discussed letter of January 1, 1892, to Godfrey. Brisbin, in conversation with Terry on the *Far West* said: "Why not put my cavalry with Custer's and go yourself in command?" He replied: "Custer is smarting under the rebuke of the President, and wants an independent command, and I wish to give him a chance to do something."

It will be noted by careful readers of the Hughes article that Ludlow admitted he was not certain he could recall the exact words Custer used in his touch-and-go meeting with him in the street. But even if he had said "got away with Stanley," did this necessarily imply that he had disobeyed orders? In the absence of other evidence it would be absurd to so conclude. If this incident is to be used as proof of disobedience we must know what Custer had actually done to justify this interpretation. And this is what we are now setting out to discover.

The first piece of evidence that comes under consideration is a letter of General Stanley to his wife, dated July 1, 1873, in which we find the following passage: "I had a little flurry with Custer as I told you I probably would. We were separated 4 miles, and I intended him to assist in getting the train, his own train, over the Muddy River. Without consulting me he marched off 15 miles, cooly sending me a note to send him forage and rations. I sent after him, ordering him to halt where he was, and never to presume to make another movement without orders. I knew from the beginning it had to be done, and I am glad to have so good a chance, when there could be no doubt who was right. He was just gradually assuming command and now he knows he has a commanding officer who will not tolerate his arrogance."

Brave words! But if Stanley believed he had effectually "squelched" Custer he was badly mistaken; for on the same day Custer wrote his

The battlefield visualized during the second phase of Custer's fight. The nearest marker is within a few feet of the deep gulch used as base of attack by the Indian hordes. Custer's command post located as shown by the monument on the sky line, left of center. The break in the line of markers (center of photo) is where Lame White Man pierced the skirmish line, killed 18 to 24 "E" troopers and lost his own life.

wife a cheery letter with a trace of mockery in it for the infantry. "Good morning, my Sunbeam . . . Infantry and trains still 15 miles in the rear, stuck in the mud, they say, but probably through lack of energy, for Captain Smith took our wagons back to the main line for supplies, and returned with them loaded."

No, Custer was not in sackcloth and ashes as a result of the lecture he had received. Far from it. For he now took the offensive. Or at least so the evidence seems to indicate. Some time—probably during the first week in July—he took over command of the expedition while Stanley was too drunk to carry on. This was foreshadowed in a letter of Custer to his wife dated simply "June," but must have been written several days earlier. In this letter Custer said:

"We are now encamped 15 miles from the infantry (which suggests that Stanley with the infantry had not moved since the first of July, the date of Stanley's letter to his wife). Rosser is desperate, and cannot speak too highly of the cavalry. General Stanley is acting very badly, drinking, and I anticipate official trouble with him. I should greatly regret this, but fear it cannot be avoided. Rosser has told me

297

how badly Stanley acted last year, some days being so overcome the expedition could not go on. One morning the engineers started at the appointed hour, but Rosser, looking back from a high bluff, saw that the infantry camp was still standing. On going back he found the officers searching for the General, but in vain. Finally Major Worth told Rosser confidentially that, having found General Stanley dead drunk on the ground outside the camp, he had carried him into his own tent, though he and the General were not on good terms, for the honor of the service.

"Rosser said he told General Stanley in St. Paul before starting that he would have a different man to deal with this year, in command of the 7th Cavalry, one who would not hesitate as second in command, to put a guard over him, Stanley, if incapacitated. General Stanley, Rosser said, acknowledged that he knew this and would try to do better. But whiskey has too strong a hold on him."

Good advice, no doubt, but unlikely to establish either Rosser or Custer in the good graces of the commanding officer, though Stanley, when sober, was not only a good soldier but a kindly and considerate gentleman as well who listened to Rosser's warning in spite of the offensive threat it contained.

Turning back now to the course of events we find that Stanley put Custer in arrest after he had taken over the command of the expedition, and compelled him to march in the rear of the column for two or three days and then released him apparently as a result of Rosser's intercession. Miss Marguerite Merrington, who edited the correspondence between Custer and his wife, wrote: "General Stanley, in a fit of intoxication, caused Custer's arrest for taking over as second in command when he himself was unable to do so."

This correspondence shows that Stanley, convinced that he had been unjust in placing Custer under arrest, went to him and made more than ample apology, as is shown in a letter of Custer to his wife some time in September.

"In regard to my arrest," wrote Custer, "and its attendant circumstances, I am sorry it ever reached your ears, as I hoped—not for myself, but for those who were the cause of it, that the matter should end here.

"Suffice to say that I was placed in arrest for acting in strict conscientious discharge of what I knew to be my duty—a duty laid down expressly in Army regulations.

"Never was I more confident of the rectitude of my course, and the official propriety of my position . . . so confident that I was content to wait, knowing that I would be vindicated in the end.

"Within forty-eight hours General Stanley came to me, and apologized in the most ample manner, acknowledging that he had been in the wrong, hoping I would forget it, and promising to turn over a new leaf.

"Twice did he repeat 'I humbly beg your pardon, sir. I not only make this apology to you, but, if you desire it, will gladly do so in the presence of your officers.'

"With his subsequent faithful observance of his promise to begin anew his intercourse with me, I banished the affair from my mind. Nor do I cherish any but the kindliest sentiments towards him, for General Stanley, when not possessed by the fiend of intemperance, is one of the kindest, most agreeable and considerate officers I ever served under.

"Looking back I regard it, as do other officers, as a necessity that an issue was forced on us, and that my opposing, instead of yielding, the interests of the service were advanced.

"On one occasion whiskey was destroyed by friends of General Stanley as the only means of getting him sober. This was publicly avowed. It had no connection with my difficulty with him, although the papers coupled the two incidents together."

What Custer did not mention in this letter is that Stanley indulged in one more colossal binge before pulling himself together apparently for the duration of the expedition, as shown in a letter Custer wrote to his wife dated July 25. "Yesterday we marched at noon, but only five miles before going into camp. Everybody is chafing at the delay. We have been thirteen days at one point when three would have sufficed. Whiskey alone is the cause of it. You have no idea how this has delayed the expedition and added to the government expenses. The steamer has been detained here needlessly for ten days, at $500 a day—$5,000. General Rosser says it is a disgrace to the service."

A few days after this letter was written Custer ran into some Indians or the Indians ran into him as he marched up the left bank of the Yellowstone. After several skirmishes the Indians retreated and finally recrossed the river opposite the mouth of the Little Big Horn.

On August 4 Stanley sent a highly laudatory account of Custer's conduct in these encounters to the War Department.

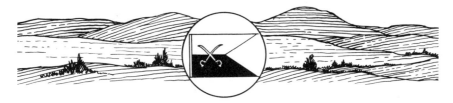

Looking west from Greasy Grass Ridge. Across the river is the site of the 3-mile long Indian Camp. At the extreme upper left dimly appear the key bluffs which highlight the "Weir Point" and "Reno fight on the hill" episodes. (Photo by Edith Kuhlman 1936).

The Battle ridge from near Custer Monument. Note Weir Point in central background. (Edith Kuhlman 1935).

DID CUSTER DISOBEY GENERAL TERRY'S ORDERS

What we seem to have, then, is that there was no disobedience on the part of Custer during the Stanley expedition; and hence no precedent foreshadowing intended disobedience in Custer's remarks to Ludlow. Even if Custer used the exact phrases he is said to have used it is by no means conclusive proof that he intended to "swing clear of Terry" without the latter's consent. When he "got away with Stanley" he had done so, as far as the evidence indicates, by obtaining Stanley's consent to push ahead with his cavalry and the surveying crew without a succession of precise orders that would tie him too closely to the slower moving infantry. Of course if Stanley had remained sober it is not likely that any serious friction would have arisen on this score.

A reasonable construction of Custer's "got away with Stanley" is that he would be able to persuade Terry to give him a free hand with his cavalry, the strategic and most mobile part of the command. It was notorious that Indians were hard to catch and that infantry were good for nothing here unless they, the Indians, could be pinned down. And actually they rarely were caught even by cavalry except during the winter months. Crook, Custer, Miles all understood this perfectly, and so, I believe did Terry. The criticisms of Terry that were current after the battle was that he was too slow, chiefly because he carried too much impedimenta.

And now, for an overall view and a sane judgment of the whole Stanley-Custer, Custer-Ludlow episode, I can do no better than to quote an enlightening passage from a letter recently received from Don Russell of the *Chicago Daily News*, a student who can see the forest in spite of the trees, and as nearly free of bias as it is humanly possible to be, and as well informed on Western history, I believe, as anyone now living.

The passage in question runs as follows: "I have never read Stanley, although seeing it much quoted. That was a queer business, and probably both were at fault, but Stanley did a lot of drinking and couldn't complain too much. I would follow you on the Ludlow story. Sure Custer wanted to cut loose with the cavalry, *but I don't think he was running out.* If you once get the idea clearly in mind that no one expected any huge number of Indians, and expected them to run—which they might have done anyway had they been given half a chance—and that the whole idea of anyone—Terry, Gibbon and all concerned—was merely to find the Indians, a lot is explained. It is usually assumed that the idea was to bring the three columns of Crook, Custer, and Terry-Gibbon together in one battle against this immense mass of Indians. Actually the idea was to draw these troops around them so they could not wander off somewhere else. Terry's order did not contemplate a meeting on a battlefield but he was concerned that the Indians not slip out beyond Custer in a direction that would be far away from Gibbon—and not knowing just where Crook was, he was not counting much on that column, except possibly it would cut off retreat to the south."

There is conclusive evidence that this overall idea did exist. Colonel Hughes referred to it briefly, but failed to develop it because it was inconsistent with his narrow thesis that Custer was not free to maneuver according to the circumstances as he found them.

On May 29th General Sheridan wrote General Sherman:

"As no very correct information can be obtained as to the location of the hostiles, and as there would be no telling how long they would stay in any one place if it was known, I have given no instructions to Generals Crook and Terry, preferring that they should do the best they can under the circumstances . . . as I think it would be unwise to make any combinations in such territory as they would have to operate in, as hostile Indians in any great number cannot keep the field in a body, or at most ten days. I therefore consider, and so do Terry and Crook, that each column will be able to take care of itself, and of chastising the Indians should it have the opportunity . . . I presume the following will occur: General Terry will drive the Indians toward the Big Horn valley and General Crook will drive them back towards Terry; Colonel Gibbon moving down on the north side of the Yellowstone, to intercept if possible such as may want to go north of the Missouri to Milk River. The result of these three columns may force many of the hostile Indians back to the agencies on the Missouri River and Red Cloud and Spotted Tail agencies."

That Terry was acting on this suggestion is fairly clear, as is indicated in the kind of instructions he issued to Custer emphasizing the importance of guarding against escape of the Indians around his left flank.

To this general, overall conception Terry added the idea that the Indians might be cornered somewhere along the Little Big Horn. This was not a bad idea, and the attempt might have succeeded had not the Indians unwittingly spoiled it by departing from their usual route up the Little Big Horn and on to their usual hunting grounds on the well-watered plateau at the headwaters of the Rosebud, the Little Big Horn and the several branches of the Tongue. But, as the Cheyennes later explained to Dr. Marquis, this year the Indians turned downstream for the purpose of hunting antelope on the benchlands opposite the mouth of the Little Big Horn. It was this unexpected move that upset Terry's applecart and was, at the same time, the reason Custer did not continue his march up the Rosebud. Terry, Gibbon

and Custer were, no doubt, aware that this plan might fail, in which case there might be long marches in "pursuit of the Indians." Custer in particular made this very plain in a letter he wrote to the New York *Herald* a few hours before he started up the Rosebud. He called his mission a "scout," and that he would follow the Indians back to their agencies even if he should be forced to subsist his command on game and horse meat. This, it will be noted, was exactly what Sheridan had in mind in his advice to the commanders in the field. Are we to suppose that Terry had not discussed this with Custer and Gibbon? Is it not implied in his expressed fear that the Indians might escape past his left flank? And if they did escape what was Custer to do? Let the Indians go and himself keep on around the head of the Rosebud Mountains and on down the Little Big Horn?

More about this later. And now to be finally done with the Hughes innuendo in connection with the 1873 expedition, it may be admitted that there is a thin sort of plausibility in the Hughes discussion connecting the Stanley-Custer misunderstanding with later events, the real cause leading to the latter's temporary suspension from command of his regiment and the substitution of General Terry for Custer as commander of the expedition as a whole, was something quite different; and had Custer been as slippery a politician as some of his critics have described him, instead of the plain-speaking soldier he actually was, the tragedy on the Little Big Horn might never have occurred. For, as is well known, in the plan of campaign as originally drawn, Custer, an experienced Indian fighter, had been designated commander of the whole expedition instead of General Terry whose experience in Indian warfare was practically nil, as he frankly admitted even to so notorious a windbag as Major James S. Brisbin.

That Custer had been indiscreet in his testimony before the Clymer Committee; that he had been misinformed on a number of things that came under discussion, may be admitted; but the chief evils he was attacking were only too real and he described them clearly before the committee (see Appendix A), calling attention to the outrageous graft involved in the appointment of traders at the army posts on the upper Missouri, as the more diplomatic General Hazen had done under cover a few years before without getting anywhere. The charges by Hazen and Custer have never been refuted. They have been buried under a mountain of verbiage that does not touch the real issue, namely the extortionate prices charged by the post traders selected by certain politicians working in the interest of Belknap's campaign for a senatorship from the state of Iowa. These parasitic intermediaries robbed the traders of most of their profits and compelled them to raise their prices to make any profit at all.

Belknap's scheme to get something for nothing was, many years after the event, described—with the joker left out—by General George A. Forsythe in a letter to Dr. Cyrus Townsend Brady, which is here reproduced in part as follows.

"For some reason Custer, one of the most splendid soldiers that ever lived, hated General Belknap, the Secretary of War. He was a good hater, too. When General Belknap was imprisoned and undergoing trial Custer wrote that he knew certain things regarding the appointments of post-traderships on the upper Missouri River, which things the prosecution thought were what was needed to insure conviction. As a matter of fact, Custer did not know anything. He had heard disappointed men who had failed to get such traderships curse Belknap and say that they knew Belknap had sold the traderships to the appointees. It was not so. Belknap had given these appointments to certain Iowa politicians for their friends, in order to secure influence in the next campaign for United States Senator from Iowa, as he had determined to try for a senatorship from that state.

"It was within his right to make these appointments and there was really nothing wrong in doing so. Of course the disappointed applicants were furious, and especially certain men who had served with Belknap during the Civil War and who thought they had a claim on him. They could not tell lies fast enough about Belknap and especially to Custer, who was thoroughly honest and believed what he said. This is what Custer thought he knew.

"Custer was summoned to Washington, of course, When he was questioned by the House Committee of prosecution it was apparent that he did not know anything. His evidence was all hearsay and not worth a tinker's dam."

Gall's Warriors Gathering for the Final Rush. From an original painting by Linde Berg in the Karl May Indian Museum, Dresden, Germany.

This letter is both enlightening and disappointing, not to say astonishing; for it betrays a naivete and a moral blindness one would not expect to find in the hero of the Beecher Island fight and a member of General Sheridan's staff. He calls Custer one of the "finest soldiers that ever lived," who was nevertheless so dumb that he "did not know anything" about what was going on right under his nose. His statement before the Clymer Committee was all "hearsay and not worth a tinker's dam." He does not explain how he came to know all this in spite of the fact that all hearsay is good for nothing. In this he follows the Custer critics, who themselves could not have had much of anything except hearsay to go on, and yet pretend that they know all about the activities of both Custer and Belknap—in fact everything that happened in connection with the Belknap impeachment proceedings, and much more they had neither heard nor seen.

All this, the whole *prima facie* case, is the veriest nonsense repugnant to logic and plain common sense. Its sole object was to conceal the real point at issue, namely the shameful graft involved in Belknap's subterfuge, the interposition of the parasitic go-betweens who selected the traders on the military reserves and then robbed them of most of their profits, compelling them to raise their prices to the occupants of the posts who were forbidden to buy anything whatsoever anywhere *in or outside the limits of the reserves, except from the traders.* When a troop commander at Fort Lincoln bought some supplies at St. Paul and sold them at cost to his people the trader, R. C. Seip, protested

305

to Belknap against this breach of the monopoly. Belknap then sent Custer a curt note with some circulars in which the monopoly was explained, and that was that. Or so it seemed. But it was not the end of it.

So here they were, the occupants of the post all neatly sewed up and forbidden to buy as much as a pinch of snuff except from the trader who added the graft money to his gross profits to the price of his goods in order to make any profit at all. (See Appendix A for further details.)

Custer finally went to Seip for a showdown on the matter of prices and learned that the annual profits of the business were about $15,000 but that, after having satisfied the demands of Generals Hedrick and Rice—Belknap's hatchet men—he had left only about $2500 to $3000. The real victims, of course, were the occupants of the posts; man, woman and child sold "down the river."

Dr. Brady did not print all of Forsythe's letter. What he did print leaves the impression that the graft existed only among the Iowa politicians. We know definitely, however, that the same extortions were practiced at a number of other posts in the West, both north and south. This leaves room for an interesting speculation concerning Belknap's ambition. Was he building up a political machine that might finally land him in the White House? A senatorship was a good stepping-stone to the Presidency. If this was not his final goal, why bother about politics outside the state of Iowa? Or did he really believe that these insatiable leeches he had turned loose on the helpless occupants of the army posts served them better than had the sutlers appointed by the officers who looked after the welfare of their men and promptly corrected any abuses as soon as they were discovered?

It was never definitely established whether or not Belknap ever received any of this dirty money, though both his first and his second wife received fairly large sums. But from the moral point of view it makes little, if any, difference who received it; for the evil effects of extortions registered in the lives of the occupants of the posts no matter who got the money. No amount of gloss or sophistry can wipe out this fact.

We do not know how General Belknap justified to his own conscience this breach of the fundamental mores of our people—of any civilized people. What we do know is that a long and bloody war loosens the moral fiber of many persons as it hardens the fibers of others. The post-war era was characterized by widespread corruption in which many persons sold their birthright for a mess of potage, and most of them probably did not know that they were doing so. But Belknap clearly did know that his action delegating the appointments to traderships to his political supporters was off color. If he had not felt so he would have

appointed the traders himself to protect the occupants of the posts against exploitation.

We are now nearly done with the long and dreary *prima facie* case against Custer, whose testimony before the Clymer Committee had greatly offended Grant, so much so that when Custer called to take the obligatory leave he refused to see him, a crude discourtesy that led to some repercussions which, though understandable, brought no credit to the Administration.

When Custer made this call he already knew that he was not to be in command of the *expedition;* which did not necessarily mean that he would not go in command of his *regiment.* In fact he could not have been sent in command of the expedition because Gibbon outranked him.

The following confidential dispatch, though undated in the copy we have, must have been sent late on the evening of April 29, 1876. It shows that when Custer called on the President the latter had already decided to suspend him from command. We shall show in a moment that Sheridan and Terry had solved the vexing problem of priority in an exchange of telegrams on April 28 and 29, whereas the cabinet did not meet until evening of the latter date.

The Confidential Dispatch

"Confidential. I telegraphed you yesterday that Secretary Taft would address a communication to impeachment managers looking to my early return to my command. The suggestion was made to Secretary through General Sherman. The Secretary stated to General Sherman he would write the letter after Cabinet meeting, but at the latter he mentioned his intention to the President who directed him not to write the impeachment managers requesting my discharge, but to substitute some other officer to command expedition. I saw Sherman's dispatch and the reply to Sheridan. I at once sought an interview with the managers of impeachment and obtained from them authority to leave. Would have started this evening but General Sherman suggested that I delay until Monday in order to see the President."

Custer followed this advice and one of the first things that happened was, figuratively speaking, a slap in the face when he tried to see the President. Custer seems to have taken this in his stride, as it were. But the next thing that came his way was a real "haymaker."

General P. H. Sheridan, Chicago, Illinois.

> I am at this moment advised that General Custer started last night for St.
> Paul and Fort Abraham Lincoln. He was not justified in leaving Washington
> without seeing the President and myself. Please intercept him and await
> further orders; in the meantime let the expedition proceed without him.
>
> (Signed) W. T. Sherman.

> Should Lieutenant Colonel Custer not be intercepted here you will take
> such steps as will secure his detention at St. Paul until further orders from
> higher authority.
>
> (Signed) R. C. Drum.

In spite of this order the plain truth is that Custer had been very
careful to observe the rules for the coming and going of officers who
had business in Washington. When he arrived to testify in the Belknap
case he called on Grant, and was informed that the President was "abed
with a cold." He left his card and departed. Not having been able to
see the President he wrote him a letter requesting a personal interview.
No answer. After his arrest he sent the following dispatch to Sherman:

> Chicago, Ill., May 4, 1876.
>
> Gen. W. T. Sherman, Washington.
>
> I have seen your dispatch to General Sheridan directing me to await
> orders here and am at a loss to understand that portion referring to my de-
> parture from Washington without seeing you or the President as I called at
> the White House at 10 A. M. Monday, sent in my card to the President and
> with the exception of a few minutes' absence at the War Department I re-
> mained at the White House awaiting an audience with the President until
> 3 P. M., when he sent me word that he could not see me. I called at your
> office at about 2 P. M., but was informed by Col. McCook that you had not
> returned from New York but were expected in the evening. I called at your
> hotel at 4 P. M., and about 6 P. M., but was informed by the clerk that you
> had not returned from New York. I requested Colonel McCook to inform
> you of the substance of the above and also that I was to leave at seven that
> evening to join my command. While at the War Department that day I also
> reported the fact of my proposed departure to the Adjutant General and the
> Inspector General of the Army and obtained from them written and verbal
> authority to proceed to my command without visiting Detroit as previously
> ordered to do. At my last interview with you, I informed you that I would
> leave Washington Monday night to join my command, and you, in conversa-
> tion replied that it was the best thing I could do: Besides you frequently
> during my stay in Washington called my attention to the necessity of my
> leaving as soon as possible.
>
> (Signed) G. A. Custer.

This telegram put Sherman on something like a "spot"; for there
can be little, if any, doubt that his sympathy, generally speaking, was
with Custer rather than with Grant. Writers hostile to Custer have
represented Sherman as being resentful over Custer's conduct in Washington. This is not true. Custer's letters to his wife show conclusively
that Sherman was on the friendliest terms with him. He invited him
to breakfast when he arrived to testify in the Belknap impeachment

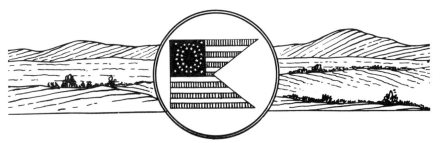

proceedings; introduced him with high praise to the Secretary of War; praised him highly for his writings; and after the battle denied that Custer had disobeyed his orders on the Little Big Horn.

Sherman may have felt that Custer was unwise in talking as freely as he did, as is to be inferred from his advice to him after he had been restored to command of his regiment. It was good advice and at the same time something in the nature of a "sop" to the President who had plenty of troubles of his own without trying to punish Custer for his testimony before the Clymer Committee. And Sherman was not likely to forget Custer's fight against Belknap's corruptions. He had, at an earlier date, fought in the same cause and lost. As I sense Sherman, he was just as clear in his thinking as he was profane in his speech, and not likely to be thrown off balance by any man who, whatever his station in life might be and however great his service to his country, had lost his judgment, as his order placing Custer under arrest and suspension from command, seemed to show, not to mention his crude infraction of the courtesies in the ceremony of "taking leave."

Up to this point there was a reason why Custer could not go in command of the expedition. But that reason no longer existed after Sheridan had, on April 28, persuaded Terry to take over the command of the expedition and thus opened the way for Custer to go in command of his regiment. And right at this point the President intervened with the order of arrest and suspension which completely nullified Sheridan's sensible suggestion. Why did he do this? If the reader will turn back to Sherman's order he will see that the only reason given is that Custer had not seen "The President and myself." To this Custer replied with a short summary of the facts and the case against him collapsed, the finishing touch being given by General Terry, who on May 6 sent the following telegram to the President:

> In forwarding the above (Custer's letter to the President) I wish to say, expressly, that I have no desire whatever to question the orders of the President or of my military superiors. Whether Lieutenant Colonel Custer shall be permitted to accompany the column or not I shall go in command of it. I do not know the reason upon which the orders given rest; but if these reasons

309

do not forbid it, Lieutenant Colonel Custer's services would be very valuable with his regiment.

So Terry did not know the reasons for Custer's suspension. The precious innocent! What was wrong with him? He had received all the telegrams in connection with the case as far as Custer was concerned, and they were plain enough for any person of average intelligence to understand; and we will have to admit that Terry possessed at least average intelligence. In fact he possessed a good deal more than that, and proved it in the very telegram in which he makes himself appear as next thing to a moron by pretending that he does not now know what all the fuss over Custer was about.

What is the answer to this? The answer is that he knew that Custer's suspension from command rested on a "frame up." But he knew also that it would be ill-advised to say so flatly. So he got the idea across with the absurd statement that he did not know the reasons for the orders given. This was "calling" Grant and Sherman with a vengeance, and both of them must have, secretly at least, admired the way it was done. Neither Grant nor Sherman was dumb, and they probably wanted an easy way out anyway; for the flimsiness of the case would have been detected sooner or later, and it was better to get out while the getting was good. And Grant, who was the source of the order, was not *naturally* vindictive, and was sure to experience some qualms sooner or later; for that is the way of decent human nature.

Of course I may be "forty miles west" in this speculation. The reader can try it on for himself and see where he comes out.

End of Prima Facie.

Appendix

THE FOLLOWING PASSAGE from Custer's testimony describes the nature of the monopoly held by traders at the army posts. Custer testified as follows:

I found on investigation that the tradership held by Mr. Dickey was held, as most of them are, by another person, Mr. Wilson managing the business and Dickey being a one-third partner, and a man named Jack Morrow, on the Platte River, owning the other third. Mr. Seip then became the trader, and the prices that were charged the officers and soldiers became so exorbitant that as many as could purchased what they could elsewhere. They did so until Mr. Seip made a written complaint and forwarded it to the Secretary of War, claiming that under the privilege which he held as trader, nobody, no officer even, had a right to buy anything elsewhere or bring it there, but must buy everything through him. The question was carried up through my headquarters. The point came up this way: A captain who desired to provide these articles for his men at a lower rate, purchased in St. Paul some of the classes of articles usually furnished by the trader, and kept them on hand and let his men have them at cost. Mr. Seip learned of this and made a protest to the Secretary of War. I forwarded Mr. Seip's letter, and in return, among other replies that came back, was this, calling my attention to circulars issued from the War Department, prescribing the rights and privileges of traders. Referring to these circulars it says:

"Copies of both are hereto attached. The first one contains this clause: 'They will be allowed the exclusive privilege of trade upon the military reserve to which they are appointed, and no other person will be allowed to trade, peddle or sell goods, by sample or otherwise, within the limits of the reserve!' That clause is plain, clear, and explicit, and means what it says.

"In the opinion of the Secretary of War these circulars are clear

The Seventh Cavalry's Regimental Standard of 1876. This flag was carried by the regiment on its march from the Yellowstone to the Little Big Horn. It is now exhibited at the Custer Battlefield Museum.

312

enough for anyone to understand who desires to do so, and he has only to repeat the statement made previously many times, that any violation of either of these circulars on the part of post-traders, if reported to the Department, as it should be, will be promptly acted upon by him.

Wm. W. Belknap
Secretary of War.

War Department. December 1, 1874.

"Official copy respectfully furnished the commanding officer Fort Abraham Lincoln, D. T., in answer to his indorsement of the third ultimo on letters of Mr. R. C. Seip, post-trader, of October 29, 1874. "By direction of the Secretary of War:

"E. D. Townsend
Adjutant General.

"A. G. Office, December 7, 1874."

This captain was prohibited from furnishing his men with those articles, and he was compelled to purchase from the post-trader whatever the men or himself or his family required. Do you want anything further?

Q. State all that you know about the matter. A. In regard to the manner in which the post-traderships were conducted, particularly that one at Fort Abraham Lincoln, attention was called to the fact, and it was a matter of common report and common information among the officers and men, that the trader had to pay a tax to outside people; but it was impossible to trace this tax until this break in the ring. I then sent for the trader at my post, and told him that he might as well confess what had been going on, because the matter was going to be made public anyhow, and although I could not prove it, I knew that that post had been paying a heavy tax outside and I wanted him to tell me. He then told me that they estimated their yearly profits at $15,000; that about one third of it was paid to Hedrick, of Iowa, that another portion of it was paid to a man named General Rice, who was supposed to be an intimate friend of the Secretary of War in Washington, and that the division of these profits was such that the trader was finally left with but about $2,500 to $3,000 out of the $15,000. I asked him then if he knew of any other person to whom this money was paid. He

313

said he knew positively only what he paid to Rice and Hedrick, but he was always under the impression that a portion of it went to the Secretary of War.

By Mr. Robbins:

Q. He professed not to know that, however? A.—Yes, sir, said he: "I am not a voluntary witness. I shall answer whatever I am asked, but I shall not tell anything that I am not asked to tell"; so I did not pursue the investigation further, thinking there might be other means by which he could be made to tell what he knows.

A Brief Summary of Colonel Hughes' Evasions and Patent Falsehoods

1. It is not true that Custer, on the evening of the 22nd of June, believed that he might have to meet 2400 warriors, as Hughes' juggling makes him say. Custer put the maximum at 1500.

2. It is not true that on the evening of June 24 Custer possessed no evidence about the location of the Indian camp other than the orders he carried implied or suggested.

3. It is not true that on the evening of the 24th Custer was still 40 miles from the enemy. Measurements on Terry's map show 23 miles, straight-line distance. On the modern survey it is 22 miles. By the trail it was a few miles more.

4. It is not true that on the evening of the 24th Custer was "not nearly in contact" with the enemy.

5. It is not true that on the 27th of June the officers consulted by Terry estimated the numbers of warriors at a maximum of 1500.

6. It is not true that Custer, on the evening of the 24th, determined to attack on the 25th.

7. It is not true that Terry, when he made out Custer's orders, be-lieved the Indians to be where they were later found, namely, within about 15 miles of the mouth of the Little Big Horn.

8. It is not true that Custer could have continued his march up the Rosebud on the 25th and been in position to attack at dawn on the 26th.

9. It is not true that Custer's remarks to Ludlow *necessarily* fore-shadowed disobedience.

10. It is probably true that, after Terry had fully informed himself

of the facts as Custer had found them on the evening of the 24th of June, he no longer believed that disobedience had occurred.

11. It is certain that Hughes was not convinced that Custer had disobeyed his orders, as is proved in the next to the last paragraph in his narrative, which reads as follows: "In no way do I intend to assail General Custer, but it has been forced upon me that his error in disobeying the orders of his superior must be made plain. *What reasons he had—what justification he might have shown, are known to no one living?*" (Italics our own.)

So, at last he confesses that he does *not* know what reasons Custer had in making use of the discretion enjoined in his orders. How shall we explain this slip of the pen that destroys his whole case against Custer? Was it the "wee small voice" that must have tormented him from the beginning? The voice that had already spoken in the quotation: *De mortuis nil nisi bonum?* (Of the dead say nothing unless it be favorable.) "The truth shall make us free" whether in the Here or the Hereafter.

But the very fact that he felt the sting of conscience proves that he was not wholly lost to grace.

Mileage Record on Trip To Rosebud June 14, 1953

By the author, Dr. Charles Kuhlman, speedometer reading made by his youngest daughter, Edith, now Mrs. Robert R. Rachmanow

Speedometer Readings:		Distance between places In Miles	Notes
545.3	HOME START, BILLINGS, MONT.		
608.3	CENTER OF CROW AGENCY	63	
609.9	ENTRANCE TO BATTLEFIELD	1.6	
614.2	GARREY OWEN	4.3	
624.8	IONIA	10.6	
629.2	LODGE GRASS	4.4	
642.5	WYOLA	13.3	
654.5	PARKMAN, WYOMING	12.0	
657.5	OHLMAN	3.0	
669.3	MONARCH	11.8	
675.4	JUNCTION, SHARP LEFT TURN	6.1	This is where the road
695.9	DECKER, MONTANA	20.5	began the circle back.
700.1	LUNCH. FORK TO THE LEFT	4.2	
704.5	BATTLE OF ROSEBUD SIGN	4.4	
712.7	KIRBY	8.2	
722.9	BIG THOMPSON CREEK	10.2	Coming in from the
725.7	DAVIS CREEK	2.8	west. Wide flat valley
726.9	JUNCTION, TO BUSBY	1.2	running S. W., nearly
728.8	BUSBY	1.9	south.
730.7	*BACK TO JUNCTION FROM BUSBY	1.9	*I took this note only
747.3	BATTLEFIELD TURN FROM THE HIGHWAY	16.9	for the record from
831.8	HOME AGAIN	286.5	the junction to the
		ROUND	Battlefield entrance.
		TRIP	

Note by author: Add 3/10 miles for every 5 miles to correct speedometer.

This gives a mileage of 134 from Garry Owen up Little Big Horn and around by Parkman to head of Rosebud down to Busby, approximate site of Custer's camp on evening of June 24.

134 miles is the distance Custer would have been forced to march to get from Busby to Indian camp if he had continued up Rosebud, etc. according to Hughes! ! !

THE CUSTER LIBRARY

The Custer Myth
by W. A. Graham

❧

Legend into History and
*Did Custer Disobey Orders
at the Battle of the Little Big Horn?*
by Charles Kuhlman

❧

*The Reno Court of Inquiry:
Abstract of the Official
Record of Proceedings*
by W. A. Graham

❧

The Story of the Little Big Horn
by W. A. Graham

❧

Troopers with Custer
by E. A. Brininstool

❧

With Crook at the Rosebud
by J. W. Vaughn